Studies in Canon Law and Common Law in Honor of R. H. Helmholz

STUDIES IN COMPARATIVE LEGAL HISTORY

Studies in Canon Law and Common Law in Honor of R. H. Helmholz

Edited by Troy L. Harris

The Robbins Collection

Berkeley

Robbins Collection Publications
Berkeley Law
University of California at Berkeley
Berkeley, California 94720
(510) 642-5094 fax: (510) 642-8325
www.law.berkeley.edu/robbins

ISBN 978-1-882239-23-8

Library of Congress Cataloging-in-Publication Data

Studies in canon law and common law in honor of R. H. Helmholz / edited by Troy L. Harris.
    pages cm. — (Studies in comparative legal history)
Includes bibliographical references.
ISBN 978-1-882239-23-8 (alk. paper)
1. Law—History. 2. Law—England—History. 3. Canon law—History. I. Harris, Troy L., editor. II. Helmholz, R. H., honouree.
  K561.S7884 2015
  340.5094—dc23
                                                          2015011915

Contents

Preface

Troy L. Harris

Richard Helmholz is a scholar, mentor, and gentleman. That he is a scholar is obvious to anyone who has visited his faculty page on the University of Chicago Law School web site and seen his list of publications and other achievements. Indeed, a glance at the bibliography accompanying this volume confirms that his scholarly output has been prodigious. At the same time, Dick has an enviable knack for addressing a variety of subjects—from the history of marriage law to the work of the ecclesiastical courts to the privilege against self-incrimination—with sophistication and rigor, while keeping a light touch and remaining accessible.

Proving once again that nothing succeeds like success, his peers have recognized his achievements and added to his list of honors. He is or has been a visiting professor and fellow (on multiple occasions) at Oxford and Cambridge, a Guggenheim Fellow, an Elected Member of the American Law Institute, a Fellow of the British Academy, of the Royal Historical Society, and of the American Academy of Arts and Sciences, along with many other recognitions and awards. He has served in numerous leadership capacities in professional and scholarly organizations, including the American Bar Foundation, the American Council of Learned Societies, the American Society for Legal History, the Institute of Medieval Canon Law, and the Selden Society. Perhaps not surprisingly, his stature as a scholar has led to a number of appointments to editorial positions such as Brill Publishers' Series on Medieval Law and its Practice, the series Comparative Studies in Continental and Anglo-American Legal History, the *Ecclesiastical Law Journal*, the *Journal of Law, Philosophy and Culture*, the *Revista General de Derecho Canónico y Derecho Eclesiástico del Estado*, and the *Rivista Internazionale di Diritto Comune*. Simply stated, the man is ubiquitous.

Richard Helmholz is perhaps best known as an historian of the Roman canon law in medieval and early modern England. Precisely because his area of scholarship lies at the intersection of multiple lines of inquiry, his contributions are recognized by historians whose paths might otherwise never cross: historians of Roman civil law, of English common law, of medieval and early modern European law, of medieval and early modern English society. The variety of contributions in the present volume is an apt reflection of the range and depth of his influence.

And yet Dick's reputation as a scholar—available to anyone with an internet connection—is only part of the story, and not even the best part. Several of us count Dick as a mentor; all of us know him to be a gentleman. Whether commenting on a colleague's work-in-progress (as many readers can confirm) or directing the dissertation of a somewhat overawed graduate student (as I myself can attest), he has been unfailingly generous with his time, constructive in his criticism, and humble in his delivery.

This volume of essays is a modest effort to recognize the variety of Richard Helmholz's accomplishments. As will be obvious, the contributions acknowledge and build upon his scholarship as a legal historian. What will not be apparent is the enthusiasm with which each author accepted the invitation to honor him, the regret of those who were unable to contribute, and the genuine affection and admiration they all expressed toward our mutual friend. Indeed, if a gentleman is measured by the number of his friends, Dick is a gentleman of the first order. On behalf of my fellow contributors, those who provided enthusiastic encouragement along the way, and those who will profit from this volume and the work that inspired it, we offer this slight tribute to a great scholar, mentor, and gentleman.

Contributors

Sir John Baker Q.C. is Emeritus Downing Professor of the Laws of England, and Honorary Fellow of St Catharine's College, Cambridge.

Paul Brand is an Emeritus Fellow of All Souls College, Oxford and Professor of English Legal History in the University of Oxford.

Professor Norman Doe is Director of the Centre for Law and Religion, Cardiff University (Wales), specializes in church law, and studied legal history under T. G. Watkin (at Cardiff), and Walter Ullmann and S. F. C. Milsom (at Cambridge).

Charles Donahue, Jr., is the Paul A. Freund Professor of Law at the Harvard Law School, where he teaches both English and Continental European legal history.

Thomas P. Gallanis is the Associate Dean for Research, the N. William Hines Chair in Law, and a Professor of History at the University of Iowa.

Troy L. Harris is Associate Professor of Law at the University of Detroit Mercy School of Law.

Mark Hill Q.C. is Honorary Professor at the Centre for Law and Religion, Cardiff University; Extraordinary Professor at Pretoria University; Visiting Professor at King's College, London; and Consultant Editor of the *Ecclesiastical Law Journal*.

David Ibbetson is Regius Professor of Civil Law in the University of Cambridge and President of Clare Hall.

David Johnston was formerly Regius Professor of Civil Law in the University of Cambridge and is now a Q.C. in practice at the Bar in Scotland.

ix

Mia Korpiola is Professor of Legal History at the University of Turku, Finland.

Laurent Mayali is Lloyd M. Robbins Professor of Law and Director of the Robbins Religious and Civil Law Collection at Berkeley Law and Directeur d'Études at the École Pratique des Hautes Études, Sciences Religieuses.

M. C. Mirow is a Professor of Law at Florida International University College of Law, Miami, Florida.

Simon Pulleyn was trained in and taught Classics at Oxford before qualifying in and practicing law in the City of London and later taking the LL.M. in Canon Law at Cardiff, where he concentrated on the medieval and Reformation periods.

Philip Reynolds teaches at Emory University in Atlanta, where he is Aquinas Professor of Historical Theology and a senior fellow of the Center for the Study of Law and Religion.

Professor Jonathan Rose is a Professor of Law and the Willard H. Pedrick Distinguished Research Scholar Emeritus, Sandra Day O'Connor College of Law, Arizona State University.

Joshua C. Tate is Associate Professor of Law at the Dedman School of Law, Southern Methodist University.

John Witte, Jr. is Robert W. Woodruff University Professor of Law and Director of the Center for the Study of Law and Religion at Emory University.

Reinhard Zimmermann is Director at the Max Planck Institute for Comparative and International Private Law and Professor at the Bucerius Law School, Hamburg.

Richard Helmholz: Bibliography 1969–2015

1969

"Bastardy Litigation in Medieval England." *American Journal of Legal History* 13 (1969), 360.

"Canonists and Standards of Impartiality for Papal Judges Delegate." *Traditio* 25 (1969), 386.

1971

"Canonical Defamation in Medieval England." *American Journal of Legal History* 15 (1971), 255.

1972

"Abjuration *Sub Pena Nubendi* in the Church Courts of Medieval England." *Jurist* 32 (1972), 80.

1974

Marriage Litigation in Medieval England. Cambridge: Cambridge University Press, 1974.

1975

"*Assumpsit* and *Fidei Laesio.*" *Law Quarterly Review* 91 (1975), 406.

"Infanticide in the Province of Canterbury During the Fifteenth Century." *History of Childhood Quarterly* 2 (1975), 379.

"Writs of Prohibition and Ecclesiastical Sanctions in the English Courts Christian." *Minnesota Law Review* 60 (1975), 1011.

1976

"Ethical Standards for Advocates and Proctors in Theory and Practice." In *Proceedings of the Fourth International Congress of Medieval Canon Law*, ed. S. Kuttner. Monumenta iuris canonici, Series C, Subsidia, vol. 5. Vatican City: Biblioteca Apostolica Vaticana, 1976.

1977

"Support Orders, Church Courts, and the Rule of *Filius Nullius*: A Reassessment of the Common Law." *Virginia Law Review* 63 (1977), 431.

1978

"Roman Law of Guardianship in England, 1300–1600." *Tulane Law Review* 52 (1978), 223.

1979

"Debt Claims and Probate Jurisdiction in Historical Perspective." *American Journal of Legal History* 23 (1979), 68.

"The Early Enforcement of Uses." *Columbia Law Review* 79 (1979), 1503.

1981

"The Writ of Prohibition to Court Christian before 1500." *Medieval Studies* 43 (1981), 297.

Review: David M. Smith, ed., *English Episcopal Acta I: Lincoln 1067–1185* (1980). *American Journal of Legal History* 25 (1981), 251.

1982

"Bibliography of Eighteenth-Century Legal Literature." *Journal of Legal Information* 10 (1982), 242.

"Excommunication as a Legal Sanction: The Attitudes of the Medieval Canonists." *Zeitschrift der Savigny-Stiftung für Rechtsgeschichte* 99, Kan. Abt. 68 (1982), 202.

Review: "Advances and Altered Perspectives in English Legal History" (*On the Laws and Customs of England: Essays in Honor of Samuel E. Thorne*, ed. Morris S. Arnold et al.). *Harvard Law Review* 95 (1982), 723.

Review: Paul R. Hyams, *Kings, Lords and Peasants in Medieval England: The Common Law of Villeinage in the Twelfth and Thirteenth Centuries* (1980). *Speculum* 57 (1982), 621.

1983

Canon Law and English Common Law. London: Selden Society, 1983. Reprinted in *Selden Society Lectures: 1952–2001.* Buffalo: William S. Hein and Co., 2003.

"Adverse Possession and Subjective Intent." *Washington University Law Quarterly* 61 (1983), 331. Reprinted in Richard H. Chused, ed., *A Property Anthology.* Cincinnati: Anderson, 1983.

"Bankruptcy and Probate Jurisdiction before 1571." *Missouri Law Review* 48 (1983), 415.

"Crime, Compurgation and the Courts of the Medieval Church." *Law and History Review* 1 (1983), 1.

"The Early History of the Grand Jury and the Canon Law." *University of Chicago Law Review* 50 (1983), 613.

"Equitable Division and the Law of Finders." *Fordham Law Review* 52 (1983), 313.

1984

Editor with Thomas A. Green: *Juries, Libel and Justice: The Role of English Juries in Seventeenth and Eighteenth-Century Trials for Libel and Slander.* Los Angeles: William Andrews Clark Memorial Library, University of California, Los Angeles, 1984.

"*Legitim* in English Legal History." *University of Illinois Law Review* (1984), 659.

Review: *Guide to American Law: Everyone's Legal Encyclopedia* (1983–). *International Journal of Legal Information* 12 (1984), 137.

Review: C. R. Cheney, *The Papacy and England, 12th–14th Centuries* (1982); C. R. Cheney, *The English Church and Its Laws, 12th–14th Centuries* (1982); Charles Duggan, *Canon Law in Medieval England* (1982). *American Journal of Legal History* 28 (1984), 90.

1985

Editor: *Select Cases on Defamation to 1600.* Selden Society 101. London: Selden Society, 1985.

"Recurrent Patterns of Family Law." *Harvard Journal of Law and Public Policy* 8 (1985), 175.

"Wrongful Possession of Chattels: Hornbook Law and Case Law." *Northwestern*

University Law Review 80 (1985), 1221. Reprinted in *A Property Anthology*, ed. Richard H. Chused. Cincinnati: Anderson, 1993.

Review: Georges Duby, *The Knight, The Lady and The Priest: The Making of Modern Marriage in Medieval France* (1983). *Commonwealth* 112 (1985), 27.

Review: Kenneth Pennington, *Pope and Bishops: The Papal Monarchy in the Twelfth and Thirteenth Centuries* (1984). *Speculum* 60 (1985), 1011.

1986

"The Conference on British Legal Manuscripts." *Journal of Legal History* 7 (1986), 341.

"More on Subjective Intent: A Response to Professor Cunningham." *Washington University Law Quarterly* 64 (1986), 65.

"The Sons of Edward IV: A Canonical Assessment of the Claim that They Were Illegitimate." In *Richard III: Loyalty, Lordship and Law*, ed. P. W. Hammond. London: Richard III and Yorkist History Trust, 1986.

"Usury and the Medieval English Church Courts." *Speculum* 61 (1986), 364.

Review: Ralph V. Turner, *The English Judiciary in the Age of Glanville and Bracton, c. 1176–1239* (1985). *Albion* 18 (1986), 479.

1987

Canon Law and the Law of England. London: The Hambledon Press, 1987.

"Damages in Actions for Slander at Common Law." *Law Quarterly Review* 103 (1987), 624.

Review: Joseph H. Lynch, *Godparents and Kinship in Early Medieval Europe* (1986). *Manuscripta* 31 (1987), 118.

1988

"*Si quis suadente* (C.17 q.4 c.29): Theory and Practice." In *Proceedings of the Seventh International Congress of Medieval Canon Law*, ed. Peter Linehan. Monumenta iuris canonici, Series C, Subsidia, vol. 8. Vatican City: Biblioteca Apostolica Vaticana, 1988.

Review: Jon Bruce and James Ely, Jr., *The Law of Easements and Licenses in Land* (1988). *Vanderbilt Law Review* 41 (1988), 1357.

Review: *The Guide to American Law Yearbook 1987* (1987). *International Journal of Legal Information* 16 (1988), 39.

1989

"Spain." In *The Records of the Medieval Ecclesiastical Courts*, ed. Charles Donahue, Jr. Berlin: Duncker & Humblot, 1989.

1990

Roman Canon Law in Reformation England. Cambridge: Cambridge University Press, 1990.

"Continental Law and Common Law: Historical Strangers or Companions." *Duke Law Journal* (1990), 1207.

"Contracts and the Canon Law." In *Towards a General Law of Contract*, ed. John Barton. Berlin: Duncker & Humbolt, 1990.

"The Education of English Proctors." In *Learning the Law: Teaching and the Transmission of Law in England, 1150–1900*, ed. Jonathan Bush and Alain Wijffels. London: The Hambledon Press, 1990.

"Origins of the Privilege against Self-Incrimination: The Role of the European *Ius Commune*." *New York University Law Review* 65 (1990), 962.

1991

Editor with Christopher Robert Cheney and Peter Stein: *Notai in Inghilterra Prima e Dopo la Riforma.* Milan: Giuffrè, 1991.

Editor with C. W. Brooks and P. G. Stein: *Notaries Public in England since the Reformation.* Norwich: Erskine Press, 1991.

"Conflicts between Religious and Secular Law: Common Themes in the English Experience, 1250–1640." *Cardozo Law Review* 12 (1991), 707.

Review: Marilyn Stone, *Marriage and Friendship in Medieval Spain: Social Relations According to the Fourth Partida of Alfonso X* (1990). *Manuscripta* 35 (1991), 232.

1992

Editor: *Canon Law in Protestant Lands.* Berlin: Duncker & Humblot, 1992.

"Bailment Theories and the Liability of Bailees: The Elusive Uniform Standard of Reasonable Care." *University of Kansas Law Review* 41 (1992), 97.

"The English Law of Wills and the *Ius Commune*." In *Marriage, Property and Succession*, ed. Lloyd Bonfield. (Berlin: Duncker & Humbolt, 1992).

"The Library in Guercino's Portrait of a Lawyer." *Atti e memorie. Accademia Clementina* 30–31 (1992), 184.

"Use of the Civil Law in Post-Revolutionary American Jurisprudence." *Tulane Law Review* 66 (1992), 1649.

Review: Reinhard Zimmermann, *The Law of Obligations: Roman Foundations of the Civilian Tradition* (1990). *Duke Journal of Comparative and International Law* 2 (1992), 309.

1993

"And Were There Children's Rights in Early Modern England? The Canon Law and Intra-Family Violence in England, 1400–1993." *International Journal of Children's Rights* 1 (1993), 23.

"Harold Berman's Accomplishment as a Legal Historian." *Emory Law Journal* 42 (1993), 475. Reprinted as "The Character of the Western Legal Tradition," in *The Integrative Jurisprudence of Harold J. Berman*, ed. Howard O. Hunter (Boulder, Colo.: Westview, 1993).

"Married Women's Wills in Later Medieval England," In *Wife and Widow in Medieval England*, ed. Sue Sheridan Walker (Ann Arbor: University of Michigan Press, 1993).

Review: *The Guide to American Law Supplement 1992* and *The Guide to American Law Supplement 1993* (1993). *International Journal of Legal Information* 21 (1993), 186.

Review: Rosalio Jose Castillo Lara, ed., *Studia in Honorem Eminentissimi Cardinalis Alphonsi M. Stickler* (1992). *Zeitschrift der Savigny-Stiftung für Rechtsgeschichte* 110, Kan. Abt. 79 (1993), 463.

Review: Alan Watson, *Roman Law and Comparative Law* (1991). *Zeitschrift für europäisches Privatrecht* 1 (1993), 639.

1994

"The Bible in the Service of the Canon Law." *Chicago-Kent Law Review* 70 (1994), 1557.

"Excommunication in Twelfth Century England." *Journal of Law and Religion* 11 (1994), 235.

"Legal Formalism, Substantive Policy, and the Creation of a Canon Law of Prescription." In *Prescriptive Formality and Normative Rationality in Modern Legal Systems: Festschrift for Robert Summers*, ed. Werner Krawietz. Berlin: Duncker & Humblot, 1994).

"The Origin of Holographic Wills in English Law." *Journal of Legal History* 15 (1994), 97.

"Other Diocesan and Lesser Church Courts." In *The Records of Medieval Ecclesiastical Courts*, Part II, ed. Charles Donahue, Jr. Berlin: Duncker & Humblot, 1994.

"The Transmission of Legal Institutions: English Law, Roman Law, and Handwritten Wills." *Syracuse Journal of International Law and Commerce* 20 (1994), 147.

Review: *The Guide to American Law Supplement 1994* (1994). *International Journal of Legal Information* 22 (1994), 285.

Review: David M. Becker, *Perpetuities and Estate Planning: Potential Problems and Effective Solutions* (1993). *International Journal of Legal Information* 22 (1994), 87.

Review: Eileen Spring, *Law, Land and Family: Aristocratic Inheritance in England, 1300 to 1800* (1993). *Journal of Legal Education* 44 (1994), 140.

1995

"Ecclesiastical Lawyers and the English Reformation." *Ecclesiastical Law Journal* 3 (1995), 360.

"Der *Usus modernus Pandectarum* und die Ursprunge des eigenhandigen Testaments in England." *Zeitschrift für Europäisches Privatrecht* 4 (1995), 769.

Review: Eric Josef Carlson, *Marriage and the English Reformation* (1994). *Journal of Ecclesiastical History* 46 (1995), 726.

Review: Hans Erich Troje, *Humanistische Jurisprudenz: Studien zur europäischen Rechtswissenschaft unter dem Einfluß des Humanismus* (1993). *Sixteenth Century Journal* 26 (1995), 1068.

Review: Rudolf Weigand, *Die Glossen zum Dekret Gratians* (1991). *Church History* 64 (1995), 458.

1996

The Spirit of Classical Canon Law. Athens, Ga.: University of Georgia Press, 1996).

"Canon Law as a Means of Legal Integration in the Development of English Law." In *Die Bedeutung des kanonischen Rechts für die Entwicklung einheitlicher Rechtsprinzipien*, ed. Heinrich Scholler. Baden-Baden: Nomos Verlagsgesellschaft, 1996.

"The Learned Laws in Pollock and Maitland." *Proceedings of the British Academy* 89 (1996), 145.

"Les officialités anglo-saxonnes et la culture juridique latine: approches historiennes." *L'Année canonique* 38 (1996), 97.

"Shopping Center Leases and Law School Courses." *Legal Education Newsletter: ABA Real Property, Probate and Trust Law Section* 1 (1996), 8.

Review: Ludwig Schmugge, *Kirche, Kinder, Karrieren: Päpstliche Dispense von der unehelichen Geburt im Spätmittelalter* (1995). *Journal of Ecclesiastical History* 47 (1996), 744.

Review: J. L. Barton, *The Mystery of Bracton* (1993). *Zeitschrift der Savigny-Stiftung für Rechtsgeschichte* 113, *Kan. Abt.* 82 (1996), 427.

Review: James A. Brundage, *Medieval Canon Law* (1995). *Journal of Legal History* 17 (1996), 92.

Review: *L'Église et le droit dans le Midi, 13e–14e siècles,* ed. Henri Gilles (1994). *Church History* 65 (1996), 81.

Review: *The Folger Library Edition of the Works of Richard Hooker,* Vol. VI, Pts. 1 and 2, ed. W. Speed Hill (1993). *Renaissance Quarterly* 49 (1996), 649.

Review: Rudolf Weigand, *Liebe und Ehe im Mittelalter* (1993). *Zeitschrift der Savigny-Stiftung für Rechtsgeschichte* 113, *Kan. Abt.* 82 (1996), 426.

1997

Edited with Albert Alschuler, Charles Montgomery Gray, and John H. Langbein: *The Privilege Against Self-Incrimination: Its Origins and Development.* Chicago: University of Chicago Press, 1997.

"Excommunication and the Angevin Leap Forward." *Haskins Society Journal* 7 (1997), 133.

"The Legal Framework of the Church of England: A Critical Study in a Comparative Context." *Texas Law Review* 75 (1997), 1455.

"Records and Reports: the English Ecclesiastical Courts." In *Case Law in the Making: The Techniques and Methods of Judicial Records and Law Reports,* ed. Alain Wijffels. Berlin: Duncker & Humblot, 1997.

"The Universal and the Particular in Medieval Canon Law." In *Proceedings of the Ninth International Congress of Medieval Canon Law,* ed. Peter Landau and J. Müller. Monumenta iuris canonici, Series C, Subsidia, vol. 10. Vatican City: Biblioteca Apostolica Vaticana, 1997.

Review: John Hudson, *The Formation of the English Common Law: Law and Society in England from the Norman Conquest to Magna Carta* (1996). *Albion* 29 (1997), 461.

1998

Editor with Reinhard Zimmermann. *Itinera Fiduciae: Trust and Treuhand in Historical Perspective.* Berlin: Duncker and Humblot, 1998.

"Harboring Sexual Offenders: Ecclesiastical Courts and Controlling Misbehavior." *Journal of British Studies* 37 (1998), 258.

"Realism and Formalism in the Severance of Joint Tenancies." *Nebraska Law Review* 77 (1998), 1.

"Religious Liberty in Western Thought." *Ethics* 109 (1998), 215.

"Spanish and English Ecclesiastical Courts." *Studia Gratiana* 28 (1998), 415.

Review: J. H. Baker, *Monuments of Endless Labours: English Canonists and their Work, 1300–1900* (1998). *Catholic Historical Review* 84 (1998), 710.

"The Canons of 1603: The Contemporary Understanding." In *English Canon Law: Essays in Honour of Bishop Eric Kemp*, ed. Norman Doe, Mark Hill, and Robert Ombres. Cardiff: The University of Wales Press, 1998.

1999

Editor with D. Barlow Burke and Ann M. Burkhart: *Fundamentals of Property Law*. Charlottesville, Va.: Lexis, 1999.

"The Canon Law." In *Cambridge History of the Book in Britain*: Volume III, 1400–1557, ed. Lotte Hellinga and J. B. Trapp. Cambridge: Cambridge University Press, 1999.

"Magna Carta and the *ius commune*." *University of Chicago Law Review* 66 (1999), 297.

Review: Giovanni Chiodi, *L'interpretazione del testamento nel pensiero dei Glossatori* (1997). *Zeitschrift der Savigny-Stiftung für Rechtsgeschichte* 129, Kan. Abt. 85 (1999), 570.

Review: *Royal Writs Addressed to John Buckingham, Bishop of Lincoln, 1363-1398, Lincoln Register 12B*, ed. A. K. McHardy (1997). *Journal of Legal History* 20 (1999), 137.

2000

"Brian Simpson in the United States." In *Human Rights and Legal History: Essays in Honour of Brian Simpson*, ed. Katherine Donovan and G. R. Rubin. Oxford: Oxford University Press, 2000.

"Independence and Uniformity in England's Manorial Courts." In *Seigneurial Jurisdiction*, ed. Lloyd Bonfield. Berlin: Duncker & Humblot, 2000.

"The *litis contestatio*: Its Survival in the Medieval *ius commune* and Beyond." In *Lex et Romanitas: Essays for Alan Watson*, ed. Michael Hoeflich. Berkeley: The Robbins Collection, 2000.

"Scandinavian Law and English Law: An Historical Sketch and a Present Opportunity." In *Family, Marriage and Property Devolution in the Middle Ages*, ed. Llars Ivar Hansen. Tromsø: Department of History, University of Tromsø, 2000.

Review: Franck Roumy, *L'Adoption dans le droit savant du XIIe au XVIe siècle* (1998). *Zeitschrift der Savigny-Stiftung für Rechtsgeschichte* 117, Kan. Abt. 86 (2000), 575.

Review: *Prefaces to Canon Law Books in Latin Christianity: Selected Translations, 500–1245*, ed. Robert Somerville and Bruce C. Brasington (1998). *Law and History Review* 18 (2000), 460.

Review: Peter Stein, *Roman Law in European History* (1999). *Ecclesiastical Law Journal* 51 (2000), 367.

Review: Patrick Wormald, *The Making of English Law: King Alfred to the Twelfth Century* (1999). *Albion* 32 (2000), 274.

2001

The ius commune *in England: Four Studies.* Oxford: Oxford University Press, 2001.

"Money and Judges in the Law of the Medieval Church." *University of Chicago Law School Roundtable* 8 (2001), 309.

"Richard Hooker and the European *ius commune.*" *Ecclesiastical Law Journal* 6 (2001), 4. Reprinted in *Tudor England: An Encyclopedia*, ed. Arthur F. Kinney and David Swain. New York: Garland, 2001.

"The Roman Law of Blackmail." *Journal of Legal Studies* 30 (2001), 33.

Review: *Repertorium bibliographicum institutorum et sodalitum iuris historiae*, ed. M. Duynstee, R. Feenstra, and L. Waelkens (2000). *Tijdschrift voor Rechtsgeschiedenis* 69 (2001), 411.

Review: D. J. Ibbetson, *Historical Introduction to the Law of Obligations* (1999). *Journal of Legal History* 22 (2001), 72.

Review: Jane E. Sayers, *Original Papal Documents in England and Wales from the Accession of Pope Innocent III to the Death of Pope Benedict XI (1198–1304)* (1999). *Zeitschrift der Savigny-Stiftung für Rechtsgeschichte* 118, Kan. Abt. 87 (2001), 543.

2002

"Discipline of the Clergy: Medieval and Modern." *Ecclesiastical Law Journal* 6 (2002), 189.

Review: *'Lex mercatoria' and Legal Pluralism: A Late Thirteenth-Century Treatise and Its Afterlife*, ed. and trans. Mary Elizabeth Basile, Jane Fair Bestor, Daniel R. Coquillette and Charles Donahue, Jr., (1998). *Speculum* 77 (2002), 137.

Review: Frederik Pedersen, *Marriage Disputes in Medieval England* (2000). *Journal of Ecclesiastical History* 53 (2002), 363.

2003

"Canonical 'Juries' in Medieval England." In *Ins Wasser geworfen und Ozeane durchquert: Festschrift für Knut Wolfgang Nörr*, ed. Mario Ascheri. Cologne: Böhlau, 2003.

"Canonical Remedies in Medieval Marriage Law: The Contributions of Legal Practice." *University of St. Thomas Law Journal* 1 (2003), 647.

"Christopher St. German and the Law of Custom." *University of Chicago Law Review* 70 (2003), 129.

"Judges and Trials in the English Ecclesiastical Courts." In *Judicial Tribunals in England and Europe, 1200–1700*, vol. 1, ed. Maureen Mulholland and Brian Pullan. Manchester: Manchester University Press, 2003.

"Natural Human Rights: The Perspective of the *Ius Commune*." *Catholic University Law Review* 52 (2003), 301.

"El privilegio y el *ius commune*: de la edad media al siglo XVII." *Cuadernos de doctrina y jurisprudencia penal* 15 (2003), 269.

Review: *Twelfth-Century English Archidiaconal and Vice-Archidiaconal Acta*, ed. B. R. Kemp (2001). *Ecclesiastical Law Journal* 7 (2003), 91.

2004

Canon Law and Ecclesiastical Jurisdiction from 597 to the 1640s. The Oxford History of the Laws of England, Vol. 1. Oxford: Oxford University Press, 2004.

Roman Canon Law in Reformation England. Cambridge: Cambridge University Press, 2004.

Editor with D. Barlow Burke and Ann M. Burkhart. *Fundamentals of Property Law*, 2nd edition. Newark, N.J.: LexisNexis, 2004.

"Clerke, Francis." In *Oxford Dictionary of National Biography*. Oxford: Oxford University Press, 2004.

"The *Ius Commune* and Sanctuary for Insolvent Debtors in England." In *Panta Rei: Studi dedicati a Manlio Bellomo*, ed. Orazio Condorelli. Rome: Il Cigno, 2004.

"Lyndwood, William." In *Oxford Dictionary of National Biography*. Oxford: Oxford University Press, 2004.

"The *Mitior Sensus* Doctrine." *Green Bag* 7 (2004), 133.

"Undue Delay in the English Ecclesiastical Courts (circa 1350–1600)." In *The Law's Delay: Essays on Undue Delay in Civil Litigation*, ed. C. H. van Rhee. Antwerp: Intersentia, 2004.

Review: Andreas Richter, *Rechtsfähige Stiftung und Charitable Corporation: Überlegungen zur Reform des deutschen Stiftungsrechts auf der Grundlage ein-*

*er historisch-rechtsvergleichenden Untersuchung der Entstehung des modernen
deutschen und amerikanischen Stiftungsmodells* (2001). *Tijdschrift voor Rechtsgeschiedenis* 72 (2004), 160.

2005

"The Law of Charity and the English Ecclesiastical Courts." In *Foundations of
   Medieval Ecclesiastical History: Studies Presented to David Smith*, ed. Philip-
   pa Hoskin, Christopher Brooke, and R. B. Dobson. Woodbridge: Boydell,
   2005.
"Natural Law and Human Rights in English Law: From Bracton to Blackstone."
   Ave Maria Law Review 3 (2005), 1.
Review: Paul Brand, *Kings, Barons, and Justices: The Making and Enforcement of
   Legislation in Thirteenth-Century England* (2003). *Albion* 36 (2005), 665.
Review: James A. Brundage, *The Profession and Practice of Medieval Canon Law*
   (2004). *Journal of Ecclesiastical History* 56 (2005), 765.

2006

"Foreword." In R. B. Outhwaite, *The Rise and Fall of the English Ecclesiastical
   Courts, 1500–1860.* Cambridge: Cambridge University Press, 2006.
"Thomas More and the Canon Law." In *Medieval Church Law and the Origins of
   the Western Legal Tradition: A Tribute to Kenneth Pennington*, ed. Wolf-
   gang Muller and Mary Sommar. Washington, D.C.: Catholic University of
   America Press, 2006.
"Ockham's Razor in American Law." *Companions and Crossroads: Essays in Honor
   of Shael Herman. Tulane European and Civil Law Forum* 21 (2006), 109.
"The *Ratio decidendi* in England—Evidence from the Civilian Tradition." In *Ratio
   Decidendi: Guiding Principles of Judicial Decisions*, ed. William Hamilton
   Bryson and Serge Dauchy. Berlin: Duncker and Humblot, 2006.
"Scots Law in the New World: Its Place in the Formative Era of American Law."
   In *Miscellany Five*, ed. Hector MacQueen. Stair Society 52. Edinburgh:
   The Stair Society, 2006.
Review: David D'Avray, *Medieval Marriage: Symbolism and Society* (2005). *English
   History Review* 121 (2006), 1444.
Review: Elizabeth M. Makowski, *"A Pernicious Sort of Woman": Quasi-Religious
   Women and Canon Lawyers in the Later Middle Ages* (2005). *Law and Histo-
   ry Review* 24 (2006), 676.
Review: Paul Mitchell, *The Making of the Modern Law of Defamation* (2005). *Jour-
   nal of Legal History* 27 (2006), 211.

2007

Marriage Litigation in Medieval England (Cambridge University Press, 2007).

"Children's Rights and the Canon Law: Law and Practice in Later Medieval England." *Jurist* 67 (2007), 39.

"Sir Daniel Dun, All Souls College, and the Civil Law," in *All Souls under the Ancien Régime: Politics, Learning, and the Arts, c. 1600–1850,* ed. S. J. D. Green and Peregrine Horden. Oxford: Oxford University Press, 2007.

"The Law of Nature and the Early History of Unenumerated Rights in the United States," *University of Pennsylvania Journal of Constitutional Law* 9 (2007), 401.

"Marriage Agreements in Medieval England." In *To Have and To Hold: Marrying and its Documentation in Western Christendom, 400–1600,* ed. Philip Reynolds & John Witte, Jr. Cambridge: Cambridge University Press, 2007.

2008

"Canon Law." In *New Oxford Companion to Law,* ed. Peter Cane and Joanne Conaghan. Oxford: Oxford University Press, 2008.

"*Quoniam Contra Falsam* (X 2.19.11) and the Court Records of the English Church." In *Als die Welt in die Akten kam. Prozeßschriftgut im europäischen Mittelalter,* ed. Susanne Lepsius and Thomas Wetzstein. Frankfurt am Main: Klostermann, 2008.

"Western Canon Law." In *Christianity and Law: An Introduction,* ed. Frank Alexander and John Witte, Jr. Cambridge: Cambridge University Press, 2008).

Review: Peter D. Clarke, *The Interdict in the Thirteenth Century: A Question of Collective Guilt* (2007). *Catholic Historical Review* 94 (2008), 800.

2009

Editor with Vito Piergiovanni: *Relations between the* ius commune *and English Law.* Soveria Mannelli: Rubettino, 2009.

Editor with W. David H. Sellar: *The Law of Presumptions: Essays in Comparative Legal History.* Berlin: Duncker & Humblot, 2009.

"Bonham's Case, the Law of Nature, and Judicial Review." *Journal of Legal Analysis* 1 (2009), 324.

"English Law and the *Ius Commune:* The Law of Succession." In *Relations between the Ius Commune and English Law,* ed. Richard. H. Helmholz & Vito Piergiovanni. Soveria Mannelli: Rubbettino, 2009.

"A Note on French and English Officialities on the Eve of the Council of Trent."

In *Mélanges en l'honneur d'Anne Lefebvre-Teillard*, ed. Bernard d'Alteroche. Paris: Éditions Panthéon-Assas, 2009.

With W. David H. Sellar: "Presumptions in Comparative Legal History." In *The Law of Presumptions: Essays in Comparative Legal History*, ed. Richard. H. Helmholz and W. David H. Sellar. Berlin: Duncker & Humblot, 2009.

"The Saga of *Van Valkenburgh v. Lutz*: Animosity and Adverse Possession in Yonkers." In *Property Stories*, ed. Gerald Korngold and Andrew Morriss. 2nd ed. New York: Foundation Press, 2009.

"Response to Hadley Arkes." *Symposium—A Common Morality for the Global Age: In Gratitude for What We are Given: Questions of Historical Development. Journal of Law, Philosophy and Culture* 3 (2009), 221.

Review: James Q. Whitman, *The Origins of Reasonable Doubt: Theological Roots of the Criminal Trial* (2008). *University of Illinois Law and History Review* 27 (2009), 203.

2010

The Spirit of Classical Canon Law. Paperback ed. Athens, Ga.: University of Georgia Press, 2010.

Editor with D. Barlow Burke and Ann M. Burkhart: *Fundamentals of Property Law*. 3rd ed. New Providence, N.J.: LexisNexis, 2010) .

"Alberico Gentili e il Rinascimento. La formazione giuridica in Inghilterra." In *Alberico Gentili. Atti dei convegni nel quarto centario della morte*. Vol. 2. Milan: Giuffrè, 2010.

"Citations and the Construction of Procedural Law in the *Ius Commune*." In *The Creation of the* Ius Commune: *From* Casus *to* Regula, ed. J. W. Cairns and Paul de Plessis. Edinburgh: Edinburgh University Press, 2010.

"Conscience in the Ecclesiastical Courts." In *Proceedings of the Thirteenth International Congress of Medieval Canon Law*, ed. Peter Erdö and Sz. Anzelm Szuromi. Monumenta iuris canonici., Series C, Subsidia, vol. 14. Vatican City: Biblioteca Apostolica Vaticana, 2010

"Human Rights in the Canon Law." In *Christianity and Human Rights: An Introduction*, ed. Frank Alexander and John Witte, Jr. Cambridge: Cambridge University Press, 2010.

"*Scandalum* in the Medieval Canon Law and in the English Ecclesiastical Courts." *Zeitschrift der Savigny-Stiftung für Rechtsgeschichte* 127, Kan. Abt. 96 (2010), 258.

"Were the English Ecclesiastical Tribunals Courts of Law?" In *Law and Private Life in the Middle Ages*, ed. Per Andersen. Copenhagen DJØF Publishing, 2010.

Review: John H. Langbein, R. L. Lerner, and Bruce Smith, *History of the Common*

Law: *The Development of Anglo-American Legal Institutions* (2009). *American Journal of Comparative Law* 58 (2010), 486.

2011

Editor: *Three Civilian Notebooks, 1580–1640.* Selden Society 127. London: Selden Society, 2011.

"Matrimonial Litigation In Pre-Reformation Scotland: A Brief Comparison With The Continent." In *Famiglia e religione in Europa nell'età moderna: studi in onore di Silvana Seidel Menchi,* ed. G. Ciapelli. Rome: Edizioni di Storia e Letteratura, 2011.

"Natural Law And The Trial Of Thomas More." In *Thomas More's Trial By Jury,* ed. H. A. Kelly, Louis W. Karlin and Gerard Wegemer. Woodbridge: Boydell, 2011.

"Regulating The Number Of Proctors In The English Ecclesiastical Courts: Evidence From An Early Tudor Tract." In *Law As Profession And Practice In Medieval Europe: Essays in Honor of James A. Brundage,* ed. M. H. Eichbauer and Kenneth Pennington. Farnham, Surrey: Ashgate, 2011.

"University Education and English Ecclesiastical Lawyers 1400–1650." *Ecclesiastical Law Journal* 13 (2011), 132.

Review: Robin Hickey, *Property and the Law of Finders* (2010). *Legal Studies* 3 (2011), 511.

2012

La Magna Carta del 1215: alle origini del costituzionalismo inglese ed europeo. Rome: Aracne, 2012.

"Annuities and Annual Pensions." In *Laws, Lawyers, and Texts: Studies in Medieval Legal History in Honour of Paul Brand,* ed. Susanne Jenks, Jonathan Rose, and Christopher Whittick. Leiden: Brill, 2012.

"The Canon Law of Annual Pensions: A Brief Historical Study." In *Recto Ordine procedit magister: Liber amicorum E. C. Coppens,* ed. L. Berkvens et al. Brussels: Koninklijke Vlaamse Academie van België voor Wetenschappen en Kunsten, 2012).

"The Law of Slavery and the European *Ius Commune.*" In *The Legal Understanding of Slavery: From the Historical to the Contemporary,* ed. Jean Allain. Oxford: Oxford University Press, 2012.

"Religion And Succession In The History Of English Law." In *Der Einfluss religiöser Vorstellungen auf die Entwicklung des Erbrechts,* ed. Reinhard Zimmermann. Tübingen: Mohr Siebeck, 2012.

Review: Will Adam, *Legal Flexibility and the Mission of the Church: Dispensation and the Economy in Ecclesiastical Law* (2011). *Journal of Ecclesiastical History* 63 (2012), 795.

Review: Karl Shoemaker, *Sanctuary and Crime in the Middle Ages, 400–1500* (2011). *Journal of Ecclesiastical History* 63 (2012), 588.

Review: Sam Worby, *Law And Kinship In Thirteenth-Century England* (2010). *English Historical Review* 127 (2012), 144.

2013

Kanonisches Recht und europäische Rechtskultur. Tübingen: Mohr Siebeck, 2013.
"Baptism in the Medieval Canon Law." *Rechtsgeschichte/Legal History* 21 (2013), 118.
"Hugh Davis (1632–1694)." *Ecclesiastical Law Journal* 15 (2013), 344.
"Judicial Review and the Law of Nature." *Ohio Northern University Law Review* 39 (2013), 417.
"Richard Zouche." *Ecclesiastical Law Journal* 15 (2013), 204.
"Roger, Bishop of Worcester (c 1134–1179)." *Ecclesiastical Law Journal* 15 (2013), 75.
Review: Martin Bertram, *Kanonisten und ihre Texte (1234 bis Mitte 14. Jh.): 18 Aufsätze und 14 Exkurse* (2013). *Catholic Historical Review* 99 (2013), 546.

2014

"Sir Daniel Dun (c 1545–1617)." *Ecclesiastical Law Journal* 16 (2014), 205.
"Sir Leoline Jenkins (1625–1685)." *Ecclesiastical Law Journal* 16 (2014), 351.
"Natural Law and Religion: Evidence from the Case Law." In *Law and Religion: The Legal Teachings of the Protestant and Catholic Reformations*, ed. Wim Decock, Jordan J. Ballor, Michael Germann, and Laurent Waelkens. Göttingen: Vandenhoeck & Ruprecht, 2014
"William of Drogheda (c 1200–1245)," *Ecclesiastical Law Journal* 66 (2014), 16.

2015

Natural Law in Court: A History of Legal Theory in Practice. Cambridge, Mass.: Harvard University Press, 2015 [forthcoming].
"Richard Rudhale (c 1415–1476)" *Ecclesiastical Law Journal* 17 (2015), 58.

Limitation of Actions:
The Curious Case of Classical Roman Law

David Johnston

INTRODUCTION

This paper is concerned with what is often called the statute of limitations. The topic seems appropriate in an essay to celebrate Dick Helmholz's remarkable contribution to the history of canon law and of the common law, not least because he has himself written on the topic in canon law.[1] In part of his discussion of the approach to limitation periods adopted in classical canon law, Helmholz observes:

> Much as happens today, when courts apply statutes of limitations by starting the period only from the moment when the party had a realistic chance to sue, usually the moment when the event came to his attention, the canon law did not look simply to the existence of the injury. Until the petitioner's ignorance of the existence of his cause of action was lifted, the limitations period ordinarily did not start. The

---

1. R. H. Helmholz, *The Spirit of Classical Canon Law* (Athens, Ga., 1996), esp. 174–99; cf. also R. H. Helmholz, "Legal Formalism, Substantive Policy, and the Creation of a Canon Law of Prescription," in W. Krauwietz, N. MacCormick and G. H. von Wright, *Prescriptive Formality and Normative Rationality in Modern Law* (Berlin, 1994), 265–83.

ius commune took over this approach. Any other must have seemed mechanical and unfair.[2]

The approach adopted in canon law accords with a pattern typical of modern legal systems. That, as Helmholz notes, is for time to start to run against a claimant from the time when he had knowledge of the facts necessary to initiate a claim. In some systems, time may start to run from an earlier date if the court takes the view that, with the exercise of reasonable diligence, the claimant could have acquired the necessary knowledge earlier; and in some systems there are two parallel limitation (or prescription) provisions, on the one hand a short period which starts to run on the date the claimant has the necessary knowledge and, on the other, a much longer one which runs from the date of the loss and has no regard to the state of the claimant's knowledge.[3]

It is easy to understand why in so many systems it is thought to be unfair and inappropriate for a claim to be subject to limitation before the claimant even learns of its existence. But a regime of this kind contrasts so strongly with the position in Roman law that it seems to be worth exploring a little further to see whether such fundamental differences can be understood.

CLASSICAL ROMAN LAW

We need to begin by recognizing that our knowledge of the position in classical law depends on sources which are remarkably few and far between. Since the workings of time limits in formulary procedure were of no practical importance once the *cognitio* system of procedure had superseded it, texts from the *Corpus Iuris Civilis* give little away about how the earlier system worked.

The starting point, however, is that some but by no means all actions were subject to a time limit. Actions based on the *ius civile* were in principle

---

2.   Helmholz, *Spirit* (n. 1), 92.

3.   See e.g. in Scotland, Prescription and Limitation (Scotland) Act 1973 sections 6, 7 and 11(3); in England, Limitation Act 1980 section 14A(6)–(8); in Germany, BGB art. 199 I; in France, *Code civil* art. 2224; more generally, *Draft Common Frame of Reference* III.-7:301.

perpetual.[4] Actions based on the praetor's edict were mostly subject to a time limit of one year. But there were exceptions, for which it is difficult to identify any single rationale.[5] They apparently included actions that were regarded in essence as vindicating a right under *ius civile*; Gaius describes them as imitating the civil law, and the two examples he gives are of *bonorum possessio* and *furtum manifestum*.[6] In the Digest, Paul, referring to Cassius, observes that praetorian actions *quae rei persecutionem habeant* are granted after a year, while others are limited to a year. He gives as examples *bonorum possessio* and the *actio Publiciana, quae ad exemplum vindicationis datur*.[7] The distinction intended is apparently between actions directed at recovery of property and those directed at a penalty. Although this is not the place to attempt the (probably impossible) task of listing precisely which actions were and which were not subject to a time limit, it is important to realize that in classical Roman law the issue of a time limit simply does not arise in relation to a large range of actions. The point goes well beyond what can be described as actions based on the *ius civile* and extends to many important praetorian remedies.[8]

One further point has to be noted: the praetor's edict contained an *exceptio temporis* or *exceptio annalis*. According to Lenel, it was worded "unless it is more than a year since the claimant was able to sue;" he assigns to its discussion only one text, D. 44.3.1, from book 74 of Ulpian's commentary *ad edictum* (see below).[9] As Lenel points out, this *exceptio* cannot have

---

4.   M. Amelotti, *La prescrizione delle azioni in diritto romano* (Milan, 1958), 23–6; M. Kaser, *Das römische Privatrecht.* 2nd ed., vol. 2. (Munich, 1975), 71–2.

5.   See e.g. W. W. Buckland, *A Textbook of Roman Law*, 3rd ed. by P. Stein (Cambridge, 1963), 689–91.

6.   Gaius, *Inst.* 4.110–111.

7.   Paul 1 ed. D. 44.7.35 pr. Cf. Amelotti (n. 4), 26 ff.

8.   For discussion, see A. Ubbelohde, *Uber die Berechnung des tempus utile der honorarischen Temporalklagen* (Marburg, 1891), 20–28. E.g. the following are expressly stated to be perpetual: *nautae caupones stabularii* (Ulp. 18 ed. D. 4.9.7.6); *de his qui effuderint vel deiecerint* (Ulp. 23 ed. D. 9.3.5.5); *actio exercitoria* (Ulp. 29 ed. D. 14.1.4.4); *actio institoria* (Ulp. 28 ed. D. 14.3.15); *damnum infectum* (Ulp. 53 ed. D. 39.2.17.3); *rerum amotarum* (Paul 37 ed. D. 25.2.21.5). Some actions were perpetual to the extent of surviving enrichment only: e.g. *dolus* (Gai. 4 ed. prov. D. 4.3.28); *fraus patroni* (Ulp. 43 ed. D. 38.5.3.1); *fraus creditorum* (Ulp. 73 ed. D. 42.8.10.24).

9.   O. Lenel, *Das Edictum Perpetuum*, 3rd ed. (Leipzig, 1927), 505: *si non plusquam annus est, cum experiundi potestas fuit.*

been designed for use in praetorian actions which were anyway subject to a one-year time limit, since their own particular formulae would already have incorporated that time limit. Instead he observes that the *exceptio* was intended for the numerous cases in which the one-year limit rested on "practice and jurisprudence."[10] Unfortunately he does not give any further or better particulars about what these numerous cases were.[11] Yet, as Gaius emphasizes, the principle was clear: actions under *ius civile* were perpetual. Equally, numerous praetorian actions were as a matter of fact perpetual. It would make no sense to describe these actions as perpetual if the *exceptio* was routinely available in a wide range of them. It therefore seems most likely that it was instead available only in specific circumstances where the praetor was persuaded that such a limit was appropriate; and where there was a sufficient issue on the facts to require the question when the claimant had become able to sue (his *experiundi potestas*) to be determined by a judge. In short, although we have no means of being certain, it seems reasonable to take the view that the *exceptio* would have been granted only *causa cognita*.

The jurists provide us with little more than hints about how the time limits operated in practice. But there is enough to arrive at the view that, for those actions in which the point arose at all, the time limit was a serious issue. That emerges from some juristic discussion about the court calendar. Certain days in the calendar were *dies nefasti*, and on those the magistrate would not exercise jurisdiction.[12] During periods when crops were harvested and grapes were picked (*messis vindemiarumque tempore*), the magistrate would administer justice only in relation to matters which were about to be extinguished by death or by time. Examples of rights which would be extinguished by death are actions for theft, under the *lex Aquilia*, for *iniuria*, and for other delicts: as penal actions these would lapse on the death of the wrongdoer; if before his death they had reached *litis contestatio*, the obliga-

---

10.   Lenel (n. 9), 505: "die zahlreichen Fälle, wo die Annalbeschränkung auf Praxis und Jurisprudenz beruhte."

11.   Equally unfortunately, the leading modern textbook simply paraphrases Lenel's own comment and adds nothing further: M. Kaser and K. Hackl, *Das römische Zivilprozessrecht*, 2nd ed. (Munich, 1996), 320, n. 59.

12.   Ibid., 202–3.

tion would be perpetuated.[13] Ulpian goes on to explain that the same applies if the matter is about to be lost through lapse of time or the time limit for the action to be brought is about to expire (*si res tempore periturae sunt aut actionis dies exiturus est*).[14] This refers to the possibility that the right of action would be extinguished by lapse of time during the harvest vacation.

For present purposes the main points to take from Ulpian's discussion are: (1) that at least some actions were subject to a time limit; (2) that the reckoning of time for purposes of calculating when the time limit expired took no account of the harvest vacation; if it had done, there would have been no need for the magistrate to deal with cases of this kind as a matter of urgency; (3) if the right of action was extinguished during the harvest vacation, the claimant could no doubt seek *in integrum restitutio*. But, as Ulpian points out in agreement with Celsus, although the position might be different for holidays declared specially, relief by way of *in integrum restitutio* should not be granted to a claimant in relation to regular periods of holiday: he should have arranged his affairs so that he did not fall foul of the holiday period.[15]

When did time start to run? In the works of the Roman jurists there is frequent reference to the notion of *dies utiles* or an *annus utilis*. One of the texts excerpted from Ulpian even begins by stating that since the issue of *dies utiles* arises frequently, it is necessary to consider the meaning of the expression "ability to sue" (*experiundi potestas*).[16] As Ulpian goes on to explain, *experiundi potestas* involves the satisfaction of three requirements: (i) the claimant must be able to sue; (ii) there must be a defendant to be sued; and (iii) the magistrate must be available. So far as the first is concerned, Ulpian mentions as impediments to the claimant being able to sue that he is being held by enemies, away on state business, in prison, or detained abroad by a storm. This raises a purely objective question: whether it is possible for the claimant to bring the action or give instructions for it to be brought. Although (perhaps oddly) Ulpian does not mention the question of lack of

---

13.   Call. 1 ed. mon. D. 44.7.59.

14.   Ulp. 2 ed. D. 2.12.3 pr.; cf. Ulp. 4 omn. trib. D. 2.12.1 pr., 2.

15.   Ulp. 12 ed. D. 4.6.26.7: *...sollemnium enim feriarum rationem haberi non debere, quia prospicere eas potuerit et debuerit actor ne in eas incidat....*

16.   Ulp. 74 ed. D. 44.3.1: *Quia tractatus de utilibus diebus frequens est, videamus quid sit experiundi potestas....*

legal capacity, it seems reasonable to assume that a person who was either under age or mentally incapable of proceeding would be regarded as lacking *experiundi potestas.*

As for the second and third points, Ulpian gives no further information whatsoever. The second evidently requires that there be either a defendant or someone representing him. What is not discussed is the case that the claimant does not know who the proper defendant should be. As Savigny pointed out, the defendant would be able to impede the bringing of the claim if he was unknown, in hiding, had fled, or was otherwise absent and unrepresented. Savigny notes too that, in a case of theft or the *actio vi bonorum raptorum,* it might easily come about that the claimant did not know whom to sue.[17] We therefore have to recognize that in principle, depending on the breadth of interpretation given to the notion that there was no defendant to defend, the one-year time limit may have been significantly extended. But on the state of the evidence there is simply no way of knowing.

There are just a few cases in which there is a suggestion that the claimant's state of knowledge might have had a bearing on when time starts to run. One instance is that of *calumnia,* loosely translated as vexatious litigation. Gaius deals with the case where one person has paid another to sue a third.[18] The question is whether the time limit should run from the date the money was paid or the date the victim discovered that it was paid. Gaius concludes that, while the victim was in a state of ignorance, he cannot be said to have had *experiundi potestas,* and so the year should run from the date on which he acquired knowledge of the payment. The situation is so special that it is difficult to regard it as a significant exception to the general rule: in particular, given that the victim would have no means of knowing about the payment or the arrangement between two other people, it is difficult to see how a remedy of this sort could have had any effect in practice unless the one-year time limit ran from the date of knowledge rather than the date of payment.[19]

17.   F. C. v. Savigny, *System des heutigen römischen Rechts,* vol. 4 (Berlin, 1841), 430, §189.

18.   Gai. 4 ed. prov. D. 3.6.6.

19.   Cf. Amelotti (n. 4), 57.

Another relates to the interdict *quod vi aut clam*. Here, in a discussion of a number of peculiarities about the one-year time limit for bringing proceedings for this kind of interdict, Ulpian considers the case of a construction put up in a place that is difficult of access or underground or underwater.[20] He concludes that *causa cognita* the one-year defense may be repelled. Here the position is not quite the same as in the case of *calumnia*: depending on the circumstances, the claimant's contention about the practical unavailability of the interdict might be persuasive or the opposite. So it seems entirely appropriate that the question whether the limit should apply should be determined after hearing argument, *causa cognita*.

A third, more problematic case is concerned with the *actio redhibitoria*, where under the aedilician edict the time limit was six months. In one of his *responsa*, Papinian advises that a buyer who was unaware of a latent defect in a slave, namely that he was a fugitive, cannot be regarded as having had *experiundi potestas*.[21] This text is problematic because it conflicts with clear statements elsewhere, from the very same context of latent defects in slaves, that the six-month time limit runs from the date of sale (or in the case of warranties, *dicta promissave*, the date on which they were given).[22] It is true that the defect of being a fugitive slave is a rather unusual one: if the slave had fled on some occasion prior to the sale, it would be difficult nevertheless to maintain that the defect still subsisted at the time of the sale, albeit it might (if disclosed) have had a bearing on the price; on the other hand, if the slave had never fled prior to the sale but did so afterwards, it would be difficult to say that any subsequent flight was caused by a defect that existed at the time of the sale.[23] While one can see that this kind of situation raises unusual problems, it is probably best to treat this case as one that simply cannot be reconciled with the remaining texts.[24]

20. Ulp. 71 ed. D. 43.24.15.5; cf. Amelotti (n. 4), 58, 89–90.

21. Pap. 12 resp. D. 21.1.55; C. 4.58.2 (A.D. 239); *Pauli Sententiae* 2.17.5.

22. Ulp. 1 ed. aed. cur. D. 21.1.19.6.

23. Cf. G. Impallomeni, *L'editto degli edili curuli* (Padua, 1955), 11 ff.

24. Cf. Impallomeni (n. 23), 229–30. Amelotti (n. 4), 71–2, while critical of a later part of D. 21.1.55, finds no fault with the central part just mentioned and places emphasis on (i) the fact that it is a single *responsum*; and (ii) Papinian's well-known independence of mind and concern for equity.

There therefore seems little reason to doubt that, except in most unusual cases, time started to run against a claimant when he had *experiundi potestas* and not when he knew he had a right of action.

A final question arises whether, once the claimant had *experiundi potestas* and time had started to run, it simply continued from that date for a year, or whether any day on which the claimant as a matter of fact did not have *experiundi potestas* was deducted from the reckoning. Ubbelohde, in a close study of the (few) relevant texts, concludes that *annus utilis* meant a continuous year running from the date when the requirements of *experiundi potestas* were first met.[25] So, for example, time would continue to run even when somebody was orchestrating a delay to the commencement of proceedings[26] or when the claimant was absent.[27]

POST-CLASSICAL ROMAN LAW

We may now turn to post-classical developments. These can be covered more briefly than the classical position, since the profile of the law of limitation is much less obscure and the contours are, from the perspective of modern legal systems, fairly familiar. The purpose of this very short section is largely to point up the contrasts with the classical regime.

The background to what became a general law of limitation of actions is to be found in the institution of *longi temporis praescriptio*, which emerged not in Rome but in the provinces.[28] It was a means of recognizing and protecting the possession of a person in relation to provincial land, to which *usucapio* did not apply. Under the Severan emperors it became an accepted legal institution, although its recognition by the jurists was somewhat piecemeal. Unlike *usucapio* it was (at least originally) not a mode of acquisition but instead a type of negative or extinctive prescription. Although that evidently changed, so that it became regarded in effect as a kind of acquisitive prescription, it is the original notion of negative prescription

25. Ubbelohde (n. 8), 47.
26. Paul 4 ed. D. 2.7.4 pr.; Jul. 2 dig. D. 2.10.3—there were other remedies to deal with such problems.
27. Pap. 3 quaest. D. 36.1.51.
28. M. Kaser, *Das römische Privatrecht*. vol. 1. 2nd ed. (Munich, 1971), 424–5; see further J. Partsch, *Die longi temporis praescriptio im klassichen römischen Rechte* (Leipzig, 1906); D. Nörr, *Die Entstehung der longi temporis praescriptio* (Cologne, 1969).

which accounts for its significance in the background to the development of a law of limitation of actions. It was on these foundations that Theodosius II proceeded to build.

The post-classical history—in fact really the starting point—of a general law of limitation of actions in Roman law begins with a constitution of Theodosius II in A.D. 424.[29] This constitution for the first time imposed on all *actiones perpetuae* (that is, all those which were not already subject to a time limit) a period of limitation of 30 years.[30] This constitution, a number issued by later emperors,[31] and a series issued by Justinian,[32] together lay out a comprehensive law of limitation of actions. Many of its features are strikingly similar to those of modern legal systems; equally striking is an almost total lack of any connection between them and the classical law that had gone before. Here it will be enough to mention three key points.

First, the starting date for the running of the new uniform prescriptive period was the date on which the claim had arisen:[33] so, for example, for *vindicatio*, it was the date on which another person had acquired the property in question. For an obligation, it was the date on which the defendant had failed to perform his obligation or more generally the date on which an obligation had become enforceable. Since a conditional obligation or one subject to a term (*dies*) was not enforceable until the condition had been purified or the term had arrived, the running of time did not begin until then.[34] In the event of interruption, a new period of limitation would have to start from day one.

Second, time ran continuously, and there was no suspension of the limitation period on grounds of *fragilitas sexus*, absence, or military service.

29. *Cod. Theod.* 4.14.1 (also transmitted as C. 7.39.3, although the text is abbreviated and interpolated). For the detail, the present discussion being merely a paraphrase, see esp. Amelotti (n. 4), 211–60; Kaser (n. 4), 71–2.

30. There were some exceptions: e.g. actions subject to a 40 or 100 year period and some which were imprescriptible: see Amelotti (n. 4), 231–2.

31. Nov. Valent. 27 (A.D. 449); Nov. Valent. 35 (A.D. 452); C. 7.39.4 (Anastasius; A.D. 491); C. 7.39.7 (Justinus; A.D. 525).

32. C. 7.39.8 and C. 4.32.26 (A.D. 528); C. 7.39.9 (A.D. 529); C. 7.40.1 and C. 1.2.23 (A.D. 530); C. 7.40.2, C. 7.40.3, C. 2.40.5, and C. 8.39.4 (A.D. 531); Novels 9 (A.D. 535), 111 (A.D. 541), and 131 ch. 6 (A.D. 545).

33. For terminology such as *ex quo competere coepit* [*actio/persecutio*], see e.g. C. 7.39.3.1; C. 7.39.7.1; C. 7.40.1.1d.

34. C. 7.39.7.4–4a, 7.

The sole exception was that time did not run against a pupil until he or she came of age.[35] This straightforward position was introduced by Theodosius II and confirmed by Justinian.

Third, the limitation period could be interrupted by raising an action.[36] Where, owing for example to the absence of the prospective defendant or his being under age, that was not possible, it could be interrupted by lodging a formal notice with the provincial governor, bishop or *defensor civitatis*, or making a declaration before witnesses.[37] It could also be interrupted by the defendant's acknowledgment, for example by reissue of a loan document or paying interest on a debt, and no doubt by other forms of part performance.[38]

This is no more than an outline of the main features of the post-classical regime. While later constitutions innovated on points of detail, the broad picture remained more or less the same from Theodosius II to Justinian. And it is a picture very different from that of classical times. Closer exploration than is possible in this paper might reveal something about the impetus for introduction of a general period of limitation of 30 years. For the present it seems reasonable to see it, as others have done, as prompted by a concern for legal certainty.[39] The clarity of the new rules would undoubtedly assist in that regard even although, for the individual prospective defendant, a limitation period of thirty years would represent a regrettably lengthy period of uncertainty.

COMPARISONS AND CONCLUSIONS

In modern terms, classical law involved a rather harsh limitation regime, with the important qualification that it applied only to a limited class of actions. This brings out what to modern eyes is the most curious feature of the classical law: on the one hand, many actions were in principle not subject to limitation at all, with the consequence that a defendant would

35.   C. 7.39.3.1a.
36.   C. 7.39.3.1.
37.   C. 7.40.2.
38.   C. 7.39.7.5a; 7.39.8.4.
39.   Amelotti (n. 4), 212; T. Honoré, *Law in the Crisis of Empire* (Oxford, 1998), 107–8 (Honoré attributes *Cod. Theod.* 4.14.1 to Sallustius.)

never gain the reassurance that sufficient time had passed so that litigation could not be initiated against him; on the other, for those actions that were subject to a time limit, the limit was very short; the claimant's knowledge of the cause of action was irrelevant; and time ran continuously from the moment at which he was first able to proceed.[40]

Any conclusions are necessarily tentative, given the paucity of evidence. But the oddities implicit in these contrasting dilemmas for the litigants suggest rather strongly that the classical jurists did not in fact conceive of the one-year time limit as a limitation period at all. We know, by contrast, that they were fully conscious of the policy justifications in favor of *usucapio*: Gaius explains that it was introduced "so that ownership of property should not be uncertain for too long;"[41] while Neratius explains it on the grounds "that there should be some end to litigation."[42] These policies are equally applicable to a regime of limitation of actions, but neither is mentioned in that context. The curiosities of the classical system seem to be more readily explicable on the ground that it was thought appropriate that praetorian remedies, the creation of a magistrate whose jurisdiction was limited to one year, should not themselves last for longer than a year.[43] This, of course, is not to say that the one-year time limit applicable to any given action was coterminous with the magistrate's own year of office. That analysis is plainly impossible, since the period of office would usually not be co-extensive with one year measured from a claimant's *experiundi potestas*; equally, if this were the rationale, all praetorian actions should have been limited to a year, but they were not.[44] Instead the suggestion here is two-fold: first, that it was thought appropriate to have a time limit on a magistrate's remedies which was the same length as the period for which he himself held office; second, that it was the term of office that prompted the introduction of time limits on certain actions, rather than a perception that

---

40. There might be circumstances in which a claimant could obtain *in integrum restitutio* against loss of his cause of action, but that could not be relied upon as a matter of course: cf. Ulp. 12 ed. D. 4.6.26.7.

41. Gaius, *Inst.* 2.44: *ne rerum dominia diutius in incerto essent.*

42. Ner. 5 membr. D. 41.10.5: *ut aliquis litium finis esset.*

43. Cf. Ubbelohde (n. 8), 54.

44. Cf. Amelotti (n. 4), 52–3.

fairness between the parties required that actions be subject to limitation after the passage of a year.

If these reflections are along the right lines, then in modern terms the one-year time limit is to be conceived not in terms of limitation of actions but as a rule of administrative or public law limiting the exercise of a magistrate's jurisdiction. While that characterization may appear to make little practical difference, it does seem to explain the unusual features of the classical system better than an analysis in terms of limitation of actions. Here are five reasons.

First, it is consistent with what would otherwise be a very surprising omission: the omission of the classical jurists to analyze when time starts to run against a claim.[45] As noted earlier, the surviving classical analysis is in terms of the objective question when a claimant first became able to sue, and the three prerequisites are identified as the existence of a claimant, a defendant, and a magistrate. Nothing is said about when a right was infringed or an obligation was incurred. We cannot be sure but we certainly cannot assume that the jurists would also have asked when the cause of action arose.

Second, so far as we can judge, for the purpose of identifying when time started to run against a claim, the classical jurists were generally not interested in the claimant's state of knowledge.

Third, in the surviving texts of the Roman jurists there is no discussion of the policy questions which are invariably raised in connection with limitation of actions. These include such things as the need to balance the interests of the parties; the need in the public interest to achieve legal certainty and avoid protracted litigation; and accordingly the appropriateness of penalizing the negligence of a dilatory claimant and protecting a defendant against arbitrary delay by a claimant.

All three of these points would be expected to receive at least some attention in a system that was consciously balancing the equities between the parties by means of a limitation period. But if the time limit is conceived in

---

45. A caveat is necessary: discussion of that kind may simply have been lost in the compilation of the Digest, although it is difficult to see why it would have been deliberately jettisoned, since it would in all likelihood have followed the same approach as the post-classical constitutions (above, n. 34).

essence as one applicable to the magistrate's jurisdiction, it is much easier to understand why the points are not considered.

Fourth, the approach suggested here is consistent with the quite separate time limits that applied to actions after they had been raised. Here a distinction was drawn between *iudicia legitima* and *iudicia imperio continentia*. Actions of the first kind lapsed if judgment had not been pronounced within 18 months of the date the parties joined issue, *litis contestatio*.[46] *Iudicia imperio continentia* depended on the *imperium* of a magistrate and remained effective only for as long as the magistrate who had authorized them retained *imperium*; this meant that an action of this kind could never last longer than one year and, depending at what point in the magistrate's year of office it was authorized, it might last considerably less. These were not limitation periods in the modern sense; instead what they required, once proceedings had commenced, was that they be completed within a certain period. For present purposes, however, these rules are interesting because they attest the concern of the classical jurists to link the jurisdiction of the magistrate with the validity of the legal remedies he granted.

Fifth, the same point can be made simply by a comparison with the post-classical regime of limitation of actions, elaborately worked out in the rules set out in particular in titles 7.39 and 7.40 of Justinian's Code. Here the question when time started to run was answered by reference to an objective test, when a right was infringed or an obligation was either incurred or breached. Clear rules on what constituted interruption of the limitation period were established, including such complexities as the application of the rules to cases involving multiple creditors or debtors;[47] and the effect of interruption by an action which was subsequently abandoned for a lengthy period.[48] Clear rules about the running of time and the very limited circumstances in which it did not run (pupillarity) were laid down. These are precisely the kinds of questions that we find in modern legal practice. Perhaps the main point of difference is that no regard was paid to the ques-

---

46. Gaius, *Inst.* 4.104–105; cf. Kaser/Hackl (n. 11), §51 III; E. Metzger, *Litigation in Roman Law* (Oxford, 2005), 114–17.

47. C. 8.39(40).4(5) (A.D. 531).

48. C. 7.39.9 (A.D. 529).

tion when the claimant knew that he had a cause of action; but this hardly seems unfair when the limitation period was anyway thirty years.[49]

The main point, however, is that all of these issues are important when the law is seeking to balance the equities between competing parties. On the other hand, when the perspective is not that of limitation, with its concomitant requirement of even-handedness between the parties, but instead a question of administrative or public law about the temporal extent of a magistrate's jurisdiction, it is much easier to understand why for classical law there was no need for close analysis of when rights accrued, knowledge was obtained, or interruptions took place.

In an essay in honor of Dick Helmholz it would have been good to arrive at more exciting or compelling conclusions. But the texts are what they are. In a broader perspective, however, the picture this short study presents is interesting because it is one that is relatively unusual in the history of Roman law and its legal tradition. First, it is clear that a coherent and well-crafted law of limitation of actions was developed entirely in post-classical times, with virtually no contribution from classical juristic thought. Second, that post-classical law went on to influence the law of prescription and limitation in canon law, in the *ius commune* more widely, and in many modern legal systems. Third, the rather unfamiliar lack of classical texts in this area of law is best (so it is argued) attributed not to accident in the preservation or textual transmission of classical juristic works but to a reality about classical Roman law and procedure: that system quite simply did not operate with the concept of limitation of actions. Its time limits were instead conceived in terms of limits on the jurisdiction of the magistrates who administered the law.[50]

49. It may be for the same reason that matters that Ulpian considered relevant impediments to a claimant being able to sue are entirely disregarded in post-classical law: see above at n. 16.

50. My thanks to Ernest Metzger for reading a draft of this paper.

Episcopal Power and Royal Jurisdiction in Angevin England

Joshua C. Tate[1]

Although scholars have expressed a wide range of opinion on the extent to which the *ius commune* might have influenced the early English Common law, there is general agreement that the great European reception of Roman law in the later Middle Ages did not cross the English Channel. Even Charles Sherman, whose maximalist case has yet to be matched, acknowledged that the impact of Roman law in England was "limited in character as compared with the Continental reception."[2] Perhaps the best explanation for this is the timing thesis offered by R. C. van Caenegem: because England developed an efficient, centralized legal system at such an early stage, the increasingly sophisticated commentaries and glosses on Roman and Canon law texts that emerged from the thirteenth century onward were of limited use to the royal justices in England.[3]

1.   For helpful comments, I am grateful to Paul Brand, Charles Donahue, and those who attended my presentations at the 2013 annual meetings of the American Society for Legal History and the Australian and New Zealand Law and History Society; the Third Biennial Conference of the European Society for Comparative Legal History; and law faculty workshops at Torcuato Di Tella University, the Legal Research Institute of the National Autonomous University of Mexico (IIJ-UNAM), and the Mexico Autonomous Institute of Technology (ITAM).
2.   Charles P. Sherman, "The Romanization of English Law," *Yale Law Journal* 23 (1914), 329.
3.   R. C. van Caenegem, *The Birth of the English Common Law*, 2nd ed. (Cambridge, 1988), 90–91.

If the precocious development of the English Common law system explains its resistance to the Continental reception, it does not follow that the entrenchment of royal justice in England was a foregone conclusion by the thirteenth century. The Angevin reforms were not universally popular, and criticism of royal justice became particularly strong during the reign of King John, whose consistent presence in England after the loss of his Continental possessions and assertive governance style led to frequent personal interventions in the operation of the royal courts.[4] John's actions may have contributed to the development of the concept of rule of law, as there is evidence of a backlash on the part of some royal justices who may have resented the king's interference with their work.[5] The most famous product of John's ineffective leadership was, of course, the Great Charter of 1215, several clauses of which addressed the need for fairness in judicial proceedings.

It is one of the great ironies of history that the king responsible for what may be the world's most important constitutional document is remembered as one of England's least effective rulers. This inconsistency might be explained, in part, by the fact that key features of Magna Carta reflect not a recognition of ancient English customs and restraints on royal power, but a reception of certain principles from the *ius commune*. In 1999, Richard Helmholz made a vigorous argument that the *ius commune* played a significant role in the shaping of Magna Carta.[6] The case for influence is particularly strong with regard to Clause 22, dealing with the amercement of clerks, Clause 27, regarding the disposition of chattels on intestacy, and Clause 55, dealing with unjust fines and amercements.[7] If the *ius commune* played a role in the development of Magna Carta, this prompts two questions. First, why was this critical constitutional moment not an occasion for the English royal courts to embrace more features of Roman and Canon

---

4.   John Hudson, *The Formation of the English Common Law: Law and Society in England from the Norman Conquest to Magna Carta* (New York, 1996), 220–24.

5.   John Hudson, *The Oxford History of the Laws of England, Volume II, 871–1216* (Oxford, 2012), 846.

6.   R. H. Helmholz, "Magna Carta and the *ius commune*," *University of Chicago Law Review* 66 (1999), 297–371.

7.   See Helmholz, "Magna Carta," 329–58; see also John Hudson, "Magna Carta, the *ius commune*, and English Common Law," in *Magna Carta and the England of King John*, ed. Janet S. Loengard (Woodbridge, 2010), 103–04.

law? Second, why did the ecclesiastical courts not seize this opportunity during the years leading up to the Great Charter to claim jurisdiction over matters that were subject to overlap between the two systems?

This article will attempt a partial answer to the second of these questions, which is not entirely unconnected with the first. With regard to one particular area—rights of presentation to churches—that was a locus for jurisdictional conflict between the royal and ecclesiastical courts, the records from one of England's most important dioceses suggest that what might have been an opportunity for an ecclesiastical court to seize more power during the king's moment of weakness was instead marked by a deliberate abdication of responsibility made possible by the king's shrewd appointment of a compliant bishop. The register of Hugh of Wells shows traces of what seems to have been a more aggressive approach of his predecessor bishops of Lincoln in patronage disputes, and a less loyal bishop might have built on that precedent to successfully lure lay plaintiffs back into the episcopal court. Instead, the bishop deferred to the jurisdiction of the king's courts and did not attempt to reassert his ancient privileges. As a result, after the constitutional crisis provoked by King John had passed, the supremacy of the king's courts over important patronage disputes was permanently secured.

The Law of Patronage and Jurisdictional Conflict

Both the English royal courts and the church claimed jurisdiction to decide disputes over patronage to churches. The position of the English kings was stated in the first clause of the constitutions of Clarendon, in which Henry II proclaimed that all advowson disputes belonged in the royal courts regardless of the parties involved.[8] By contrast, Canon law claimed that patronage disputes ought to be decided in ecclesiastical courts, making exceptions only for cases where the advowson was appurtenant to an estate

---

8. *De advocatione et presentatione ecclesiarum, si controversia emerserit inter laicos, vel inter clericos et laicos, vel inter clericos, in curia domini regis tractetur et terminetur.* D. Whitelock, M. Brett and C. N. L. Brooke, ed., *Councils and Synods with Other Documents Relating to the English Church,* I (Oxford, 1981), Part II, 878–79.

and a secular court had jurisdiction over the estate. [9] The English royal courts were unconcerned with these principles of Canon law, but there was little the bishops could do about it unless they were prepared to face the wrath of the Angevin kings, which, as the example of Thomas Becket made clear, was a dangerous proposition indeed. On the other hand, the bishops could and did decide which priests had the right to particular benefices, and those determinations were difficult to entangle from the underlying advowson disputes.[10]

For the most part, the English bishops did not interfere with the exercise of royal jurisdiction regarding advowson disputes. In order for a bishop to challenge royal authority, it was necessary for at least one of the parties to be dissatisfied with the procedures offered in the king's courts, or for the dispute to drag on long enough for the Third Lateran Council to be invoked. Although some interpretations of the Council allowed a bishop to fill a benefice if a dispute in the secular court was not resolved within four months, the royal court records suggest that the English bishops adopted a more conservative approach and waited six months before taking action.[11] The expedited procedures made possible by the assize of darrein presentment limited the opportunities of bishops to exercise their authority under the Council.[12] The early plea rolls do contain examples where bishops became involved in patronage disputes, such as a dispute between Fulk d'Oyri and the abbot of Crowland in Trinity Term 1194.[13] The parties were ultimately given license to concord, with a notation that the bishop of Lincoln had to be present for any agreement.[14] However, that case involved a claim to present to a vicarage and an associated pension owed to the abbot, and

9.   Peter Landau, *Jus Patronatus: Studien zur Entwicklung des Patronats im Dekretalenrecht und der Kanonistik des 12. und 13. Jahrhunderts* (Cologne, 1975), 207–10; see also R. H. Helmholz, *The Oxford History of the Laws of England, Volume I: The Canon Law and Ecclesiastical Jurisdiction from 597 to the 1640s* (Oxford, 2004), 478–79 (citing X 2.1.3).

10.   J. W. Gray, "The *Ius Praesentandi* in England from the Constitutions of Clarendon to Bracton," *English Historical Review* 67 (1952), 481–508.

11.   Joshua C. Tate, "The Third Lateran Council and the *Ius Patronatus* in England," in *Proceedings of the Thirteenth International Congress of Medieval Canon Law: Esztergom, 3–8 August 2008*, ed. Peter Erdö and Sz. Anzelm Szuromi, Monumenta Iuris Canonici, C.14 (Vatican City, 2010), 598–600.

12.   Tate, "Third Lateran Council," 595–98.

13.   14 Pipe Roll Society 7, 10 (Trin. 1194) [hereinafter PRS].

14.   14 PRS 28 (Trin. 1194).

Hugh of Avalon's assertion of his jurisdiction was understandable in that context.[15]

If King John had been content to allow the royal courts to follow their standard procedures, the triumph of the royal courts in the jurisdictional conflict over advowson disputes would be easily understood. As in other contexts, however, John was prone to intervene personally in certain advowson cases of particular interest to him. For example, in Easter Term 1201, King John ordered his justices not to hear an assize of darrein presentment brought by Robert de Buillers and his wife Hillary against William of Firsby, archdeacon of Stow, until his preferred candidate, Roger de Beaumont, was accepted by the chapter of Lincoln as bishop to replace the recently deceased Hugh of Avalon.[16] Similarly, in Hilary Term 1203, King John prohibited a lawsuit from being heard concerning the church of St. Decuman's as long as the bishop of Bath had taken the sign of the cross.[17] In Trinity Term 1208, a dispute over the church of Wimpole in the diocese of Ely between Saer de Quenci, earl of Winchester, and Robert de Insula was abruptly called to a halt with the explanation that "the lord king does not want the lawsuit to proceed (*dominus rex non vult quod loquela illa procedat*)."[18]

In many of these cases, there might have been good reasons for John's decisions. It made sense to wait for the appointment of a bishop of Lincoln before deciding an important dispute where the bishop had, as in the case from Easter Term 1201, been vouched to warrant.[19] There are other instances in the rolls in which a party was excused from appearance or given other relief on the grounds that he had taken the cross.[20] In light of his brother's absence from England during his reign, however, King John's personal in-

15.　Joshua C. Tate, "Competing Institutions and Dispute Settlement in Medieval England," in *Law and Disputing in the Middle Ages: Proceedings of the Ninth Carlsberg Academy Conference on Medieval Legal History 2012*, ed. Per Andersen et al. (Copenhagen, 2013), 244.

16.　1 Curia Regis Rolls 442 (Pas. 1201) [hereinafter CRR]; *The Life of Saint Hugh of Lincoln*, trans. Herbert Thurston (London, 1898), 565–66.

17.　2 CRR 179 (Hil. 1203).

18.　5 CRR 231 (Trin. 1208).

19.　1 CRR 442 (Pas. 1201).

20.　See, e.g., 3 CRR 193 (Mich. 1204) (party excused from appearance); 7 CRR 297 (Mich. 1214) (losing party pardoned of an amercement).

volvement in these and other cases might have been perceived by the losing parties as an interference with the regular course of justice. As explained by Doris Stenton,

> John was but performing an ancient royal duty. But in the last ten years of the twelfth century the administration of justice had been carried on with but little reference to the king himself. It had been a time when the king's court was growing rapidly in popularity. The practice of eyres had been elaborated and the court at Westminster had become the centre of a highly organised judicial system, which depended on the Justiciar whose writ ran as the king's. The accession of a king who knew England as well as Henry II had known it, who was as interested in legal problems as Henry II had been, meant that Justiciar and Judges alike found that they had a master. [21]

The best evidence that John's involvement in the royal courts at the beginning of his reign was not perceived as a positive development is the Great Charter itself, which famously insists that John will not sell, deny, or delay right or justice to any person.[22] That line would have been superfluous unless at least some of the losing parties in royal cases felt aggrieved by John's personal dispensation of justice, and such litigants would presumably have been open to a viable alternative. In some cases, episcopal courts might not have been a practical option, but those bishops who were able to offer justice in advowson disputes might have found willing customers in those subjects of King John who were frustrated by his rule. Why did the ecclesiastical courts not seize the opportunity during the years leading up to the Great Charter to claim the jurisdiction granted to them under Canon law? To answer this question, it is helpful to turn to the diocese of Lincoln, which offers some of the earliest detailed records of day-to-day diocesan proceedings involving vacant churches.

---

21. Doris Mary Stenton, "King John and the Courts of Justice," in *Pleas before the King and His Justices, 1198–1202*, I, Selden Society 67 (1948), 86.

22. *Nulli vendemus, nulli negabimus aut differemus rectum vel justiciam*. Great Charter of 1215, Clause 40.

Patronage in the Medieval Diocese of Lincoln

Although the medieval diocese of Lincoln was not the largest diocese in England, it was vast in size, including all or part of eight counties, and probably contained the largest number of religious houses in the country.[23] It is unsurprising, therefore, that the diocese of Lincoln produced a high percentage of the ecclesiastical patronage disputes brought to the royal courts. Of the advowson cases mentioned in the surviving plea rolls of Richard I, 27.6% involved churches in the diocese of Lincoln, which was tied with the diocese of Norwich. Together the two dioceses accounted for the majority of the advowson disputes in the royal courts from 1194 to 1199, with the diocese of York a distant third at 9%.[24] Over time, however, the percentage of cases involving churches from the diocese of Lincoln dropped as other dioceses began to produce more litigation in the royal courts. By the time of the last rolls from the reign of King John, the percentage of royal advowson cases involving churches in the diocese of Lincoln had dropped to 17.3%.[25] Advowson litigation brought into the royal courts by the Angevin reforms did not return to the ecclesiastical courts, notwithstanding the problems that some of King John's most powerful subjects had with his dispensation of personal justice.

In an earlier article, I argued that the high percentage of disputes between laymen and religious houses in the diocese of Lincoln during the last years of the reign of Richard I may have reflected a perceived bias on the part of Hugh of Avalon, a former Carthusian prior who would eventually be canonized, in favor of the monasteries.[26] Although Lincoln continued to produce a high number of cases involving religious houses after the death of St. Hugh in 1200, by the end of John's reign the diocese had ceased to be exceptional in that regard. Of the advowson disputes between laymen and religious houses that first appear in the surviving plea rolls from Trin-

23. David Knowles, *The Religious Orders in England, Volume 3: The Tudor Age* (Cambridge, 1959), 62.

24. Tate, "Competing Institutions," 238.

25. Out of 52 advowson cases that first appear in the published plea rolls from Trinity Term and Michaelmas Term 1214, nine involved churches in the Diocese of Lincoln. The highest number of cases, twelve, came from the diocese of Norwich, and the remaining cases were spread out more or less evenly among other dioceses.

26. Tate, "Competing Institutions," 240–44.

ity Term and Michaelmas Term 1214, five involve churches in the diocese of Lincoln,[27] but six involve churches in the diocese of York,[28] four involve churches in the diocese of Norwich,[29] and three involve churches in the diocese of Bath.[30] The simplest explanation for the change is that, by the end of King John's reign, litigants initiated advowson disputes in the royal courts as a matter of course, not to avoid a perceived bias on the part of particular bishops who presided over the ecclesiastical courts.

By the end of the reign of King John, we have a better idea of what might have been happening in ecclesiastical courts with regard to patronage disputes. The rolls of Hugh of Wells, who became bishop of Lincoln in 1209, form the earliest surviving episcopal register in England, and provide a detailed record of the activities of the bishop and his archdeacons with regard to ecclesiastical vacancies.[31] These rolls show that it was routine to hold an ecclesiastical inquest *de iure patronatus* whenever a benefice became vacant.[32] If the description in the rolls is any guide to what procedure was followed in practice, however, the nature of the inquest seems to have evolved over time. The earliest roll in the series, currently identified by the reference number "X" but known during the episcopate of Bishop Hugh as the "Vetus Rotulus," consists of thirteen membranes in two different hands.[33] As demonstrated by the careful research of David Smith, the earliest entries on the roll are the first four entries on Membrane 1 and the entries on Membrane 2, which were written by a different scribe than the other entries on the roll. This scribe, whom Smith refers to as Scribe A, used a "small and untidy hand," while the other scribe, Scribe B, wrote in

---

27.   7 CRR 135 (Trin. 1214) (Milton); 7 CRR 221 (Trin. 1214) (Ingham); 7 CRR 278 (Mich. 1214) (Asgarby); 7 CRR 302 (Mich. 1214) (Harby); 7 CRR 305 (Mich. 1214) (Morton).

28.   7 CRR 118 (Trin. 1214) (Barningham); 7 CRR 165 (Trin. 1214) (Bilton and Healaugh); 7 CRR 177 (Trin. 1214) (Attenborough); 7 CRR 260 (Mich. 1214) (South Kirkby); 7 CRR 261 (Mich. 1214) (Elvaston); 7 CRR 280 (Mich. 1214) (Adel).

29.   7 CRR 132 (Trin. 1214) (Burnham); 7 CRR 259 (Mich. 1214) (Stanninghall); 7 CRR 286 (Mich. 1214) (Barney); 7 CRR 297 (Mich. 1214) (Randworth).

30.   7 CRR 129 (Trin. 1214) (Englishcombe); 7 CRR 164 (Trin. 1214) (Stanton); 7 CRR 196 (Trin. 1214) (Brean).

31.   David M. Smith, "The Rolls of Hugh of Wells, Bishop of Lincoln 1209–35," *Bulletin of the Institute of Historical Research* 45 (1972), 155.

32.   Gray, "*Ius Praesentandi*," at 491–94.

33.   Smith, "Rolls of Hugh of Wells," at 157–60.

a hand that was "regular, neat, and more ornate." The entries written by Scribe A most likely date to 1214 and 1215.[34] One of those entries relates to the institution of a parson to the church of Stibbington:

> Master Thomas of Tyrinton, presented by the abbot and convent of Thorney to the church of Stibbington, is admitted and instituted to that church.... And this was done after an inquest by the bishop, present in that very church, determined that the church was the subject of no controversy and the abbot and convent held the advowson....[35]

Of the many entries in the roll that refer to an institution of a new parson, this is the only one that refers to an inquest having been made by the bishop relating to the advowson. Other entries in Membrane 2 refer to an inquest by the dean of Lincoln, one of the archdeacons, or another senior cleric, but also typically state that the inquest determined that the advowson of the church belonged to a specific individual or religious house.[36] This formulaic language was soon changed, however, to a more ambiguous statement of what occurred at the inquest. The following entry from Membrane 4 is illustrative:

> William of Cennor, a clerk, having been presented by the abbess and convent of Godstow to the church of Easington...was admitted and instituted as parson since everything was made clear through an inquest by the archdeacon of Oxford....[37]

---

34. Smith, "Rolls of Hugh of Wells," at 160.

35. "Magister T. de Tyrintona presentatus per abbatem et conventum de [Thorney] ad ecclesiam de Stibbingtona, ad eam est admissus et institutus in eadem.... Et facta fuit prius inquisitio per episcopum, in ipsa ecclesia presentem, quod fuit sine controversia et de advocatione dictorum Abbatis et conventus...." W. P. W. Phillimore ed., *Rotuli Hugonis de Welles, Episcopi Lincolniensis A.D. MCCIX–MCCXXXV*, Volume 1, Lincoln Record Society 3 (1913): 5–6 [hereinafter RHW].

36. RHW 1, 2–9 (entries referring to inquests by the dean of Lincoln, archdeacons of Northampton, Oxford, Bedford, and Buckingham, and official of Northampton).

37. "Willelmus de Cennora, clericus, presentatus per abattissam et conventum de Godstow ad ecclesiam de Esindone...cum omnia per inquisitionem per Archidiaconum Oxoniensem factam essent liquida...admissus est et in persona institutus...." 1 RHW 16 (membrane 4).

In most subsequent entries, the archdeacon's inquest is reported to have determined that "the matter was ready (*negotium fuit in expedito*)," giving the green light to the institution of the new parson while omitting any reference to a finding regarding to the advowson.[38] Some entries are even less specific, reducing the description of the inquest to a simple "etc."[39]

Taken by themselves, these changes in formulaic language might not indicate any significant change in the procedures being followed in the diocese with regard to vacant churches. Neither Scribe A nor Scribe B was likely to have been present at the inquests they recorded, and Scribe B may simply have chosen to be more concise in summarizing the returns he received from the clerks of the various archdeacons. In light of the significant drop in the percentage of royal advowson cases from the diocese of Lincoln from the episcopate of Hugh of Avalon to that of Hugh of Wells, however, it is at least possible that the entry relating to the church of Stibbington might be the last trace of what was once a significant involvement by the bishop in patronage disputes. Compared to the neat and ornate hand of Scribe B, the hand of Scribe A, who was responsible for the entries in membranes 1 and 2, suggests that he was either new to the role of keeping entries in the bishop's register or—more likely, given the chronology of the entries—was primarily trained to handle other administrative matters and took on the role of scribe toward the end of his career. Even if Hugh of Wells rarely intervened in such matters, Scribe A might have remembered an earlier time when Hugh of Avalon as bishop took a more aggressive approach, making determinations as to rights of presentation as a matter of course. At the least, Scribe A regarded the church as playing some role in the determination of the ownership of the advowson, whether the inquest was made by the bishop or a lower official. Scribe B preferred to elide that aspect of the inquest, perhaps sensitive to the fact that the royal courts considered advowson disputes to be within their sole jurisdiction.

KING JOHN AND HIS BISHOPS

Outside of the occasional revisionist historian, King John is not frequently mentioned as an effective administrator. In one respect, however, John did

38.   Gray, "*Ius Praesentandi*," at 492–93.
39.   See, e.g., RHW 1, 12 (membrane 3); RHW 1, 63 (membrane 9).

have some success: he was able to appoint bishops to two of the most important dioceses in England who proved to be loyal allies or, at the least, not thorns in King John's side. Hugh of Wells was one of those bishops. Neither a scholar nor a holy man, Hugh joined the chancery of King John in 1199 and continued to serve the king until his election to the bishopric of Lincoln in 1209. Hugh broke with King John following the latter's excommunication, which may have facilitated his confirmation notwithstanding suspected election irregularities and other malicious rumors. However, Hugh never caused the sort of problems for John that his predecessor Hugh of Avalon caused for Henry II, and he is remembered primarily as a competent administrator who served his diocese efficiently for many years. Hugh also served as a royal justice on several eyres during the reign of Henry III, John's successor.[40]

It is unsurprising that a bishop with the background of Hugh of Wells would have little interest in reasserting claims under Canon law that conflicted with the longstanding royal position that advowson disputes belonged in the king's courts. Moreover, Hugh of Wells was not the only loyal clerk whom King John was able to successfully appoint to a high ecclesiastical office. John de Gray, bishop of Norwich from 1200 to his death in 1214, was, like Hugh, a clerk in King John's service before his elevation to the episcopate. When the pope excommunicated King John, John de Gray was one of only two bishops to remain loyal to the king, the other being Peter des Roches, bishop of Winchester.[41] The confidence of King John in the administration of his bishop of Norwich might explain a curt entry from the plea rolls of Hilary Term 1203 dismissing a lawsuit over the advowson of the church of Kettleston, in the diocese of Norwich, "by order of the lord king (*per preceptum domini regis*)," without further explanation.[42] A loyal bishop like John de Gray would have taken extra care to avoid any decisions that might have incurred the king's displeasure; thus, the possibility of a jurisdictional conflict would have been of only theoretical importance in that relationship.

40. David M. Smith, "Wells, Hugh of (d. 1235)," *Oxford Dictionary of National Biography* (Oxford, 2004), http://www.oxforddnb.com/view/article/14061.
41. Roy Martin Haines, "Gray, John de (d. 1214)," *Oxford Dictionary of National Biography* (Oxford, 2004), http://www.oxforddnb.com/view/article/11541.
42. 2 CRR 163 (Hil. 1203).

Disputes regarding advowsons were a small, albeit important, part of the business of the early royal courts. If the bishops had managed to seize jurisdiction over advowsons in the tumult leading up to Magna Carta, it would have been a small and possibly short-lived victory. Any account of the success of the English Common law, however, must take into account not only the fact that the early Common law courts were successful in attracting litigants, but that they were able to keep that business through the end of the reign of one of England's least popular kings. Had the Common law been less fair or efficient, the royal courts might have suffered the same fate as Star Chamber in a later age. The true genius of the Angevin legal reforms was their resilience in the face of the worst enemy of the rule of law: powerful men who do not understand the limits of their power.

The Common Lawyers of the Reign of Edward I and the Canon Law

Paul Brand

It is during the reign of King Edward I (1272–1307) that we first see clearly groups of professional lawyers practicing in the lay courts, and especially in the royal courts, in England and can identify many of their members. It is also then that we first see those lawyers being treated as members of a legal profession through the imposition of controls over their admission to practice, provision being made for their training and education, and the imposition and enforcement of rules of professional conduct on members of these groups.[1] Law reports (which begin at the very end of the previous reign but first survive in any quantity only in this reign) begin to give us a clear picture of the activities not just of these professional lawyers (or, more specifically, of their elite, the serjeants) but also of the justices who presided over the main royal courts, participating in arguments and making judgments on the basis of their knowledge and expertise in the English Common Law.[2] Our initial impression when looking at this world of the English Common Law courts and their lawyers and justices is just how different it is from the world of the English ecclesiastical courts and their lawyers and judges. It is not just that the English Common Law had its own

1. Paul Brand, *The Origins of the English Legal Profession* (Oxford, 1992), chapters 5–8.
2. Paul Brand, *Observing and Recording the Medieval Bar and Bench at Work: The Origins of Law Reporting in England* (London, 1999).

distinctive set of procedures, separate area of competence and applicable legal rules, but also that its lawyers and justices were separately trained. Indeed, they even used a different language in court from the legal experts of the ecclesiastical courts: Anglo-Norman French, as opposed to the Latin of the ecclesiastical courts. But even if these were different worlds, they were not, and could not be, worlds hermetically sealed from one another. For all but two short periods in the reign the chief justices of the Common Bench (the main court for civil litigation) were themselves clerics.[3] Three of the four longer-term chief justices (master Roger of Seaton, John of Mettingham and Ralph de Hengham) also held ecclesiastical benefices. The fourth, Thomas Weyland, did not; indeed he was enough of a layman to have married two wives and to have fathered a number of children. But he had been ordained a clerk and his original clerical status may have helped to save his life when he was accused in 1289–90 of being an accessory after the fact to a murder committed by his servants.[4] All of these men other than Weyland seem likely to have acquired, and indeed needed, some knowledge of canon law for their ecclesiastical office holding. It is probable that master Roger of Seaton had even studied canon law at university. He had certainly performed functions for two successive bishops of Durham which required him to be expert in it.[5] During the first half of Edward's reign (to 1289) ordained clerics, all with ecclesiastical livings, also accounted for a majority of other judicial appointments to the Common Bench. Such appointments continued to be made after 1289, although clerics became less predominant in the second half of Edward's reign. These clerical justices included at least one man (master Ralph of Farningham) whom the evidence suggests may have been a university trained lawyer expert in the learned laws.[6] Another justice, master John Lovel, although never a justice of the Common Bench, did hold the senior clerical post of keeper of rolls and writs in that court and was a justice of one of the two eyre circuits from 1292 to 1293 and a justice of King's Bench for a short period in 1293–4. Master John is prob-

---

3.   The two periods were 1273 when Gilbert of Preston was chief justice, and Michaelmas term 1289 when Ralph of Sandwich was interim chief justice.

4.   Paul Brand, *The Making of the Common Law* (London, 1992), 113–133.

5.   *Earliest English Law Reports*, I, ed. Paul Brand, Selden Society 111 (1996), cxxxv–cxxxvi.

6.   *Earliest English Law Reports*, I, cxxxix–cxl.

ably the only royal justice in this period who had been a practicing canon lawyer, and he is known to have had a period as an advocate in the Court of Arches during the 1280s.[7] As for the professional lawyers of the common law courts, there is evidence to suggest that at least three of the professional serjeants of the Common Bench, men who were also active in other courts, had been ordained to at least minor orders before they became serjeants, though none seems ever to have held an ecclesiastical benefice.[8] This does not necessarily indicate any particular knowledge of, or expertise in, canon law on their part but it may do. More significant is the fact that Edmund of Pashley, a serjeant active in the later years of the reign and well beyond, was called a "legist," a Roman lawyer. Edmund seems likely to have acquired his expertise in a university environment and will also have acquired there a knowledge of canon law. There is also evidence to indicate that at least four and perhaps as many as eight serjeants (two of whom became Common Bench justices) knew some Roman and canon law and had perhaps acquired it in the same way.[9]

The two worlds of the lay and ecclesiastical courts also came into contact, and sometimes into conflict, in other ways as well. In those contacts, as they are recorded in the official records of the king's courts and in the unofficial law reports of cases heard there, we can see some of the ways in which the justices and serjeants of the royal courts had of necessity to pick up some knowledge of canon law and its procedures. We can also sometimes glimpse their attitudes, and sometimes their prejudices, towards canon law. Take for example the issue of bastardy. The normal rule of the Common Law in this period was that whenever the question arose in the course of civil litigation about title the land as to whether a particular individual involved in the case was or was not a bastard, and therefore incapable of inheriting land or other property from his parents or from anyone else, that question was transmitted to the relevant local ordinary for him to have

7.   Brand, *Making of the Common Law*, 72, 197; CP 40/60, m. 15.

8.   Paul Brand, "The Serjeants of the Common Bench in the Reign of Edward I: an Emerging Professional Elite," in *Thirteenth Century England VII: Proceedings of the Durham Conference 1997*, ed. Michael Prestwich, Richard Britnell and Robin Frame (Woodbridge, 1999), 81–102 at 95, note 95.

9.   Paul Brand, "Legal Education in England before the Inns of Court," in *Learning the Law; Teaching and the Transmission of Law in England*, ed. Jonathan A. Bush and Alain Wijffels (London, 1999), 51–84 at 73–4.

inquiries made in an ecclesiastical court and for him then to report back to the court on the birth status of that individual.[10] There were, however, a number of exceptions to this general rule. One was when the alleged bastard was already dead at the time of the litigation. This was the situation in a formedon in the reverter case heard in the Common Bench in Easter term 1302. The claimant's title was as grandson of the original grantor of entailed land, Hugh Miller, now claiming its reversion but tracing his descent from the grantor through his father, Hugh Clerk. The warrantor of the current tenant of the land alleged that Hugh Miller also had an elder son (and heir) named Henry, who had succeeded him in the lands he held at the time of his death. Although Henry was now dead he had a living son, with a better title to the reversion. The claimant agreed that there had been such an elder son but said that he was a bastard.[11] There are five different law reports of this case. All have different versions of a speech made by chief justice Hengham in the course of pleading. In one of them he says:

> When bastardy is alleged against someone who is alive a writ will issue to the bishop to try there whether he is a bastard or not, but where one takes the exception of bastardy for someone who is dead one ought to enquire here how he was considered when he was alive, whether as a bastard or otherwise, and so you will tell us whether he was held a bastard in his life or not.[12]

A second version of the same speech in a different manuscript is slightly more specific. It seems to show Hengham's knowledge and understanding of the reasons for the different treatment of the issue of bastardy in the case of someone who was living and someone who was dead and suggests that this was something required by the procedural rules of ecclesiastical courts:

10. R. H. Helmholz, "Bastardy Litigation in Medieval England" in *Canon Law and the Law of England* (London, 1987), no. 11.

11. The case is *Philip son of Hugh Clerk of Greet v. Peter son of Peter of Greet*. The plea roll enrolment is CP 40/142, m. 27d.

12. "*Hengh'*. Quant bastardie est allegge ver un homme qe est en pleyne vie si istra bref a levesqe pur trier illok' le quel il seit bastard ou nun, mes la ou lem prent excepcion de bastardie de cely qe mort est si deit lem enquere ceyns pur quel il esteit tenu tantcum il fut en vie pur bastard ou autre e pur ceo nus dirrez vus le quel il fut tenu pur bastard en sa vie ou nun." British Library [BL] MS Add. 31826, fol. 136r.

When an exception of bastardy is alleged in the person of someone who is alive and is a party the exception will be tried in court christian and when bastardy is alleged in the person of one who is dead it will be tried in [this] court by inquest *because in court christian it is necessary for the parties to be present* and one will not enquire whether he was bastard or not but how he was considered locally during his lifetime.[13]

It was also the normal procedure when any question arose in one of the king's courts as to whether a widow who was seeking her dower had been lawfully married to the husband by whose endowment she was claiming for this question be transmitted to the relevant local ordinary for an ecclesiastical court to make inquiries and for the bishop then to certify their findings back to the justices of the king's court and for them to give judgment accordingly. There are two reported early fourteenth century Common Bench cases which demonstrate a clear perception on the part of common lawyers and justices of just how differently the common and canon law courts viewed the essential requirements for a valid marriage. In an as yet unidentified dower case heard in Michaelmas term 1304 of which there are two surviving reports, the tenant's serjeant (Ashby) wanted to except that the claimant to dower had never been coupled to her late husband at the church door, alluding to the formal marriage ceremony which the common law required for a marriage if that was to give the widow entitlement to dower.[14] The claimant's serjeant (Hampton) in response simply offered to prove that she had been coupled to him "in lawful matrimony" (with no mention of the church door) and to prove this before the ordinary. Ashby attempted to drive his opponent to say in addition in which village and church and diocese she had married, evidently trying to make her prove a ceremonial marriage. The woman's serjeant (or serjeants) resisted and, in

---

13. "*Hengham.* Quant excepcion de bastardie est allegge en la persone cely qy est en vie '<et sait partie>' la excepcion serra trie en la court cristiene e quant bastardie est allegge en la persone cely qy est mort ele serra trie en la court par enqueste '<pur ceo qe en curt christiene covient qe les parties seint presenzs>' e home ne enquerra mie le quel il fut bastard ou noun, mes coment il fut tenu en pays en sa vie." BL MS Egerton 2811, fols. 105v–106r.

14. BL MS Add. 31826, fol. 349r; Bodleian Library MS Holkham Miscellaneous 30, fol. 59r

doing so, apparently revealed their reason for doing so. The church court would consider her the wife of her late husband even if she had only been married to him by words of marriage in his chamber and even on his death bed. The presiding justice, Mallore, evidently agreed that the church courts would hold her his wife even if they had only "pledged faith" and so apparently drove her to say additionally where (in which church and village) they had been coupled. He subsequently added that, even if it were found that he had been married in a different church she would get her dower, but the clear implication is that marriage at the church door was essential.

In the second case heard in Easter term 1306 Isabel the widow of Ingram de Balliol sued Henry de Percy for her dower third of the manor of Foston by Wigston in Leicestershire. As enrolled, Henry pleaded that she was not entitled to dower since she had never been coupled to Ingram in lawful matrimony. She responded that she had been and had married him at Foston in the diocese of Lincoln. The bishop of Lincoln was instructed to inquire into the marriage. He did not report back until 1309. He then informed the court that she had been joined to him in lawful marriage but overseas and had then adhered to Ingram as her husband for quite some time thereafter.[15] There are two reports of the case and these add materially to our understanding of it.[16] The longer of the two reveals that the tenant had asked in court where the claimant was. On being told that she was present but only by attorney, he said that he had asked because she had never been in England. The lady's serjeant, however, said that her attorney had been duly received by the treasurer, Walter de Langton, as the king's writ said. The tenant then denied that Isabel had ever been coupled to Ingram in lawful marriage. Her serjeant (Pashley) denied this and asserted Isabel had been so coupled. He offered to prove this in an ecclesiastical court. It was Justice Bereford who then made him say in which bishopric she had been married and where. Bereford seems (perhaps out of court) to have suggested that Pashley had lost his client's case since she had never come to England, and thus the bishop would not be able to take cognizance

15.   CP 40/159, m. 32d. Henry de Percy had been granted in 1299 all the lands in England and Scotland which had belonged to the late Ingram and which would have been inherited by Ingram de Umfraville, the king's enemy and rebel, presumably a Bruce supporter: CPR 1292–1301, 396.

16.   The reports are YB 33–35 Edward I, 183–5; BL MS Hargrave 375, fol. 147v.

of the marriage.[17] Pashley, perhaps on the basis of his knowledge of canon law, said the contrary was true. The woman, or whoever was suing for her, would be able to secure a letter from the bishop of Lincoln to the bishop of the place where they said the marriage had taken place, even if this was out of the country, for him to investigate and report back, and the bishop of Lincoln would then certify the court, as he eventually did. One report describes this procedure as being what was required by the "law of England," the other more plausibly as what was required by the "law of Holy Church."

The church courts had a much wider matrimonial jurisdiction than this, of course, as well and there are two other cases from the last decade of the thirteenth century which show common lawyers and common law justices and (in one case) a common law jury referring to the exercise of such a jurisdiction in ways which may suggest a degree of skepticism, and even distaste, over the way that jurisdiction was, or might be, exercised. The first is a detinue of chattels case brought by Agnes the daughter of Richard de Brok against Edmund of Navestoke in 1290. She was seeking the return of chattels to the value of £66 which had been given by her father to Edmund on her marriage, now that the marriage had been annulled in the Court of Arches.[18] The annulment had been on the grounds of a prior contract of marriage which Edmund had made with Elizabeth of Ludehale. As the plaintiff's count is recorded on the plea roll it is said to have been Edmund who sued the annulment. The reports, however, suggest that her serjeant may have said only that Edmund instigated Elizabeth's suit and the jury verdict enrolled on the plea roll certainly says that although the annulment had been made at the suit of Elizabeth, it was at the instigation and procurement of Edmund. Either way this does not look like a suit initiated by the disappointed woman to whom marriage had been promised. Perhaps there really had been a prior contract of marriage and Edmund had soon repented of his marriage to Agnes and was able to use the church courts to annul the marriage and ensure his marriage to Elizabeth instead. But there may have no such prior contract. Edmund and Elizabeth may both have

---

17. This melds material from the two reports.

18. I discuss the case in "The Equity of the Common Law Courts," in *Law and Equity: Approaches in Roman Law and Common Law*, ed. E. Koops and W. J. Zwalve (Leiden, 2014), 39–53 at 39–41.

been willing to perjure themselves in order to separate Agnes and Edmund and annul the marriage and allow Elizabeth to marry him.

The second is an entry *sur disseisin* case brought by John son of Roger de Cherbourg against the warden of Merton College, Oxford, for the manor of Thorncroft in Leatherhead in Surrey. In this case John alleged that the flaw in the warden's title was its ultimate derivation from a different John de Cherbourg, who had disseised the claimant's uncle, Wigan de Cherbourg.[19] Hugh Despenser, the warden's warrantor, objected that the claimant John was not his uncle's heir, as he had claimed. Wigan had a son John who had entered the lands Wigan held at the time of his death as his heir and was still living and it was this John who was Wigan's heir. The fuller of the two reports of the case gives the response of John's serjeant (Tothby). Tothby did not say straight out that John was a bastard. What he said was that before Wigan had married his wife Agnes he had no wife by whom he had engendered a child and that Agnes had survived Wigan and their marriage had never been annulled. He therefore argued that the existence of a son of Wigan named John should not prejudice the claimant unless Hugh could say that John was not just the son of Wigan but also the son of Agnes.[20] Chief Justice Mettingham responded that Tothby should say whether or not John was legitimate. It might have been that Wigan was "of so large a conscience" that after he had married Agnes he went elsewhere and married another by whom he engendered this John (or in the second version "that he had married Agnes in the county of N. and another in the county of M."). Tothby's response was "one ought not suppose other than what law requires and we understand that law does not permit a man to have two wives at a time." This is clearly a reference to the rules of canon law but it is not one which required any more than a rudimentary knowledge of those rules. It is also one which also suggests how easily a reference to canon law rules might be incorporated into common law argumentation

19. CP 40/101, m. 124. The case is reported briefly in YB 21 & 22 Edward I, 225–7, and much more helpfully in two closely related reports in BL MS Add. 31286, fols. 217v–218r and Lincoln's Inn [LI] MS Misc. 87, fols. 5r–v.

20. "Wogan de ki seisine nus avum conte esposa une femme Agnes, avant quele Agnes unqe femme naveit par ki nule engendrure naveit, la quele Agnes survesqui Wogan e unques devorce ne se prist entre eus e ceo volum averer; par quei nus demandum jugement si il puse dire qe Johan seit fiz e heir Wogan sil ne puse dire que il fut fiz Agnes."

without any clear sense of them being separate sets of rules. Tothby then offered proof that Wigan had not had issue by any prior wife and that John was not the son of Agnes. Chief Justice Mettingham (perhaps facetiously) suggested that it was not necessarily the case that a man could not have two wives at a time: "Perhaps he had a dispensation from the Roman Curia" (*Par aventure il aveit dispensacion de la curt de Rome*). Even a clerical chief justice may have had some reservations about the extent of the papal power of dispensation.[21]

One obvious way in which the two systems came directly into conflict was through the issuing by chancery of writs of prohibition to stop litigants suing in ecclesiastical courts on matters on which the king's courts claimed a monopoly for themselves, or more generally for lay courts, and to stop ecclesiastical judges hearing and determining such cases and through writs of attachment on such prohibitions when they were disregarded, which brought plaintiffs and ecclesiastical judges to answer in the king's court. By the last quarter of the thirteenth century there had come to be a demand from the ecclesiastical side for a mechanism that would allow the resumption of the litigation in the church courts if, on the face of the record of that court, it was plain that the case was one which lay within its proper jurisdiction. Such a demand was made in the clerical complaints presented to the Easter parliament of 1285. An initial response given only by the chancellor and some of the council talked in general terms of allowing recourse in these circumstances to the justices of the Common Bench or King's Bench. A later response given by the king envisaged recourse to either of the chief justices of these courts (Ralph de Hengham or Thomas Weyland) or to the second justice of the Common Bench (William of Brunton) or to the eyre justice William of Saham, and of them advising on the basis of the *libellum vel peticionem* in the case.[22] Nothing seems to have been done to translate this into action at this time. This required a further petition, probably one submitted at the Easter parliament of 1290. This led to a royal instruction recorded on the parliament roll which gave the chief justice, evidently here

21.   After Wigan's death in 1284 there were two rival sons and heirs by two wives, one of whom was Agnes, both named John: *Earliest English Law Reports*, IV, Selden Society 123 (2006), 436–9 (89 Wilts. 22).

22.   F. M. Powicke and C. R. Cheney, *Councils and Synods with Other Documents Relating to the English Church* (Oxford, 1964), II, ii, 956, 962.

the chief justice of King's Bench alone, or the chancellor authority to write to the ecclesiastical judges after they had read the libel (*viso libello illius cause*) if they could see that the case was one for which there was no remedy from the king's chancery and authorizing them to proceed.[23] In practice only the chief justice of King's Bench seems to have been active in this matter, initially at least, and there is no evidence of the chancellor authorizing cases to proceed until the second quarter of the fourteenth century.[24] The new procedure clearly required the chief justice to know how to read a libel and to understand enough of what he was reading to translate it into the terminology of the common law courts. Only thus could he determine whether the case was one which should be allowed to proceed. The earliest case to mention a "consultation" issued by the chief justice (here Gilbert of Thornton) was one heard in the Common Bench in 1294–5, where the grounds for allowing the case to proceed were that the tithes being claimed did not amount to a quarter of the value of the church.[25] A degree of acquaintance with the procedures and forms of the ecclesiastical courts on the part of one of the serjeants of the Common Bench is also shown in two reports of a later prohibition case heard in 1303.[26] The defendant's assertion was that he had simply been claiming a mortuary and that he had a consultation from chief justice Brabazon allowing this claim, which was endorsed on the libel. The plaintiff's serjeant (Warwick) objected that the ox which the rector was claiming as his mortuary had been assigned a value or price in the libel but that this was inappropriate since the rector could not assess the price. The rector's serjeant (Harle) was able to respond both that it was necessary in court christian when claiming something to give a value just as in a lay court and also that, if the value assigned was too high, the party could make that objection in court christian. He might have been briefed on this point in advance but he sounds like a man who knew what he was talking about.

23.   For the petition see PROME, Roll 2, item 29 and the instruction see PROME, Roll 1, item 31.

24.   *Early Registers of Writs*, ed. Elsa de Haas and G. D. G. Hall, Selden Society 87 (1970), cxii–cxiv.

25.   *Select Ecclesiastical Cases from the King's Courts, 1272–1307*, ed. David Millon, Selden Society 126 (2009), 26–27 (1.20).

26.   YB 30 & 31 Edward I, 441–7; BL MS Add. 5925, fol. 152v. The record is printed in *Select Ecclesiastical Cases*, 40–43 (1.26a, 1.26b).

The two legal systems also overlapped, and sometimes came into conflict, in the area of rights over churches, the right to present incumbents to vacant ecclesiastical livings, who would only be instituted to the livings after episcopal approval. Here I want to focus in the main on one particular area, that of the right to present not to a rectory (the main post in a parish church, normally with the largest share in the church's income, and often held by a non-resident rector), but to a permanently established and endowed vicarage (the subordinate post in a parish church which might be held on a short-term contract but also might be a permanent appointment with a smaller share in the church's income, which was normally held by a resident vicar). There had long been a variety of common law remedies to establish title to the advowson of a rectory or to assert the specific right to present a rector at a particular vacancy. There was no parallel action to allow patrons to assert rights over permanently endowed vicarages until legislation of 1285, part of the statute of Westminster II, c. 6, authorized them.[27] There are two quite distinct reported cases from 1300 about the right to present to vicarages which were vacant. In both the serjeant Nicholas of Warwick invoked on behalf of his clients what seem to be canon law rules and presumptions in support of their cases. The first is an action of *quare impedit* about the right to present to the vacant Norfolk vicarage of Buxton. Of this there are two related enrolments from two successive terms and multiple reports.[28] The presentation was claimed by the prior of Sempringham, whose house had been given the advowson of the church by Hubert (II) de Rye and had then been allowed to appropriate the rectory to the benefit of the priory, but reserving four marks of revenue to support a permanent vicarage, with the consent of the bishop and his dean and chapter.[29] The initial possessory claim was made on the basis that the prior's predecessor had presented the last vicar. His opponent was the local diocesan, the bishop of Norwich, who claimed that his predecessors or the arch-

27. *Statutes of the Realm*, I, 77.

28. CP 40/133, m. 12 and CP 40/134, m. 35; BL MSS Add. 31826, fols. 168r–v and Add. 37657, fols. 18r–v; Cambridge University Library [CUL] MS Ee. 6. 18, fols. 43r–v; LI MS Misc. 87, fol. 89r.

29. *English Episcopal Acta VI: Norwich, 1070–1214*, ed. Christopher Harper-Bill (Oxford, 1990), no. 436: the grant of the church to Sempringham was made before 1170, the bishop's consent to Sempringham to appropriate was made after 1175.

bishop of Canterbury *sede vacante* had exercised the right to collate to the vicarage at every vacancy in the vicarage going back six bishops, to the time of bishop William of Raleigh (1239–43). In argument, Warwick claimed (according to one report) that it was "common law and right" (*comune ley e dreit*) (and he must be referring to canon law) that a church was a single entity with the parsonage (or rectory) and vicarage forming "one body" of the church and each annexed to each other as single advowson (*qe le eglise seit une e qe le personage e la vikarie seint cum un cors de legise e lun anex a lautre cum un avoesun*) and that they could not be severed from each other without a specialty; or (according to a second report):

> According to common law for one church there is as a rule only one advowson, so that the parsonage and the vicarage are a single entity, for the vicarage is a parcel of the parsonage, so to sever the vicarage from the parsonage would be to make two advowsons where by common law there is only one advowson and to sever the parcel from the whole and that is against common law and we do not think that he ought to be received [to claim that] without specialty.

The court seem to have been receptive to this line of argument but also found compelling the written evidence produced on behalf of the prior that the bishop's predecessor, Roger Skernyng (1266–78), had acknowledged the prior's right to present and had requested him to present the bishop's clerk to the living. The chief justice then asked the bishop's attorney to advise his client to make peace. The second case is an assize of darrein presentment about the right to present to the vacant Derbyshire vicarage of Longford, for which there is also an enrolment and three different reports.[30] The presentation was claimed by John of Longford, the patron of the rectory, on the basis of the last presentation having been made by his father Oliver. The defendant was John de Cressy, the rector of Longford, who had been himself presented to the rectory by the plaintiff. The reports show Warwick again making arguments, this time on behalf of the rector, which are apparently derived from canon law. He argued that the rector's own presentation by John had been to the whole of the church. This had included

---

30.   CP 40/131, m. 270d; BL MSS Add. 37657, fols. 45v–46r and Add. 31826, fol. 88r; LI MS Misc. 87, fols. 93r–v.

the portion John of Longford called the vicarage as well as that part the parson himself held, and that the allocation of a portion of the revenues to the vicar was a matter for the rector alone and only he and not the bishop or the patron could increase or decrease the portion. He also said that, even if John's ancestors had presented to the vicarage, that was simply by the sufferance of his predecessors and it was his obligation to recall the dispersed portion of the church's endowment and reunite it with that endowment: an obligation with its roots in canon law. The case nonetheless went to the assize for a verdict but that verdict was adjourned and is not recorded.

The common lawyers' understanding of the canon law rules about the resignation of livings is demonstrated by the reports of a debt case heard in Michaelmas term 1303. This was brought by William of Leicester, one of the clerks of the king's chancery, against Richard of Gatwick clerk, the rector of an unidentified parish church.[31] Twelve of the fourteen marks that were being claimed were claimed on the basis of a deed under which Richard had apparently promised to resign his living to William.[32] He had also agreed to pay William an annuity of four marks a year until he did so and that the sum of twelve marks was to be payable within fifteen days if he resigned his church to anyone other than William. William's main claim was to the twelve marks because he alleged that Richard had resigned the church to a third party. There were two main lines of objection or defense to this claim. One was that the contract itself was tainted with simony. Since the contract was "against the law" (*encountre la ley*) or "odious and outside the law of the land" (*odiouse e hors de ley de terre*) it was therefore void. The implication is that the contract was simoniacal because William was procuring the living for himself on the basis of a financial inducement and that the canon law prohibition of simony was somehow imported into the common law and was capable of invalidating even a written contract.

31. The reports are in BL MS Harley 25, fol. 173v (and the related BL MS Add. 35116, fol. 234r); CUL MS Ee.6.18, fols. 78r–v; BL MS Add. 5925, fol. 64r (and related version at fol. 166v). The notes are in YB 30&31 Edward I, 477 (from LI MS Hale 188) (and also in BL MS Add. 5925, fol. 151r) and BL MS Harley 25, fol. 186r (and related BL MS Add. 35116, fol. 243r). The related plea roll enrolment is CP 40/145, m. 135d but this was probably only drafted after the agreement which terminated the litigation and seems deliberately to pass over all the argument in the case and distorts the nature of the underlying dispute.

32. None of the reports mention this positive promise but the argument in them makes no sense without supposing such a promise to be explicit or implicit in the deed.

The justice (William of Bereford) who was hearing the case did not specifically rule on this point or adopt this reasoning. The second argument
rested on the canon law view that it was not properly speaking possible to
resign a benefice to anyone other than the local ordinary, or, as one of the
reports says, *quia persona debet resignare ecclesiam suam episcopo et non ad
aliam personam*. Richard's counsel argued that since the original promise
was one that it was impossible for Richard to keep this also invalidated the
agreement, one of the notes relating to the case noting that the written law
said *nemo obligatur ad imposibile*. Bereford held that if a man promised to
pay a debt if he did not do something that was impossible (and he cited as
his example a promise to pay £40 unless the promisor removed the whole
of the Tower of London and placed it in this court at Westminster within
seven days) this did not invalidate the agreement. It merely made the debt
payable all the quicker. Richard's counsel denied they were the same because he said it was impossible for Richard to have resigned to a third party
or to William. Eventually the parties settled on terms that gave William
five marks out of the fourteen which he had claimed.

In this paper I have looked at just a few of the ways in which the
English Common Law courts and the English canon law courts intersect-
ed in the reign of Edward I, largely from the perspective provided by the
English Common Law sources, the law reports and plea roll enrolments,
both of them as yet largely unpublished. In it I have tried to demonstrate
that the justices and lawyers did indeed approach the canon law and the
procedures of the canon law courts not with total ignorance or hostility, but
with some degree of understanding and on occasion a willingness to incor-
porate ideas and concepts from the canon law when they could be useful. I
have also noted some of the ways in which the background and training of
some common law justices and professional lawyers may have assisted in a
more fruitful interaction between the two systems.

These were two very different legal systems which co-existed with
each other in England and I found myself wondering as I wrote it how far
the lawyers and the judges of the English canon law courts would have understood the law and procedures of the Common Law courts in the same
period and how far they might have incorporated ideas and concepts from
it. It is a shame that this is not a question that it is easy, and perhaps even
possible, to answer.

Ethical Standards for Advocates and Proctors of the Court of Ely (1374–1382) Revisited

Charles Donahue, Jr.

One of Dick Helmholz's first articles dealt with ethical standards for advocates and proctors of the medieval English church courts.[1] Recently, the development of the medieval canonical legal profession has been given a magisterial treatment by Jim Brundage, and others have dealt with the topic as well.[2] Both Helmholz and Brundage made considerable use of the Act Book of the Court of Ely. There were good reasons for doing so. The book contains over 3,000 entries, from March of 1374 to February of 1382. Not only is the book the most comprehensive of the surviving medieval church court books, it is also remarkable for its consistency and accuracy. Its author, Robert Foxton, notary public and registrar of the court, was proud of his work, and he had something to be proud of.

The imminent publication of a complete edition of the book[3] provides an occasion to ask whether a full edition can shed more light on what has

---

1.   R. H. Helmholz, "Ethical Standards for Advocates and Proctors in Theory and Practice," in *Proceedings of the Fourth International Congress of Medieval Canon Law: Toronto, 21–25 August, 1972*, ed. Stephan Kuttner, Monumenta Iuris Canonici, C: Subsidia, 4 (Vatican City, 1976), 283–99; repr. in idem, *Canon Law and the Law of England* (London, 1987), 41–57.

2.   James A. Brundage, *The Medieval Origins of the Legal Profession: Canonists, Civilians, and Courts* (Chicago, 2008), 240, 307, 376, with references to earlier works.

3.   *The Register of the Official of the Bishop of Ely: 21 March 1374–28 February 1382*, ed. Marcia Stentz and Charles Donahue, Jr. (Cambridge, Mass., forthcoming 2015).

already been done with it on the topic of the development of the medieval canonical legal profession. This article suggests that it can, and it seems appropriate to offer it to the leading scholar of English medieval Canon law.

But first a word of caution: We cannot assume that what was happening in this court was also happening elsewhere. The proximity of the court to the University of Cambridge allowed students in law at the university to serve the court (and themselves) by taking on positions in the court. Henry Bowet, who was both an advocate of the court and the official of the archdeacon, is described as "licenciate in laws" when he makes his profession of obedience as the official of the archdeacon (39.35).[4] When he makes his last appearance in the register as a witness to his successor's profession of obedience, he is described as "doctor of civil and canon law" (54.30, 16 Jan. 1378). He later became archbishop of York. Richard Scrope is described as "inceptor of civil law," when he becomes official of the court (24.01, 16 Nov. 1375). Three years later, he is described as "professor of civil and canon law and chancellor of the university" (70.42, 25 Feb. 1378). He, too, later became archbishop of York. John Newton is a "bachelor in laws" (probably civil only) when he is admitted as an advocate of the court in (39.38, 24 Jan. 1377). When he is commissioned to be the official in succession to Scrope almost three years later, he is described as "doctor of laws" (once more, probably civil only) (78.01, 20 Sep. 1379). His later career was not so distinguished as Bowet's and Scrope's, but he spent the last 20 years of his life as treasurer of York Minster.[5] Clearly all three men earned their degrees while they were working at the court, and they were not alone. Clearly too, all three men benefited from the patronage of Thomas Arundel, the young bishop of Ely in this period, the brother of one of the most powerful men in England, and himself a future archbishop both of York and of Canterbury.

ADVOCATES

Brundage identifies nine advocates in the register.[6] There are actually only eight who are identified as such: Henry Bowet, James Cottenham, Richard

---

4.   References are to entry numbers in the forthcoming edition.
5.   John Le Neve, *Fasti Ecclesiae Anglicanae, 1300–1541, 6: Northern Province*, B. Jones, comp. (London, 1963), 14.
6.   Brundage, *Legal Profession*, 307.

Drax, John Epperston, Thomas Gloucester, William Laas; John Newton, and John Potton.[7] Brundage's count, however, is probably correct. The *acta* of the synod of 18 June 1375 are witnessed by five men who are identified as *iurisperiti*: Thomas Eltisley snr, William de Willingham, Thomas Glouces-ter, Robert Eltisley, and John Potton (18.23, 18.24, 18.25). *Iurisperitus* is an alternative for *advocatus*, and Potton and Gloucester are elsewhere identi-fied frequently as advocates of the court. Both Eltisleys seem to have been beneficed clergymen who occasionally performed functions for the court, but they do nothing that would indicate that they were advocates at the time of the register. (They may have been such in the past.) Willingham, however, appears once as commissary of the official, once as a proctor, and three times as a witness of *acta* of the official (where he appears first, even before Thomas Gloucester). All of these are functions that known advo-cates performed, and, so far as we are aware, only advocates served as com-missaries of the official where the commission involved actually conducting a court session.

While it is likely that Willingham was an advocate of the court, he probably did not remain active for long. His last appearance is as a witness of the synodal *acta* of June 1375. Henry Bowet was quite active while he was serving as an Ely lawyer, but, as we have seen, he last appears in January of 1378. Drax is mentioned only twice, and that as a witness in a case. He may not have been an active advocate during the period of our register. James Cottenham, who, like Bowet, is quite active while he was serving as an Ely lawyer, does not appear after early in 1378. Epperston appears only three times, Laas twice.

What that meant was that the lion's share of the work fell on Cotten-ham, while he remained active, Gloucester, Newton, and Potton. Lawyers like to be busy, but when Scrope basically abandoned the court (he last sits on 8 April 1378, and Newton does not become official until 22 September 1379), the advocates were confronted with ethical dilemmas of which they seem to have been aware but about which they could do little.

The basic ethical principle is stated quite early on. In entry 18.08, Thomas Gloucester and John Potton are sitting as commissaries in the ab-

---

7.   References to all of the people mentioned in this article may be traced in the Index of Persons and Places of the forthcoming edition.

sence of Nicholas Ross, who was the official at the time. In the previous session, the moving parties brought an action against a vicar *ex officio promoto*. In this session, the vicar should have replied. The entry tells us, however, *de [partium] consensu expresso datur dies in proximo ad idem, videlicet ad respondendum dicto articulo, propter absenciam iudicis quia uterque commissarius est de consilio partis promoventis*. Little or no harm was done. Ross returned to the bench in the next session. But if there were effectively no official, the fact that the advocates were also the judges could cause problems.

It happened in *Gransden/Shanbery*,[8] which was basically an appeal from a judgment of the archdeacon's official in a marriage case. At one session when Thomas Gloucester was hearing the case as commissary of Scrope, he recuses himself because he had served as advocate of one of the parties in the case (39.03). It was probably for that reason that Ross had commissioned John Potton to hear the case (entries 1.04, 10.04). But Potton apparently became ill, and the sentence that he rendered was never entered. (There is a gap in record where it should have been entered [29.02].) An appeal was taken from this sentence, however. With Scrope's departure, Gloucester was now the commissary in charge of the consistory court, but he was barred from acting in the case. Apparently, he was even barred from commissioning someone else to hear the case. The case was not resolved until John Newton became official.[9]

In *Day*, Gloucester represents the plaintiff/appellee in a marriage case appealed from the archdeacon's official (entries 6.08, 9.09). At one point in the proceedings, the appellee alleges that the process returned by the archdeacon's court is insufficient because it fails to show that Gloucester was, in fact, properly authorized as the commissary of the archdeacon's official in the case (11.06); she asks to be admitted to prove that he was. She fails of her proof in the next session, but ultimately succeeds in getting the judgment below sustained. Her ultimate success is probably the result both of the fact that Ross chose to examine the appellant *ex officio* (and may as a result have found out that the original complaint was probably true), and also of the fact that when forced to, the appellant's proctor refuses to swear that his exception of the nullity of process below (which was probably grounded

---

8.   Names of cases can be traced in the Table of Cases of the forthcoming edition.

9.   Details in Charles Donahue, Jr., *Law, Marriage, and Society in the Later Middle Ages: Arguments About Marriage in Five Courts* (New York, 2007), 256–8.

on the absence of any proof that Gloucester was duly authorized to act) was not "malicious," which seems here to mean something like the modern "frivolous" (17.05). For our purposes what this case tells us is that although someone who has represented a party cannot later act as a judge in his or her case, someone who has acted as a judge can represent one of the parties on appeal at least when the party is the one seeking to sustain the judgment below.

The advocates, then, seem to have been aware of the ethical difficulties created by their multiple roles and sought to avoid the most obvious of them. While we may pause at the fact Gloucester represented Isabel Spinner, the plaintiff/appellee in *Day*, in a case in which he had served as a judge, there was no obvious conflict of interest. He, like she, was seeking to sustain a judgment in which he had participated. Indeed, Gloucester's desire to defend a judgment in which he had participated may have ensured that a woman who does not seem to have been of high station got the best representation that the court had to offer.

The multiple roles that the advocates played may have had a more subtle effect, not one that was prejudicial to their clients, but quite the opposite. Their clients may have gotten a more favorable treatment than did others who were represented only by proctors or not represented at all. Firm evidence of this is hard to come by. The role of the advocates is hidden from the record unless they, as they sometimes did, took over in name or in fact the role of the proctor. Two cases, however, in which their appearance is recorded may be telling.

Barnwell/Tavern is an *ex officio* prosecution for adultery and incest. The incest from a modern point of view is not particularly serious; the woman, who is not said to be married, was alleged to have been the godmother of two of the married man's children. The incest, however, is probably the reason why the case is in the consistory, which did not deal, as a regular matter, with ordinary adultery cases. In the first iteration of the case, the man succeeds in purging himself of the crime, but the woman fails in her purgation. James Cottenham takes on her representation and succeeds in getting an order that she can try again to find oath-helpers. She fails again, and the case goes into abeyance. More than a year later, the new official, Scrope, renews the prosecution. This time the couple are represented by Henry Bowet. They appeal to the court of Canterbury. Then, saying that they were advised to appeal by their counsel, they renounce their appeal before Scrope and get off remarkably lightly: They are absolved of the excommunication that they had incurred for contumacy; they purge themselves of their crime (the record does not say with how many oath-helpers or of what kind); they abjure each other and "suspicious places" under a penalty of six whippings around the church and six whippings around the market of Cambridge if they violate their oath.

The same basic pattern is found in *Littleport/Lakenheath*. Simon, the vicar of Littleport, was charged by Ross *ex officio* with fornication and keeping a concubine in the vicarage.[10] Simon takes an appeal to the court of Canterbury, but does not pursue it. After Ross's death, Scrope threatens to execute Ross's sentence of excommunication for contumacy. James Cottenham appears on the vicar's behalf, and, once more, the vicar gets off remarkably lightly: He is absolved of the sentence of excommunication upon swearing to stand by the mandates of the church and paying four pence to sacrist of Ely for use of the shrine of St. Etheldreda; he denies the charge of fornication and purges himself (once more the number and quality of the oath-helpers is not mentioned); he agrees to remove the woman from the vicarage in two weeks and "to abstain from her in suspect places."

In both cases, the final proceedings take place out of session in Scrope's lodgings (but in the presence of witnesses, and, we assume, Foxton). In both cases we may suspect that the submission of the defendants was with foreknowledge that what would happen to them would not be particularly serious. In short, we suspect that their advocates "cut a deal" with the official. Compromises of criminal cases are common enough in our own day, and it should not surprise us too much that they happened in the Middle Ages. The question that we raise here is whether these compromises would have been as favorable to the defendants had they not been represented by advocates, who, as we have seen, had a close relationship with the official. John Joseph (*Joseph*), who so far as we can tell was not represented by an advocate, spent four days in gaol in Cambridge castle when he refused to perform the penance enjoined on him, and ultimately did penance.

10. The woman is charged separately with fornication both with the vicar and his chaplain. She successfully purges herself. See Donahue, *Law, Marriage, and Society*, 293 and Texts and Commentary no. 520.

The presence of advocates is not the only difference, however, between *Barnwell/Tavern* and *Littleport/Lakenheath*, on the one hand, and *Joseph*, on the other. Barnwell, Tavern, and Simon the vicar of Littleport never admit their offenses and, ultimately, purge themselves. Joseph confessed to a long-term, open, and adulterous relationship with a woman by whom he had a number of children, and then blatantly refused to do penance. There are more than suggestions of class distinctions between the defendants who got off lightly and Joseph, although those distinctions are also related to the fact that the former defendants had advocates and Joseph did not. The relationship of the advocates to the court does not fully explain the difference of result in these cases, but it helps to explain it.

PROCTORS

The proctors of the court are harder to identify than the advocates. The problem is that *procurator* is a general word for a proctor or attorney, and it is clear that many of the men are identified as someone's proctor in the register are clearly not proctors of the court in the normal sense of the term. The easiest to exclude are those who appear to take the oath of obedience on behalf of their clients at the beginning of the register or who appear at synod on behalf of their clients, and no place else. Similarly to be excluded are those who appear only as proctors for a particular religious institution. These men may well have been professionals, but they were probably working for their clients in many capacities and just happened to appear in the Ely consistory when their clients' business took them there.

At the other end of the spectrum are those who are identified as "proctors general of the consistory," and who appear many times in the court on behalf of different clients, most of them local men and women of the diocese. There are six men so identified in the register, and we list them here in the order of the number of different people whom they represent: John de Wiltshire (178), Peter Caprik (158), Walter Sutton, notary public (53), Richard Pitts, notary public (31), Hugh Candlesby, notary public (22), and Richard Ferriby (11). Candlesby was also the registrar of the archdeacon, and Pitts served, at least on occasion, as commissary of the official of the archdeacon. This may help to explain why they had so many fewer representations than Wiltshire and Caprik. Sutton may also have performed other functions in his capacity as a notary. (Sutton was not admitted as general proctor until January of 1377, but Wiltshire was admitted at the same time, and he ended up having the most representations of all.) Ferriby was probably connected with the family of lawyers and administrators, a member of which, William, was keeper of king's wardrobe in 1360 and who may be the same as William Ferriby, the chief notary of Richard II.[11] Richard Ferriby's stay in Ely was short. He gets his first proxy on 7 October 1378 (64.29). He substitutes Caprik, Sutton, and William Leverton in all his cases on 3 February 1380 (84.44) and Caprik and Sutton on 3 October 1380 (93.08). The only mention of him after that (97.03) says that Caprik appeared as a substitute for him. It looks as if Ferriby tried to establish a practice in Ely and did not succeed.

There is one man who has almost as many representations as Sutton (51) and who is called "proctor of the consistory" but never "proctor general of the consistory": William Killerwick. Killerwick appears consistently as a proctor at the beginning of the register until we reach the following entry (54.33) on 14 January 1378:

> Nicholaus Walssh de Lyttelyngton' et Mabila uxor sua citati ad instanciam Ricardi Tod de eadem in causa diffamacionis, parte actrice per Johannem Wiltesshir', clericum, procuratorem suum apud acta constitutum, parte rea vocata et preconizata, quidam Willelmus Killerw'c, asserens se procuratorem eorum, ostendit quamdam litteram et peciit se admitti ad occupandum pro eis. Et quia eidem Willelmo tanquam nobis et officio nostro ingrato et rebelli in nostra audiencia alias interdiximus officium procurandi quousque iuramento interposito admitteretur in procuratorem generalem dicti consistorii nostri si forte in eventum admitti mereatur, ideo ipsos Nicholaum et Mabilam pronunciamus minus sufficienter comparuisse ipsosque reputamus contumaces, reservata ulteriori pena usque ad proximum et decernimus ipsos fore premuniendos ad proximum ad comparendum per se vel procuratores de gremio consistorii existentes.

---

11.   T. F. Tout, *Chapters in the Administrative History of Mediaeval England* (Manchester, 1928–37), 6.148 and n. 1.

In modern terms, Scrope disbarred Killerwick for his contempt, which is not recorded in the register, and he never appears again.

Another "disbarment" occurs on 23 February 1380 (85.44), this time by Newton of William Leverton. Leverton first appears as a proctor on 17 March 1379, when he appears as "proctor by letter" on behalf of priest who is bringing a violence case (72.34). In the next session, he appears in two different cases on behalf of the official of the archdeacon, the defendant in cases of appeal *ex officio*, with Foxton expressing some doubt about his authority to do so (*qui se dicit procuratorem*; entries 73.11, 73.12). He also appears in the same session, seemingly without challenge, on behalf of a defendant in defamation case (73.40). He does not appear again until 22 September 1379 when he is called as a witness by the appellant in one of the cases brought against the official of the archdeacon (78.12) and as the proctor, along with Hugh Candlesby, for a group of parishioners suing their rector for deprivation of service (78.43). He appears once again, representing the defendant in a marriage case, on 3 November (80.32).

On 14 January 1380 one of the parishioners and on 2 February 1380 another of the parishioners appear before the official saying that they never appointed Candlesby and Leverton to be their proctors in the deprivation case, that they never had any intention of moving such a case, and that the dean of Cambridge sealed their proxy without their authority (83.49). They expressly revoke the authority that Candlesby and Leverton pretend that they have. Candlesby and Leverton are to be called to answer the charge that they represented the parishioners without authority and concocted a false proxy.

The disbarment, which occurs two sessions later, was almost certainly prompted by this event, but it is not the ground given for the disbarment:

> Cum quidam Willelmus Leverton' clericus officium procuratoris generaliter et publice exercens, in consistorio nostro recusans subire admissionem nostram ad dictum officium in eodem consistorio exercendum monitusque per nos ad iurandum de observando consuetudines et statuta dicti consistorii et curie nostre. Et quia hoc facere recusavit, ideo nos officialis Elien' officium procuratoris in dicto consistorio nostro amodo exercendum interdiximus sub hac forma.

There follows a formal sentence of disbarment (85.44). Leverton never appears again.

The category of "proctor general of the consistory" occurs before Scrope became official. Richard Pitts so describes himself in a substitution that he gave to Cottenham and Bowet in the very first set of *acta*. Peter Caprik does the same in substitutions during Ross's tenure. The phrase does not come into more general use, however, until early in Scrope's tenure (24 Jan. 1377, 39.38), when he conducted a formal admission ceremony in which he appointed Newton and Laas as advocates and Sutton and Wiltshire as *procuratores generales* of the court. The oath that both the advocates and the proctors took is then entered in full (39.39). One other admission ceremony is recorded in the register, this time only of an advocate (Epperston) and much more briefly (58.24). Otherwise it would seem that admission was done more informally and not recorded in the register, but it almost certainly was done. There is no reason to doubt, for example, that Ferriby was admitted as a proctor general.

What were the privileges of a proctor general? They were clearly not so broad as those that are today associated with admission to the bar of a particular court and those of the serjeants of the Common Bench in this period: an exclusive right of audience. Many men appear as proctors of a single client without challenge. Very few, however, appear more than once, and those who do are relatively easy to explain.

Robert Foxton, the registrar, appears as a proctor for 36 named individuals or institutions. None of these representations is in a contentious matter. He represents a large number of beneficed clergy and religious houses in swearing obedience to the bishop at the beginning of the register and a smaller, but still significant, number of religious houses at synod.

William Bridge represents 11 individuals. He received a substitute proxy from Wiltshire (43.38), and all of his representations are of Wiltshire's clients in the following session or the one thereafter. He is probably the rector of Teversham who was commissary general of the archdeacon (54.24 and 72.43).

John Hostler represents 9 individuals. Most of his appearances occur during Ross's tenure, and virtually all of his appearances are as a substitute, mostly for Richard Pitts. He may have been Pitts' apprentice. The one exception to both generalizations is entry 52.19 (3 Dec. 1377), where he appears as proctor for the plaintiff in a marriage and divorce case *litteratorie constitutum sub manu publica, signo et subscripcione Ricardi Pyttes clerici, notarii publici, consignata.* If we can believe the recorded appearances *ut prius,* he continued to represent the plaintiff in a complicated case, which finally resulted in a sentence in her favor on 23 May 1379 (74.17). This is the last that we hear of him as a proctor. He is called apparitor of the archdeacon in entry 38.17 and apparitor of the Cambridge deanery in entry 55.31 (but the citation is on behalf of John Potton as archdeacon's official). In this instance he gets into substantial trouble for citing someone outside his jurisdiction and within the jurisdiction of the priory of Anglesey. He has to hand over the staff of his office, but then it is restored to him (55.35). We last see him produced as a witness in a marriage case where he is described in English as "Somenor" (89.38). Like Ferriby, and perhaps Bridge, Hostler looks like someone who was trying to establish himself as a proctor of the consistory, but either did not succeed or got diverted by other opportunities.

John Dunham has all the hallmarks of an apprentice (he may also have been a law student). He is described as a *mandatarius* of the official (Scrope). This sounds rather grand, but it is clear from the entry (67.35) that what it means is that he was commissioned to deliver an inhibition mandate from the official to the official of the archdeacon, John Pinxton. Pinxton gave Dunham a hard time, and Scrope backs him up by citing Pinxton for disobedience and contempt. In *Caprik* (3) Dunham joins with Peter Caprik in suing for his salary against John Frost jnr. Here he is described as a *mandatarius* of the consistory, and, once more, that probably means is that he delivered the inhibition mandate to the archdeacon's official in the appeal proceedings that were part of *Fisher/Frost.*

Dunham is the beneficiary of two proxies, one given by Margaret Halle to John Wiltshire and to him (66.34), the other given by Hugh Martin to Peter Caprik, Walter Sutton, and to him (73.44). Both result in some confusion. In the first session in which the parties in *Halle* appear by their proctors (68.30), Wiltshire is representing the defendant, Thomas Carlton, and Dunham substitutes Peter Caprik for himself as Margaret's proctor. Thus it remains, so far as we can tell, for the rest of the case. Whether Foxton simply got it wrong in entry 66.34 and then insisted on the substitution so that the record would cover his mistake, or whether Wiltshire betrayed his client, leaving Dunham holding the bag, we cannot tell. Dunham, however, seems to have done the right thing. He may not have had the ability to undertake Margaret's case by himself, and he should not have been doing so, even if he could do it, when he was so closely associated with the much more senior proctor who was on the other side.

What happens in *Martin* is even stranger. In the first entry in the case, both Hugh Martin, the appellant in a marriage case who had been ordered by the archdeacon's official to marry the appellee, and Clarissa Edmond, the appellee, appear personally (73.09, 21 Apr. 1379). She gives a proxy to Caprik and Wiltshire in entry 74.38 (26 May 1379). The next entry in the case (74.09, 23 May 1379) records that Hugh does not appear and that Clarissa appears by Wiltshire. Entries on 10 June (75.09) and 30 June (76.09) record that Hugh did not appear and Clarissa appeared *ut prius*, presumably by Wiltshire. On 21 July (77.09) Hugh is recorded as appearing personally and Clarissa *ut prius*. The case is continued to 31 July when the process from the archdeacon's court finally appears, and the parties are given the next session to speak against it. That session occurred on 22 September (78.10) when we are told that Hugh appeared personally and that Dunham appeared for Clarissa! This is, of course, a serious breach of basic legal ethics, if it is to be believed. If it is not, i.e., that it is a mistake and that Dunham actually appeared for Hugh, then he did a bad job, because this was the session at which he was supposed to object to the process held before the archdeacon. Neither party raises any objection, however, and the case is set down for sentencing. No further appearances of proctors are recorded, but it seems likely that Hugh was getting some legal help, because he later proposes an exception that ultimately leads to testimony being taken (82.09). Eventually, Newton calls Clarissa in personally to respond to questioning (86.08). He eventually quashes the sentence of the archdeacon's official at a session at which both parties are said to have appeared personally (92.06).

The proctors did not do a very good job here, even if we assume that they were offering some advice in the background. It certainly looks as if it was Newton's proactive behavior that lead to the ultimate resolution. Since neither of the parties seems to be of particularly high station, an explanation for the proctors' behavior may lie in the fact that the parties could not afford anything more.

Other proctors who represent only a couple of clients have patterns that are similar to Dunham's. John Doke, who, like Hostler, is described as the apparitor of the deanery of Cambridge (5.15), represents two clients at the beginning of the register in cases that other proctors had brought close to a conclusion (13.03, 14.02). John Flamstead receives, along with Richard Pitts, a proxy from two men toward the end of register (94.32). Neither is recorded as their proctor in the case for which the proxy seems to have been made (*Barton* (3)). At the beginning of the register Simon Godrich, who is described as the original proctor, substitutes Killerwick as the proctor for a couple who are appealing from the archdeacon and disappears (18.17, 18.18). Once more at the beginning of the register, Roger Sterling, along with Killerwick and Doke, receives a substitution from Caprik (15.15). Pursuant to this substitution, Sterling appears once in four different cases, in two of these perhaps twice (16.03, ?17.03; 16.04, ?17.04; 16.05, 16.07).

The question, then, is what did William Leverton do other than what a number of others seem to have been doing? There was certainly no rule that someone who was not a proctor general could not represent more than one party in the consistory. There was no school for proctors; they learned on the job. Bridge, Hostler, and, perhaps, Dunham all seem to have been trying to become proctors general. That may have been the case with some of those in the previous paragraph as well. What Leverton did not do, as the others did, was associate himself with one or more of the existing proctors general as he was working his way into the system. He tried to insinuate himself into the ranks of the proctors, first, by representing a single person from whom he had a written proxy, then by asserting, an assertion that Foxton questioned, that he was authorized to represent the archdeacon's official. He was probably trying to take advantage of the fact that the court was being run by commissaries, Scrope having departed without resigning his position.

There is some evidence that Leverton tried to play the game right. On 3 February 1380, the day after the second of his two Kingston clients had disowned his proxy, he got appointed, along with Caprik and Sutton, as a substitute for Ferriby (84.44), but it was too late. Ferriby was already on his way out, and so was Leverton. He was "disbarred" 20 days later. (After Leverton's disbarment, Ferriby returns long enough to issue another substitute proxy to Caprik and Sutton, excluding Leverton [93.8].)

We may suspect that Leverton's real patron was Hugh Candlesby. Candlesby is the proctor general associated with Leverton in the disastrous Kingston representation. Candlesby was not a good man to have as your patron; he was, as the modern phrase goes and as we shall see shortly, "ethically challenged." But as we have already noted, Leverton's association with Candlesby and the false proxies in *Kingston* (4) are not the stated ground for his disbarment. Newton says that he offered Leverton the position of general proctor if he would take the oath. This he refused to do, so he was interdicted from appearing in the court.

The question is whether we should believe this when we strongly suspect that the real reason for Leverton's disbarment was his involvement in the Kingston affair. Perhaps we should. We have already seen that Scrope seems to have tightened the court's grip on the admission of proctors and advocates. The oath may have been new in his regime, or at least this form of oath, and the appellation "proctor general" gets much more play in his period. Leverton's attempt to move into the ranks of the proctors may have been his, and perhaps Candlesby's, means of testing whether this new control by the court would continue in the new regime. Newton answered that question on 23 February 1380 (85.44): if you want to want to represent clients regularly in my court, you are going to have to take the oath. On those conditions, Leverton wanted none of it.

There is another reason why we might believe that Newton offered Leverton the oath which Leverton refused to take. The matter of the Kingston representation was still pending. If Leverton took the oath, he would clearly subject himself to the discipline of the court. Leverton, we might surmise, knew that he had no defense to the charges that he concocted a false proxy.[12] Better to walk away from the situation than subject one's self to discipline and then be disciplined for concocting a false proxy.

---

12.   It is, of course, possible that the charges of concocting a false proxy were themselves false or that the situation was more ambiguous than the charges make them out to be. They were never proven, and only two of the four parishioners involved make them. We are inclined, however, to think that the charges may be substantially true. A case that seems similar to the one brought against the vicar in *Kingston* (4) had been brought earlier (*Kingston* (2)). The vicar purges himself in that case, and it is plausible that the parishioners had no desire to revive it. The vicar in *Kingston* (4) seems genuinely puzzled. He asks for legal help, and two advocates of the court are assigned to him (78.43).

From Newton's point of view, this was also a better way of proceeding. The charges against Candlesby and Leverton had not been proven. To disbar Leverton on the ground of the charges would probably require that they be proven. Better to offer him the oath with reasonable confidence that he would not take it. That gets rid of Leverton and establishes the proposition that the new regime will continue to follow the policy of the old one.

This method of proceeding also avoids having to proceed against Candlesby. Why that might be deemed desirable is a question easier to ask than to answer. The judgment of history, including that of the present writer, on Hugh Candlesby has not been kind. Margaret Aston described his "behaviour as far from exemplary"; Michael Sheehan called him "a rather sinister man."[13] Yet both Scrope and Newton kept him, as Scrope says in another context, *in gremio consistorii* as a proctor general. Perhaps this is the time briefly to rehearse the evidence.

The first indication that we get that Candlesby was in any trouble comes early in the register when Ross is still official (*Candlesby (2)*; 18.28, 24 May 1375). Candlesby is charged with having seized from the court's mandatary a court mandate sent to the dean of Cambridge and having refused to return it, in contempt of the jurisdiction of the bishop and official. He appears and claims he did not seize and contemptuously hold the mandate, but retained it, copied it, and gave it to the dean immediately afterwards. He submits to the court's grace in so far as he was delinquent, and at the request of the archdeacon's official, his penance is pending on the condition of his good behavior (*sub gestura sua*). In the previous entry (18.27), the dean of Cambridge had been let off on similar terms for having failed to execute the mandate.

These cases are part of a much larger ongoing dispute between the consistory court and the court of the archdeacon. What an examination of the whole register has to say about that must be saved for another occasion. Suffice it to say here that we should be careful not assume that relations be-

---

13.   Margaret Aston, *Thomas Arundel: A Study of Church Life in the Reign of Richard II* (Oxford, 1967), 125–6. Michael M. Sheehan, "The Formation and Stability of Marriage in Fourteenth-Century England: Evidence of an Ely Register," *Mediaeval Studies* 33 (1971), 228–63, in idem, *Marriage, Family, and Law*, 38–76, at 53; Donahue, *Law, Marriage, and Society*, entries gathered under *Candelesby* in the Subject Index.

tween the two courts were always as strained as they were at the time when
these contempt citations were issued. They come right around the time of
a synod in which Ross issued a massive injunction against the archdeacon's
court, accusing it violating numerous provisions of Canon law (18.24).

As registrar of the archdeacon, Candlesby could be expected to defend the prerogatives of the archdeacon's court. Sometimes his defense of
those prerogatives seems to go beyond the bounds of what was acceptable.[14]
In a seemingly straightforward defamation case (*Lovely*) in which the rector of Maulden (Beds.) is suing a man of Little Eversden for defamation,
Candlesby, representing the defendant, excepts to the libel on the ground
that by custom in Ely diocese the jurisdiction of this case belongs, at least
as a matter of first instance, to the archdeacon and not to the consistory
(*ipsius cause cognicionem saltim primariam non ad nos sed ad archidiaconi
Elien' ipsiusque officiali et ministros pertinere et pertinere debere solum et in-
solidum ex consuetudine laudabili ut asseruit et legitime prescripta et hactenus
pacifice observata*). Scrope rejects this argument in strong language: *ipsas ex-
cepciones tanquam manifeste fictas et falsas ac falso conceptas duximus reicien-
das*. Scrope orders Candlesby to reply to the libel. Candlesby refuses and
departs from the court in contempt. Scrope excommunicates him. Later in
the day, when everyone's tempers had cooled, Candlesby returns, asks to
be absolved, is absolved, and substitutes Wiltshire for himself as proctor
(26.12). One can imagine that this substitution might have been a condition
of the absolution.

In 1376–7, Candlesby was charged with being the illegal farmer of a
church (*Candlesby/Wilburton*). He defends on the ground that as a cleric,
he could be a farmer of a church and that in his case an express license from
the bishop was not necessary, and the case is ultimately dropped.

In the same period, Candlesby was the defendant in a marriage case
(*Pattishall/Candlesby*). The plaintiff eventually admitted she had no proof,
and so Candlesby won the suit, but in the meantime he illegally had his
marriage to another woman solemnized. At a minimum we may say that in
this case he does not look good. The illegal solemnization may have been no
more than the product of his confidence, which ultimately proved correct,

---

14.   Aston, *Arundel*, 125–6, 142–3.

that he would prevail in the suit, but the plaintiff's ultimate confession that she had no proof could have been the product of coercion or bribery.[15]

There can be little doubt that Scrope sought to tighten his control over the proctors. He got rid of Killerwick. Perhaps he sought to get rid of Candlesby as well, but Candlesby evaded his grasp. He became a proctor general, and that, paradoxically, may have made him more difficult to get rid of.

We can have little doubt that both Scrope and Newton would have liked to get rid of Candlesby. To us it seems that they had grounds to do so, but there were problems with establishing those grounds. The charge in *Candlesby/Wilburton* in 1376–7 that he illegally farmed a church was not proved. The charge of illegal solemnization in *Pattishall/Candlesby*, which Candlesby confessed, led to Scrope's reserving the penance to himself on the condition of the former's good behavior (*sub gestura sua*) (37.27). Scrope may have preferred this to disbarment. By doing this he kept the archdeacon's registrar in his power. After this, however, Candlesby was accused of impeding an alms-seeker who had been authorized by the consistory (*Potton/Candlesby*). He was allowed to get off simply by denying the charge. One would have thought that the accusation of concocting a false proxy would have been the last straw. We might speculate that Candlesby had friends in high places, but there is no direct evidence of that. What we see on the record is that Newton was able to rid himself and the court of a man who was probably Candlesby's protégé, but could not get rid of the man himself.

Margaret Aston suggested that Candlesby's ultimate downfall came about when he, along with others associated with the archdeacon, participated in the violence of 1381.[16] Her evidence for his participation in those events is perhaps not as powerful as she thought. It may illustrate that in addition to friends Candlesby also had enemies in high places. Be that as it may, on 30 October 1381 (107.01), he is referred to in the register as "former registrar [of the archdeacon]." He may have been deprived as a result of the events of that summer, but he also could have been deprived because of

---

15. See Donahue, *Law, Marriage, and Society*, 273–4 and Texts and Commentary nos. 481–4.

16. Aston, *Arundel*, 125–6.

a change in administration in the court. By the end of the register Richard
Pitts is being referred to as registrar of the archdeacon (110.26).

We have seen that with the possible exception of Candlesby, Scrope's
administration seems to have led to a tightening of control over the proctors. What did the proctors get in turn for their submission to this tightening of control? As we have seen, they did not get a monopoly, but they did
get, it would seem, an assurance that they would be protected from competition as a regular matter. This almost certainly allowed them to maintain,
perhaps to raise, their fees. It also almost certainly ensured that men who
worked at it full time, like Caprik and Wiltshire, could accumulate an impressive number of representations over the course of the register. Finally,
they got, if our analysis of the proctors who did not become general proctors is correct, some control over new admissions to their ranks.

There was one more privilege that was, if not unique to general proctors, shared by them: the ability to sue for their salaries in a court with the
procedures of which they were quite familiar. At the end of register, an
ordinance is entered that made these procedures easier for them than it was
for the ordinary run of litigants (113.29). The ordinance probably codifies
procedures that had been being followed for some time. Salary cases occur
before Scrope made his move to enhance the office of proctor general, a
move that seems to date to January of 1377. Candlesby brings a salary case
in his capacity as registrar of the archdeacon (*Candlesby (1)*); an ordinary
chaplain brings one for his salary (*Stow (1)*); Potton and Caprik bring one
in their capacity as advocate and proctor of the consistory (*Potton/Capr-
ik*); Bowet brings one in his capacity as an advocate (*Bowet*). After Scrope
makes his move, however, when the proctors are suing for their salaries,
they always describe themselves as proctors general of the court, as Caprik
had not before, and no one except officers of the court brings a salary case:
Caprik (1), *Pitts*, *Caprik (2)*, *Candlesby (3)*, *Candlesby (4)*, *Caprik (3)*, *Foxton
(2)*, *Sutton (5)*.

Scrope's move should probably be seen as one in the direction of in-
creasing professionalization of the proctors, perhaps also of the advocates.
They were subject to more professional discipline; they gained some control
over admission to their ranks, and some protection against competition. The
result was probably that fewer people could afford their services. The number of litigants who appear *pro se* in the register seems quite large. The proc-

tors were probably willing to offer these litigants some help for more modest fees. The sophistication shown by some *pro se* litigants is remarkable.[17]

Whether Scrope's move increased the competence or the professional ethics of the proctors is a more difficult question to answer. The level of competence of the proctors throughout the register seems quite high. Except for Candlesby, obvious ethical violations seem rare. Wiltshire may have abandoned his client in *Halle*. He would have been entitled to do so if he thought her case unjust. His behavior, however, does not look good when he then proceeded to represent her opponent. He made up for it, at least to some extent, by having the man whom we suspect was his apprentice get the most experienced proctor that the court had to represent her. The case ultimately, like many other defamation cases, ended in *pax* (73.29). Dunham looks as if he appeared for the wrong person in *Martin*. That was probably just a mistake, either Dunham's or Foxton's. Dunham was a very junior proctor, not yet admitted as a proctor general, and he never appears again.

Court-enforced discipline is evident in areas other than the two notable "disbarment" cases. In the middle of a very long marriage case in which one of the parties has died and which seems to be going nowhere, the proctors for the remaining parties (Pitts and Caprik) allege that their proxies have been revoked by these parties, who have not appeared for some time. They want to withdraw from the case. Gloucester, the commissary sitting on the case, tells them that they cannot do this. It is after the *litis contestatio*, and it is not clear that the proxies have been revoked. The proctors soldier on (45.03), though it is unclear whether they are present at the massive series of continuations that follows after that before the case is finally resolved, some three years later (86.03). Sometimes a well-placed oath administered by the judge to the proctor allows the case to move on. We have already seen one case in which the proctor (Caprik) refuses to swear that the exception that he has raised is not "malicious" (17.05), and this refusal allows the court to proceed to a conclusion in the case. In another case the court makes the proctor (unnamed) swear that he will use "diligence" to get the witnesses produced. It works; the witnesses are produced in the next session (4.05, 5.05).

17.   See Donahue, *Law, Marriage, and Society*, 240–1, 300.

CONCLUSION

There is nothing that we have found in the Ely register that should upset the existing accounts of the development of the canonical legal profession. What a detailed study does illustrate, however, is how gradual and serendipitous the process was. Take away a young, vigorous, and reform-minded bishop who happened to have a major university with a law faculty in his diocese, and none of this might have happened. Take away an ambitious and impatient rising law professor who hit upon the idea of conducting a formal admission ceremony for advocates and general proctors, and what we see over the course of eight years might not be nearly so visible, and might not have happened. Take away a more patient, but somewhat rigid, successor to the law professor, what Scrope began might not have continued. And, of course, take away Robert Foxton and the dramatically serendipitous survival of his register, we would not know anything about what Scrope and Newton did.

The Evolution of the Common Law

Thomas P. Gallanis[1]

Evolution means change over time. From the work of Charles Darwin and others, we know that species evolve. So too, though in different ways, do human societies. In this essay, I focus on one aspect of the evolution of human society—the evolution of law[2]—and on one system of law in particular: the Common law of England.

How and why did the Common law evolve?

The prevailing answer to this question comes from the scholarship of England's greatest living legal historian, Professor S. F. C. Milsom.[3] So substantial has been his contribution to our understanding of the development of the Common law that he has rightly been described as "the most

---

1.   This essay is a lightly revised version of my Donald M. Sutherland Memorial Lecture in Legal History, given at the University of Iowa in March 2011. It is a pleasure to thank Hallie Goodman (Class of 2014) for research assistance and the University of Iowa Law School for research support. Participating in this *Festschrift* for Professor Helmholz—my teacher and mentor—is a special pleasure.

2.   For some of the many prior studies on this general theme, though with varying approaches, perspectives, and areas of focus, see Peter Stein, *Legal Evolution: The Story of an Idea* (Cambridge, 1980); Allan C. Hutchinson, *Evolution and the Common Law* (Cambridge, 2005); David M. Rabban, *Law's History: American Legal Thought and the Transatlantic Turn to History* (Cambridge, 2013).

3.   See especially S. F. C. Milsom, *A Natural History of the Common Law* (New York, 2003); S. F. C. Milsom, *Historical Foundations of the Common Law*, 2nd ed. (London, 1981).

significant historian of English law since [the founder of the discipline, Professor Frederic] Maitland."[4]

For Professor Milsom, the main agent of common-law evolution was the individual lawyer representing his client.[5] The lawyer's intention was not to change the law but simply to win the case. Nonetheless, the effect was legal change. In Professor Milsom's words,

> There was no legislative mind, no view from above, no substantive law to be viewed, not even much of a system. Legal thinking was about the procedural possibilities open to individual lawyers in a world of intellectual free enterprise, and the convolutions were not intended to change 'the law' or indeed intended at all: they were the cumulative residue of innumerable tiny twists, each intended only to serve the client of the day.[6]

How exactly did this work? Here again are Professor Milsom's words:

> The life of the Common law has been in the abuse of its elementary ideas. If the rules of property give what now seems an unjust answer, try obligation.... If the rules of contract give what now seems an unjust answer, try tort. Your counterfeit will look odd to one brought up on categories of Roman origin; but it will work.... And so the legal world goes round.... Lawyers have always been preoccupied with today's details, and have worked with their eyes down. The historian, if he is lucky, can see why a rule came into existence, what change left it working injustice, how it came to be evaded, how the evasion provided a new rule, and sometimes how that new rule in its turn came to be overtaken by change. But he misunderstands it all if he endows the lawyers who took part with vision on any comparable scale, or attributes to them any intention beyond getting today's client out of his difficulty.[7]

4.   David Ibbetson, "Book Review, Milsom, *A Natural History*," *Law Quarterly Review* 120 (2004), 696.

5.   This argument is especially prominent in Milsom, *Natural History*.

6.   Milsom, *Natural History*, xvi, 27.

7.   Milsom, *Historical Foundations*, 6–7.

Note two features of this explanation of legal change. First, there is little role for what today we would call the executive or legislative branches of government. In Professor Milsom's view, the king—and, later, Parliament—played at best a minor role in the medieval and early modern development of the Common law, and their effect on the law was primarily unintentional. In Professor Milsom's words:

> The largest changes have never been deliberate. Even when large consequences follow from a legislative act, one can be sure they were not intended. The legislator addresses a problem small enough to be identified: what may happen is that the current of events catches on to his remedy and produces a larger diversion. The current may catch on anything. Its force is that of clients coming to lawyers with what seems to common sense like a case, although the law is against them. All the lawyer can do for one hit by a rule is to look for a way round it, make a distinction, bring some new idea to bear. If he succeeds, the rule is formally unimpaired. If the route that the special facts of his client's case enabled him to take can be used by others, the result may be reversed, but the rule remains. Even when it is abolished or forgotten, its shape will be seen in the twisting route by which it was circumvented.[8]

There is also a second feature of Professor Milsom's approach to the evolution of the Common law that we should notice. The viewpoint is internal to the legal system; it focuses on the process of litigation and the role of lawyers in that process. The approach gives little attention to external forces—political, social, or economic. The approach also puts aside the intellectual movements of the day, except insofar as those movements were already internal to the practice of the Common law. This minimizes the potential role of external or foreign ideas—for example, ideas emanating from the universities, where the study of law meant not the Common law but the Roman and Civil law and the Canon law of the Christian Church.

In this description of Professor Milsom's evolutionary approach, you can detect the beginnings of a critique. Let me make the critique more explicit by discussing three examples of legal change.

8. Ibid., 6.

I.

The first example comes from the twelfth century and the law of land. The example concerns what is known as the "assize of novel disseisin."

The word "assize" has multiple, interconnected meanings in English legal history.[9] For present purposes, "assize" can refer to a royal writ—meaning a written order from the king, sealed with the king's seal—and it can also refer to the legal procedure authorized by that writ.[10] This dual meaning is present in the "assize of novel disseisin." The assize was a royal writ by which a plaintiff could initiate legal proceedings in the king's court to complain of a recent dispossession of land (a "novel disseisin").[11] Here is the sample language of the writ:

> The king to the sheriff of [location], greeting. A. has complained to us that B. unjustly and without judgment disseised him of his free tenement in [location] after the first passage of the lord King Henry, son of King John into Gascony [or other recent event]. And therefore we command you that, if A. shall give you security for pursuing his claim, then cause the tenement to be reseised of the chattels which were taken therein and cause the same tenement with the chattels to be in peace until the first assize when our justices shall come into those parts. And in the mean time cause twelve free and lawful men of that neighborhood to view the tenement, and cause their names to be put onto the writ, and summon them by good summoners that they be before the said justices at the said assize ready to make recognition thereon. And put by gage and safe pledges the aforesaid B., or if he shall not be found his bailiff, that he may be there then to hear the recognition. And have there the summoners, the names of the pledg-

---

9.   For a description of the meaning of "assize" see, for example, J. H. Baker, *An Introduction to English Legal History*, 4th ed. (London, 2002), 20–22, 233–234; Paul Brand, *The Making of the Common Law* (London, 1992), 138–141; Donald W. Sutherland, *The Assize of Novel Disseisin* (Oxford, 1973).

10.   Sutherland, *Assize of Novel Disseisin*, 1–42; Milsom, *Historical Foundations*, 119–124.

11.   For discussion about the role of this royal writ see, for example, Sutherland, *Assize of Novel Disseisin*, 2–3 and Milsom, *Historical Foundations*, 139.

es, and this writ. Witness [my self at Westminster on the _____th day
of [month] in the _____th year of our reign.][12]

What was the purpose of this writ, which first appeared around the
1160s during the reign of Henry II?

The orthodox answer, prior to Professor Milsom, was that the assize
of novel disseisin was designed by Henry II or his advisers as a general protection of possessors of land against wrongdoers. In the words of Professor
Maitland:

> In the first age of its operation, the novel disseisin seems to have been
> directed against acts which could be called ejectments in the strictest
> sense of the word, though…any persistent interference with posses-
> sion might fall within it. English law was perfectly ready to say with
> the Roman text that, if a man goes to market and returns to find on
> his land an interloper who resists his entry, he has been ejected.[13]

Professor Donald Sutherland followed Maitland's view. Professor
Sutherland wrote: "The central concern of the assize was with disseisins
of land. It prohibited men from ejecting one another from fields and buildings, woods and meadows…."[14]

Why was a royal remedy necessary? Why not handle the matter at
a more local level—for example, in the court of the plaintiff's feudal lord?
The orthodox answer, prior to Professor Milsom, was that the assize of
novel disseisin was a deliberate move on the part of Henry II or his advisers
to protect rights in property and, probably also, to advance the jurisdiction
of the royal courts. In the words of Professor Sutherland:

> The protection of freehold property rights must have been the pri-
> mary purpose [of the assize]…. [But b]ehind this concern…may have
> lain a deeper purpose. Henry II and his ministers may have been aim-
> ing to exalt the king's authority. They opened the king's court to every

12.   Baker, *Introduction to English Legal History*, 545.
13.   Fredrick Pollock and Frederic William Maitland, *The History of English Law
Before the Time of Edward I* (Cambridge, 1898; repr. 1969) 2, 53–54.
14.   Sutherland, *Assize of Novel Disseisin*, 11.

freeman however humble by offering him there the protection of the assize. This detracted from the jurisdiction both of feudal lords and of sheriffs in their county courts and instead brought the business before the king himself or before those specially appointed commissioners of his from headquarters, the justices.... Most of all, it cut off the feudal lord's power to make his own decisions on his own principles in dealing with his free tenants.... All these effects were in fact produced by the assize, and from what we know of Henry II and his government it is easy to believe that they planned it this way.[15]

Enter Professor Milsom, who challenged the orthodox answer as being inconsistent with the language of the writ.[16] He asked the fundamental question: who was "A" and who was "B"? The orthodox interpretation suggested a horizontal relation, as one tenant dispossessed another. But Professor Milsom argued for a vertical interpretation: B was A's feudal lord.[17] For Professor Milsom, the words of the writ were crucial. "Disseisin" meant the undoing of seisin, and "seisin" referred to the creation of a feudal bond between the tenant and his lord.[18] Thus, only A's lord could disseise A, typically for failing to fulfill A's feudal obligations. And the standard practice of lords, before reaching that ultimate sanction of disseisin of land, was to confiscate some of the recalcitrant tenant's personal property, hence the reference in the writ to "reseisin of the chattels which were taken therein." Moreover, the writ speaks of summoning B "or if he cannot be found his bailiff." Only a lord—not another tenant or a random interloper—was likely to have been wealthy enough to have a bailiff. And most crucially, the writ speaks of B acting "without judgment." Only a feudal lord—again, not another tenant or an interloper—would have had the right to hold a court and issue a judgment. Thus, the writ must have been directed at lords who disseised tenants without using the lords' own proper procedures.

This led Professor Milsom to a very different view of the writ's purpose. The writ was not designed to protect property rights nor to advance royal jurisdiction by moving litigation from feudal courts into royal courts,

---

15.   Ibid., 30, 33–34.
16.   See, for example, Milsom, *Historical Foundations*, 137–143.
17.   Ibid.
18.   Ibid.

though over time it had these unintended effects. Rather, it was aimed more narrowly at feudal lords who did not follow proper procedures through their own courts but instead disseised their tenants without a legal judgment. In Professor Milsom's words, the assize "came into being in a framework in which lords were still in control of their lordships, and in which therefore the king's court could seek only to control the doings of lords. The purpose of this control was not, and could not be, in any sense 'anti-feudal': it was to prevent and correct departures by lords' courts from the accepted body of feudal custom."[19] This brings us to one of Professor Milsom's most famous phrases: that the assize was designed simply "to make the seigniorial structure work according to its own assumptions."[20]

Professor Milsom's interpretation is brilliant and elegant. However, it does not completely correspond to the historical realities of England in the twelfth century nor to what we know of Henry II.

First, the word "disseisin" had a broader meaning in the twelfth century than the undoing of a feudal bond between lord and tenant. We can see this in a writ, dated between 1135 and 1152, in which Queen Matilda alleged that Malcolm of St. Liz and his son Walter had disseised[21] Matilda's own tenants.[22] And the assize of novel disseisin was broader in another sense too: it was a remedy not only for actual dispossession but also for substantial interference with the use of land—what today we would call nuisance.[23] This suggests a remedy protecting property rights more generally than just the right of a tenant against his feudal lord.

Second, the assize of novel disseisin was the product of legislation— meaning a royal enactment.[24] It was not an organic development within the Common law[25] but instead a decision of royal policy.

19. Ibid., 124.
20. S. F. C. Milsom, *The Legal Framework of English Feudalism* (Cambridge, 1976), 186.
21. *Regesta Regum Anglo-Normannorum 1066–1154*, vol. 3, ed. H. A. Cronne and R. H. C. Davis (Oxford, 1968), no. 239d, 86.
22. I am indebted to Professor Ibbetson for this reference. See Ibbetson, "Book Review," 696.
23. Sutherland, *Assize of Novel Disseisin*, 11.
24. Ibid., 5–8.
25. Ibbetson, "Book Review," 696.

Third, the surviving evidence going back to the reign of Henry's grandfather, Henry I, indicates that the feudal jurisdictions were not sovereign unto themselves but instead were heavily bound by well-defined custom. Tenants enjoyed "considerable security of tenure"[26] while alive, and the tenant's right to transmit property by inheritance at death was almost always respected by the feudal lord.[27] Moreover, royal supervision ensured compliance with feudal custom. As Professor John Hudson observed, "Henry I was sufficiently involved in [feudal] affairs not only to affect individual cases, but to force lords to take the possibility of royal involvement into account in their regular dealings with their tenants."[28] Professor Milsom's picture of a world, prior to the assize, in which "lords were in control of their lordships" is not consistent with these realities. In the words of Professor Hudson, "the Anglo-Norman world was not one of autonomous lordships but of considerable royal involvement."[29]

This brings us to Henry II. The thirteenth century treatise known as *Bracton* describes the assize of novel disseisin as "*multis vigilis excogitatam et inventam*"[30]—devised and invented after many watchful nights. This echoes one of Henry II's own clerks, Walter Map, who described his king as "a subtle deviser of novel judicial processes."[31] Whether the assize was Henry II's invention or that of his advisers we cannot be sure. But Henry II was actively involved in the transformation of royal justice that occurred during his reign.

It must be remembered that Henry II became king by invasion. His grandfather, Henry I, who had been an able and strong monarch, died in 1135, and was succeeded (after some maneuvering) by Stephen, accurately described as "the most genial of the Norman kings and the least com-

---

26. John Hudson, *Land, Law and Lordship in Anglo-Norman England* (Oxford, 1994), 275.

27. Ibid., 130.

28. Ibid., 131.

29. Ibid., 253. See also John Hudson, *Oxford History of the Laws of England, Volume II: 871–1216* (Oxford, 2012), 609–614.

30. *Bracton on the Laws and Customs of England*, ed. George E. Woodbine, vol. 3, (Cambridge, Mass., 1977), fol. 164b (III, 25). For an additional discussion of *multis vigilis excogitatam et inventam*, see Brand, "'Multis Vigilis Excogitatam et Inventam': Henry II and the Creation of the English Common Law," in *Making of the Common Law*, 78–102.

31. W. L. Warren, *Henry II* (Berkeley and Los Angeles, 1973), 360.

petent."[32] Stephen's reign was marked by ongoing battles with Henry I's daughter Matilda, who was supposed to be the heir. There was little royal control and much baronial freedom—too much, in fact. The period was rightly described as "a true and terrible Anarchy."[33] By 1148, Matilda had retired to the Continent, and the future Henry II was approaching adulthood.

In 1153, Henry II invaded England—it was a "largely bloodless"[34] invasion—and Stephen agreed in the Treaty of Winchester that Henry II would become the next king. Nine months later, Stephen's death enabled that provision in the treaty to be carried into effect. The newly crowned Henry II saw himself very much in the mold of Henry I: a strong king who would restore order and centralized control. Henry II's leading modern biographer, Professor W. L. Warren, put it this way: "That the development of the English Common law owed much...to Henry II personally...can hardly be put in doubt."[35] The assize of novel disseisin "emerged from [Henry's] close attention to English affairs [during the period from] 1163–1166."[36]

Thus, the stronger view is that the assize of novel disseisin was not a modest measure with consequences largely unintended. Rather, the assize was part of the plan of Henry II and his advisers to centralize justice in the courts of the king and to develop laws and procedures common to the entire country.[37]

II.

Let me now turn to my second example, from the late thirteenth century and the law of crime. In his textbook on the *Historical Foundations of the Common Law*, Professor Milsom begins the section on crime with two

---

32.   C. Warren Hollister, Robert C. Stacey and Robin Chapman Stacey, *The Making of England to 1399*, 8th ed. (Boston, 2001), 172.

33.   David Crouch, *The Beaumont Twins: The Roots and Branches of Power in the Twelfth Century* (Cambridge, 1986), 138.

34.   Hollister et al., *Making of England*, 177.

35.   Warren, *Henry II*, 359–361.

36.   Ibid., 359.

37.   For further analysis, see Hudson, *Oxford History*, 528–536, observing (on p. 536) that "the attitudes of the Angevin reformers were very significant" but also that "developments were far from pre-determined."

memorable sentences: "The miserable history of crime in England can be shortly told. Nothing worth-while was created."[38] What Professor Milsom means by this arresting observation is that, during the formative periods of the Common law, the substantive law of crime—meaning the law of felony, the serious crime that would have been of interest to the king's court, rather than handled in local courts—did not have the opportunity to develop. The felony defendant would be accused, the jury would render its yes-or-no verdict, and the defendant would stand convicted or acquitted.[39] Unlike the private law of land, contract, or tort, the details of the law of felony could not evolve because, in Professor Milsom's words, there was no "discussion [of the kind] by which law develops as an intellectual system."[40] The development of substantive criminal law was stunted in large part by the absence of lawyers. As Professor Milsom rightly observed: "Until relatively modern times the lawyer was not even allowed to play any real part [in trials for serious crime]; and even if he had been, few defendants could have paid him."[41]

The rule in the royal courts prohibiting or severely restricting the use of lawyers for the defense in matters of felony—but not in lesser matters, which we would today call misdemeanor and known in an earlier era as trespass—has long been an anomaly within the Common law. Writing in the middle of the eighteenth century, Sir William Blackstone admitted that it was a puzzle. He wrote: "For upon what face of reason can that assistance be denied to save the life of a man, which yet is allowed him in prosecutions for every petty trespass?"[42] Three generations earlier, the same question did not get much of an answer from Lord Chief Justice Jeffreys, who is reported to have said this in the trial of Thomas Rosewell in 1684:

> For, there are abundance of cases in the law, which seem hard in themselves; but the law is so, because the practice has been so, and we cannot alter the practice of the law without an act of parliament.

38. Milsom, *Historical Foundations*, 403.
39. Ibid., 407–413
40. Ibid., 403.
41. Ibid.
42. William Blackstone, *Commentaries on the Laws of England*, vol. 4 (Oxford, 1979), 349.

I think it is a hard case, that a man should have counsel to defend himself for a two-penny-trespass, ...but if he steal, commit murder or felony, ...he shall [not] have counsel...: But yet you know as well as I, that the practice of the law is so; and the practice is the law."[43]

Professor Milsom is absolutely right to make a connection between the absence of lawyers and the stunted evolution of the corresponding substantive criminal law. But he did not ask the next question: What explains the absence of lawyers?

I have tackled this question in a recent article[44] and offer a summary of the argument here. The absence of lawyers is most plausibly linked to a particular understanding of the royal prerogative during the reign of Edward I.

The earliest reported instance in England of a request for the assistance of counsel being denied in a criminal trial is found in the report of a rape case heard in Yorkshire in the early 1290s:

It was presented by the twelve of Ewcross that Sir Hugh son of Henry ravished a girl in [location] and took her to his manor in the same vill, and knew her against her will.

....

Justices. Sir Hugh, it has been presented to us that you ravished such a woman in [location] and took her to your manor, as above, and knew her against her will. How do you wish to acquit yourself of it?

Hugh. Sir, I ask that I may have counsel, lest I be taken unawares in the King's Court for lack of counsel.

Justices. You should know that the King is a party in this case and sues *ex officio*, whence in this case the laws do not allow that you should have counsel against the King where he sues *ex officio*. If [indeed] the woman were to act against you would have counsel against her, but not against the King.

....

43. T. Howell, *Cobbett's Complete Collection of State Trials*, vol. 10 (London, 1816), 267.

44. Thomas P. Gallanis, "Making Sense of Blackstone's Puzzle: Why Forbid Defense Counsel?," *Studies in Law, Politics, and Society*, 53 (2010), 35–57.

Moreover the law should be universal and equal and the law is that where the King is a party *ex officio* that one against whom the King acts *ex officio* should not have counsel against the King. And if against the law we were to grant you counsel and the country [meaning, the jury] should decide in your favor, as might happen with God's help, it would be said that you had been acquitted by favor of the justices and therefore we do not dare to do this nor should you desire this....[45]

It is important to put this case in historical context. The case was heard in the second half of the reign of Edward I, shortly after his return from overseas, away from the governance of England.[46] Upon his return, he conducted a ruthless purge of the royal judiciary, dismissing most of the judges and imprisoning many of them.[47] The judges hearing the case of Sir Hugh were the remaining or newly installed judges, eager to keep on the king's good side.

Lawyers as well as judges had reason to be wary of Edward I, who was highly skeptical of the legal profession.[48] Professional lawyers in the royal courts can be traced to the time of Edward I's father, Henry III,[49] but it was during Edward I's reign that a recognizable legal profession emerged. Edward I's reign saw the "first legislation specifically concerned with the behavior of"[50] lawyers. This was Chapter 29 of the Statute of Westminster I (1275), summarized by Professor Paul Brand as follows: "Any [lawyer] convicted of conduct amounting to deceit or collusion...was to be imprisoned for a year and a day and permanently barred from practice.... [A]nd the king was to impose a stiffer penalty in any case where the gravity of the offence seemed to require it."[51]

Additional concerns about attorneys were evidenced in an ordinance of the Epiphany parliament of 1292 giving the justices of the Common

---

45. BL MS Add. 31826, fols. 206v–207r. I thank Professor Jonathan Rose for sharing with me his transcription of the manuscript. See also YB 30 & 31 Edward I (Rolls Series), 530.

46. Gallanis, "Making Sense of Blackstone's Puzzle," 43.

47. M. Prestwich, *Edward I* (New Haven, 1997), 229.

48. Gallanis, "Making Sense," 43–44.

49. Paul Brand, *The Origins of the English Legal Profession* (Oxford, 1992), 23–25.

50. Ibid., 120.

51. Ibid.

Bench the power to limit the number of attorneys practicing there and in a royal mandate of June 1292 declaring the "fraud and malice of many of [the attorneys]."[52] Professor G. O. Sayles has "plausibly connected" the ordinance and mandate to a "general enquiry into the misconduct of attorneys, the results of which…no longer survive."[53]

In addition to the regulation of lawyers, the control of crime was a matter of on-going and significant concern to Edward I, as evidenced by the Statute of Westminster I in 1275[54] and the Statute of Winchester in 1285.[55]

Combine a receptive judiciary, the persistent problem of serious crime, a strong and determined monarch—described as physically "impressive" with a "violent temper"[56]—and the monarch's substantial concerns about lawyer misconduct—and also, I suspect, concerns about some lawyers being too good at representing their clients—and we have the ingredients for a restriction on the use of defense lawyers in trials for serious crime.

An important question is whether the prohibition of lawyers was new in the 1290s or whether the justices were re-emphasizing a principle that had emerged earlier. It is hard to know. The justices, speaking to Sir Hugh, implied that the prohibition was already established. They described counsel as something "the laws do not allow" [*iura non patiuntur*] and "against the law" [*contra legem*]. But what law(s)? The justices did not say. The reference to *iura* is unhelpfully, perhaps deliberately, vague. The references to *lex* or *legem* likewise offer little help: there is no surviving evidence of a statutory or royal prohibition.

Either way, the connection remains between the prohibition on lawyers and the judges' understanding of the royal prerogative. Also relevant was the climate in the wake of Edward I's return from overseas. Here a crucial point must be noticed. In the absence of a statutory or other written

---

52. Ibid., 115.

53. Ibid. See also *Selected Cases in the Court of King's Bench*, ed. G. O. Sayles, V, Selden Society 76 (1958), lxiii.

54. E.g., procedures for trial of homicide; *prisone forte et dure* for accused felons refusing trial. See 3 Edw. I, chs. 11, 12 (1275).

55. From the preamble: "Forasmuch as from day to day, robberies, murthers, burnings [and thefts] be more often committed than have been heretofore…." 13 Edw. I, *Stat. Wynt.* (1285).

56. Michael Prestwich, "The Art of Kingship: Edward I, 1272–1307," *History Today* 35, no. 5 (1985), 108, 111.

prohibition against defense counsel, the justices in the 1290s likely had legal room to maneuver. They could have granted Sir Hugh's request. But in the aftermath of the purge, they declined to do so. The fear of being accused of improper conduct—and punished—is palpable in their words: "it would be said that you had been acquitted by the favor of the justices and therefore we do not dare to do this."[57]

Whether the prohibition on lawyers was new or newly reinforced, the fact remains that the prohibition henceforth was in place. It would remain in place until a crack in the dike appeared in the eighteenth century,[58] followed by a statute in 1836 allowing full defense by counsel.[59]

What this discussion reveals is that the development of the Common law, or in some instances the lack of development, cannot be fully explained by reference to the internal dynamic of the Common law itself. External factors, including the role of the monarch, must be taken into account.

III.

Let me now turn to my third and final example, taken from the law of contract in the sixteenth century.

To use the word "contract" in the modern sense would be an anachronism. In the medieval period, actions in the king's courts on what we would today call a contract—an agreement or an exchange of promises—would typically arise either under the action of covenant or the action of debt.[60] By 1321, the king's judges had limited the action of covenant by declaring that the only acceptable evidence of a covenant was a written document bearing a seal.[61] For plaintiffs who did not have this kind of evidence but who still

---

57. Gallanis, "Making Sense of Blackstone's Puzzle," 41, citing to BL Add. MS 31826, fols. 206v–207r.

58. John M. Beattie, "Scales of Justice: Defense Counsel and the English Criminal Trial in the Eighteenth and Nineteenth Centuries," *Law and History Review* 9 (1991), 221, 227; T. P. Gallanis, "The Rise of Modern Evidence Law," *Iowa Law Review* 84 (1999), 543–544.

59. Prisoners' Counsel Act of 1836, 6 & 7 Will. 4, ch. 114 (1836).

60. Milsom, *Historical Foundations*, 242–282.

61. Baker, *Introduction to English Legal History*, 319.

wanted to sue to enforce an agreement in the royal courts, the standard method was to use the action of debt.

Thus, in the fourteenth and fifteenth centuries, the action of debt was the principal means by which agreements were enforced in the king's courts. But there was very little substantive law. As Professor Milsom rightly observed: "If...somebody had sat down about 1500 to write an account of 'the law' behind the action of debt, there would not have been a great deal to write about."[62] Why not? Why, over the centuries, had a sophisticated law of debt not evolved? The answer is that the procedural mechanisms for determining whether or not the defendant owed a debt did not provide the opportunity for substantive questions to arise. The plaintiff would assert his claim, the defendant would make a general denial—"*nil debet*," meaning "he owes nothing"—and then the claim would be decided, either by an inscrutable jury or by "wager of law,"[63] a procedure requiring the defendant simply to produce a certain number of people willing to swear that the defendant had answered truthfully. Either way, the result was a yes-or-no verdict. In the words of Professor Milsom: "What matters about this is its consequence in inhibiting legal development. Term after term and century after century disputes of every kind were hidden under *non debet*. And it is not only that the facts are hidden from us today. The legal questions that they might have raised were hidden from legal examination at the time."[64] This crucial point connects nicely to one of Professor Milsom's most well-known aphorisms: "[L]egal development consists in the increasingly detailed consideration of facts."[65]

So how did our modern law of contract evolve, if the facts were buried in the action of debt and could not be raised to the surface for discussion and elaboration? The answer, as Professor Milsom has rightly noted, is that, in the sixteenth century, plaintiffs—meaning, the plaintiffs' lawyers—increasingly stopped using the action of debt and instead used

62. Milsom, *Historical Foundations*, 256.

63. Baker, *Introduction to English Legal History*, 74; R. H. Helmholz, *The ius commune in England: Four Studies* (Oxford, 2001), 84–88.

64. Milsom, *Historical Foundations*, 256.

65. S. F. C. Milsom, *Studies in the History of the Common Law* (Ronceverte, W. Va., 1985), 171.

a different action, the action of assumpsit.[66] Assumpsit was a variety of the long-standing action for trespass. Trespass actions in the king's courts were divided into two major categories: trespass *vi et armis* (trespass allegedly committed by the defendant "with force and arms" which violated the king's peace and thus naturally fell within the jurisdiction of the royal courts) and trespass on the case (in which the plaintiff did not allege "force and arms" but instead specified the particular facts of the defendant's trespass). Assumpsit was a variety of trespass on the case. The word "assumpsit" simply refers to an undertaking. If the defendant had undertaken—for example, to perform a service —and had caused damage to the plaintiff in performing it, then the plaintiff could sue in trespass, specifying the facts of the undertaking. By way of example, consider the following writ for assumpsit, alleging negligence by a carrier:

> The king to the sheriff of [location], greeting. If N. shall give you security for pursuing his claim, then put by gage and safe pledges T. that he be [before our justices at Westminster on such a day] to show why, whereas the same T. at the vill of [location] had undertaken [*assumpsisset*] safely and securely to carry a certain pipe of wine belonging to the selfsame N. from the aforesaid vill of [location] to the vill of [location]: the aforesaid T. carried the pipe so carelessly and improvidently that in default of the selfsame T. the pipe was cracked, that the same N. lost the great part of the aforesaid wine, to the damage of the selfsame N. ten marks,[67] as he says. And have there the names of the pledges and this writ. Witness [my self at Westminster on the _____th day of [month] in the _____th year of our reign.][68]

A difficulty with the action of assumpsit in the fifteenth century was that it was limited in scope. It was clear that the action could be used to sue for an undertaking performed badly. But what about the *failure* to perform an undertaking—nonfeasance, rather than malfeasance? This was a debated question, but the Year Book reports suggest that throughout the fifteenth century mere nonfeasance would not support an action of as-

---

66. Milsom, *Historical Foundations*, 295–304.
67. A mark was 2/3 of a pound, so ten marks was a substantial fine.
68. Baker, *Introduction to English Legal History*, 547.

sumpsit.[69] As Professor Milsom wrote in one of his memorable phrases: "not doing is no trespass."[70]

By the early sixteenth century, however, the Common law had reversed course: actions of assumpsit for nonfeasance were permitted.[71] Thus was assumpsit launched on the path to become a more general remedy for breach of contract.

Why had this happened? Professor Milsom is right to point to the influence of plaintiffs and their lawyers. From the plaintiff's perspective, the action of assumpsit had several advantages over the old action of debt. One of these was that the method of proof was always trial by jury; the defendant could not acquit himself simply with the oath-helpers of wager of law. Another advantage for the plaintiff was that the action of assumpsit, being a species of trespass, could be heard in the Court of King's Bench, whereas the action of debt could be heard only in the Court of Common Pleas. Both were royal courts, but the King's Bench had more effective mechanisms for ensuring that the defendant would appear at trial.

This was an era in which the Court of King's Bench and the Court of Common Pleas competed for business—and for the fees generated by litigation.[72] The King's Bench had an incentive to widen the scope of the action of assumpsit in order to gain more business from the party who selected the forum, namely the plaintiff.[73]

One of the consequences of the shift from the action of debt to the action of assumpsit was that the facts of the case were no longer hidden and could form the basis of legal discussion. Consider, for example, a central question in modern contract law: What consideration, if any, is needed to support an enforceable contract? In context of the action of debt, such a question would almost never have arisen, so it is not surprising that the royal judges in the fifteenth century did not have an answer. Indeed, we can see considerable confusion on the point in the Year Book report of a

69. Ibid., 334.

70. S. F. C. Milsom, "Not Doing is No Trespass," *The Cambridge Law Journal* 12 (April 1954), 105–117.

71. Milsom, *Historical Foundations*, 277–279.

72. Daniel Klerman, "Jurisdictional Competition and the Evolution of the Common Law," *University of Chicago Law Review* 74 (2007), 1184.

73. Ibid., 1191.

discussion on an action for debt in the year 1458.[74] The plaintiff alleged that the defendant had agreed to pay him a sum of money in exchange for the plaintiff's marriage to the defendant's daughter. The plaintiff did marry the daughter, but the defendant refused to pay. The plaintiff brought an action of debt in the royal Court of Common Pleas. Two of the justices were of the opinion that the plaintiff had shown a *quid pro quo* sufficient to maintain an action of debt; three of the justices said that he had not. In the end, the case was not decided but instead was "adjourned"—a standard way to avoid having to reach a decision in the event of disagreement.

In the context of the action of assumpsit, questions of consideration arose routinely and needed to be resolved, hence the evolution of the doctrine of consideration from the sixteenth century. In Professor Milsom's words, "[t]he Common law had been pushed into greatness because its practitioners could not quite stop each other talking about what had actually happened."[75]

Professor Milsom's approach to legal evolution is persuasive about why the Common law of contract was stunted before the beginning of the sixteenth century and why rules of contract law, for example the doctrine of consideration, evolved thereafter. But what Professor Milsom's approach does not persuasively answer is why the substantive rules reached this particular answer rather than another.[76] The Common law courts needed to determine whether a marriage constituted consideration, but why should the answer be yes rather than no, or no rather than yes?

Here, we must look beyond the internal workings of the Common law. And it is here that Professor Milsom's analysis loses steam. He suggests that the substantive rules were "primarily" borrowed from lower jurisdictions: the "Common law judges would look to the circumstances in which agreements were enforceable in [the] local courts."[77] I agree that the evolution was at least in part a transplantation of ideas—but why and how from the local courts? What about other bodies of law, such as Roman,

---

74. Y.B. Mich. 37 Hen. VI, fo. 8, pl. 18, reprinted and translated in Sir John Baker, *Baker and Milsom, Sources of English Legal History*, 2nd ed. (Oxford, 2010), 263–265.

75. Milsom, *Studies in the History of the Common Law*, 189.

76. I am indebted to Professor Ibbetson for this point. Ibbetson, "Book Review," 696.

77. Milsom, *Historical Foundations*, 358.

civil, and ecclesiastical law? On the subject of consideration, these are likely to have been more influential.

The early sixteenth century saw the publication of the legal treatise commonly known as *Doctor and Student*, written by the Common lawyer Christopher St. Germain.[78] It was written in the form of a dialogue between a doctor of divinity—trained in the university, hence familiar with Civil and Canon law—and a "student" of English law, meaning a barrister. Among the many topics discussed was the juristic notion of *causa* or "cause," which in the Civil and Canon law was prerequisite to an enforceable contract. A promise made without *causa* was unenforceable: it was a naked pact (a *nudum pactum*) on which no legal action would arise: *ex nudo pacto non oritur actio.* This maxim, discussed in *Doctor and Student*,[79] was well known to common lawyers and likely formed part of the raw material used to fashion the English doctrine of consideration. We can see this most visibly in a report of a case from 1565 in which the lawyer for the defendants— namely, the barrister and law reporter Edmund Plowden—makes the following argument, blending both the Latin maxim and the English idea of consideration:

> If I make a contract with another that if he will marry my daughter I will give him £20...I have nothing thereby; and if one were to have no regard to nature it would be said *nudum pactum, et ex nudo pacto non oritur actio.* But sir, my daughter is hereby advanced, and that is consideration enough for me.[80]

This example demonstrates that the common lawyer was nowhere near as insular as once described by Professor Maitland, who famously remarked that "the English lawyer...knew nothing and cared nothing for any system but his own...."[81] In reality, common lawyers, like Edmund Plowden and many others, were influenced by ideas from other legal systems. A full

---

78. *St. German's Doctor and Student*, ed. T. F. T. Plucknett and J. L. Barton, Selden Society 91 (1974).

79. Ibid., 228–233.

80. *Sharington v. Strotton* (K.B. 1565), reprinted in Baker, *Sources of English Legal History*, 525.

81. *The Collected Papers of Frederic William Maitland*, ed. H. A. L. Fisher, I (Cambridge, 1911), 488.

account of the evolution of the Common law must take on board those external influences.

IV.

Let me now turn from specific examples to the overall theme of the Common law's evolution. Professor Milsom tackles this theme directly in the book that is the summary of his life's work, *A Natural History of the Common Law*. In the idea of a natural history of law, there is much to commend. Legal systems, no less than biological species, have origins and evolution. We can learn much from examining the emergence and development of a legal system, and the system of the English Common law in particular.

For Professor Milsom, the Common law's natural history emphasizes its gradual, unintentional—indeed, almost accidental—development. Just as a species evolves through a gradual series of almost unnoticed changes, so too for Professor Milsom did the Common law evolve through a series of tiny decisions made by individual lawyers trying to win the case for the particular client at hand.

This is as far as Professor Milsom takes the analogy between legal and biological evolution. Is there something more that the analogy can teach us? I believe that there is. There are two features of biological evolution that we should keep in mind when investigating the history of the Common law.

The first is that biological evolution is not always gradual. Darwin emphasized this in the first edition of his *On the Origin of Species*. He wrote: "Species of different genera and classes have not changed at the same rate...."[82] From the perspective of geologic time, where the smallest unit of chronology spans millions of years, some evolutionary developments occurred slowly, some almost overnight. To describe this phenomenon, Professor Richard Dawkins has coined the term "variable speedism."[83] Currently there is a debate among biologists about whether evolution alternates only between bursts of change and periods of stasis, with essentially no speeds in between or whether the rate of change is merely, in Professor

82.   Charles Darwin, *On the Origin of Species* (London, 1859), 313.
83.   Richard Dawkins, *The Blind Watchmaker* (Harlow, Essex, 1986), 245.

Dawkins's words, "fluctuat[ing] continuously from very fast to very slow and stop, with all intermediates…[and] no particular reason to emphasize certain speeds more than others."[84] Either way, the point to notice is that evolution can happen quickly.

The second feature of biological evolution that is revealing for the history of the Common law is that the forces prompting evolutionary change are often external to the affected species. Of the four principal mechanisms of evolutionary change—mutation, migration, natural selection, and genetic drift[85]—the first three require us to keep external forces in mind. Mutations are changes in an organism's DNA; they can arise internally through errors in DNA replication or externally through the effect of radiation, chemicals, and other organisms—such as viruses—with the ability to alter DNA sequences. Migration occurs when individual organisms move from one population to another, thereby altering the frequency of genetic characteristics in the new population; the migration is typically prompted by external pressures causing the individual organisms to relocate. Natural selection is a process by which genetic mutations are favored if they enhance the organism's ability to reproduce; the organism's evolutionary fitness depends on its success at responding to and overcoming external impediments.

What then are the lessons for legal history that we learn from evolutionary biology? We learn that change can be rapid as well as gradual. And we learn that change can be prompted and shaped by factors, pressures, ideas, and individuals outside the legal system.

V.

The distinction is often made between internal and external legal history. Succinctly described by Professor David Ibbetson, the distinction is this. Internal legal history "deals with law on its own terms, its sources are predominantly those thrown up by the legal process—in England, that is, the

---

84. Ibid., 245–246.
85. For discussion, see Benjamin A. Pierce, *Genetics: A Conceptual Approach*, 4th ed. (New York, 2012), 704–715.

records of courts, law reports, and legal treatises…."[86] External legal history, in contrast,

> is the history of law as embedded in its context, typically its social or economic context. It[s] sources are not, or not simply, those thrown up by the legal process; nor, commonly, is its focus the law. In so far as it might be said to be the history of law in action, it is the action that matters.[87]

The history of the Common law must combine internal and external approaches. Only through this combination will we explain the Common law's evolution in all its rich complexity.[88]

---

86. David Ibbetson, "What is Legal History a History Of?" in *Law and History: Current Legal Issues*, vol. 6, ed. Andrew Lewis and Michael Lobban (Oxford, 2004), 34.

87. Ibid., 33.

88. For a leading article sounding this theme, see R. H. Helmholz, "Continental Law and Common Law: Historical Strangers or Companions?," *Duke Law Journal* 1990, no. 6, 1207–1228. See also Thomas P. Gallanis, "Reasonable Doubt and the History of the Criminal Trial," *University of Chicago Law Review* 76 (2009), 941, 951–952; *Relations Between the* ius commune *and English Law*, ed. Richard H. Helmholz and Vito Piergiovanni (Soveria Mannelli, 2009).

Clergy and the Abuse of Legal Procedure in Medieval England

Jonathan Rose

INTRODUCTION[1]

The Common law's emergence as a mechanism for dispute resolution created the potential for individuals to misuse litigation to implement their self-interest, thereby perverting the justice system. These abuses prompted numerous complaints to the king and council, parliament, and chancery seeking a remedy. Parliament attempted to mitigate these problems with the enactment of various statutes dealing with the abuse of legal procedure.[2] These prohibitions included those directed at conspiracy, maintenance, champerty, and embracery. These statutes produced a significant amount of litigation in medieval England. Among all these abuses and offenses, maintenance emerged as the most common subject of complaint and the word commonly used to denote these types of wrongful conduct.

---

1.   The author wishes to express appreciation of John Baker, Charles Donahue, and Wendy Rose for their comments and assistance. As usual, the author bears full responsibility for the article's analysis and conclusions as well as all its errors.

2.   P. H. Winfield, *The History of Conspiracy and Abuse of Legal Procedure* (Cambridge, 1921). G. O. Sayles, "Conspiracy and Allied Offenses," in *Select Cases in the Court of the King's Bench*, III, Selden Society 58 (1939), liv–lxxi.

The clergy[3] were involved in these abuses and actions, both as perpetrators and victims. The records of litigation in the plea rolls reveal this involvement.[4] The objective of this essay is to study these activities as they related to members of the clergy. This topic seems a fitting one in a book to honor Professor Richard Helmholz, given his renown as a leading scholar of the Canon law as well as a pioneer in identifying the relationship between the *ius commune* and the Common law. The essay also provides an opportunity to use Professor Helmholz's own scholarship regarding Common law litigation dealing with ecclesiastical subjects.

THE CLERGY AND COMMON LAW LITIGATION

Numerous legal principles deal with the relationship between the medieval English church and the English state. Various statutes and canon and Common law doctrines implicate these matters. But the Church was not just a formal institution, but like all institutions was populated by numerous people, who carried out its quotidian functions. Nothwithstanding their religious lives, these members of the clergy were also part of the broader English society. As Edward I said in 1279, "the *communitas cleri* live under our rule no less than the rest of the people."[5] Both in their ecclesiastical capacities and as members of communities where they lived and worked, the clergy had many interactions with the secular institutions

---

3.   The terms, "clergy' and "cleric" are not clearly defined nor used uniformly. In this essay, these terms are used expansively as it appears in the clergy-laity divide. These terms used to include all those designated as "clerk" in court records or other legal documents as well as those designated as "abbess," "abbot," "archbishop," "bishop," "brother," "chaplain," "deacon," "dean," "friar," "master,' "monk," "parson,""prebendary," "presbiter," "priest,""prior," "prioress," "rector," or "vicar." Technically, neither abbesses nor prioress, as women, were "clergy." But their religious offices make their involvement in maintenance and other litigation as well as petitions relevant to the subject of this essay. Also, absent further information in the source, there is some ambiguity whether those called masters were clerics or whether the title just designated someone with a university education.

4.   This essay draws on a larger research project, which will be the subject of a forthcoming book, *Maintenance in Later Medieval England* (Cambridge University Press).

5.   As quoted in J. H. Denton, "The Clergy and Parliament in the Thirteenth and Fourteenth Centuries," in R. G. Davies and J. H. Denton, eds., *The English Parliament in the Middle Ages* (Manchester, 1981), 102.

and individuals that involved them in the every day life of that world.[6] As Professor Helmholz pointed out, "the two orders lived side by side."[7] In addition, the church and clergy were involved in substantial commercial activity "as landowner, as purchaser, and as employer and consumer," which involved unavoidable entanglement with the secular world.[8] Moreover, clergy were participants in the political life of the realm as evidenced by the summoning of the spiritual lords and the participation of other clergy or their proctors in Parliament and in their roles as clerks of various royal officials.[9] Perhaps, even more important, they also functioned as staff in the departments of state such as the Chancery and Exchequer and as judicial officials in Chancery and as justices of the peace.[10] In addition, they exercised royal authority as holders of private franchises.[11] They also undertook various tasks as instructed by the crown that involved dealing with lay persons.[12] Those activities brought the church and clergy into contact with the secular world in manifold ways. All these contexts held a potential for conflict,[13] which could involve the Common law and the clergy as participants in litigation in the secular courts.[14]

6. One interesting notion was the expectation that they take part in the "sporting life of their friends and neighbors." J. R. H. Moorman, *Church Life in England in the Thirteenth Century* (Cambridge, 1945), 148.

7. Richard Helmholz, "Civil Jurisdiction and the Clergy," in Richard Helmholz, *The ius commune in England: Four Studies* (Oxford, 2001), 194.

8. R. N. Swanson, *Church and Society in Late Medieval England* (Oxford, 1989), 228–42.

9. "The Clergy and Parliament in Thirteenth and Fourteenth Centuries," in Davies and Denton, *The English Parliament in the Middle Ages*, 88–108.

10. Swanson, *Church and Society*, 187–88. 123–24, 187–88.

11. Like other private franchises, ecclesiastical franchises were the target of *quo warranto* proceedings. Ibid., 122–39.

12. A. K. McHardy, "Clerical Taxation in Fifteenth-Century England: The Clergy as Agents of the Crown," in R. B. Dobson, ed., *The Church, Politics and Patronage in the Fifteenth Century*, 168 (Gloucester, 1984).

13. Such conflicts could be community and not personally based and could be pervasive and extended. Gervase Rosser, "Conflict and Political Community in the Medieval Town: Disputes Between Clergy and Laity in Hereford," in T. R. Slater and Gervase Rosser, *The Church in the Medieval Town* (Aldershot, 1998), 20–42; Norman Tanner, *The Church in Late Medieval Norwich, 1370–1532* (Toronto, 1984), 141–58.

14. See, e.g., R. L. Storey, "Clergy and the Common Law in the Reign of Henry IV," in R. F. Hunnisett and J. B. Post, *Medieval Legal Records Edited in Memory of C. A.*

Professor Helmholz has shown that although Canon law had a principle known as *privilegium fori*, which attempted to preclude secular court
jurisdiction over the clergy in civil matters, it had little or no effect.[15] As he
noted, the English Common law, lawyers, and judges rejected that principle.[16] In England, these Canon law rules were a "dead letter."[17] "Clerics were
suing and being sued in personal actions brought in the temporal forum
from the earliest days of the Common law" and it became "routine."[18] He
said that it was likely that the clergy were commonly involved in Common law litigation "concerning debts, lands, personal property, and other
temporal matters."[19] This litigation occurred both with respect to matters
related to their ecclesiastical offices and activities and to matters having no
religious dimensions. Robert Palmer's study of the social status of litigants
in Court of Common Pleas 1465 showed that "the Common law was relevant to a very broad sector of society" with ecclesiastics constituting about
7% of the plaintiffs and 5% of the defendants and with religious magnates
about 5% of the plaintiffs and 1/% of the defendants.[20] In a broader survey
of the clergy as litigants in litigation in the Court of Common Pleas from
1275–1563, he found that "the absolute number of clergy who brought cases at Common law was extremely high from the mid-fourteenth into the
fifteenth century." Specifically, he determined that beneficed clerics and
chaplains were plaintiffs in almost 1500 total actions for the years 1347, 1386,
and 1417. Religious institutions initiated another 650 actions during those

---

F. Meekings (London, 1978), 341–408. Due to "perpetual disputes and quarrels," Thomas
Cantilupe, bishop of Hereford "found it necessary to keep five advocates in the King's
bench as well as proctors and attorneys in other courts." Moorman, *Church Life in England*,
171. Moorman did not make clear what he meant by "advocates" in the King's Bench.

15.   Helmholz, "Civil Jurisdiction and the Clergy," 187–239. His essay is really the
seminal investigation of this topic as English legal historians have largely ignored this matter. Ibid., 190–94. This principle was also known as *jurisdictio racione persone*.

16.   Ibid., 191–93, 216, 225–37. He noted, however, the use of bishops rather than
royal sheriffs to serve process on clerical defendants in litigation in the royal courts. Ibid.,
225–37. He, called them "quasi royal officers" and "ecclesiastical sheriffs." Ibid., 231, 237.

17.   Ibid., 223.

18.   Ibid., 237–38.

19.   He noted further that the clergy were involved in these civil matters more than
they were in felonies and that clerics were on both sides of some actions. Ibid., 189.

20.   "The Social Status of Litigants in the Court of Common Pleas: 1465," http://
aalt.law.uh.edu/ELHOv/Status.html.

same years.[21] In these years, he found more generally that the number of enrollments for three years totaled almost 3400 individual actions, accounting for 15% of all litigation in 1347, 18% in 1386, and 14% in 1417.[22] Despite the church's concern about its jurisdiction and intrusion by the secular courts, the medieval English clergy were not reluctant to use the Common law courts to assert their rights and vindicate their claims. As Swanson stated,

> Clerics were just as litigious as their lay compatriots if not more so. They sought remedies against each other and laymen. If the state offered such remedies they would happily use its machinery. Clerics therefore appear as plaintiffs in many actions before the secular courts which, if the church claims were enforced, would have gone to its courts.[23]

Like other litigants, they pursued their actions where remedies were most likely available.[24] That forum was often a secular court, where clerics "would happily use its machinery" and would ignore "the claims of the church courts if they did not offer the desired remedy."[25] Palmer has demonstrated the church's substantial reliance on the Common law, identifying

---

21. "Clerics as Litigants," http://aalt.law.uh.edu/ELHOv/Clerics.html. Palmer used a narrower definition of "cleric" than used in this essay. He stated that "Clergy" in this context is used in the sense that the plea rolls seem to use it: not any clerical person in orders, but only those clerical persons who are rectors or vicars or of higher status (thus chaplains were not "clergy"). Ibid.

22. "Clerics as Litigants 2," http://aalt.law.uh.edu/ELHOv/Clerics2.html. He stated that "the decline in the percentage that enrollments with clerical plaintiffs bore to all litigation indicate a high point in the late fourteenth century, when 18% of litigation had a clerical plaintiff, down then to a low of 11% right before the Reformation, with a collapse of such cases after the Reformation. The exclusion of the clergy from commerce and the limitations applied to pluralism decreased their economic standing and thus the occasions they would have to bring suits at Common law." Ibid.

23. Swanson, *Church and Society*, 187–88; W. A. Pantin, *The English Church in the Fourteenth Century* (Cambridge, 1955), 127–30.

24. Jones argued that the "popular demand for justice" was a motivating force as litigants, pursuing "personal gain or advantage," "were taking their legal difficulties to whatever power could solve them, regardless of the pretensions of the crown or church." W. R. Jones, "The Two Laws in England: the Later Middle Ages," *Journal of Church and State* 11 (1969), 115.

25. Ibid.

numerous actions in both the Common and King's Benches.[26] "The sheer volume of litigation brought by the clergy made the court of common pleas one of the most important venues for handling the mundane problems of the church."[27] As Professor Helmholz has shown, this litigation was "part of the long-continuing absorption into the Common law of remedies once available only in the court of the church."[28]

Writs of prohibition were a primary mechanism that facilitated this process.[29] Private litigants used these writs to prevent litigation against them in the ecclesiastical courts.[30] The clergy were among the "keenest seekers" of such writs.[31] It reflected "the gradual process of conflict, accommodation, correction, and growth that characterized spiritual and secular jurisdiction in the thirteenth and fourteenth centuries."[32] These develop-

---

26. Robert Palmer, *Selling the Church: The English Parish in Law, Commerce, and Religion, 1350–1550* (Chapel Hill, 2002), 50–54.

27. Ibid., 52.

28. Richard Helmholz, "Annuities and Pensions," in Susanne Jenks, Jonathan Rose and Christopher Whittick eds., *Laws, Lawyers, and Texts: Studies in Medieval Legal History in Honour of Paul Brand* (Leiden, 2012), 80.

29. Writs of prohibition have been a subject of Professor Helmholz's own scholarship. Richard Helmholz, "The Writ of Prohibition to Court Christian before 1500," in Richard Helmholz, *The Canon Law and the Law of England* (London, 1987), 59–76; "Writs of Prohibition and Ecclesiastical Sanctions in the English Courts Christian," in ibid., 77–117. The clergy repeatedly complained about the "overly expansive use of writs of prohibition." Helmholz, "Annuities and Pensions," 78; J. Robert, Wright, "The Conflict Between the Courts, and Clerical Grievances," in J. Robert Wright, *The Church and the English Crown, 1305–1334: A Study Based on the Register of Archbishop Walter Reynolds*, 178–94 (Toronto, 1980); W. R. Jones, "Bishops, Politics, and the Two Laws: The *Gravimina* of the English Clergy, 1237–1399, *Speculum* 42 (1966), 209–45. Cardinal Flahiff initially explored this subject, which apparently had been neglected, in some detail some time ago. G. B. Flahiff, "The Writ of Prohibition to Court Christian in the Thirteenth Century, Part I," *Mediaeval Studies* 6 (1944), 261–313; Flahiff, "The Writ of Prohibition to Court Christian. Part II," Mediaeval Studies 7 (1945), 229–90.

30. David Millon has recently discussed both the procedural and substantive aspects of writs of prohibitions and has collected numerous royal courts actions involving the use of such writs. David Millon, *Select Ecclesiastical Cases*, Selden Society 126 (2009).

31. J. H. Baker, *Introduction to English Legal History*, 4th ed. (Bath, 2002), 128; Flahiff, "The Use of Prohibitions by Clerics," *Mediaeval Studies* 3 (1941), 101–116.

32. Helmholz, "Annuities and Pensions," 84. Initially the writ of *Circumspecte Agatis* and the *Articuli Cleri* were used to define the boundaries of secular and spiritual jurisdiction. Subsequently, the Statute of *Praemunire* enabled aggrieved parties to seek

ments regarding the jurisdictional conflicts contributed significantly to the involvement of the clergy in litigation in the secular courts in various contexts.[33]

The clergy's ecclesiastical activities created numerous occasions for contact with the Common law. Matters such as patronage, benefices, pensions, and tithes, which were the subject of commercial activity, could be viewed as forms of property.[34] As result, as Professor Helmholz discussed, English law subjected them to the Common law rather than ecclesiastical jurisdiction.[35] Patronage was a contentious subject and "an important

---

penalties for litigation inappropriately instituted in the church courts. Baker, *Introduction*, 128–29, 144–45, 438. These developments have been a longstanding subject of scholarly interest. See, e.g., J. H. Denton, "The Making of the *Articuli Cleri* of 1316," *English Historical Review* 101 (1986), 564–95; E. B. Graves, "The Legal Significance of the Statute of Praemunire of 1353," in C. H. Taylor, ed., *Anniversary Essays in Medieval History by Students of Charles Homer Haskins* (New York, 1929), 57–80; E. B. Graves, "Circumspecte Agatis," *English Historical Review* 43 (1928), 1–20; W. T. Waugh, "The Great Statute of Praemunire," *English Historical Review* 37 (1922), 173–205.

33. The thirteenth and fourteenth centuries were an active period of these jurisdictional conflicts and they occurred in a variety of contexts and legal actions. For a detailed study, see W. R. Jones, "Relations of the Two Jurisdictions: Conflict and Cooperation in England during the Thirteenth and Fourteenth Centuries," in *Studies in Medieval and Renaissance History* VII (Lincoln, 1970), 79–210. The secular courts might also be involved in excommunication. But in such instances, the relationship between ecclesiastical and royal authorities was cooperative rather than contentious as in the areas of jurisdiction conflict. Swanson, *Church and Society*, 179–81; F. Donald Logan, *Excommunication and the Secular Arm in Medieval England: A Study in Legal Procedure from the Thirteenth to the Sixteenth Century* (Toronto, 1968); Brian Woodcock, *Medieval Ecclesiastical Courts in the Diocese of Canterbury* (Oxford, 1952), 93–97. Spiritual and royal authorities also cooperated in the prosecution of heretics. H. G. Richardson, "Heresy and the Lay Power under Richard II," *English Historical Review* 51 (1936), 1–28. Overall, Jones seemed to have taken an expansive view of the cooperation between ecclesiastical and royal authorities. Jones, "The Two Laws," 111–31.

34. See, e.g., W. A. Pantin, "Patronage and the Use of Benefices," in W. A Pantin,., *The English Church in the Fourteenth Century* (Cambridge, 1955), 30–46; Margaret Harvey, "The Benefice as Property: An Aspect of the Anglo-Papal Relations During the Pontificate of Martin V, 1417–31," in W. J. Sheils and Diana Wood, eds., *The Church and Wealth: Studies in Church History* (Oxford, 1987), 161–73.

35. Unlike the *ius commune* and Canon law, jurisdiction under the English Common law was determined by the subject matter involved in the litigation and not by the status of the parties. Helmholz, "Civil Jurisdiction," 193, 200–5, 223, 231, 239.

aspect of the crown's jurisdiction."[36] Benefices "integrated the incumbent into his locality" and sometimes this created conflicts with their neighbors, which resulted in litigation.[37] Although the right to appoint beneficed clergy belonged to the bishop, advowsons, the right to nominate a cleric for appointment, the more important role in this complicated process, was subject to royal jurisdiction.[38] Royal jurisdiction over such matters expanded and these conflicts often ended up in the royal courts. Advowson rights "produced substantial conflict and much litigation" and the Common law developed various writs such as *darrein presentment, quare impedit,* and *quare non admisit* to protect this form of property.[39] Actions based on these writs could involve the clergy in Common law litigation. The extension of royal patronage increased this possibility with the bishops as defendants in some actions.[40] In commenting on the growth of patronage, Swanson argued that "the concept of patronage as a piece of property, subject to process in the royal courts, also aided the changes, with the crown's lawyers ruthlessly extending their master's patronal rights, by use of the writs of *Quare impedit...* and *Quare non admisit....*"[41] The developing complexity over patronage rights likely "made such disputes even more subject to Common law determination."[42]

The pension obligations of religious institutions also became a subject of the Common law, which in some instances resulted in actions in the royal courts.[43] The emergence of secular jurisdiction over pensions is an

---

36. Millon, *Select Ecclesiastical Cases,* ci–cviii.

37. Swanson, *Church and Society,* 63–64.

38. Professor Helmholz has explored this topic and the potential for the conflict between ecclesiastical and royal authorities. "Benefices and the *Ius Patronatus,*" in Richard Helmholz, *The Canon Law and Ecclesiastical Jurisdiction from 597 to the 1640s, The Oxford History of the Laws of England,* I (Oxford, 2004), 477–91.

39. Palmer, *Selling the Church,* 17–23.

40. Joel Rosenthal, "Kings, Continuity and Ecclesiastical Benefaction in Fifteenth-Century England," in Joel Rosenthal and Colin Richmond, ed., *People, Politics, and Community in the Later Middle Ages* (Gloucester, 1987), 161–75.

41. Swanson, *Church and Society,* 72–76.

42. Ibid., 142–44.

43. The monetary support for chantries could pose similar problems. Helmholz, *The Canon Law and Ecclesiastical Jurisdiction,* 369; Swanson, *Church and Society,* 61, 64, 68. See generally A. Hamilton Thompson, *The English Clergy and Their Organisation in the Later Middle Ages* (Oxford, 1947), 132–60.

interesting example of how Common law remedies displaced those that were initially and exclusively available in the ecclesiastical courts. Professor Helmholz has ably detailed the process and illustrated how the Common law writ of annuity as a basis for pension actions emerged.[44] Although a remedy for collecting pension arrears was available in the church courts through *causae annuae pensione*, clergy and other litigants began to use writs of prohibitons against actions for arrears in those courts. Although initially, despite the preclusion of ecclesiastical jurisdiction, the Common law lacked an alternative remedy, one was developed based on the Canon law remedy. Professor Helmholz noted that 75% of the initial writs of annuity involved spiritual pensions and, thus, the secular remedy served the same function as that which was available under Canon law.[45]

The church was involved in substantial economic activity and, as in the world at large, money could always result in disputes and litigation.[46] Palmer has described the attributes of "the parish as a commercial entity."[47] Tithes were one dimension of that nature, providing the economic resources for the rector and his family.[48] Professor Helmholz has described tithes, another subject of his scholarship,[49] as "the basic ecclesiastical tax paid by the laity."[50] Tithes were a matter that could also produce conflict and legal disputes.[51] "Clashes between incumbents and tithe-payers were fairly

44. Helmholz, "Annuities and Pensions," 69–85.

45. Ibid., 80–81.

46. Swanson, *Church and Society*, 191–251. J. Gilchrist, *The Church and Economic Activity in the Middle Ages* (London, 1969). Also church officials acted as collectors of clerical taxes payable to the crown. This activity could involve in legal disputes in the process of rendering accounts at the Exchequer and the use of secular remedies to deal with recalcitrant payors. McHardy, "Clerical Taxation," 172–73. For major dispute in 1441 over the collection of taxes by the Prior of Leeds, during the course of which the crown sought to distrain the archbishop of Canterbury for contempt although he was ultimately exonerated, see M. Hemmant, *Select Cases in the Exchequer Chamber before All the Justices of England*, Selden Society 71 (1933), 84–95.

47. Palmer, *Selling the Church*, 30–47.

48. Swanson, *Church and Society*, 211–17

49. Helmholz, *The Canon Law and Ecclesiastical Jurisdiction*, 433–65.

50. Ibid., 433. Church rectors were also taxpayers and "were among the most important contributors to both papal and royal taxes." May McKissack, *The Fourteenth Century, 1307–1399* (Oxford, 1959), 302.

51. See, e.g., J. A. F. Thomson, "Tithe Disputes in Later Medieval London," *English Historical Review* 78 (1963), 1–17.

common."[52] In discussing these conflicts, Professor Helmholz said, "yet discord there was—in abundance.... One eventual result of discord was jurisdictional, breaking the church's monopoly on litigation over tithes."[53] He observed that "once the tithe was severed from the harvest, it became a temporal matter."[54] Their sale and lease made them a form of property and could subject disputes about them to litigation in the secular courts.[55] Palmer identified numerous types of disputes over tithes that resulted in litigation in the court of common pleas.[56] John Baker also identified actions regarding tithes in the Court of the Star Chamber.[57] The Common law action of trespass *de bonis asportis* was used to resolve disputes over tithes.[58]

Another form of payment to parishes was mortuaries. Although not the subject of substantial scholarship, Professor Helmholz has provided a detailed treatment.[59] He defined a mortuary as "a customary offering made to one's parish church at one's death." As he and other scholars have noted, these payments were strongly disliked and resented by the laity and burdened them at an emotionally and financially difficult time.[60] Along with tithes, they "provided the commonest reason for conflict between the cleric and parishioner."[61] Although mortuaries were the subject of litigation in the ecclesiastical courts,[62] their nature as a lay good or chattel, as Professor Helmholz noted, subjected them to common jurisdiction through writs of

---

52. Swanson, *Church and Society*, 212.

53. Helmholz, *The Canon Law and Ecclesiastical Jurisdiction*, 433. He discussed the Canon law litigation over tithes, ibid., 440–50.

54. Helmholz, "Annuities and Pensions," 78.

55. Swanson, *Church and Society*, 64, 144.

56. Palmer, *Selling the Church*, 31–39.

57. J. H. Baker, *Oxford History of the Laws of England*, VI, 1483–1558 (Oxford, 2003), 198–99.

58. Millon, *Select Ecclesiastical Cases*, cviii–cxvi.

59. Richard Helmholz, "Mortuaries and the Law of Custom," in Richard Helmholz, *The ius commune in England: Four Studies* (Oxford, 2001), 135–86.

60. Helmholz, "Mortuaries," 145; Palmer, *Selling the Church*, 42; Swanson, *Church and Society*, 216.

61. Swanson, *Church and Society*, 216.

62. Helmholz, "Mortuaries," 170–77.

prohibition or trespass or detinue actions, which would again involve the clergy in Common law litigation.[63]

Ecclesiastical institutions possessed great quantities of land, which "inevitably led to many disputes which were intensified by the medieval passion for litigation."[64] Ecclesiastics as landlords presented numerous potential for conflicts and disputes.[65] Actions for annual rent in various contexts to which the clergy and religious institutions were parties were a matter for the Common law.[66] The practice of clergy of leasing prebends produced numerous conflicts over money, which resulted in litigation in the Common law courts to collect arrearages. Robert Palmer has made a substantial study of this commercial activity, which was widespread until it was curtailed by a 1529 statute.[67] His study identified numerous parish leases, fifty of which involved leases made between 1270–1488, that resulted in Common Bench litigation.[68] Prior to the Black Death, landlords brought numerous account actions against the bailiffs that they had hired to manage the parishes.[69] After the Black Death, leasing became more common and absentee rectors and vicars leased the parishes to both clerical and lay tenants.[70] In litigation regarding the leases, remedies were sought through the normal Common law actions available to lessors and lessees.[71]

Nor was the involvement of clergy in Common law litigation limited to their ecclesiastical offices and activities. Various types of activities by the clergy led to civil actions in the royal courts. As Professor Helmholz noted, the clergy were regularly sued in the Common law and local courts

63.   He opined that he thought that this occurred less often than in the other areas of jurisdictional conflict. Ibid., 177–80. Nevertheless, Palmer found a number of actions involving mortuaries in the records of the royal courts. Palmer, *Selling the Church*, 42–47.

64.   Moorman, *Church Life in England*, 171. In addition, enforcement and manipulation of the Statute of Mortmain, which governed grants of land to the church, could give rise to disputes with royal authorities and Common law litigation. Sandra Raban, *Mortmain Legislation and the English Church, 1279–1500* (Cambridge, 1982), 72–129.

65.   Swanson, *Church and Society*, 202–26, 238–42.

66.   Millon, *Select Ecclesiastical Cases*, lxxxviii–ci.

67.   Palmer, *Selling the Church*, 48–142.

68.   Ibid., 263–73.

69.   In three Michaelmas terms in 1328, 1338, and 1345, there were respectively thirty-three, thirty-six, and thirty-six such actions. Ibid., 75–79, 255–58.

70.   Ibid., 79–111.

71.   Ibid., 112–42.

and "pleas of debt and trespass and other personal actions brought against them were quite common."[72] The clergy were involved in numerous credit transactions, both as lenders and borrowers.[73] They also engaged in various types of commercial transactions that resulted in litigation.[74] The clergy also acted as executors for decedents in dealing with money claims involving the latters' estates. The activities in all these contexts likely resulted in actions in the secular courts, most likely in actions of debt and account.[75] Palmer has noted that the substantial increase in Common Bench actions to collect money may have contributed to an increase in clerical plaintiffs in that court in the fourteenth century.[76] The clergy were also involved possessory disputes, as reflected in assizes of novel dississein or trespass.

The clergy were involved in a wide range of trespass disputes. One of the most common was trespassory rape actions. Numerous clerics were defendants in statutory actions by husbands for the rape and abduction of the latters' wives and the taking of their goods.[77] Dunn stated that "the clergy were accused of ravishment more than any other group" and "over-represented among defendants in such actions."[78] Many of these actions involved

---

72. Helmholz, "Civil Jurisdiction," 223.

73. Swanson, *Church and Society*, 234–37.

74. Dyer noted that such activities resulted in actions involving debt, trespass, and detention of chattels in the borough courts. Christopher Dyer, "Trade, Towns and the Church: Ecclesiastical Consumers and the Urban Economy of the West Midlands, 1290–1540," in T. R. Slater and Gervase Rosser, ed., *The Church in the Medieval Town* (Aldershot, 1998), 70–71. Heath cited a number of examples: Peter Heath, *The English Parish Clergy on the Eve of the Reformation* (London, 1969), 37, 43, 147, 161, 162, 185.

75. Some of these action may have been in manor courts. Elaine Clark, "Debt Litigation in a Late Medieval English Vill," in J. A. Raftis, ed., *Papers in Medieval Studies: Pathways to Medieval Peasants* (Toronto, 1981), 247–79.

76. Palmer, "Clerics as Litigants," http://aalt.law.uh.edu/ELHOv/Clerics.html.

77. Statute Westminster II, cc. 34–35 (1285), *Statutes of the Realm*, I, 87–88; J. B. Post, "Ravishment of Women and the Statutes of Westminster" in J. H. Baker, ed., *Legal Records and the Historian* (1978), 150–64; "Sir Thomas West and the Statute of Rapes," 1382, *Bulletin of the Institute of Historical Research* 53 (1980), 24–30.

78. She said that they accounted for one-third of the defendants in the abduction actions, where the occupational status of the defendant was identified although they made up only two per-cent of the English population. Caroline Dunn, *Stolen Women in Medieval England: Rape, Abduction, and Adultery, 1100–1500* (Cambridge, 2013), 180. She discussed actions against clerics in detail, 180–90; she also noted some of the allegations were false and retaliatory, ibid., 161–62; 188–90. For a detailed study of the clerical population of me-

consensual relationships and not forcible intercourse. Some of the actions also may have been intended to enforce clerical norms, using the law to punish clergy for breaking the vow of celibacy by committing fornication or adultery. Although there was no action for defamation in the King's Bench or Common Bench until the sixteenth century, clergy were parties in defamation actions in local courts as Professor Helmholz has shown.[79]

Criminal actions against the clergy were a longstanding, controversial subject, reaching back to the debate between Henry II and Archbishop Thomas Becket over "criminous clerks."[80] Although a compromise was achieved that permitted clerics to be turned over to their ordinaries for canonical purgation, this "benefit of clergy" did not prevent them from being indicted.[81] As the plea rolls show, they were indicted for homicide and other felonies and targets of appeals of felony.[82] In particular, the King's Bench records contain numerous presentments and appeals of clergy for felonious rape, which were not consensual like the trespass actions and which specially alleged carnal knowledge and forcible conduct. Dunn stated that clergy "were frequently cited in rape allegations."[83] In sum, the clergy, both with respect to their ecclesiastical and other activities were frequent plaintiffs and defendants in Common law litigation.

---

dieval England, see Josiah Russell, "The Clerical Population of Medieval England," *Traditio* 2 (1944), 177–212.

79.   Richard Helmholz, *Select Cases on Defamation to 1600*, Selden Society 101 (1985), 36.

80.   J. G. Hudson, "Constitutions of Clarendon, Clause 3, and Henry II's Reforms of Law and Administration," in Jenks, Rose, and Whittick, *Laws, Lawyers and Texts*, 1–19; Baker, *Introduction*, 128–29; Heath, *The English Parish Clergy*, 119–33.

81.   Helmholz, *The Canon Law and Ecclesiastical Jurisdiction*, 511–14; Baker, *Introduction*, 513–15.

82.   To the extent that occupations could be identified, clerics constituted the largest percentage of those accused of homicide in thirteenth century England. James Given, *Society and Homicide in Thirteenth-Century England* (Stanford, 1977), 82–83. The felony actions against clergy included treason, the most serious criminal offense. Storey, "Clergy and the Common Law," 353–408.

83.   Dunn, *Stolen Women*, 180.

THE CLERGY AND ABUSE OF LEGAL PROCEDURE

The involvement of clergy in abuse of legal procedure can be divided into two chronological periods. The first period, which begins in the late thirteenth century and extends through the reign of Edward III, involves the initial development of legal remedies for abuse of legal procedure, primarily those for conspiracy and champerty. The nature of the litigation in the second period, which begins with the reign of Richard II and extends through the fifteenth century, is quite different. The actions in that period are primarily private and crown maintenance actions, likely as a result of a 1377 statute, which made maintenance of another person's litigation generally illegal.[84] This essay will focus on the first period.[85]

Starting in the late thirteenth century, several enactments provided a basis for legal remedies against those who misused the legal system through conspiracy, maintenance, and champerty. These provisions created a legal basis for both jury presentments and private actions directed at conspiracy.[86] As to the former, the articles of the Eyre included a chapter in 1279 instructing the justices to inquire as to conspiracies, which enabled jury presentments for conspiracy.[87] In addition, the 1293 Ordinance of Conspirators and the authorization of a writ of conspiracy provided a basis for

84. "No Counsellors, Officers, or Servants nor any other person within the Realm Engand, of whatsoever Estate or Condition, shall henceforth take nor sustain any quarrel by maintenance in the country, or elsewhere upon a grevious pain." I Rich. II, c. 4, *Statutes of the Realm*, II, 2–3 (1377).

85. The actions discussed in this essay are contained in the plea rolls of The National Archives, Public Record Office in the records of the King's Bench (KB 27), Common Bench (CP 40), and the Justices of the Eyres (JUST 1). Citations to National Archives documents CP 40, KB 27, and JUST 1 refer to the digital archive assembled by Robert C. Palmer and Elspeth K. Palmer, *The Anglo-American Legal Tradition* http://aalt.law. uh.edu/, hereafter AALT. Individual citations will provide the AALT image number.

86. Winfield, *The History of Conspiracy*, 1–130; Sayles, "Conspiracy and Allied Offences," *Select Cases in the Court of the King's Bench* III, liv–lxxi; Alan Harding, "The Origins of the Crime of Conspiracy," *Transactions of the Royal Historical Society*, 5th ser., 33 (1983), 89–108.

87. Helen Cam, "Studies in the Hundred Rolls: Some Aspects of Thirteenth-Century Administration," in Paul Vinogradoff, ed., *Oxford Studies in Social and Legal History*, VI (1921; repr., New York, 1974), 58–101; Sayles, "Conspiracy and Allied Offences," lvii.

private actions against conspirators.[88] This offense involved two or more individuals who joined together, often by oath, to engage in some form of wrongful conduct. Although the actions involve a large variety of factual situations, many of the actions involved conspiring to have an innocent person charged with a crime. Moreover, some actions involved conspiracy to engage in maintenance or champerty or combined accusations of conspiracy and maintenance. As a result, the plea rolls contain numerous presentments and private actions regarding conspiracy.

Maintenance was viewed as a longstanding and pervasive problem in medieval England.[89] As a legal concept, it involved providing assistance or support in the litigation of another person.[90] Champerty was a special form of maintenance in which the maintainer, in return for the assistance, entered a covenant with the party to the action to receive all or part of the money or land in dispute if the action were successful. These two types of conduct were the targets of numerous statutes.[91] The initial prohibitions were contained in the 1275 Statute of Westminster I.[92] Chapter 25 prohibited champerty by the officers of the king and Chapter 28 made the main-

---

88.   Ordinance of Conspirators: I *Rot. Parl.* 96, 21 Edw. I (1293) (1767–77); ed. Paul Brand, in *The Parliament Rolls of Medieval England (PROME)*, ed. C. Given-Wilson et al., http://www.sd-editions.com/PROME. Authorization of the writ of conspiracy: *Statutes of the Realm* I, 316; KB 27/137, m. 12 (1293), AALT img. no. 1841.

89.   Winfield characterized maintainance, like conspiracy and champerty, as an "abuse of legal procedure," *The History of Conspiracy*, 131.

90.   There was a social concept of maintenance, which was broader and less well-defined than the legal one. In the former, the word, maintenance, was used to denote various types of wrong doing, not limited to the legal forms of maintenance, and often related to litigation or legal issues, which were alleged to undermine legal rights and security of property. The petitions to the king and his council, parliament and chancery were the most common manifestation of this notion, but it appeared also in medieval literature, religious works, and private letters.

91.   There were over fifteen enactments between 1275 and 1542. The primary enactments were *Articuli Super Cartas*, 28 Edw. I, st. 3, c. 11 (1300), *Statutes of the Realm*, I, 139; Statute of Conspirators, 33 Edw. I, *Statutes of the Realm*, I, 216 (Statutes of Uncertain Date); 4 Edw. III, c. 11 (1330), *Statutes of the Realm* I, 264; 20 Edw. III, cc. 4, 5 and 6 (1346), *Statutes of the Realm*, I, 304–05; 1 Rich. II, c. 4 (1377), *Statutes of the Realm*, II, 2–3.

92.   There was an earlier statute prohibiting champerty by serjeants in the London courts. *Liber de Antiquis Legibus: Cronica Maiorum et Vicecomitum Londonariorum*, ed. T Stapleton, Camden Society, original series, 34 (1846; repr. New York, 1968), 42–43. The impact and significance of this statute are not clear.

tenance of quarrels in the king's courts by royal clerks and sheriffs illegal.[93] The 1285 Statute of Westminster II reiterated the prohibition on champerty by officials more specifically.[94] Whatever their political and rhetorical impact, it is not clear that these initial provisions resulted in much royal or private enforcement. However, the 1300 *Articuli Super Cartas* extended the prohibition on champerty to all persons.[95] As a result of this statute, many private champerty actions were instituted.

Conspiracy, Maintenance, and Champerty Actions

During this period, clergy were both plaintiffs and defendants in a number of conspiracy and champerty actions. In studying these actions, it is important to note that accusations in the records are only allegations and what is charged is not always what actually happened.[96] More commonly, the clergy were defendants rather than plaintiffs in these types of actions.[97] In the 1293 Eyre of Kent, three clerics—a monk, a chaplain, and a clerk—

93. Statute of Westminster I, cc. 25, 28, 33, 3 Edw. I (1275), *Statutes of the Realm*, I, 33–34.

94. "The Chancellor, Treasurer, Justices, nor any of King's council, nor clerk of the Chancery, nor of the Exchequer, nor of any Justice or other Officer, nor any of the Kings's house, Clerk nor Lay shall not receive any Church, Advowson of a Church, Land, nor tenement in Fee, by Gift, nor by Purchase, not to Farm, nor by Champerty, nor otherwise, so long as a plea is before us, or before any of our Officers; nor shall take no Reward thereof; And he that doth...either himself, or by another or make any bargain shall be punished at the K's pleasure, as well he that purchaseth, as he that doth sell." Statute of Westminster II, 13 Edw. I, c. 49 (1285), *Statutes of the Realm*, I, 95.

95. "Because other officers not bound by earlier Champerty statute., no Officer nor any other, for to have part of the thing in plea, shall not take upon him that is the Business that is in Suit; nor none upon any such Covenant shall give up his right to another." *Articuli. Super Cartas.*, 28 Edw. I, st. 3, c. 11, *Statutes of the Realm*, I, 139.

96. As is the case with all litigation records, the parties' pleas and other allegations are much more common than an actual verdict or judgment in the cases. The latter will be noted when they are available.

97. Conspiracy: Just 1/376, m. 69d (1293), AALT img. no. 3479 ; KB 27/140, m. 42 (1294), AALT img. no. 2606; KB 27/148, m. 8d (1296), AALT img. no. 765; KB 27/150, m. 6d (1297), AALT img. no.98; KB 27/150, m. 34d (1297), AALT img. no. 158. Champerty: CP 40/149, m. 213d (1304), AALT img. no. 1369; CP 40/149, m. 283 (1304), AALT img. no. 600; CP 40/154, m. 63 (1305), AALT img. no. 130; KB 27/350, m. 78 (1347), AALT img. no. 3640; KB 27/351, m. 83 (1348), AALT img. no. 1795; KB 27/352, m. 76 (1348), AALT img. no. 2559; KB 27/353, m. 55d (1348), AALT img. no. 6599.

were among fifty individuals who were presented as conspirators and as maintainers of parties in various courts. The jury found all the defendants guilty.[98] Another action involved an aggressive parson who was present-ed for forcibly ejecting a widow from her land and then at his own cost maintaining the plaintiff in an assize of novel dissesin against the widow in return for having the land.[99] Perhaps the most heinous conduct involved the indictment of John of Tintern, the abbot of Malmesbury, and his fellow monk, John of Rodborn, for conspiring to procure the killing and actually killing several men. Moreover, the abbot ordered the beating and wounding of others and the abduction of one of the victims' wife, who renounced her husband, who had built a fortress to protect his wife from the abbot, and she "lived continuously with the abbot, knowing the abbot to be a felon and of bad character."[100]

Clergy were also charged for maintaining and assisting those who had been charged with felonies. Brian of Grey, knight and fellow broth-er of the prior of St. John of Jerusalem, was charged with supporting and maintaining felons and other wrongdoers and being a common maintainer of quarrels. In one instance, he took 10 marks to maintain a man indicted for murder and threatened to beat the coroner who refused to conceal and withdraw the indictment. In another instance, he took a thief arrested by

98. Just 1/376, m. 69d (1293), AALT img. no. 3479. All the defendants paid fines which ranged from £40 to 1/2 mark. The monk's fine was 20 marks, paid by his abbot, the chaplain's 1/2 mark, and the clerk's 1 mark. In another presentment, the parson of the church of Moor Munkton was among a number of men confederating together to main-tain each other's pleas. They were permitted to make fines and went quiet. KB 27/355, m. 3 (1349), AALT img. no. 7781.

99. He was also presented for another assault of a man and the abduction of a woman. He obtained a pardon for his offenses. KB 27/353, m. 52d (1348), AALT img. no. 6592.

100. KB 27/352, m. 130 (1348), AALT img. no. 2674. The record also notes that the abbot and his predecessor, Adam de la Hoke had been involved in a dispute over money that had belonged to the Depensers and in the turmoil during the reign of Edward II and had received a pardon for their offences during that period. *Cal. Pat. Rolls,* 7 Edw. III, 1345–48, 558; R. B. Pugh, and Elizabeth Crittall, ed., "House of Benedictine monks: Abbey of Malmesbury," *A History of the County of Wiltshire* 3, British History Online, http://www.british-history.ac.uk/report.aspx?compid=36532. According to the plea roll record, the oyer and terminer justices apparently refused to accept the earlier pardon and the abbot and his fellow monk made a fine with the king for £500 and were pardoned for the above offenses.

the constable and permitted him to escape. He also procured a man to be indicted, and he took 10 marks from the man to maintain and assist him.[101] In a notorious series of activities involving the abduction of the wealthy widow, Margery Poyninges, in which a number of men were charged with treason, homicide, and other felonies,[102] Thomas of Litherland, prior of Burcough was accused of being of counsel to those men and maintaining and receiving them.[103] Clerics were also presented for rescuing felons from prison and also for saving them from the gallows, an offense which raises interesting moral issues.[104]

But private parties brought numerous conspiracy actions as well, some of which also were against the clergy. One of the most interesting actions was a plea of conspiracy and trespass that Thomas Lewknor and Lucy, his wife, brought against John, the parson of the church of Souldern for several types of wrongful conduct, including champerty and maintenance.[105] They alleged that he conspired with the defendant and the jurors

101. Brian was charged with numerous other offenses, including numerous assaults, extortion, abductions, and thefts, some of which involved clerical victims. Despite his massive campaign of wrongdoing, Brian obtained a charter of pardon and a surety of peace. He sought to be delivered from prison, but the record is incomplete. KB 27/461, m. 6 rex (1376), AALT img. no. 154. In 1370, Brian de Grey was appointed as an attorney by the attorneys of the prior of the hospital to act in their place. Cal. Pat. Rolls, 15 Edw. III, 1370–74, 4, 8.

102. The event involved an attack on Beaumes manor, Berkshire by John Dalton, knight and numerous others. Two people were killed and others wounded. Cal. Pat. Rolls, 7 Edw. III, 1345–48, 310–11, 312, 384. For a detailed discussion of the event, see Lady Russell, Swallowfield and Its Owners (London, 1901), 39–47; Nora Alexander, "The Raid on Beaumes Manor, Shinfeld, Berks, Good Friday, 1347," Berkshire Archeology Journal 35 (1931), 144–53.

103. Thomas obtained a pardon. 27 KB/357, m. 23d (1349), AALT img. no. 9009. A number of men came forth and asserted Thomas' innocence. Cal. Pat. Rolls, 7 Edw. III, 1345–48, 436. The plea rolls contain a number of records regarding these indictments.

104. JUST 1/710, m. 57 (1285), AALT img. no. 9601 (prison). In the 1285 Oxford Eyre, six men, who were condemned to death, were rescued by clerics, who took them to the church of St. Giles, where they abjured the realm. JUST 1/710, m. 57 (1285), AALT img. no. 9601–02; JUST 1/710, m. 57d (1285), AALT img. no. 9601–02; . JUST 1/710, m. 57f (1285), AALT img. no. 9723–24. A later action provided more detail of the rescue. It said that the cord by which the convicted felon hung, half-alive, was cut by a cleric and the felon taken to a church where he resumed life. KB 27/455 (1374), AALT img. no. 338.

105. KB 27/140, m. 42 (1294), AALT img. no. 2606. This action is also included in Sayles, ed., Select Cases in the Court of the King's Bench, III.

in a land action they had brought, which prevented the prosecution of the action. Other acts of conspiracy of which they accused him included preventing them from obtaining services from their tenants, abducting the wife's daughter and advising her to bring an action of mort d'ancestor for a manor that he would obtain by champerty if she were successful, advising a man to implead them for a debt of which he would also have champerty, procuring a man to bring an assize of novel dissesin against them and maintaining that plea, and procuring the jurors in similar action against them that he also maintained. The parson asserted numerous defenses, two of which presented interesting legal issues. First, he alleged that two of the accusations were not actionable by a writ of conspiracy. Other writs were available for the abduction and an action based on a judicial writ of conspiracy, therefore, need not be answered. Likewise, in the assize against them, a writ of conspiracy could not be used to quash the adverse verdict, which still stood firm. As to the allegations of champerty and maintenance, he acknowledged that he provided assistance to various parties as alleged, but said it was permissible as "it is lawful for anyone in the realm to help his friends in their rights in the lord king's court" and some of those he assisted were "his parishioners and he advised them on their rights and gave them his help as it was lawfully permissible for him to do."[106] Apart from the allegations of champerty, which he did not explicitly deny or justify, his justifications likely made his assistance permissible.[107]

As was the case with most champerty actions, the actions where clergy were defendants frequently involved maintenance of action involving a dispute over real property. For example, a man and his wife sued the parson of the church of St. Michael, Coney Street, York, for maintaining an action regarding a messuage in York in which the champerty plaintiffs were defendants, by virtue of which the parson would have the messuage.[108] Two similar actions were brought, one against the prior of the hospital of St. John of

---

106. As a result, the plaintiffs were given permission to withdraw their plea and the parson went without day.

107. These justifications likely reflected longstanding social norms. These norms and permissibility of his justifications are discussed in greater detail in the forthcoming book.

108. CP 40/149, m. 213d (1304), AALT img. no. 1370.

Jerusalem and another against the parson of church of St. Savior, York.[109] One action involving land combined allegations of conspiracy, champerty and forgery. The defendant enlisted a cleric to bring an assize of novel disseisin, for which the cleric paid the defendant 10 marks and the right to the land if he were successful. The cleric participated with the defendant in fabricating a verdict, which was presented to the jurors in the assize, which caused the plaintiff to lose the land.[110]

Clergy were also plaintiffs in conspiracy actions,[111] but not as frequently as they were defendants. In one action, a chaplain sued a man who was his counsel, being paid a half mark a year to attend to all his business, for conspiracy involving his disloyalty. After being retained, his counsel procured a man to sue the plaintiff, who was the lessee of the altarage of a church, in an ecclesiastical court regarding the lease and took 40s. from the man to assist him against the chaplain, his client, who then lost the altarage. The defendant also sued the plaintiff for various debts that the plaintiff alleged were fabricated.[112] In another action, a parson sued a man that he had sued in an ecclesiastical court and the jurors who had presented him in the sheriff's tourn. Although the plaintiff claimed he had been advised by the king's court to sue in the court Christian, he was nevertheless amerced 40s., which he paid. The jurors responded that they were re-

109. CP 40/149, m. 283 (1304), AALT img. no. 600; CP 40/154, m. 63 (1304), AALT img. no. 130. All three actions were based on the 1300 *Articuli super Cartas*, 28 Edw I, st. 3, c. 10 and are in the *audita querela* form. There were also four mesne process entries regarding an action in which one of the defendants was a chaplain involving land in Gloucester. See note 108 infra.

110. It is unclear to what action the verdict pertained. The plaintiff did allege that he had attempted to levy a fine regarding his purchase of the land, but was unable to do so because of harassment. Although the cleric was a participant in the conspiracy, champerty, and forgery, he was not a defendant in the action. KB 27/138, m. 49d (1293), AALT img. no. 2274. This action is also included in G. O. Sayles, ed., *Select Cases in the Court of the King's Bench* II, Selden Society 57 (1938), 168.

111. I only identified one instance where a cleric, in this case the abbot of Hayles, was a plaintiff in champerty action. The action involved maintenance of *scire facias* action on a fine regarding a mill, by which the champerty defendants, one of whom was a chaplain, would have the mill. The action is evidenced only by four mesne process entries. KB 27/350, m. 78 (1347), AALT img. no. 3640; KB 27/351, m. 83 (1348), AALT img. no.1795; KB 27/352, m. 76 (1348), AALT img. no. 2559; KB 27/353, m. 55d (1348), AALT img. no. 6599.

112. The defendant denied the allegations and the action was sent to the jury. KB 27/150, m. 14d (1297), AALT img. no. 116.

sponding to articles in the tourn, one of which inquired of suits in the court Christian, to which they truthfully responded, as they were required, by presenting the plaintiff and did not do so by malice or conspiracy.[113] Clergy were also sometimes on both sides of the case.[114]

In some actions, clergy were not accused as defendants, but they were the beneficiaries of conspiracy, champerty, or maintenance. A jury presented that several men conspired to maintain each other's enterprises and that one of them took £10 from a vicar to procure his acquittal for a murder that he committed, took 11 marks annually from a chaplain to beat a man, and took 11 marks from the same chaplain for maintenance in preventing his indictment for murder.[115] A collector of tolls of Beverly, who had been the underbailiff and custodian of the archbishop of York's prison and the king's coroner, was presented for maintaining the false pleas of two chaplains.[116] Further, two men were presented for making various threats of bodily harm and death, including threatening a man, on pain of losing his life and members, to cease being of counsel to a prior, whom they undertook to maintain.[117]

Those charged with maintenance also took money from clerics to have innocent men indicted. For example, William of Poppleton, parson of the church of Harewode, and others took £20 to indict those whom master Ralph of Turville wished to indict for trespass to the archbishop of York and procured an inquisition for five marks, which indicted various men, from whom substantial fines were extorted.[118] In an action involving the

---

113. All the parties put themselves on the jury. KB 27/150, m. 14d (1297), AALT img. no. 116.

114. E.g. KB 27/148, m. 8d (1296), AALT img. no. 765 (prior v. parson); KB 27/350, m. 78 (1347), AALT img. no. 3640 (abbot v. chaplain); KB 27/164, m. 15d (1301), AALT img. no. 1564 (prior v. rector).

115. Nevertheless, the chaplain was indicted. The conspirator was found guilty. KB 27/273, m. 26 rex (1328), AALT img. no. 321. Conspirators also caused a lay brother of the abbot of Fontaignes to be falsely indicted. KB 27/355, m. 5 (1349), AALT img. no. 7785.

116. KB 27/354, m. 42 rex (1348), AALT img. no. 7217.

117. They further pursued the man to a market and searched his house to kill him and for the next six months, he said that he no longer dared to be in the country. KB 27/312, m. 20 rex (1338), AALT img. no. 326.

118. The defendants said that they could not deny the charges and they were permitted to make fines with the king. KB 27/355, m. 4 (1349), AALT img. no. 7783. In contrast, John Vavasor, who charged as a "common maintainer of false pleas and a common

obligation to repair a bridge, the abbot of Pershore was a beneficiary of a conspiracy by an ambidextrous lawyer against the abbot of Westminster.[119] In addition, three clerks were charged with conspiring to have a man falsely excommunicated by procuring another man to impersonate the victim and be summoned to appear before the archdeacon of London.[120] Moreover, clergy might also be victims of conspiracy.[121]

Consistent with the earlier discussion of the clergy's frequent resort to secular courts and their remedies, clergy used the writ of conspiracy to resolve disputes over ecclesiastic matters. For example, the chief lord of lands, which he had seized as a result of their unlawful alienation in mortmain, brought action against the master of the hospital of St. Bartholmew, two other clerics, and another man for conspiring to avoid the statute. The master, to whom the lands had been alienated by the chief lord's tenant, conspired with the other clerics to oust the chief lord and procured the tenant to enfeoff the nonclerical defendant by making a false charter to him, by virute of which he successfully gained possession of the lands by an assize of novel disseisin against the chief lord, who was ousted as a result.[122] In another action, the prior of Belvoir sued a conspiracy action against Master William, the parson of the church of Harby and a clerk of the prior and the convent of Belvoir, in a dispute over an advowson. After the parson

---

conspirator," was found not guilty of taking £20 from Master Ralph to have same men indicted for a trespass, perhaps the same one as it was to William le Zouche, archbishop, and who made a £200 fine with the archbishop. The jury found John not guilty. KB 27/354, m. 71d (1348), AALT img. no. 7449. William de Popel was also presented for conspiring to indict several innocent men for breaking out of prison. Again he said that he was unable to deny the charges and made a fine. KB 27/355, m. 2d (1349), AALT img. no. 8086.

119.   The jury presented that the lawyer, who took money from both abbots, conspired with a clerk in fraudulently counterfeiting a sealed sheriff's return of a jury panel to substitute a different panel and in accusing and convicting the abbot of Westminster for failing to repair the bridge. The lawyer said he was unable to deny the charges and made a fine with the king and the sheriff was ordered to arrest the clerk. KB 27/352, m. 32 (1348), AALT img. no. 2745.

120.   As result of the archdeacon's order to the victim's rector, the victim was summon to appear and regained his status, claiming he lost 100s. by the conspiracy. KB 27/532, m. 4 rex (1248), AALT img. no. 2690.

121.   A jury presented that two men conspired to maintain each other's enterprises and caused a vicar to be falsely indicted for several felonies, of which he was subsequently acquitted. KB 27/273, m. 26 rex (1328), AALT img. no. 321.

122.   KB 27/150, m. 34d (1297), AALT img. no. 158.

unsuccessfully requested to be presented to a vacancy, he procured the lady of Belvoir to disturb their presentee, procured himself to be presented and promised to keep the lady harmless and refund all her expenses, and procured the lady and her bailiffs to distrain his animals and ploughs so that the prior's land lay uncultivated and unplanted. Master William denied the conspiracy and said he was a clerk and of counsel to the lady and advised her on the advowson and the prosecution of her other legal matters.[123] A prior sued a rector for conspiring with a vicar regarding the collection of taxes on behalf of the king. The jury found that defendant had conspired with vicar, as alleged by the prior, to misrepresent the prior's account rolls by fabricating another roll to show that the prior had witheld money in deceit of the king. The prior was exonerated and the jury found the rector guilty of conspiracy.[124]

Actions Involving Other Legally Related Wrongdoing

Actions involving legally related wrongdoing, but not related to conspiracy, champerty nor maintenance, can be considered another type of abuse of legal procedure. The clergy were involved in actions regarding this conduct.[125] Bribery was one type of such wrongdoing. When it involved jurors, the medieval offense was known as embracery.[126] Although it was mentioned in the 1293 Ordinance of Conspirators, several statutes enacted during the reign of Edward III specifically prohibited it.[127] Perhaps the most significant was a 1364 statute, which authorized a private party to sue on behalf of the king and himself for ten times the amount of the bribe, with the

---

123. KB 27/148, m. 8d (1296), AALT img. no. 765.

124. The prior claimed that rector acted to destroy the prior and his house. The jury found that the rector had unsuccessfully solicited other rectors to join in his conspiracy and awarded the prior £200 in damages, which the court reduced to £100, for the damage sustained by his disgrace and slander and the deterioration of his house. KB 27/164, m. 15d (1301), AALT img. no. 1564. This action is also included in Sayles, ed., *Select Cases in the Court of the King's Bench* III.

125. I identified twenty-five such actions during this period.

126. In his seminal study, Winfield treats it as form of such abuse. Winfield, *The History of Conspiracy*, 161–75.

127. Ibid., 162–63; W. S. Holdsworth, *A History of English Law*, III (London, 1966), 399–400.

fine split equally.[128] As a result, numerous actions based on a writ of *decies tantum* resulted. Clerics, who had acted as jurors, were sued in actions on such writs.[129] In another action, a prior gave food and drink to a defendant in such an action.[130] Livery, another form of prohibited conduct, was often associated with maintenance and retaining.[131] Clerics also gave livery in violation of the statute. For example, in a plea of trespass brought by an abbot, the defendant successfully challenged the array as biased for the abbot since it was arraigned by the sheriff of Lincoln, who wore the abbot's livery.[132]

Clerics, who were acting as lawyers, were charged with wrongdoing, similar to the misconduct of secular lawyers. The chaplain of Wollaston complained that Robert, the rector of the church Twywell and revenue collector of the bishop of Lincoln, was his counsel in all his business sued against the vicar of Wollaston and accused Robert of taking 100s. from his adversary. The chaplain said that Robert "fraudulently annihilated" his business and was "a common ambidexter."[133] Master Robert of Neweham, proctor in the court Christian, also called a "common ambidexter, outdid Robert, taking 10s. from his client's opponent, but also summoned a man to that court to respond to a false plea by a woman, for whom he was the proctor and took 10s. from each of them.[134] In an egregious instance of corruption, a jury presented that a man was sued by a woman in a false plea, which was prompted by her proctor, a vicar, and a notary, before the archbishop

---

128. 38 Edw. III, st. 1, c. 12 (1364), *Statutes of the Realm*, I, 384–85.

129. E.g. CP 40/423, m. 317d (1366), AALT img. no. 1488 (two chaplains); CP 40/461, m. 451d (1376), AALT img. no. 1925 (chaplain). Clerics also brought such actions. E.g. KB 27/423, m. 45d (1366), AALT img. no. 662 (abbot).

130. KB 27/455, m. 133d (1374), AALT img. no. 645. In another action, a cleric was indicted for assaulting a juror and threatening to kill him. The juror claimed that he was attacked for acknowledging the truth in an action where the cleric had been indicted for trespass to a prior and that juror and his fellow jurors no longer dared to appear because of their fear of the cleric. KB 455, m. 4d rex (1374), AALT img. no. 660.

131. E.g., 1 Rich. II, cc. 4, 7, 9 (1377), *Statutes of the Realm*, II, 3; 13 Rich. II, st. 3, 74–75; J. M. W. Bean, *From Lord to Patron* (Pittsburgh, 1989), 143–46, 200–11; J. R. Maddicott, "Law and Lordship: Royal Justices as Retainers in Thirteenth- and Fourteenth-Century England," *Past & Present*, Supplement 4 (1978), 66.

132. KB 27/420, m. 8d (1365), AALT img. no. 279.

133. KB 27/313, m. 4 rex (1338), AALT img. no. 230.

134. Robert paid a fine. KB 27/354, m. 35 rex (1348), AALT img. no. 7204.

of York. After the matter was put in arbitration, those three men managed to be designated as the arbitrators and, on the advice of two of the arch-bishop's clerks, decreed that the man pay the woman £30, of which 100s. were promised to the clerks, 10 marks to the vicar, who was the chief judge, 100s. to the proctor, and 40s. to the notary.[135] Clergy were also presented for misconduct in their judicial capacities. An official of the church of St. Cuthbert, Hoveden and two clerks were presented for acting as counsel for plaintiffs and defendants in pleas before them.[136]

Finally, a number of clergy, like royal and other secular officials, were presented for misusing their office, often for extortion. Several actions ac-cused them of charging excessive fees for performing the functions of their offices. A number of these actions involved the fees for proof of wills and testaments in the probate process.[137] The clergy also used their offices to extort money from other clerics charged with fornication and adultery.[138] In another action, a church official, together with two chaplains and a sum-moner, extorted fines from people, disregarding those fixed by the asses-

135. The defendant in the plea paid £10 of the £30 adjudged against him. The wom-an and the three men presented said that they could not deny the charges and made a fine with the king. KB 27/355, m. 10d, AALT img. no. 8103.

136. They were also charged with holding pleas of debt and covenant not related to testaments nor marriage in violation of the royal statute as well as being presented for numerous other types of wrongdoing. KB 27/355, m. 3d, AALT img. no. 8089.

137. KB 27/355, m. 4 (1349), AALT img. no. 7785 (collector of spiritual dues arch-bishop of York); KB 27/355, m. 11 (1349), AALT img. no. 7796 (clerks & officials archbishop of York); KB 27/355, m. 8d (1349), AALT img. no. 8098 (vicar who was also a dean & his clerk); KB 27/355, m. 8d (1349), AALT img. no. 8098 (dean). In one action, a master was presented for taking 20s. by extortion from a vicar and commonly taking from the rectors and chaplains of a deanery, totaling £100. KB 27/355, m. 8d (1349), AALT img. no. 8098. In all these action, the defendants did not deny the accusations and were permitted to make fines with the king. In another action, it was presented that a rector and collector of dues for the bishop of Lincoln by color of his office took goods worth 19 marks of a former vicar and broke the vicar's testament, which had been shown to him. KB 27/313, m. 4 rex, AALT img. no. 230.

138. In one action, a master and official of the diocese of Richmond not only extort-ed money for proof of testaments, he extorted various vicars and prebends of his deanery and harassed those guilty of fornication or other spiritual offenses and extorted fines from them for their reform. KB 27/356, m. 4d (1349), AALT img. no. 8588. In another action, a master extorted 20s. from a vicar and commonly took from the rectors and chaplains of a deanery and extorted fines from the chaplains and others impleaded for fornication or adultery. KB 27/355, m. 8d (1349), AALT img. no. 8098.

sor of fines and further profited by charging innocent people with usury and other crimes.[139] But, of course, the offices were not always guilty of the charges. For example, the chancellor of the bishop of Lincoln was found not guilty when sued by a man for using his office to summon a man to correct his soul and ignoring jury findings of the man's innocence and unjustly harassing him until he made a fine with the chancellor.[140] Other clergy were also accused of engaging in fraudulent activities.[141]

Finally, some actions alleged that the clergy were involved in various other types of wrongdoing connected with litigation. In one action, the king alleged that a master Robert had schemed to avoid an adverse judgment by suing the clerk, who was presented and installed by the archbishop of York, in a plea outside the realm of England.[142] In another action, a woman and her husband sued a chancery clerk and others for colluding to deprive the woman of her dower and deceive the Common Bench by a

139. They also collaborated to have a commissioner grant a separation between a husband and wife on the condition that the wife make an appeal before the official, which caused them to profit. The defendants said that they could not deny the charges and were permitted to make a fine with the king. KB 27/355, m. 3d (1349), AALT img. no. 8089. The underbailiff and custodian of the archbishop of York's prison was charged with using his office large fines for various false and fictitious causes. KB 27/354, m. 42 rex (1348), AALT img. no. 7217.

140. The man alleged that the chancellor asserted that he had been accused of raping another man's wife which the man denied and two juries agreed. Nevertheless, he alleged that the chancellor ignored those findings and refused to deliver the man until he made a fine of 6s. 8d. The jury found the chancellor not guilty. KB 27/356, m. 40d ((1349), AALT img. no. 8653.

141. The crown sued a vicar and clerk asserting that prior to being charged with felonious killing of a man, the felon gave his lands to a vicar and clerk so he could avoid their forfeiture for felony and that he continued to take the profits after the allegedly fraudulent transfer. The defendants alleged that they made the transfer openly and in good faith. KB 27/455, m. 16d rex (1374), AALT img. no. 687.

142. Roger of Blakeston had recovered the advowson to the prebendary of Thorp in the church of the Blessed Peter of Hoveden against the prior of Durham. Master Robert sued the clerk presented regarding his receipt of the presentation, claiming it impugned his right. After Robert was outlawed because of his nonappearance, a man appeared on his behalf and said Robert was out of the country in the service of the king. As result, it was found that he was unaware of the process against him and received a pardon both of his outlawry and trespass. KB 27/357, m. 1 rex (1349), AALT img. no.8848. Roger sued Robert for the latter's trespass since the king's pardon did not negate that right. KB 27/357, m. 31d (1349), AALT img. no. 8994.

fraudulent writ of *dedimus potestatem* appointing attorneys for the defendant in the dower action.[143]

LITIGATION PATTERNS

This section will explore the patterns of litigation discussed above as well as identifying the patterns in the later period. Two conclusions follow from the examination of these actions regarding the clergy and abuse of legal procedure. First, the involvement of the clergy in such actions was significant. But that, I think, should not be surprising, given that they were generally involved in a substantial amount of Common law litigation, as indicated earlier in this essay. More specifically, the clergy were involved as plaintiffs, defendants, victims, or beneficiaries of conspiracy, champerty, or maintenance in 20% of the actions and 18% of the actions involving other legally related wrongdoing.[144] In the later period, 1377–1485, the clergy were also involved in actions involving abuse of legal procedure. The litigation during that period consisted primarily of private and crown trespassory maintenance actions.[145] Clergy were involved on one or both sides in 23% of those actions. They accounted for 15% of all the plaintiffs and 8% of the all defendants.[146]

143. Master Richard, the chancery clerk, colluded with two men, scheming to trick the king's court and fraudulently oppress the dower plaintiffs by impleading the writ in the Chancery before the clerk to appoint the two men as attorneys for the dower defendant. All of this was unknown by the defendant who had been living outside of England for three years or more. Presumably their collusion would invalidate any action taken by the attorneys in the Common Bench dower action. Although the dower defendant would be the beneficiary of this and may have been the mastermind of this scheme, he was not sued in the action, which is only a mesne process entry. CP 40/423, m. 33 (1366), AALT img. no. 66.

144. I have collected about 160 conspiracy, champerty, and maintenance actions during this period. I am grateful to Professor Paul Brand for providing references to many of these actions during the reigns of Edward I and Edward II. I have collected 147 actions involving other legally related wrongdoing during this period.

145. During this period, I have identified 692 maintenance and champerty actions. Of this total, private maintenance actions consisted of 57% of the actions, crown trespassory actions 35%, champerty actions 5%, criminal maintenance actions 2.5%, private and private conspiracy actions .4%.

146. It is difficult to compare these statistics with those in early period. During the later period, unlike the earlier one, it is possible to identify the status or occupations of the

Clergy were also active participants in petitioning the king and his counsel to complain about maintenance and abuse of power and lordship and as the targets of those complaints.[147] Clergy were named in 36% of such petitions in the early period, of whom 43% were petitioners and 57% targets. Thus, in all these contexts, the involvement of the clergy was significant.[148]

Finally, it is interesting to examine the composition of the clergy involved in these different contexts. With reference to the early period, in the actions relating to conspiracy, champerty, and maintenance, forty-six individual clerics were either parties to the actions or otherwise connected to them. Although there were nine types of clergy were identified, parsons were the most common (11), followed by clerks (8), chaplains (6), and masters (5). Scholars have often divided up clergy into two types. Thirty-nine different clerics, representing thirteen different types, were involved in the actions regarding other legally related wrongdoing. Clerks (9), masters (8), and chaplains (7) were the most common. In the later period, 183 clerics were identified as parties to the maintenance and champerty actions.[149] Although fourteen different types were involved, clerks (92) and chaplains

---

defendants as result of the 1413 Statute of Additions, which required that information. 1 Hen. V, c. 5 (1413), *Statutes of the Realm*, II, 171.

147. I have collected 165 of such petitions to the king and his council during the early period. The National Archives Public Record Office has created a series that contains these petitions denominated "Special Collections: Ancient Petitions," SC 8. Denton asserted that such petitioning by clergy was an area of their activity that had been disregarded. Denton, "The Clergy and Parliament in the Thirteenth and Fourteenth Centuries," 97–98.

148. Although the involvement in the three contexts regarding legal actions is relatively consistent, one needs to be cautious in drawing any inferences from that fact. Different methods of collection were used in gathering these actions. With respect to the conspiracy, champerty, and maintenance actions in the early period, systematic chronological sampling was used for those during the reign of Edward III, but not those for the reigns of Edward I. The same sampling approach produced of actions of other legally related wrongdoing for the reign of Edward III, but there was no attempt to collect such actions for the reigns of Edward I and II. Systematically chronological sampling was used for the later period, 1377–1485, but a much larger volume of records was examined and the search was confined to actions relating to maintenance and champerty. The extent of involvement was much higher with regard to clerical involvement in petitioning. That difference might be explained by the nature of the documents, petitions as compared with legal actions, and by the fact that all of the petitions were searchable by words.

149. Forty-nine were plaintiffs and 134 were defendants.

Table 1. Clerical Involvement in Abuse of Legal Procedure

Type of Clergy	Plaintiff or Victim	Defendant or Beneficiary	Total	Actions
EARLY PERIOD				
Conspiracy, Champerty & Maintenance				
Regular Clergy	3	10	13 (28%)	
Secular Clergy	3	30	33 (72%)	
	6 (13%)	40 (87%)	46	32/160 (20%)
Other Legally Related Wrongdoing				
Regular Clergy	3	2	5 (13%)	
Secular Clergy	4	30	34 (87%)	
	7 (18%)	32 (82%)	39	26/147 (18%)
Petitions				
Regular Clergy	16	18	34 (45%)	
Secular Clergy	17	25	42 (55%)	
	33 (43%)	43 (57%)	76	60/165 (36%)
LATER PERIOD				
Maintenance & Champerty				
Regular Clergy	13	13	26 (14%)	
Secular Clergy	36	121	157 (86%)	
	49 (27%)	134 (73%)	183	160/692 (23%)

(43) constituted the great majority (74%). During the early period, seventy-six individual clerics representing fifteen types of clerics, were either petitioners to the the king and his council (33) or targets of those petitions (43). The most common were abbots (19), clerks (14), bishops (12), and priors (9).[150]

150. Among the petitioners were an abbess and a prioress.

Another way to view the clergy involved in the abuse of legal procedure is whether they were regular clergy such as abbots, priors, monks or secular clergy such as parsons, chaplains, clerks, rectors, and vicars.[151] Unlike the regular clergy who lived in monasteries or other religious houses, the secular clergy were more proximate to the lives and activities of their parishioners and frequently lived among them. Thus, one would expect that the latter would be more connected with litigation involving the abuse of legal procedure. In the litigation in both periods, that expectation is largely well founded. In the early period, secular clergy constituted 72% of those involved and regular clergy 18%. In the actions during that period involving other legally related wrongdoing, secular clergy accounted for 87% of the involved clerics and regular clergy 13%. In the later period, secular clergy constituted 86% and regular clergy 14%. Despite the predominance of secular clergy, the involvement of regular clergy was much lower, but perhaps not insignificant. The picture is quite different with respect to petitioning. In that context, secular clergy made up 55% of the petitioners or targets and regular clergy 45%. The differing nature of petitions and their function may explain this difference.

The second conclusion is that the nature and pattern of all these types of actions regarding the clergy were, by and large, quite similar to those involving secular litigants. As legal remedies for abuse of legal procedure at the end of the thirteenth century, the conspiracy actions in the case of both types of litigants, predominated, with regard to both presentments and private actions. Moreover, the conspiracy actions cover a wide variety of types of wrongdoing, but the most common are conspiring to have a person charged with a criminal offense or victimized by a false plea. In both instances, champerty actions involve land and are not nearly as common as conspiracy actions. Moreover, all or almost all of such actions are brought by private litigants and there is little or no evidence of crown enforcement of the statutes prohibiting champerty. Further, in both situations, main-

---

151. With some clergy, complete accuracy in categorization is not possible. This is especially true with masters and maybe also with clerks. Moreover, in a particular instance, any individual cleric could be connected with either type of clergy. In classifying masters and clerks, I have relied, to the extent possible, on the information and context of the record in the individual action. As a result of that, most of the masters and clerks were classified as secular clergy, which might not be completely accurate.

tenance actions limited to unlawful support or assistance of a litigant are infrequent. Private maintenance actions are rare, and most actions alleging maintenance are combined with conspiracy or other accusations.

The same conclusion holds true for the actions involving other legal related wrongdoing. Both secular and religious officials were sued for extortion and the wrongful use of their offices. Religious lawyers like secular ones were sued for ambidexterity and other unethical conduct in their representational capacities. Clergy who served on secular juries were charged like other jurors with taking bribes. Both clergy and nonreligious individuals were involved in actions as perpetrators or victims of various types of wrongdoing in litigation. Also abuse of legal procedures related to religiously related issues like advowsons and mortmain were regularly litigated in the royal courts by clerical litigants just as there were by secular litigants. Moreover, the clergy were involved in litigation in the secular courts involving wrongdoing in the courts Christian and wrongdoing by ecclesiastical lawyers no differently than the actions in the royal courts by secular litigants to police and punish similar wrongful lawyers and conduct related to litigation in those courts.

CONCLUSION

In sum, much of the litigation regarding the clergy and the abuse of legal procedure reflected significant clerical involvement, and the litigation was quite similar to that in which secular litigants were participants.

The Private Life of Archbishop Johannes Gerechini: Simulated Marriage and Clerical Concubinage in Early Fifteenth-Century Sweden[1]

Mia Korpiola

INTRODUCTION

The Danish-born Archbishop Johannes Gerechini [Jens Gerekesson Lodehat] of Uppsala (ca. 1378–1433) apparently had a knack for making enemies. During his archiepiscopate 1408–21, he managed to anger not only his cathedral chapter and the Dominicans of Stockholm but also his former patron, King Erik of Pomerania (r. 1397–1439), who ruled over all three Scandinavian kingdoms.[2] At this point, the secrets of his private life started to unravel and become public as his opponents collected evidence of his misdeeds and his purported breaches of canon law.

In 1419, King Erik called a meeting in Copenhagen, which ended in Gerechini's incarceration, but he managed to escape and reach the pope. In 1420, Archbishop Johannes of Riga was appointed by the pope to investigate the accusations and adjudicate in the case. After a struggle of some

---

1.   An early version of this article was presented at the Carlsberg conference "Law and Private Life in the Middle Ages" in Copenhagen on 30 April 2009. I would like to thank the participants for their feedback and discussion.

2.   The three crowns of Denmark, Norway, and Sweden were united under one Danish ruler during the period of the so-called Union of Kalmar. This personal union lasted from 1397 to 1523 with several interruptions and internal upheavals.

years, Gerechini first resigned his see in 1421 for annual financial compensation at least until he received another preferment. However, he was deposed by Pope Martin V (r. 1417–31) in 1422. After this, he still accompanied King Erik on trips abroad and was sent on diplomatic missions before
he was nominated as Bishop of Skálholt in Iceland in 1426. His tumultuous
life ended in 1433, when he is said to have been lynched by being drowned
in a sack in a river near his cathedral in connection with power struggles in
Iceland in which England was involved.[3]

We know about Gerechini's private-turned-public-life first and foremost through a single document, written by a public notary at the behest of
the Uppsala chapter in July 1419. The deposition of the archbishop's second
cousin, Jeppe Niklisson, and his wife, Margareta Jakobsdotter Piil, reveals
how Gerechini wished to have her as his concubine.[4] First, the Archbishop
broke Margareta's engagement or marriage to another man. He then arranged an elaborate simulated wedding between Margareta and Jeppe to
avert suspicion before Margareta came to live in the archbishop's household
as his kinsman's wife. Gerechini and Margareta had two children together, while Jeppe and Margareta, fearing incest, never consummated their
marriage.

This article will analyze the facts of the case of Archbishop Johannes
Gerechini from two perspectives: the validity of the simulated marriage
against the general background of the canon law concerning matrimony
and clerical concubinage, especially in the Swedish context. But before em-
barking on either of these two main objectives, I will put the case in its political context in the power struggle between archbishop, king, and chapter
in early fifteenth-century Sweden as these special circumstances led to the
preservation of the case to the present. The result was the "biggest history
of scandal in the annals of the archdiocese of Uppsala."[5]

---

3.   Claes Gejrot, ed., *Vadstenadiariet: Latinsk text med översättning* (Stockholm,
1996), 166–67; Beata Losman, "Johannes Gerechini," in *Svenskt Biografiskt Lexikon* [here-
after *SBL*] 20 (Stockholm, 1973–1975), 215–16; cf. Thelma Jexlev, "Gerechini, Johannes," in
Dansk biografisk lexikon, 3rd ed., 5 (Copenhagen, 1980), 153.

4.   Carl Silfverstolpe, ed., *Svenskt diplomatarium* [*SD*] III (Stockholm, 1885–
1920), 586–88.

5.   Yngve Brilioth, *Svenska kyrkans historia 2: Den senare medeltiden 1274–1521*
(Stockholm, 1941), 308.

ARCHBISHOP JOHANNES GERECHINI:
THE INFAMOUS FIGUREHEAD OF THE SEE OF UPPSALA

Jens Gerekesson had had a promising start to his ecclesiastical career. A scion of the noble Danish house of Lodehat and nephew of Petrus Johannis, bishop of Roskilde, he had studied at the University of Paris in 1401 and law at Prague in 1404. A canon of Roskilde, he had worked as Chancellor to King Erik of Pomerania, whose chancery proved to be a springboard to bishoprics both for himself and Magnus Tavast (ep. 1412–1450), future bishop of Turku.[6] Gerekesson had not been the choice of the Uppsala chapter, which had elected its *praepositus* Andreas Johannis as the new archbishop on 24 March 1408. However, this did not deter the king from nominating Jens as his candidate for the archiepiscopal see of Uppsala. In the spring of 1408, delegations from both candidates appeared in Rome to seek the papal confirmation of Gregory XII (r. 1406–1415), which the King's candidate received. The schism meant that the position of Gerechini as the new archbishop was only considered secure in 1410 after the confirmation of (anti-)Pope John XXIII (1410–15).[7]

Indeed, the fact that he was Danish, and had been nominated for political reasons by the king against the will of the chapter must have clouded Gerechini's start as archbishop of Uppsala. Moreover, his limited pastoral and capitular experience also raised concerns at the start of his archiepiscopal career—as, ironically enough, did his knowledge of canon law.[8] The disputes regarding his predecessor's estate and will were ongoing, seemingly only definitely settled in 1423.[9] It seems that one of the bones of contention between King Erik and his new archbishop came to be the independence of the Church from the crown. When Johannes Gerechini called for a provincial council in 1412, he justified this with the many adverse developments in the position of the Church. The ecclesiastical liberties were

---

6.   Kr. Erslev, "Gerechini, Johannes," in: *Dansk biografisk lexikon* 5 (Copenhagen, 1891), 596; Jexlev, "Gerechini, Johannes," 153; Losman, "Johannes Gerechini," 215; Ari-Pekka Palola, *Maunu Tavast ja Olavi Maununpoika—Turun piispat 1412–1460* (Helsinki, 1997), 141–44.

7.   Beata Losman, *Norden och reformkonsilierna 1408–1449* (Gothenburg, 1970), 50–52.

8.   Brilioth, *Svenska kyrkans historia* 2, 307–08.

9.   Losman, *Norden*, 53–54, 89 n. 10.

being restricted, faith had become lukewarm, and ecclesiastical discipline
was no longer respected. Moreover, the list of taxes demanded from the
Church and its tenants in blatant contravention of its privileges was long.
Indeed, the provincial statute issued at the council referred to the familiar problem that the laity handed down sentences in questions relating to
ecclesiastical property. The clergy complained that it had long been silent
because of the lack of justice and in default of royal assizes, but this did not
mean that they accepted such sentences. No layman had jurisdiction over
ecclesiastical property. All sentences given by laymen to the detriment of
the church's property were declared null and void in accordance with canon
law.[10] There is a certain irony that the 1412 statutes also heralded a stricter
policy against lay concubinage and regulated the criteria for people wishing
to marry *in facie ecclesiae*.[11]

Gerechini also presided over the council of Arboga, again issuing
provincial statutes, in 1417.[12] However, only later did King Erik withdraw
his support from the archbishop in connection with Danish disputes between Erik and the bishop of Roskilde in which Gerechini sided with the
bishop.[13] This led to his downfall.

One of the major entanglements during Gerechini's episcopacy was
related to his breach of the peace of a Dominican convent in 1417 when he
led a posse of armed men into its refectory. There they caught a Stockholm
vicar, Johannes Junge, wounding him and dragging him out of the convent.
Only miraculously did Junge, who had obviously angered the archbishop
by allegedly engineering an appeal against the archbishop at the papal curia, escape among the crowd in the marketplace.[14] It has been assumed that
this was connected to the famous case of Helleka Horn, a wealthy Stockholm widow, coveted as a wife by two Stockholm burghers and involved
in a lengthy lawsuit in the ecclesiastical courts. The sentence of the archbishop favoring the widow and upholding the validity of her second marriage was finally reversed to favor the appellant, the first husband Lubert

---

10.   Carl Silfverstolpe, ed., *SD* II (Stockholm, 1879–1887), 541–44, esp. 544; Losman, *Norden*, 57–59.

11.   Ibid., 542.

12.   Silfverstolpe, ed., *SD* III, 273–74; Losman, *Norden*, 68–70.

13.   Jexlev, "Gerechini, Johannes," 153.

14.   Losman, *Norden*, 67.

Kortenhorst. This case has been researched in detail. What seems obvious is that Gerechini tried to suppress appeals to Rome against his sentence.[15]

Because the long rivalry between the pro- and anti-royal parties in Sweden resulted in the victory of the latter "nationalistic" party in 1523, Gerechini remained the foreign villain, unjustly nominated by the Danish king to the Swedish archdiocese and later deposed because of his "wicked life" (*onda leffuerne*).[16] This account was later repeated in late nineteenth- and twentieth-century national romantic Swedish historiography. G. Djurklou described him in the most vivid terms with little support in contemporary or even near-contemporary sources:

> His private life, besides, was far from suited to a man of the cloth. In his castles and manors, he lived almost like a Turkish pasha in his harem, constantly banqueting with mostly female but noble guests, and devoted himself to the wildest lecheries. Tyrannical, bold and ruthless beyond all limits, he inspired such fear that neither the ecclesiastical nor the secular authorities, not even the members of his own chapter, who were constant eyewitnesses hereto, dared to put an end to his wild rampage....[17]

According to such sternly moralist and national romantic researchers, the rioting of this reckless and unrestrained sexual predator was only stopped by the little man, a Swedish hero. "The truth of the old proverb, a small tussock often upsets a great loaded cart, was fully confirmed here."[18] Or as Lizzie Carlsson put it, "so, finally the simple Stockholm burgher Ludbert emerged victorious after years of unrelenting and goal-ori-

---

15.   Silfverstolpe, ed., *SD* III, 472–79; Lizzie Carlsson, *"Jag giver dig min dotter:"* *Trolovning och äktenskap i den svenska kvinnans äldre historia*, II (Lund, 1972), 111–18; Mia Korpiola, "The Two Husbands of Helleka Horn: Interpreting the Canon Law of Marriage in Late Medieval Sweden," in *"Panta rei": Studi dedicati a Manlio Bellomo* 3, ed. Orazio Condorelli (Rome, 2004), 153–81; Losman, *Norden*, 73–78. See also Losman, *Norden*, 67.

16.   Olavus Petri, "En Swensk cröneka," in *Samlade skrifter* IV (Uppsala, 1917), 147.

17.   G. Djurklou, "Jöns Gerekesson ärkebiskop i Uppsala 1408–1421: Kulturbild från konung Eriks af Pommern dagar," *Historisk tidskrift* 14 (1894), 194.

18.   Djurklou, "Jöns Gerekesson," 195.

ented struggle against the once mighty and ruthless royal favourite Jöns Gerekesson...."[19]

Gerechini undoubtedly transgressed against canon law and committed crimes and mortal sins. But although his reputation as an archbishop has traditionally been extremely bad, some researchers have seen some mitigating circumstances in his archiepiscopate. Beata Losman observed that he was financially exploited by King Erik of Pomerania.[20] Even Gabriel Djurklou, who condemned his character and life so eloquently, credited him with zeal in protecting the ecclesiastical liberties and issuing synodal statutes.[21] In fact, King Erik of Pomerania probably considered Gerechini too independent-minded an archbishop, preferring a more malleable candidate instead of someone who defended the Church's liberties against secular powers.[22]

AN ARCHIEPISCOPAL *MÉNAGE À TROIS*: SIMULATED MARRIAGE AND SUPERVENIENT AFFINITY

As mentioned above, it was first and foremost the political intrigues intended to oust Archbishop Gerechini that made his private life so public. But even before this, the Archbishop's domestic arrangements must have been causing suspicions among some. Gerechini, his second cousin Jeppe Niklisson and Margareta Jakobsdotter Piil had formed a curious *ménage à trois*. The notarial instrument tells us that Margareta had originally been married to Sigurd the Shoemaker in Stockholm, which, with its over 4,500 inhabitants, was by far the most populous town in the diocese of Uppsala and the capital of the kingdom of Sweden.[23] Piil's first marriage followed the typical Swedish marriage process through a betrothal (*desponsata legittime fuerat*) followed by cohabitation when Sigurd moved in with Margareta to live in her house (*qui in domum ipsius mulieris animo cohabitandi ingressus fuerat*).[24] No solemnization *in facie ecclesiae* was mentioned even if

19.   Carlsson, *"Jag giver dig min dotter,"*118.

20.   Losman, *Norden*, 85.

21.   Djurklou, "Jöns Gerekesson," 192–93.

22.   Losman, *Norden*, 66, 87, 110; Jexlev, "Gerechini, Johannes," 154.

23.   Marko Lamberg, *Dannemännen i stadens råd: Rådmanskretsen i nordiska köpstäder under senmedeltiden* (Stockholm, 2001), 21.

24.   Silfverstolpe, ed., *SD* III, 586–88.

the Church had been actively campaigning for more than a century for the banns to be read and the parish priest perform the actual marriage rite.[25]

For some reason not mentioned in the document, the validity of the marriage of Margareta and Sigurd had been called into question and investigated by the archbishop. An annulment had followed. We do not learn why the marriage was annulled or on whose initiative. However, the document mentions that it was done perfunctorily (*perfunctorie separata*).[26] The document implies that the archbishop abused his position as judge so that he could have his way with Margareta, who was not the only female party in a matrimonial cause with whom Gerechini was thought to have had inappropriate dealings. In the case of the bigamy of the widow Helleka Horn, the Archbishop was alleged to have had improper dealings with her when examining and adjudicating the case, keeping her by his side at his ship and at his archiepiscopal manor of Arnö for a week before his initial judgment in her favor.[27]

As for Margareta, the intentions of the archbishop were no mere allusion as it was said outright that Gerechini had taken a fancy to her. According to the document, he then concocted a cunning and sophisticated plan to have her introduced into his household under the pretext of marriage. His kinsman Jeppe Niklisson was to contract with her, but in name only. When they would thereby have a socially acceptable excuse to introduce Margareta to the archiepiscopal household, Gerechini could then take her as his concubine. Jeppe would also be reckoned the father of all Margareta's children, possibly sired in the future by the Archbishop. However, Jeppe was under instructions not to touch Margareta. The notion was turned into a plan of action, demonstrating considerable knowledge of canon law, which was realized accordingly.[28] The couple got engaged (*per tradicionem annuli desponsauit*) after which the marriage was solemnized by the archbishop's trusted secretary. They had also acted as if they had consummated

25. Mia Korpiola, *Between Betrothal and Bedding: Marriage Formation in Sweden, 1200–1600* (Leiden, 2009), esp. 204–29.

26. Silfverstolpe, ed., *SD* III, 586–88.

27. Silfverstolpe, ed., *SD* III, 474: "dictus dominus archiepiscopus ad octo dies… recepit dictam Hillecham ad propriam nauem suam et deducit eam ad curiam suam archiepiscopalem Arnøø et de Arnøø vsque ad ciuitatem Vpsalensem…." See also Brilioth, *Svenska kyrkans historia* 2, 331.

28. Silfverstolpe, ed., *SD* III, 586–88.

the marriage.[29] However, whether or not they had actually contracted marriage or not depended mainly on whether they consented freely to actually marrying each other and whether they had expressed their consent.

As is well known, the development of canonical marriage law in the second half of the twelfth and early thirteenth centuries put the free and expressed marital consent of the parties firmly at the heart of the canon law of marriage. No rituals, solemnities or consummation were necessary for a valid marriage if two persons free to contract with each other voluntarily expressed their present-tense consent to marry each other.[30] There were no impediments such as consanguinity or affinity between Jeppe, who came from the diocese of Roskilde in Denmark, and Margareta from the diocese of Uppsala, as she had not had sexual relations with the archbishop prior to her marriage.

It was claimed that Gerechini had told Jeppe to simulate the exchange of consent and wedding, but by no means really consent or have sexual relations with Margareta.[31] This seems to have gone according to plan. When the officiating cleric asked Jeppe whether he wished to marry Margareta, he had not answered in the affirmative as he had no wish to marry her. Thus, he had mumbled "mum mum." Margareta, in her turn, had had matrimonial intentions, but had remained silent when asked for her consent.[32]

How is one to interpret this? The canon law of marriage insisted on the mutual consent of the parties, the expressed intention to get married. This inward will had to be expressed by words or outward signs. As Peter Lombard (ca. 1096–1164) had put it, if a person consented mentally to the marriage, but had failed to express it by words or some other unequivo-

---

29. Silfverstolpe, ed., *SD* III, 586–88.

30. See, e.g., the concise description in R. H. Helmholz, *Marriage Litigation in Medieval England* (Cambridge, 1974), 26–28.

31. Silfverstolpe, ed., *SD* III, 586–87: "volo quod te simules eam desponsare et ducere apparenter in vxorem, sed nullo modo in matrimonium consencies nec vmquam ei commisceberis...."

32. Silfverstolpe, ed., *SD* III, 587: "si iuxta patrie morem a sacerdote benedicente interrogaretur an ipsam Margaretam habere vellet vxorem, quod ad hanc interrogacionem nullatenus affirmatiue responderet, sed quod diceret leuiter musitando: mum mum, et quod nullo modo in matrimonio consentiret...tempore suscepte benediccionis ad interrogacionem sacerdotis benedicentis tacuit, habuit tamen intencionem pro matrimonio."

cal signs, this consent alone did not make a marriage.[33] As the *Liber Extra* expressed it, mere consent sufficed for a legitimately contracted marriage, but words or equivalent gestures were required for proving it. Thus, the deaf and the mute could also validly contract matrimony through signs and gestures, even without spoken words.[34] Contrariwise, if lack of consent was not expressed by words or by other signs and no force had been employed, there was no way out of the marriage.

On the other hand, the contrary scenario was also possible as people could utter the words of consent without having the will or intention to marry. As Peter Lombard had written, words of consent were spoken without the heart wanting it (*verbis explicant quod tamen corde non volunt*). Merely using the proper set of words without the accompanying will or a mental reservation did not invalidate a marriage unless force or fraud (*si non sit coactio ibi vel dolus*) had been used.[35] One could make a mental reservation about marriage, for example, when only wanting to bed a woman without actually wanting to wed her or remain with her. In such a case the marriage would be considered valid.[36]

Thomas of Chobham (ca. 1160–1233~1236) discussed mental reservations under the rubric *De ficte contrahentibus* in his influential *Summa Confessorum*. Thomas started by restating the canonical position that verbal consent alone did not suffice, and had to be accompanied by consent of the mind (*consensus in matrimonio debet esse non solum verborum sed etiam animorum*). However, mental reservations prevented the union from being a valid marriage in the eyes of God, while the Church would consider the expressed words of marriage as binding. How was this apparent dilemma to be resolved? God who knew everything could also adjudicate in hidden

---

33. *Magistri Petri Lombardi Sententiae in IV libris distinctae*, II (Grottaferrata: Collegium S. Bonaventurae Ad Claras Aquas, 1981, dist. xxvii, 3: "Item si consentiant mente, et non exprimant verbis vel aliis certis signis; nec talis consensus efficit matrimonium."

34. X 4.1.23; X 4.1.25: "Solo consensu legitimo contrahitur matrimonium, sed verba requiruntur quoad probationem...vel alia signa aequipollentia."

35. *Magistri Petri Lombardi Sententiae*, dist. xxvii, 3.

36. Rudolf Weigand, "Liebe und Ehe bei den Dekretisten des 12. Jahrhunderts," in *Love and Marriage in the Twelfth Century*, ed. Willy van Hoecke and Andries Welkenhuysen (Leuven, 1981), 46.

and secret cases, but man could only judge manifest and expressed things.[37] Similarly, if one party used unclear expressions or a false identity to deceive the other party and without the genuine will to get married, the union was to be regarded a marriage in the ecclesiastical court if subsequent consummation had taken place. Nevertheless, the matter would be deemed differently in the penitential forum.[38] According to the canon law maxim, the Church could not judge secret matters (*de occultis ecclesia non iudicat*).[39] In addition, for the exchange of consent to form a valid marriage, both parties had to want the marriage and its consequences.

Obviously, the union of Margareta and Jeppe was considered not to have been valid from the start because of a lack of expressed consent. Yet, despite the originally simulated character of the union, if the couple had afterwards consented to it or had intercourse with each other voluntarily, this would have ratified the marriage and validated it.[40] However, here both parties denied that they had ever consummated their union after solemnization. Even this had been simulated, as Jeppe and Margareta wanted to create the believable facade of a marriage while knowing that they risked incest because of Margareta's budding relationship with Gerechini, Jeppe's kinsman in the third degree of consanguinity. As they wished to avoid incest, they never had sex (*nunquam se carnaliter adinuicem cognouerunt timore incestus committendi*). Thus, they spent the two first nights of the marriage in the same bed only for appearance's sake and while their cronies were there (*solum ad satisfaciendum apparencie hominum…post recessum sodalitium suorum surgens ab ea*), and never *nudus cum nuda* as ecclesiastical court records sometimes put it. Instead, Jeppe said that he was half-dressed, wearing boots when sharing the same bed for a short while (*vir…cum caligis et semiuestitus per breuem morulam*). After this, Jeppe slept far away from her, alone in another house (*in alia domo fuit solitus pernoctare*), while Margareta pursued her liaison, resulting in the birth of two children by her archiepiscopal lover.[41]

---

37.   Thomas of Chobham, *Summa confessorum*, ed. F. Broomfield (Louvain, 1968), Q. VIIa, cap. v.

38.   X 4.1.26.

39.   X 5.3.33: "si excessus eorum esset ecclesiae manifestus, quae non iudicat in occultis, poena essent canonica feriendi."

40.   Cf. X 4.1.21.

41.   Silfverstolpe, ed., *SD* III, 587.

This document was not part of the court protocol of an annulment process as it describes the couple as already separated. The impediment of affinity (*affinitas per illicitum coitum*) between Margareta and Jeppe seems to have been the justification of the decision to dissolve the marriage. This impediment was only created between them after their simulated and invalid marriage. However, the notarial instrument emphasizes that Jeppe and Margareta were not in collusion to rid themselves of each other. Jeppe was described as sighing and crying (*cum suspiriis et lacrimis*) and he had also taken an oath to speak the truth and avoid malice or collusion (*prestitis itaque de veritate dicenda et malicia ac collusione vitandis a partibus iuramentis*). However, the document emphasized the truth of Jeppe's story by insisting that he related voluntarily and freely, but out of a bad conscience (*sponte, clare ac libere et ex certa sciencia et dolorosa consciencia*), the facts that he knew. The same applied to Margareta, but she also confessed with "female shame" (*licet cum muliebri verecundia*). It also stressed that the annulment of the marriage by the *officialis* of Uppsala had been done *ex officio* (*dominum officialem instabat…propter certas et inauditas causas per eundem exprimendas per ecclesisie iudicium separaret*). Moreover, both Jeppe and Margareta gave assurances that, notwithstanding the affinity between them, they would very willingly remain married to each other (*libentissime in coniugio remanerent*).[42] Thus, Gerechini's plan seems to have been successful, since the marriage seemed outwardly valid, incest was avoided, and the presumption of paternity (*pater est quem nuptiae demonstrant*) meant that the children were taken to be the husband's.

CLERICAL INCONTINENCE IN MEDIEVAL SWEDEN

Clerical celibacy had been enforced throughout Catholic Europe by implementing the demands of the Gregorian Reform, especially since the twelfth century. The Second Lateran Council of 1139 addressed the question of clerical marriage, prohibiting it. Referring to the impurity of these "temples of God, vessels of the Lord and sanctuaries of the Holy Ghost" caused by sex, its canons 6–8 forbade all those in higher orders, monks, nuns and professed lay brothers from marrying or keeping spouses or con-

---

42. Silfverstolpe, ed., *SD* III, 586.

cubines. Disregarding the canon entailed penance, and loss of benefice and position followed. Four decades later, the Third Lateran Council targeted clerics who "in open concubinage kept their mistresses in their houses" in particular. The clerics were either to discard their lovers and lead a celibate life or be stripped of their ecclesiastical office and benefice. In 1215, the Fourth Lateran Council still deemed it necessary to order clerics to live continent lives. Recalcitrants were to be punished with loss of benefice and permanent defrocking in the worst cases, and the penalties were extended to prelates who failed to put an end to such iniquities.[43]

In Scandinavia, clerical marriage was widespread. Unlike Denmark, where there were revolts for and against clerical celibacy in the twelfth century, no such dramatic events seem to have taken place in medieval Sweden[44]—probably because clerical celibacy was not yet strictly prohibited. Moreover, the establishment of Christianization in Sweden was not completed until about 1200. In 1248, the papal legate, William of Sabina, arrived in Sweden to supervise the arranging of the Church in Sweden in accordance with the requirements of canon law. In connection with his visit, a provincial council was organized under his supervision at Skänninge in 1248, interpreted as a sign that Sweden had become a part of Catholic Europe.[45]

In the spirit of the Gregorian Reform, William of Sabina complained of the abominable state of the Swedish church. He blamed this largely on the fact that the sons of deceased priests, or failing them, other close male relatives, inherited all the chattels of the church of which they had been in possession. Consequently, the council of Skänninge forbade priests thereafter from acknowledging their future natural sons born of their

43. E.g., Norman P. Tanner, ed., *Decrees of the Ecumenical Councils 1* (London, 1990), 198, 217–18, 242; James A. Brundage, *Law, Sex, and Christian Society in Medieval Europe* (Chicago, 1987), esp. 214–23, 251–53, 314–19, 342–43; Hendrik Callewier, "Canon Law and Celibacy: The Sexual Urges of the Secular Clergy in Fifteenth-Century Bruges," in *Law and Private Life in the Middle Ages: Proceedings of the Sixth Carlsberg Academy Conference on Medieval Legal History 2009*, ed. Per Andersen, Mia Münster-Swendsen and Helle Vogt (Copenhagen, 2011), 181–90.

44. Birgit Sawyer and Peter Sawyer, *Medieval Scandinavia: From Conversion to Reformation, circa 800–1500* (Minneapolis, 1993), 172–73.

45. Anne-Sofie Gräslund, "Religionsskiftet i Norden," in: *Kyrka, samhälle, stat. Från kristnande till etablerad kyrka*, ed. Göran Dahlbäck (Helsinki, 1997), 11–13.

present wives or concubines within a year, or of any future concubines. If the priest-fathers died intestate, the sons were deprived of any property their father or the church owned on threat of excommunication. No such penalty was imposed on existing sons or children born during the year of respite. Intestate succession of priests was a mortal sin, robbery or theft (*rapinam vel furtum*), according to the statute, and only by restitution could they make their peace with God. Priests could licitly dispose of their inherited or personally donated property, or goods they had acquired though the work of their hands or learning, through a will only. Other property belonged to the Church. More severe punishment of priestly concubines was also on the council's agenda. Priests were forbidden to marry or to keep concubines publicly or in residence. All new concubines were to incur major excommunication. Existing wives and concubines had one year to renounce their sin and separate, after which time the obstinate were banned. Priests continuing to associate and live with such excommunicated women were also anathema. Only priests and concubines past their fifties were exempted if they got an episcopal dispensation. This could only be received if thought appropriate provided they vowed chastity to the bishop, deposited a considerable financial bond for a possible relapse and never again slept in the same house or under the same roof.[46] In fact, papal legates also arranged councils in Spain in the 1220s, intending to abolish and penalize clerical concubinage. These conciliar statutes were supplemented by local synodal statutes in the 1240s.[47]

This drastic attempt to purge the clergy of their mistresses and children was, however, bound to fail because the country would have suffered from an acute shortage of priests. The decision was revoked only ten years later by Alexander IV (r. 1254–61) in answer to Archbishop Laurentius of Uppsala's supplication. The Pope admitted that the punishments of the

46. Johan Gustaf Liljegren, ed., *Diplomatarium Suecanum* [hereafter DS] I (Stockholm, 1829), 330–31; Bertil Nilsson, "A Fight against an Intractable Reality: The Efforts at Implementing Celibacy among the Swedish Clergy during the Middle Ages," in *Sacri canones servandi sunt: Ius canonicum et status ecclesiae saeculis XIII–XV*, ed. Pavel Krafl (Prague, 2008), 602–04; Åke Ljungfors, "Mötet i Skänninge 1248," *Kyrkohistorisk Årsskrift* 50 (1950), 4–13. Unlike the slightly earlier Danish statutes, these did not threaten sinning priests with deprivation of benefices.

47. M. A. Kelleher, "'Like Man and Wife:' Clerics' Concubines in the Diocese of Barcelona," *Journal of Medieval History* 28 (2002), 352.

council of Skänninge had been too strict and permitted its abolition in the diocese of Uppsala. Only in the following year was the revocation extended to the whole of the Swedish church province, and the penalties slightly relaxed.[48] Later provincial and synodal statutes still repeatedly discussed the punishment of concubinous clerics, their concubines and children, but the Church had to establish a *modus vivendi* with the "intractable reality"[49] of the embarrassing but inevitable priestly concubines and families.[50]

It is hardly surprising that Johannes Gerechini was not the only cleric guilty of breaking his vow of celibacy or keeping a concubine. In fact, even some other bishops had been accused of sexual misconduct. In the 1340s, Bishop Bo of Växjö (ep. 1320–43) had been strongly suspected of incontinence and thus causing a grave scandal (*criminum incontinencie...vehemens suspicio et graue scandalum laborabant*) among other crimes, even though there seems to have been little tangible proof (*nichil probatum*) of sexual crime. The interlocutory decree determined that the number of compurgators Bishop Bo had to produce would be decided later, at the next provincial council.[51] However, in 1280 bishop Ascer of Växjö (ep. 1261–87) had been found guilty of overstepping his rights to demand money from his diocesans and fornicating with four different women after his accession to the see of Växjö. Lucia and Ingegerd had been single and Cecilia and Ingrid married.[52]

Indeed, it easy to agree with the assertion of Beata Losman that the complicated arrangements Gerechini had to orchestrate suggest that public episcopal concubinage no longer existed in Sweden at that time.[53] Why would the lower clergy have led an impeccable life if their superiors flouted the celibacy rule? In some cases, clerical sexual crime was punished. In 1341, Olof, the former rural dean (*praepositus*) of Ångermanland and vicar of a church in Enköping, gave a part of his lands to the House of the Holy

48. Liljegren, ed., *DS* I, 389–90; Ljungfors, "Mötet," 31; Nilsson, "A Fight," 604–04.

49. Nilsson, "A Fight."

50. Emil Hildebrand, Sven Tunberg and Ernst Nygren, eds., *DS* VI (Stockholm, 1878–1959), 184; Silfverstolpe, ed., *SD* II, 579; H. Reuterdahl, ed., *Statuta synodalia veteris ecclesiæ sveogothicæ* (Lund, 1841), 58–59, 118–19; Nilsson, "A Fight," 606–12.

51. Bror Emil Hildebrand, ed., *DS* V (Stockholm, 1858 and 1865), 58–59.

52. Joh. Gust. Liljegren, ed., *DS* II (Stockholm, 1837), 655.

53. Losman, "Johannes Gerechini," 216.

Ghost in Stockholm as atonement for his and his former loyal servant Ragna's sins.[54] The joint atonement may have been for the couple's illicit relationship, and Olof had possibly lost his deanery because of it. Depriving clergymen of their benefices was a matter in which the bishop could only adjudicate with the consent and advice of the cathedral chapter.[55] There are instances of defrocked priests from medieval Sweden, but sexual crime was usually punished by fines. Cases of serious sexual crime committed by priests, such as incest with spiritual kinswomen, violations of maids, and adultery, were occasionally dealt with surprising leniency.[56]

Later in the fifteenth century, the conciliar movement and the church councils set out to reform the Church from within. Despite suggestions that celibacy be abolished for the lower clergy, the decrees of the Council of Basle from 1435 once more attacked the rather ineffectively pursued question of clerical concubines by forbidding the keeping of concubines on pain of fines and loss of benefice. Emulating this example, later fifteenth-century synodal statutes in France, the Low Countries, and Denmark, as well as Swedish provincial and synodal statutes also decreed more severe penalties for clerics—including those suspected of concubinage.[57]

The attitudes of the laity towards breaches of clerical celibacy were ambiguous. Having one's wife or daughters seduced and impregnated by monks or parish priests was probably seldom seen as a tempting prospect. Most laymen may have accepted clerical concubines as a lesser evil, saving their own women from priests "who honored the Virgin Mary in the morning, but embraced Venus at night."[58] The town of Stockholm seems to have experienced sufficient incidents of lecherous clerics sleeping with married townswomen. What irritated the town fathers was the immunity of the clergy in such cases, and the town decided to inquire at the next meeting of the Estates whether it had competence to arrest clerics taken in

54. Hildebrand, ed., *DS* V, 73–74.

55. Kauko Pirinen, *Turun tuomiokapituli keskiajan lopulla* (Helsinki: Suomen Kirkkohistoriallinen Seura, 1956), 93.

56. Sara Risberg and Kirsi Salonen, eds., *Auctoritate Papae: The Church Province of Uppsala and the Apostolic Penitentiary 1410–1526* (Stockholm, 2008), e.g., no. 95, 205–06.

57. Brundage, *Law, Sex, and Christian Society*, 536–39; Callewier, "Canon Law," 183–84; Losman, *Norden*, 143, 145, 251–52; *Statuta*, ed. Reuterdahl, 166, 175–76, 182.

58. Sawyer and Sawyer, *Medieval Scandinavia*, 172.

the act with married women.[59] As the ecclesiastical court records have not survived, and the town courts had no jurisdiction over incontinent clerics, there are hardly any documented cases of clerics involved in sexual crime, apart from a few sporadic documents.

Although "monk's whore" was considered a very slanderous expression in late medieval Sweden, "priest's whore" also appears.[60] Possibly the housekeeper or concubine of the parish priest was a more integral part of the community, and her quasi-marital status was tacitly upheld in society. A priest's monogamous union may have posed no threat to the community, as his concubine could be equated to his wife. Priests were also referred to by the word "herr," a title also used for nobility or lords, and his higher status may have contributed to his housekeeper's. Monks, however, usually lived in their own community, separated from the world by the monastic rule and were unable to offer women semi-permanent and stable positions, lodging, food and clothes. Their encounters were usually bound to be furtive and clandestine. These factors probably contributed to the particularly pejorative sense of "monk's whore."

As M. A. Kelleher has suggested, "clerics' concubines and their children...were not necessarily marginalised within their communities" even if they were denied "official status in law."[61] This probably applied to medieval Sweden as well, where the communities were small. Some Swedish evidence suggests that individual clerics actually bequeathed property to their concubines without acknowledging them as such in their wills. In a number of wills, wealthy testators remembered a housekeeper (villica)[62]—while some even had several housekeepers in their service, managing different manors. A cow (vacca) or a tunic (tunica) seems to have been the custom-

59.   Emil Hildebrand, ed., Stockholms stads tänkeböcker 1474–1483 samt burspråk (Stockholm, 1917), 30 May 1478, 172.

60.   E.g., Erik Noreen and Torsten Wennström, eds., Arboga stads tänkebok I (Uppsala, 1935), 12 Oct. 1467, 270; Erik Noreen and Torsten Wennström, eds., Arboga stads tänkebok II (Uppsala, 1938–39), 13 Feb. 1486?, 281.

61.   Kelleher, "'Like man and wife'," 359.

62.   The Latin villica is usually translated as female administrator, overseer or housekeeper or the wife of a male overseer, with the special sense of wet-nurse of royal children: J. F. Niermeyer and C. van de Kieft, Mediae latinitatis lexicon minus 2, 2 ed. (Darmstadt, 2002), 1439, 1441.

ary bequest to such a servant.[63] In some wills, the property was unusually valuable to be given to a mere servant. Naturally, absolute proof is usually lacking as the women are not introduced in the documents as concubines. For example, at the town court of Kalmar, Johannes de Borgh, *perpetuus vicarius ecclesie kalmarnensis*, bequeathed three cows to his *focaria*[64] Ragnild for her work (*pro suis laboribus*) in 1410. In addition, he seems to have ceded to her and her son Henrik some lands with buildings, utensils and cattle. At the same time, he also gave fifty Swedish marks "in ready money" (*quinquaginta marchas sweticas in prompta pecunia*) for the use of "his little ones" (*paruulis suis*), Henrik and Elisabeth.[65] These were major bequests of property.

Canon Nils Cristinesson of Uppsala, whose matronymic may hint that he himself was of illegitimate birth, and canon Johannes Westfal of Åbo (ca. 1307–1385) both willed away real estates to women who had been in their service. The "discreet matron" Helena Offradsdotter, Nils's housekeeper (*villica*), was granted a piece of land with several houses (*fundum suum quem idem dominus Nicolaus sibi legauit, in sua vltima uoluntate...vna cum domibus in ipso situatis*) within the town of Uppsala sometime before 1329.[66] "Matron" Elin (*cuidam matrone Elene nomine racione sui longi et fidelis seruicii*) received three pieces of land in Räntämäki in 1368 for her long and faithful service to Johannes Westfal.[67] The value of the property makes one wonder whether the bequests were meant as means of guaranteeing the surviving long-term partner's upkeep after the demise of the other, or, in Westfal's case, were part of a retirement settlement. Canon Westfal was about to climb the ecclesiastical career ladder as he became the *praepositus* of the Turku chapter in 1368 when the incumbent, Johannes Petri, was

---

63. E.g., Jan Axelsson et al., eds., *DS* IX (Stockholm, 1970–2000), 581.

64. While the Latin *focaria* has the more classical sense of cook or housekeeper, Niermeyer and van de Kieft give three senses for the word: soldier's wife, concubine and clerical concubine in the *Mediae latinitatis lexicon minus* 1, 573. Similarly, the provincial statute of Lund from 1345 used "focarie et concubine" synonymously in reissuing the prohibition by the papal legate, Cardinal Otto, against clerical concubinage, Hildebrand, ed., *DS* V, 451–52.

65. 1410, Ivar Modéer and Sten Engström, eds., *Kalmar stads tänkebok* (Uppsala, 1945–49), 20–21.

66. Bror Emil Hildebrand, ed., *DS* IV (Stockholm, 1853 and 1856), 125, 131.

67. Axelsson et al., eds., *DS* IX, 471.

elected bishop. In 1370, Westfal himself became bishop, and it may be that the discreet retirement of a long-time housekeeper (or concubine) was necessary for his advancement to higher ecclesiastical posts.[68]

Nevertheless, while inherited land was to be kept within the kin group and alienating land required more formalities, it may have been more common to bequeath chattels. In 1378, Johannes Petri, canon of Strängnäs and vicar of Vadsbro, made his will in preparation for traveling to Rome. Among other legacies, he left his housekeeper Kristina a handsome donation in chattels: six cows, ten sheep, several metal cauldrons and pots and a generous collection of household textiles, including a "better" tablecloth and towel, as well as several bolsters, mattresses and sheets.[69] In his will from 1368, Lydbrekt Petersson, vicar of Torsåker, remembered his housekeeper (deghio)[70] Ramfrid, after the usual and generous bequests to churches, fellow clerics, relatives and friends. She was to receive eight ells of cloth from Brabant and fifteen ells of cloth from Werwicq, a well-equipped bed, a grey fur lining for a cloak, a silver spoon, a pound of flour and malt each and two cows.[71] Knut, vicar of Svanshals, left his villica Helena a cow, a bull, a horse, eight ells of cloth from Courtrai plus some other property in his mid-fourteenth-century will.[72] In 1454, Ervast and Ingemar the Shoemaker witnessed that the priest Jönis of Arboga had given his dea Katarina a hooded cloak worth nine marks before he left for Rome so that she "would serve him the more faithfully."[73]

In the medieval Swedish categorization of the status of illegitimate children, the children of priests, monks and nuns were ranked the lowest. Together with children born in incest or adultery, they were explicitly grouped as "whore children" (horbarn), adulterines, in medieval Swedish

---

68. On Westfal, see, e.g., Jarl Gallén, "Johannes Westfal," in: SBL 20, 227. See also Liljegren, ed., DS I, 541.

69. Claes Gejrot et al., eds., DS XI (Stockholm, 2006–11), 516.

70. K. F. Söderwall gives the secondary meaning of the Swedish word forsea or forsia, housekeeper or female overseer in his Ordbok öfver svenska medeltids-språket I [(Lund, 1884–1918), 184, 299], but as its other synonym, deghio or deye, is translated as housekeeper, girl or mistress, it is also somewhat tainted with the same double meaning.

71. Jan Axelsson et al., eds., DS IX, 438.

72. Hildebrand, Tunberg and Nygren, eds., DS VI, 513.

73. Noreen and Wennström, eds., Arboga stads tänkebok I, 27 March 1454, 24.

town law.[74] While natural children, who could be legitimized by their parents' subsequent marriage, had only limited inheritance rights, "whore children" could inherit from neither parent nor other relatives. Intestate succession having been ruled out, wills and donations of chattels or acquired land were the only option. It is also occasionally possible to glimpse a priest donating land to his illegitimate children; since gifts of chattels were probably hardly ever documented, no evidence of them survives. In 1353, the vicar of Ekeby donated land worth eleven *örtugs* (elva örtugaland; *solidos*) to his natural son Nils. Nine witnesses (*fastar*) signed the document. In addition, two clerics, a canon of Strengnäs and the rural dean (*praepositus*) of Närke, confirmed it with their seals.[75] The two girls, Ragnild and Katarina, whom Ragvald, vicar of Mörlunda, had brought up, were in fact his children by a concubine. The girls, recipients of Ragvald's estate of Holmstentorp in the donation made in 1329, were mentioned without a patronymic only as daughters of Margareta, brought up by him (*puellis meis dilectis, ragnildi et katerine filiabus margarete penes me enutritis*). However, a much later document from 1355 confirms Ragvald's paternity: at Ragnild's entering the nunnery of Vreta, Ragvald had unlawfully given the convent (*pro introitu filie sue domine Ragnildis*) certain landed property with his daughter that he had in fact previously donated to the prebend he was holding.[76]

Clerical concubinage was a reality in late medieval Sweden, but it is difficult to assess its extent or character. Hendrik Callewier has recently argued for the late medieval Low Countries and Bruges that 45–60 percent of priests failed to live celibate lives.[77] In Sweden, the number of dispensations for sons of priests to become clerics regardless of their illegitimate birth and other references to breaches of celibacy also support the view that clerical incontinence was not the rare exception.[78] Concubinage and breach-

74. Åke Holmbäck and Elias Wessén, eds., *Magnus Erikssons stadslag i nusvensk tolkning* (Lund, 1966), Ärvdabalken (Chapter on Inheritance) 15, 61.
75. Hildebrand, Tunberg and Nygren, eds., *DS* VI, 458–59.
76. Hildebrand, ed., *DS* IV, 89; Hildebrand, Tunberg and Nygren, eds., *DS* VI, 534.
77. Callewier, "Canon Law," 185.
78. Risberg and Salonen, eds., *Auctoritate Papae*, e.g., nos. 1–2, 13–18, 21, 37–45, 48–53, 61–62, 69–72, 75, 81–82, 91, etc., 153–54, 161–63, 166, 176–79, 188–91, 193, 199, 204; Hedda Gunneng, ed., *Biskop Hans Brasks registratur* (Uppsala, 2003), nos. 39, 45, 122, 124-25, 136, pp. 131–32, 137–38, 199–200. See also Kirsi Salonen, "In their fathers' footsteps: The

es of celibacy were however seldom flaunted by the clergy, as high-profile
affairs involving violation of virgins, incest or adultery tended to irritate
the parishioners or attract the attention of ecclesiastical superiors.[79] Also
to avert attention, Margareta Piil had taken communion every Easter following the exhortation of her lover's secretary, who had solemnized her
simulated marriage and who was obviously a party to the collusion and
knew about the mortal sin she was living in.[80] The elaborate subterfuge and
simulated marriage orchestrated by Gerechini to conceal his concubinage
were necessary means.

CONCLUSION

We might never have learned anything of the private life of Archbishop
Johannes Gerechini of Uppsala without the political events that made his
opponents assiduously gather evidence against him. Consequently, the account of the curious marital arrangements of Jeppe Niklisson and Margareta Jakobsdotter has been preserved. Does the case only have curiosity
value? I argue that the life and times of Archbishop Johannes Gerechini
are instructive and certainly amount to more than merely an entertaining
story. According to Swedish standards, this was an extraordinary case preserved through unusual circumstances. As in so many other case studies
and microhistories, however, it does tell us something of normality as well.

This narrative shows that Gerechini could not overtly keep a concubine in his household, having to employ subterfuges and stratagems in
order to provide an excuse for her presence there. The simulated marriage
between Margareta and Jeppe then took place in order to provide a respect-
able facade for the archbishop's concubinage. The archbishop had allegedly told Jeppe never to consent to the marriage or to consummate it. The

---

illegitimate sons of Finnish priests according to the archives of the sacred penitentiary
1449–1523," in *Roma, Magistra Mundi: Itineraria Culturae Mediaevalis. Mélanges offerts au
Père L. E. Boyle à l'occasion de son 75e anniversaire*, ed. Jacqueline Hamesse (Louvain-la-
Neuve, 1998), esp. 361–66; Bertil Nilsson, "The Lars Vit Case: A Fragmentary Example of
Swedish Ecclesiastical Legal Practice and Sexual Mentality at the Beginning of the Fif-
teenth Century," in *Medieval Christianity in the North: New Studies*, ed. Kirsi Salonen,
Kurt Villads Jensen and Torstein Jørgensen (Turnhout, 2013), 237–60.

79.   E.g., Nilsson, "The Lars Vit Case," esp. 240–41.

80.   Losman, *Norden*, 84.

case supplies a relatively detailed description of how Margareta became the archbishop's mistress and of the simulated marriage. It does not tell us how the case was heard, and non-consummation provided justification for an annulment based on subsequent affinity. Nevertheless, it also suggests that the canon law of marriage could be used with some sophistication by medieval people to further their own personal agendas, as Frederik Pedersen has demonstrated,[81] even if these were in blatant conflict with the ethical aims of this legislation.

Despite the shameful end of his archiepiscopal career and the public scandals he created, what seems to have remained uppermost in the minds of his contemporaries some time having elapsed since his violent death was his martyrdom. We learn that Gerechini came to have the reputation of a saint, and that some miracles were ascribed to him.[82] Even the man himself would probably have found this an amusing and ironic twist to the story of his turbulent life.

81. Frederik Pedersen, "Did the Medieval Laity Know the Canon Rules on Marriage? Some Evidence from Fourteenth-Century York Cause Papers," *Mediaeval Studies* 56 (1994), 111–52.

82. Losman, "Johannes Gerechini," 216.

The Presumption of Evil in Medieval Jurisprudence

Laurent Mayali

The existence of evil is a central theme in medieval theology.[1] Ever since Augustine's reply to the question *unde malum faciamus?*, generations of doctors have debated the complex problem of evil's occurrence in Christian society.[2] The medieval discussion of good versus evil was not limited to the spiritual issues of people's sin and their eventual salvation. It also fostered a secular debate on the foundation of society and the rationale of its institutions. It is therefore not surprising that medieval canonists spent a significant amount of time considering evil's challenge to the interpretation of rules and the enforcement of the legal order. The assessment of this challenge rested upon the prevalent opinion that the role of the law was to contain or possibly eradicate the nefarious influence of evil on human affairs and prevent its harmful effect on social dealings. Faced with this task, medieval jurists and canonists in particular adopted a double-pronged strategy of prevention and repression that relied heavily upon a combination of Christian beliefs on the nature of the conflict between good and evil and the legal process, supported in part by the teachings of Roman law.

By the second half of the twelfth century, the production of short treatises on romano-canonical procedure[3] anticipated the establishment of

---

1. Paul Ricoeur, *Finitude et culpabilité, L'homme faillible* (Paris, 1960), 14–15.

2. See for instance, A. Boureau, "La chute comme gravitation restreinte. Saint Anselme de Canterbury et le mal," *Nouvelle Revue de Psychanalyse* 38 (1988), 129–145.

3. L. Fowler-Magerl, *Ordo iudiciorum vel ordo iudiciarius. Repertorien zur Frühzeit der gelehrten Rechte, Ius commune* Sonderhefte 19 (Frankfurt am Main, 1984).

an effective ecclesiastical jurisdiction that soon played a central role in the
adjudication of disputes and control of public unrest.[4] It also signaled the
institutional mutations that redefined the normative system that governed
Christian society. As Dick Helmholz rightly observed in outlining the governing principles that defined the spirit of medieval canon law, the canonists' initial pragmatism did not extend to ignoring the spiritual teachings
of the sacred texts.[5] Their more realistic approach to society's normative
challenges did not question the significance of the Church's pastoral mission,[6] nor did it deny the sacred principle of the fight against the forces
of evil. The jurists' knowledge rested upon the common belief in a model
of Christian harmony where people's faith, as Stephan Kuttner suggested,
did not dissociate the spiritual substance of human life from the temporal
necessity of the socio-political order.[7] It is within this unique normative
synthesis that the idea of evil achieved a renewed legal significance as both
a sin and a crime.[8] On one hand, in spiritual affairs, evil was a compelling
reality that occurred in various stages of people's life. On the other hand,
in legal matters, evil's effects in public order and private life were measured
by diverse sets of rules that stressed the main rationale of the legal system.
While theologians and philosophers viewed evil as a formidable challenge,
both in its origin and its scope, for the salvation of mankind, jurists considered it a source of disturbance that jeopardized the permanence of legal
institutions and the stability of public order. Keeping in mind the ultimate

4.   Gottofredo da Trano, *Summa super titulis decretalium* (Lyon, 1519; repr. Aalen,
1968), fol. 2, proemium. "Hic iudices animarum salubria querent consilia hic sub certis ru-
bricis invenient ex quibus causis irregularitas dispensabilis vel indispensabilis incurratur
et per quos valeat dispensari. Qualiter consideratis criminibus et circunstanciis peccato-
rum adhibeantur remedia conscientis sauciatis. Hic prelati et alii forenses judices instru-
entur quomodo pro tribunali oporteat iudicare."
      5.   Richard Helmhoz, *The Spirit of Classical Canon Law* (Athens, Ga., 1996).
      6.   A. Cattaneo, "Teologicidad y juridicidad de la canonistica. Klaus Mörsdorf
y su concepció de la canonistica como disciplina teológica con método jurídico," *Revista
Española de Derecho Canonico* 51 (1994), 35–49.
      7.   Stephan Kuttner, "Harmony from Dissonance. An Interpretation of Medie-
val Canon Law," St. Vincent College, Wimmer Lecture, X, 1956 (Latrobe, 1960), 1–16, now
in *The History of Ideas and Doctrines of Canon Law in the Middle Ages* (London, 1980), I.
      8.   Stephan Kuttner, *Kanonistische Schuldlehre von Gratian bis auf die Dekretalen
Gregors IX. Systematisch auf Grund der handschriftlichen Quellen dargestellt*, Studi e Testi 64
(Vatican City, 1935), 3–38.

Christian ideal of man's salvation, the decision to contain evil within legally acceptable parameters was increasingly viewed as a public necessity when the government of Christian society required the Church's redoubled vigilance.

In a recurring statement borrowed from Isidore of Seville's *Etymologies*, Gratian described statutory law (*lex*) as being "designed to inspire fear and coerce human audacity so that righteousness could withstand evilness."[9] He further supported this assertion with a reference to Augustine's definition of law's purpose as helping "good people to live in peace among the wicked ones."[10] The decretists' structural interpretation of law's institutional significance focused on its capacity to provide a stable and secure social environment. His approach differed from the theologian's moralist view that styled law as a tool for making people better. By the turn of the thirteenth century, in the wake of the ideological changes and procedural reforms introduced by the fourth Lateran Council[11] in response to the secular and religious threats to the authority of the Roman Church, Johannes Teutonnicus observed in his *Glossa ordinaria* to the *Decretum* that "Laws are not made to force people to do good," but merely "to forbid them from doing evil."[12] The two positions were eventually reconciled when, prominent decretalists such as Henrico de Segusio, the future cardinal of Ostia, and Sinibaldo Fieschi, the future pope Innocent IV, asserted canon law's authority in all religious and secular matters. "Canon Law," Hostiensis

9.   Gratian, *Decretum*, Dist. 4 c. 1: "Facte sunt autem leges ut earum metu humana coerceatur audacia:tutaque sit inter improbos inocentia, et in ipsis improbis formidato supplicio refrenetur nocendi facultas."

10.   *Glossa ordinaria*, Dist. 4 c. 1: "tutaque: ut boni inter malos quiete vivant ut C. 23 q. 5 c. 18."

11.   For instance, Lateran IV, can. 8: "Qualiter et quando debeat prelatus procedere ad inquirendum et puniendum subditorum excessus, ex auctoritatibus Novi et Veteris Testamenti colligitur evidenter, ex quibus postea processerunt canonice sanctiones, sicut olim aperte distinximus et nunc sacri approbatione concilii confirmamus."

12.   Huguccio, *Summa in decreto*, Dist 4 c.. 1: "Factae: Nam eis bene facere quis non cogitur sed male facere prohibetur ut xxiii q. v ad fidem," and "tutaque i. boni inter malos et improbos quieti uiuant ut xxxiii q. v non frustra," in Huguccio Pisanus, *Summa Decretorum*, Tom. I Distinctiones I–XX, ed. Oldrich Prerovsky, *Monumenta Iuris Canonici*, Series A, Corpus Glossatorum, 6 (Vatican City, 2006), 73; *Glossa ordinaria*, ibid., "coerceatur: nam per leges nemo cogitur bene facere sed male facere prohibetur;" cf. also *Glossa Palatina*, MS Vaticana Pal. Lat. 658, fol. 1va.

used to remind his students "combines theology with the practice of the civil law." It could thus be viewed as "the knowledge of all knowledge" since it cared for the salvation of people's soul while maintaining social peace through the enforcement of the legal order.[13] In other words, canon law combined the power of the judge with the authority of the confessor.[14] By the middle of the thirteenth century, this institutional dualism shaped the representation of the church and the beliefs of its clergy.[15] But Johannes Teutonnicus' down-to-earth opinion never ceased to influence the medieval idea of law. During the last centuries of the Middle Ages, its recurring mention was a constant reminder of law's initial purpose.

John's view found vindication in the widespread belief that a wicked human nature was bound to do evil things *ab adolescentia*.[16] Human weakness and its consequences on both prejudicial personal behavior and social unrest had long been a source of concern in Christian thought. The theological dimension of fault and its consequences influenced undoubtedly the common adherence to this belief but the newly developed legal doctrine of guilt expanded its range. As it considered the social consequences of individual behaviors, this doctrine encouraged a more factual treatment of transgressions as objective legal offenses. The emphasis placed on public order further underscored the normative autonomy of the legal system without, however, advocating a radical rupture with the ideals and values

13.   Henricus de Segusio, Hostiensis, *Summa Aurea, In primum decretalium librum Commentaria* (Venice, 1581; repr. Turin, 1965), fol. 6 n. 39, and Innocent IV, *Commentaria Apparatus in V libros decretalium* (Frankfurt, 1570; repr. Frankfurt, 1968), fol. 1: "quod in hoc volumine multi casus et articuli utiles et necessarii tam in consiliis animarum et poenitentiali foro quam in regendis et disponendis ecclesiis et rebus ecclesiasticis et prelatis."

14.   Stephan Kuttner, "Tra giurisprudenza, filosofia e diritto. La giustizia e i canonisti del medioevo," in *Lex et iustitia nell'utrumque ius. Radici antiche e prospettive attuali* (Vatican City, 1989), 83–93.

15.   Peter Landau, "Il concetto del diritto ecclesiale in prospettiva filosofico-storica," *Ius Ecclesiae* 17 (2005), 347–384.

16.   Gratian, *Decretum*, C. 12 q. 1. c. 1: "Omnis aetas ab adolescentia in malum prona est." Archidiaconus, *Super Decreto* (Lyon, 1547), Causa 12 q. 1 c. q., fol. 218ra: "Et no. quod dici consuevit quod homo pronior est ad malum quam ad bonum et hoc ideo quia malum per se potest bonum vero non nisi per gratiam. Item propter somitem impellentem ad malum. Item propter multa impedimenta boni. ç, fol. 317va, C. 12 q. 1, c. 1: "No. ex verbo prona quod dici consuevit quod homo pronior est ad malum quam ad bonum et hoc ideo quia malum per se potest bonum vero non nisi per gratiam ut de consecra dist. 4 c. fi."

embodied in religious norms.[17] Since the safeguarding of social peace was viewed as a main foundation of institutional stability, law's *raison d'être* was initially limited to insuring public safety.[18] It did not address the more private consequences of people's subjective impulses. The self-conscious acceptance of law's expected success in curbing the acts of evildoers expressed the jurists' vision of an overarching[19] legal order that opened the door to a legalist conception of justice as a process centered on the enforcement of rules. "Law (*Lex*) should be right (*recte*)" noted Johannes Teutonnicus "because in law (*ius*) what is right is even more desirable than what is just."[20]

To affirm the rectitude of legal norms required a subtle balance between the ideal of justice ideal[21] and the rigor of law.[22] On one hand, the strict adherence to law's rules and to procedure allowed for the rationalization of judges' decisions in doubtful and challenging cases. On the other hand, it also supplied a convenient explanation for the death sentences that would otherwise contravene a cleric's primary obligation not to shed blood. In such capital punishment cases, law's basic function exonerated the responsibility of ecclesiastical judges.[23] As the decretists explored the extent of judicial responsibility in sending convicted criminals to their death, they quoted Jerome's statement that. "To punish murderers, sacrileges and poisoners is not to spill blood but it is the function of the law."[24] It was pre-

---

17.   For instance, in the first half of the twelfth century, the debate between Bulgarus and Martinus on the role of the oath in establishing the authority of legal agreements, Ennio Cortese, *La norma giuridica. Spunti teorici nel diritto commune classico* (Milan, 1962), 1–35.

18.   R. Fraher, "The Theoretical Justification for the Criminal Law of the High Middle Ages: 'Rei publicae interest, ne criminal remaneant impunita,'" *University of Illinois Law Review* (1984), 577–595; R. Helmholx, *The Spirit of Classical Canon Law*, 257–283.

19.   Pierre Legendre, *Le désir pôlitique de Dieu: étude sur les montages de l'état et du droit* (Paris, 1988), 349 ff.

20.   *Glossa ordinaria*, Dist. 4 c. 2 , *honesta*.

21.   W. Ullmann, "Some Medieval Principles of Criminal Procedure," *The Juridical Review* 59 (1947), 1–28, repr. in *Jurisprudence in the Middle Ages* (London, 1980), XI: "the supreme criterion of all medieval considerations in the field of the theoretical and practical jurisprudence was the realization and the concrete manifestation of the idea of justice."

22.   Raphael Eckert, "Peine judiciaire, pénitence et salut entre droit canonique et théologie (XIIe–début du XIIIe s.)," in *Revue de l'Histoire des Religions* 228 (2001), 483 ff.

23.   For instance, Simon of Bisignano, *Summa in Decretum*, ed. Pier Aimone (Fribourg, 2007), Principium, p. 2: "quia videtur iudex non occidere sed lex."

24.   Gratian, *Decretum* C. 23 q. v c. 31.

cisely this function that defined the basic nature of the Church's legal order when it was being updated as a system of social and political governance centered on the repression of evil.[25] As observed by René Girard in the broader context of his discussion of violent punishments, the "rationalistic approach" of the judicial process was "more concerned with the general security of the community than with any abstract notion of justice."[26] The concept of rightful justice addressed these concerns, as it was never meant as the expression of a pre-modern doctrine of the rule of law. The instrumentalization of legal rules served a different purpose as dispensing justice increasingly became an administrative process. The canonists' far-reaching understanding of the Roman concept of public law as regulating and protecting religious institutions further justified the criminalization of any acts or criticisms waged against the church.[27]

Thus, by the beginning of the thirteenth century, the jurists' interpretation of law's essential function reflected the institutional shift to a repressive model that departed from the more traditional penitential archetype. As the same Johannes Teutonnicus once more observed in recapping the decretists' opinions: "You may say that in all these cases a rigor contrary to natural equity was purposefully instituted for the sake of peace or society."[28] For this latter purpose, the new criminal law and inquisitorial procedure were undoubtedly of great use. The legalistic approach to social and religious deviance served its purpose. It produced a typology of various offenses that were defined by their corresponding punishments.[29]

The shift from offense to punishment in measuring the dangerousness of various public transgressions reflected also the changing perception

25.   Pierre Legendre, "Artiste de la Raison. Remarques sur la fonction structurale du juriste" in *Law, Life and the Images of Man. Modes of Thought in Modern Legal Theory. Festschrift für Jan M. Broekman* (Berlin, 1996), 553–559; now in *Sur la question dogmatique en Occident*, I, (Paris, 1999), 193–207.

26.   René Girard, *Violence and the Sacred*, trans. Patrick Gregory (Baltimore, 1972), 22–23.

27.   *Glossa ordinaria*, Dist. 1 c. 11, publicum: "unde qui ledit sacerdotes vel res sacras ab omnibus tanquam pro publico crimine potest accusari."

28.   *Glossa ordinaria*, Dist. 1 c. 2, ius.

29.   On the canonist's definition of crime, Stephan Kuttner, *Kanonistische Schuldlehre von Gratian bis auf di Dekretalen Gregors IX* (Vatican, 1935), 4: "So bemühte sich die Wissenschaft des 12. Jahrhunderts, den rechtlichen Begriff des Strafvergehens oder Verbrechens (*crimen*) enger als den religiösen Begriff der Sünde (*peccatum*) abzugrenzen."

of evil from a subjective representation to an objective reality. Yet the control of evil was not limited to the repression of crimes and the public display of spectacular punishments designed to showcase the unforgiving might of the public authorities[30] and instill fear in people's minds.[31] In the canonists' eyes, evil's ubiquitous manifestations undermined personal status, family stability and traditional forms of solidarity that defined the social order. It also threatened the various interactions that formed the core of the feudal order. It disrupted business transactions[32] and eventually compromised the stability of the legal order. The establishment of jurisprudence as an autonomous knowledge rested upon the responses to such threats.[33] The jurists' ability to distinguish between various types of malevolent behaviors and anticipate their consequences shaped legal doctrine from the late twelfth century to the end of the thirteenth century.

This intellectual process produced a normative typology that redefined evil from a theological enigma into a legal wrongdoing.[34] It successfully mixed religious beliefs with legal reasoning as the reliance upon law's authority in defining human actions led to the formation of a distinctive model of institutional governance that considered the protection of social peace and public order on equal terms with the salvation of the faithful. For this purpose, the medieval jurists succeeded in redefining the fact-based predictability of evil into a law-based normality. The normalization of evil reflected the growing significance of legal knowledge in medieval culture. As with many other sources of people's concerns in both their private and

30.   On this punishment process and the public display of force, see Michel Foucault, *Discipline and Punish. The Birth of the Prison* (New York, 1979), 33.

31.   IV Lateran Council, can. 7, *metus poenarum*.

32.   Archidiaconus, *Super Decreto* (Lyon, 1549), Dist. 4 c. 1: "ut uidetur ex hoc quod lex cohibeat omnia mala quia non sufficienter coerceretur humana audacia nisi omnia mala cohiberentur per legem, preterea intentio legislatoris est homines facere bonos et virtuosos sed non potest esse bonus nisi ab omnibus vitiis abstineat ergo ad legem humanam pertinet omnia vitia conpescere."

33.   Apparatus in Decretum, *Ecce vicit leo*, St. Florian MS XI.605, fol. 2vb: "et hoc ostendit magister quod hanc causam canones vel leges instituendi ut bonis detur securitas....No. fuit bonis lex non posita sed propter malos"; Summa *Animal est substantia*, MS Liège 127, fol. 2ra:"quod propter malos lex etiam imposita quia bonis lex non est posita c. xix q. ii Due sunt leges."

34.   For a similar example of legal narrative see, Karl Shoemaker, "The Devil at Law in the Middle Ages," *Revue de l'histoire des religions* 228 (2011), 567–86.

public lives, legal rules and concepts supplied satisfactory answers to society's needs and people's doubts. The renewed idea of the *ius commune* as
a set of legal principles observed by various groups and communities confirmed the transition from a vague normative order to a more structured
legal system. It also served as a common language and mode of communication that contributed to the unification of disparate feudal institutions
and practices. The status of evil and its perception were definitively altered.
What was initially described as an omnipresent peril was now treated as a
legal presumption.

The change of legal paradigm was confirmed, at the end of the thirteenth century, by a rule inserted in the title *De regulis iuris* of the *Liber
Sextus* (VI 5.12.8) promulgated by Boniface VIII.[35] Much has been written
on Boniface's political pretenses.[36] His response to secular challenges to
pontifical authority defined in part the engagements of his pontificate. His
conception of the papacy's political significance relied upon the Church's
juridical culture that Gregory IX had outlined in 1234 with the promulgation of the *Liber Extra*.[37] A few decades later, the election of Innocent IV, a
former professor of law, further confirmed the legal authority of the papacy
in its political fight against Frederic II, the self-described heir of the Roman
legal legacy. Following in the steps of his famous predecessors, Boniface did
not evade his legal responsibilities. Since the end of the twelfth century, the
predominant role of the papacy in the governance of the church had produced a significant increase in the volume of decretals written in response
to the frequent queries addressed to the papal curia from all the parts of
Christendom. Gregory IX's *Liber Extra* became outdated. The promulgation of the *Liber Sextus* was intended to address this issue[38] while also
reflecting Boniface's ambition in presenting this compilation as the clear

35. Michele Begou-Davia, "Le *Liber Sextus* de Boniface VIII et les extravagantes
des papes précédents," *Zeitschrift der Savigny-Stiftung für Rechtsgeschichte, Kanonistische
Abteilung* 90 (2004), 77–191.

36. Emanuele Conte, "La Bolla *Unam Sanctam* ei fondamenti del potere papal fra
diritto e teologia," *Mélanges de l'École française de Rome* 113 (2001), 663–684.

37. Gregory IX, Bull *Rex Pacificus.*

38. Michèle Begou-Davia, "L'*inventarium iuris canonici* (1300) de Bérenger Frédol,"
Proceedings of the 13th International Congress of Medieval Canon Law, Eedsztergom 3–8
August 2008, ed. Peter Erdö and Szabolc A. Szuromi, Monumenta Iuris Canonici 14 (Vat-
ican City, 2010), 389–395.

manifest of pontifical authority. The pope's legal omniscience rested upon Roman imperial precedent. His claim that he was "holding all the law in the archive of his chest"[39] was a direct reference to Justinian's prior assertion. This is not the place to address the complex consequences of such a claim for the historical development of pontifical authority; suffice it to observe for our limited purpose that as a product of this supreme legislator, the *Liber Sextus* achieved the status of codification of the Christian legal order.[40] By the end of thirteenth century, the Roman model had been thoroughly assimilated. Ancient imperial Rome was the pontifical *communis patria*.[41] Canonists no longer needed the legitimacy of Roman legal science to assert the authority of their own law. Boniface's adoption of the imperial legislator model further added to this belief.

The composition of the *de regulis iuris* title reflected the representation of canon law as a fully autonomous legal science of government that, in Gratian's earlier words, combined *potestas* and *scientia*.[42] The presence of a similar title in Justinian's Digest points to the influence of Roman law, which had also warranted the adoption of a similar yet much shorter title in the *Liber Extra*. In the *Liber Sextus*, however, the title's structure and content give it a unique character that betrays its ultimate function as the foundation of the Church's legal order. The number of rules and their evenly distribution between Roman law's principles and canon law's original rules confirm the author's deliberate attempt to assert its universal value through a unifying process that goes beyond the initial harmonization that was advocated in the previous century. Petrus de Ancharano later captured the essence of these expectations when he observed that "of all the legal is-

---

39.   VI 1.2.1.:"Licet Romanus pontifex qui iura omnia in scrinio pectoris sui censetur habere…"

40.   Tilmann Schmidt, "Papst Bonifaz VIII als Gesetzgeber," in *Proceedings of the Eighth International Congress of Medieval Canon Law, San Diego, 21–27 August 1988*, ed. Stanley Chodorow (Vatican City, 1992), 227–246.

41.   Laurent Mayali, "*Romanitas* and Medieval Jurisprudence," in *Lex et Romanitas. Essays for Alan Watson*, ed. Michael Hoeflich (Berkeley, 2000), 121–138.

42.   Gratian, *Decretum*, dist. 20 dict. ant. C. 1: "Sed aliud est causis terminum imponere aliud scripturas sacras diligenter exponere. Negotiis diffiniendis non solum est necessaria scientia sed etiam potestas."

sues none is more common to both canon and civil law than the title on the rules of laws which captures the essence of both legal systems."[43]

Boniface's choice was not to replicate the Roman model but to establish a strong legal alternative for the governance of medieval society, partly in response to the pretenses of the secular powers and partly in accordance with the idea of the universal Church. In this context, to present the presumption of evil as a rule of law served a double purpose. It credited law with the essential task of addressing a complex and wide-ranging failing of the human condition. It also confirmed the legal authority of Church institutions.[44] Legal rules also contributed to this process. They illustrated of the rationality of the legal order. Rules did not create the law.[45] But in the eyes of the medieval jurists such as Bulgarus, they focused its substance by coalescing its diverse expressions into one unitary principle.[46] In this all-inclusive conception of the legal rule, exceptions to the rule did not challenge its unifying function nor did it undermine its authority. Rules were defined as the joining together of various cases that shared the same *ratio*.[47]

Written in a concise style, rule VIII stated "Once evil, always presumed evil."[48] As Hans Kiefner rightly observed, this expression had no precedent in Roman law and the rule was not included in the Digest's *De regulis iuris*.[49] Its origin should be traced instead to Accursius' *Glossa ordi-*

43. Petrus de Ancharano, *Super Sexto decretalium Commentaria* (Bologna, 1583), fol. 496b: "Inter ceteras autem materis iuris nulla communior est et ad utrumque ius canonicum et civile magis apta quam tractatus iste de regulis iuris ubi revolvitur totum corpus utriusque iuris."

44. For instance, recently, David Deroussin, "Remarques sur les *Regulae juris* et les principes de droit (temps modernes)," *Revue de l'histoire de droit français et étranger* 90 (2012), 195–235.

45. D. 50.17.1: "Regula est quae rem que est breviter enarrat, non ex regula ius sumatur sed ex iure quod est regula fiat. Per regulam igitur brevis rerum narratio traditur ut ait Sabinus quasi causae coniectio est quae simul cum in aliquot vitiate est, perdit officium suum."

46. K. Beckhaus, *Bulgari ad Digestorum titulum de diversis regulis iuris antiqui commentarius et Placentini ad eum additiones sive exceptiones* (Bonn, 1856; repr. Frankfurt am Main, 1967), 164

47. Peter Stein, *Regulae Iuris: From Juristic Rules to Legal Maxims* (Edinburgh, 1966), 135 ff.

48. VI 5.12.8: "Semel malus, semper praesumitur malus."

49. Hans Kiefner, "Semel malus, semper praesumitur esse malus. Bemerkungen zur Bildung von Prasumptionem im Recht des Mittelalters, insbesondere in der Glossa

naria. In a gloss on Ulpian's opinion that someone who was once guilty of calumny should not "readily been heard" in a second accusation (included in the Digest's title on "Accusations and Indictments"), Accursius observed that "someone who is once evil, is afterwards presumed evil."[50] This, he added, results from an inference from a past action to a present one. It should be noted that Accursius did not consider all the legal consequences of this presumption. It was, in his mind, akin to a series of similarly rebuttable legal presumptions (*praesumptio iuris*) that could arise during the legal process. The doctrine of *praesumptio malitiae* did not introduce new arguments to the broader debate on presumptions.[51] Accursius' comments were more descriptive than normative. The gloss listed a series of examples excerpted from various parts of the Digest while also alluding to the existence, in some cases, of the opposite presumption of goodness. This relative indifference did not reflect a lack of interest in presumptions.

By the time of the *Glossa ordinaria*, most of the questions defining this issue were already answered. From the early teachings of the Bolognese doctors in the first half of the twelfth century, medieval jurists, on both sides of the Alps, contributed to the legal theory of presumption in their exegesis of a few texts scattered in Justinian's compilations.[52] André Gouron shed new light on Placentinus' role in this discussion.[53] The nomadic Bolognese professor who had found refuge in Montpellier, where his lectures attracted the attention of the local elites, introduced a new classification of the types of presumptions with their practical consequences.[54] His decisive contribution found a receptive audience in canonist circles, where decretists such as Stephan of Tournai and the unknown author of

---

ordinaria des Accursius" *Zeitschrift der Savigny-Stiftung für Rechtsgeschichte, Kanonistische Abteilung* 78 (1961), 308–354.

50.   D. 48.2.7.3, addendum: "Nota qui semel malus est et postea praesumitur ut hic..."

51.   For a general discussion of presumptions in law see Chaim Perelman and Paul Foriers, *Les présomptions et les fictions en droit* (Brusells, 1974), 350

52.   On presumptions in a comparative perspective see *The Law of Presumptions: Essays in Comparative Legal History*, ed. Richard H. Helmholz and W. David Sellar, Comparative studies in continental and Anglo-American legal history, vol. 27 (Berlin, 2009),

53.   André Gouron, "Placentinus 'Herold' der Vermutungslehre?," in *Festschrift zum 65. Geburtstag von Professor Hans Kiefner* (Münster, 1994), 90–103.

54.   Hans Kiefner, "Qui possidet dominus esse praesumitur," *Zeitschrift der Savigny-Stiftung für Rechtsgeschichte, Kanonistische Abteilung* 79 (1962) 239–306, at p. 244–58.

the *Summa Quoniam omissis* were aware of the Provençal jurists' works.[55] R. Motzbacker has shown how the short treatise *De presumptionibus*, written by a member of Placentinus' circle in Montpellier before 1177, was used, a few years later, by Sicardus of Cremona in his first systematic study of presumptions inserted in his *Summa*. Canonists were thus able to offset Gratian's *Decretum*'s omissions and take advantage of the civilists' contribution to construct an elaborate theory of evidence.[56] Within the next half-century, early compilations of decretals remedied the lacuna in the Church's legal sources with the adoption of a title entirely devoted to presumptions. The *Liber Extra* confirmed this preference.[57] The Decretalists contributed to development of the doctrine and its diffusion in legal circles.[58] By the end of the century, however, presumptions did not seem to attract as much pontifical attention. This title was no longer included in the *Liber Sextus*. Despite this omission, presumptions formed the matter of no less than six distinct rules in *de regulis iuris* and "*Semel malus, semper praesumitur malus*" promptly attracted the canonists' interest. As Dinus de Mugello observed in his commentary,[59] the scope of the presumption of evil as a rebuttable *praesumptio iuris* or *naturae* could only be measured by comparison with the opposite presumption of good.[60] Once more, jurists were facing what appeared to be an unsolvable conflict between good and evil.[61] But

---

55. André Gouron, "Aux racines de la théorie des présomptions," *Rivista Internazionale di Diritto Comune* 1 (1990), 99–109 .

56. Rüdolf Motzenbacker, *Die Rechtsvermutung im kanonischen Recht* (Munich 1958), 507 at 104–108.

57. X 2.23. See also *Compilatio* Ia (2.16), IIa (2.15) and IIIa (2.14)

58. Richard H. Helmholz, *The Spirit of Canon Law* (Athens, Ga., 1996), 26.

59. Dinus de Mugello, *De regulis iuris* (Lyon, 1577), fol. 75–79: "huius regulae et exemplorum eius ratio est generalis quia de praeterito praesumitur in praesenti sed contra regulam et exempla videtur praesumptio iuris et naturae quia quilibet praesumitur bonus nisi probetur malus C. de inof. testamento l. omnimodo et ff. de lega. ii l. cum quidam et l. cum pater § rogo et de presump. c. dudum. Sed dic quod accidens naturae contrarium, removet effectum praesumptionis naturae."

60. Johannes Andreae, *In sextum decretalium librum commentaria* (Venice, 1581; repr. Turin, 1966), Semel malus, fol. 88–88A: "Prima glossa ponit exempla secundo quomodo hec presumptio potest dici hominis facti vel iuris sed non de iure."

61. Albericus de Rosate, *Commentarii in secundam digesti novi partem* (Venice, 1585), De regulis iuris, fol. 315vb, Semel malus semper praesumitur: "et sic haec regula vera est, ita et eius opposita quod semel bonus semper bonus presumitur."

this opposition was not expressed in theological terms. It required a legal solution as it challenged the structure of the juridical order and its natural law foundation. In this regard, the presumption of evil was not a simple *praesumptio malitiae* based on the report of a past behavior that might repeat itself in similar circumstances. What was the likelihood of goodness in a human being created in God's image? Was goodness in human beings nothing more than a rebuttable presumption? If human beings were presumed to be good by nature, wickedness would be the result of an *accidens naturae*. Could it be, then, that the latter outweighed the former, since it came afterwards, *posterior prioribus derogat*? Moreover, if being good comes from nature should it be considered as a consequence of natural law? And since natural law is immutable, should the *praesumptio naturae* be considered irrebutable? These were the questions that reflected, in the distinctive reasoning of the legal scholastic, the jurists' attempts to clearly define the scope of the presumption of evil within the legal medieval order. Having shown why the presumption of good could not avail itself of the immutability of natural law, the canonists struggled to reconcile the likely goodness of human nature with the inevitability of evil. Given its comprehensive scope, the presumption of evil would prevail. Goodness then would be the exception. This broad interpretation presented the advantage of providing a straightforward rationalization for the prevalence of malice in transactions by removing any uncertainties that might impede the legal process. It did not account, however, for various cases where honesty seemed to prevail.[62] Presumed malice was legally defined *secundum legem et canonem*.[63] But the presumption of goodness remained difficult to explain in legal terms. Its

62. Domenicus a Sancto Geminiano, *Super decretorum volumine commentaria* (Venice, 1578): homo quare praesumitur bonus sed non solvendo C. 6 q. 5, c. accusator, fol. 246vb: "Ratio est quia homo fuit creatus plenus virtutibus, unde naturaliter presumuntur ei virtutes inesse. Nec obstat per peccatum destructio, quia per sacramentum baptismi fit reparatio...Et ideo cum constet semel reparatus adhuc talis presumitur nisi probetur destructus..."; Johannes Antonius de Sancto Georgio, *Commentaria super decretorum volumina* (Pavia, 1497), Dist. 37 c. qui de mensa: "malum non presumitur a persona honesta factum sed bonum indubio" "nota quod factum a persona honesta et bona presumitur potius bonum quam malum in casu dubii"

63. Petrus de Ancharano, *Super Sexto decretalium Commentaria*, De regulis iuris, fol. 636rb: "Praesumptio malitiae est praesumptio hominis secundum legem et canonem quae procedit cum quis habet malam famam etest praesumptio facti et de preterito ad prasesens tempus et etiam praesumptio iuris..."

natural origin in human creatures was damaged by the *accidens naturae*
that changed the fate of mankind.[64] In order to have any value, any presumption of goodness required the jurists to admit either that goodness
survived the original sin—an opinion that was undermined by the recognition of the legal force of the presumption of evil—either the definition of
goodness in terms that would make it compatible with the requirements
of the legal order. By the turn of the fifteen century, and after much discussion, the second option was eventually outlined by Peter of Ancharano
since the first one could not be legally justified. Challenging the opinion
that advocated the validity of a *praesumptio bonitatis* despite evidence to the
contrary, the celebrated canonist suggested that goodness was nothing else
than the knowledge of the law and the obedience to its rules.[65] Peter's solution completed the process of legal acculturation. The problematic rapport
of good and evil was defined within the medieval legal system in a theory
of presumptions that made it possible for the jurists to manage its consequences for the social order. A few decades later, the French jurisconsult
Gui Pape reminded his readers that "This rule is famous. It deals with a
most useful matter but if someone wanted to fully discuss it, forty lectures
would not even begin to do it."[66] As far as we know Gui, whether out of
concern for his impatient audience or simply for his own sake, did not attempt to give forty lectures on that subject. By then, as we can see in Gui's
short treatise on presumptions,[67] the rule *semel malus, semper praesumitur
malus* was part of a doctrine the significance, which insured its influence

---

64. Johannes Monachus, *Glossa aurea super sexto decretalium libro addita* (Paris
1535; repr. Aalen 1968), De regulis iuris, Semel malus (summarium Philippi Probi), fol. 983:
"Item ratio huius regule liquet ex parte presumentis cuius natura corrupta malo potius
presumitur."

65. Petrus de Ancharano, *Super Sexto decretalium Commentaria*, fol. 636b: "Ista
presumptio bonitatis oritur ex observentia legum quas quilibet scire praesumitur ac tenetur etiam servare."

66. Gui Pape, *Lectura super decretales* (Lyon, 1517), fol. 194: "ista regula est no-
tabilis et habet materiam satis utilem, qui vellet expedire istam regulam non sufficerent
quadraginta lectiones."

67. Gui Pape, "De presumptionibus," *Tractatus Universi Iuris*, vol. 4 (Venice,
1584).

until today, when presumptions play a fundamental role in the conception of modern legal systems.[68]

---

68. Chaim Perelman and Paul Foriers, *Les présomptions et les fictions en droit* (Brussels, 1974), 350.

Pedro Guerrero's Treatise on Clandestine Marriage

Philip Reynolds

Pedro Guerrero was archbishop of Granada from 1546 until his death in 1576, and he was among the leading prelates at the Council of Trent during the second and third of the council's three periods. Guerrero was a keen reformer throughout this career, and he championed the cause of reform at Trent, where he led the delegation of Spanish prelates. After the council, he strove to realize Trent's disciplinary decrees in his archdiocese, as well as to assimilate the Moorish citizens of Granada more fully to the dominant Christian culture.[1] Guerrero collaborated and corresponded with Juan de Avila, a controversial reformer and preacher, and an advocate of devotional and evangelical renewal.[2] They had become acquainted as students at Alcalá in the 1520s.

Guerrero was a qualified theologian, whereas most bishops and archbishops were canon lawyers with no formal training in theology. He had studied theology at Salamanca, and he had been a professor of theology

---

1. For a comprehensive account of Guerrero's life and work, see C. Herreros González and M. C. Santapau Pastor, *Pedro Guerrero, vida y obra de un ilustre riojano del siglo XVI* (Logroño, 2012). D. Coleman, *Creating Christian Granada: Society and Religious Culture in an Old-World Frontier City, 1492–1600* (Ithaca, 2003), 145–76, describes Guerrero's work as a reformer and his role in the culture wars of Granada. H. Rawlings, *Church, Religion and Society in Early Modern Spain* (Houndmills, Basingstoke, U.K., 2002), 153–54, provides a biographical profile.

2. Coleman, *Creating Christian Granada*, 148–50. For the correspondence with Avila, see J. López Martín, *Don Pedro Guerrero: epistolario y documentación* (Rome, 1974).

there from 1531 through 1535. From 1535, he held the primary chair of theology at Sigüenza, where he was a canon of the cathedral.

Guerrero acquired a reputation for being troublesome and intransigent during the third period of the Council of Trent (1562–63).[3] According to Pedro González de Mendoza, the bishop of Salamanca, the Italian prelates hated Guerrero so much that his proposing something was sufficient reason for them to propose the opposite.[4] On January 18, 1562, Guerrero was one of the prelates who staged a protest against the papal legates' exclusive right to set the agenda and to prepare draft decrees, as defined in the principle *proponentibus legatis*.[5] Shortly after this protest, he addressed a brief treatise on the subject to the legates.[6] Guerrero was convinced that the cause of reform would be blocked unless the bishops took control of the agenda, but his fear was exaggerated, for the legates deputed the drafting of decrees to prelates. Guerrero was one of the thirteen prelates whom the legates deputed on June 21, 1563, to draft the decrees on the sacrament of marriage.[7] During the prolonged and fraught debate over whether clandestine marriages should be made invalid, Guerrero was a consistent proponent of invalidation, and he was on the winning side. The decree *Tametsi* of Session XXIV made clandestinity a diriment impediment, despite the legates' misgivings.

THE TREATISE ON CLANDESTINE MARRIAGE

At some point during those proceedings, Guerrero wrote a substantial treatise on clandestine marriage, explaining the chief arguments in play at the council as well as his own position.[8] The treatise survives in a single

---

3.   Coleman, *Creating Christian Granada*, 145–48, 166–76.

4.   Ibid., 166.

5.   Ibid., 170–71. *Concilium Tridentinum: Diariorum, actorum, epistularum, tractatuum nova collectio*, published by the Societas Goerresiana (Fribourg, 1901–) [hereafter CT], 8: 291.

6.   CT 13: 572–74.

7.   CT 9: 590–91.

8.   MS Biblioteca Universitaria de Granada, Caja B-4, 346r–383v. J. López Martín, "El voto de Don Pedro Guerrero sobre el sacramento del matrimonio en el Concilio de Trento," *Archivo teologico granadino* 44 (1981): 147–219, provides an edition (pp. 155–219), for which I am very grateful, but because it contains quite a few transcription errors, I have used the manuscript as my preferred source.

manuscript. Juan López Martín, an authority on Guerrero, identifies the hand as that of Guerrero's secretary, Juan de Fonseca: the cleric and theologian who advised Guerrero at Trent.[9] The manuscript bears marginal and interlinear notations in the hands both of Fonseca and of Guerrero himself.[10]

The relation of the treatise to the proceedings of 1563 is unclear. Guerrero refers to the proceedings in the past tense, and he writes as one who is explaining them to outsiders. This was not a position paper, therefore, designed as a contribution to the proceedings. But there is no mention in the treatise of the decree *Tametsi* of Session XXIV (Nov. 11, 1563), which was the outcome of those proceedings. Thereafter, Guerrero's chief task would have been to implement the reforms in his archdiocese. It seems, therefore, that Guerrero wrote the treatise *in medias res*. It is likely that Guerrero or his secretary (or both) worked up the treatise from the notes or written speeches that he used during the proceedings, perhaps even after the council had come to an end. The votes of the more learned prelates at the council, such as Guerrero, were detailed and carefully argued statements, presupposing extensive preparation. It is possible that Juan de Fonseca did the editing after Session XXIV without bringing the contents up to date.

The period of the contents, in contrast, is tolerably clear. On the one hand, because the treatise presupposes most of the arguments that circulated during the proceedings, it must have been composed well after July 20, 1563, when the legates put the first draft of the decrees on marriage before the prelates. On the other hand, the treatise reflects the state of the question before September of that year, for Guerrero assumes throughout that what is at stake is the invalidation both of clandestine marriages and of the marriages of minors without their parents' consent. The first two versions of the decrees on clandestine marriage (July 20 and August 7)

---

9. The *acta* record that Ioannes Fonseca, "clericus saecularis Hispanus cum archiep. Granatensi," spoke on communion under both kinds at a *congregatio theologorum* on June 22, 1562 (CT 8: 612), and likewise on the sacrament of orders on October 1, 1562 (CT 9: 31–32). He is also listed in the *acta* as one of the *sacrae theologiae doctores et magistri* who contributed to Session XIX (CT 8: 500). J. López Martín, *La imagen del obispo en el pensamiento teológico-pastoral, de don Pedro Guerrero en Trento* (Rome, 1971), includes editions of Tridentine treatises by Guerrero on ecclesiastical residence (201–301) and Juan de Fonseca on the sacrament of orders (302–45).

10. López Martín, "El voto de Don Pedro Guerrero," 148–49.

took the same approach. When the legates presented the third set of drafts to the prelates on September 5, however, these included two versions of the clandestinity decree: another version of the original, with the parental consent requirement; and a new version that eliminated all mention of parental consent but tightened up the requirements for publicity, which now included the office of the parish priest as well as the presence of other witnesses.[11] The prelates who expressed any preference in their votes, including Guerrero,[12] opted for the new version. It was this version that passed into the fourth draft and eventually became law in Session XXIV. The contents of the treatise, therefore, must belong to the period between July 20 and the second week of September. The most probable hypothesis is that they reflect the prelates' discussion of the second draft during August 11–23, for by that time the chief arguments and counterarguments were all in circulation and it was becoming clear that the two sides would never be reconciled.[13]

The treatise comprises three main sections followed by an appended essay. First, after some preliminary remarks, there is a numbered series of seven brief statements.[14] Guerrero presents these as premises,[15] but they might be better characterized as cruxes or key points. Guerrero adds some further key points after the numbered premises. Second, Guerrero presents a sequence of five extensively developed *conclusiones*, which together constitute a single five-step argument. The third section consists of objections made by the opponents of invalidation with Guerrero's replies to them. There are twelve objections, although the series is not numbered. Finally, there is an essay on the multiple senses of the terms "canon law" and "divine law." This appendix arises incidentally from Guerrero's reply to the twelfth and last objection, which happens to take Guerrero to the impediment of holy orders in the Roman and Byzantine traditions. Because some

11. CT 9: 761–62.

12. CT 9: 781/1.

13. López Martin, "El voto de Don Pedro Guerrero," 149–50, reaches the same conclusion through different reasoning.

14. Two successive premises, the fourth and fifth, are both counted as the fourth, so that the numbering is out of step from the fifth premise onwards. In the notes that follow, I add Guerrero's number in parentheses, e.g., Premise 5 (4) is the fifth premise, to which Guerrero designated the number 4 (348r, 158).

15. 346v/5 (156): "Pro clariori autem harum quaestionum enodatione sunt aliqua praemitenda."

ascribed the impediment to divine law and others to human or ecclesiastical law, Guerrero suggests that one might reconcile such disagreements by observing that the term "divine law" is equivocal, for what some call "divine law" others characterize as ecclesiastical or canon law.

The assertions by Guerrero on clandestinity that are recorded in the *acta* of the council appear in a new light when one reads the treatise. Guerrero's votes do not stand out as especially noteworthy when one reads the *acta*, but the treatise reveals that what seem to be minor or incidental remarks in the *acta* are key points in a carefully worked out theory. Many of the votes that Angelo Massarelli recorded as secretary to the council must have been abbreviated versions of what the participants actually said. Comparison of Guerrero's recorded votes with his treatise is salutary, therefore, but the record may have misrepresented him more than it did many others because some of his arguments were abstruse and difficult to follow. I shall note the chief parallels below, mainly in the footnotes. The treatise is not sufficiently organized to succeed in its own right, partly because it remains too closely related to the proceedings of the council, and partly because the author goes around in circles and seems too easily distracted by incidental considerations, although these defects may have resulted from the editing process. Nevertheless, it is full of interesting ideas and observations.

What follows is in three parts. In the first part, I shall review the circumstances of the treatise and describe Guerrero's intentions and methods. In the second part, I shall attempt coherently to reconstruct the central five-stage argument, rearranging some of the material and incorporating material from elsewhere in the treatise. Finally, I shall outline Guerrero's theory of laws. Three salient and interconnected themes run through the treatise: the twofold character of Christian marriage as both a civil contract and a sacrament; the relationship of human law to divine law; and the changeability of all human law, ecclesiastical as well as secular, which must adapt to the exigencies of each era.

GUERRERO'S INTENTIONS AND METHODS

Most Catholic prelates, canonists, and theologians during the sixteenth century agreed with the Protestants that clandestine marriages were pernicious, that they undermined familial and civic order, and that they should be suppressed as much as possible. Many of them considered the chief hazard of clandestinity to be the marriage of minors without their parents' consent, which the medieval principle of *solus consensus* made possible. Spain was no exception. In 1551, Juan de Avila wrote to Guerrero describing the appalling consequences of clandestine marriages and marriages without parental consent, urging the archbishop to pursue the matter at Trent. The only solution, in Avila's view, was to invalidate unwitnessed marriages.[16]

What should the Catholic church do about the problem? Could the church render clandestine marriages null and void, as the Protestants were doing?[17] When the general council first took up these questions, during its sojourn at Bologna in 1547, the *theologi minores*[18] were inclined to resist invalidation. Most of them considered it to be too much at variance with the principle of *solus consensus*, and it seemed to presuppose a Protestant heresy. Some of the prelates were more open to the idea, but the Bologna proceedings resulted in no substantive decrees, and the council petered out. This was the end of the council's first period.[19]

The council returned to the question during the third period. On March 11, 1562, Cardinal Gonzaga of Mantua put before the prelates twelve articles on pastoral reform, two of which were about clandestine marriages: Should they be declared null and void henceforth? And what should be the conditions that distinguish a clandestine marriage from a marriage

16.   H. Kamen, *The Phoenix and the Flame: Catalonia and the Counter Reformation* (New Haven, 1993), 279.

17.   The most comprehensive account of clandestinity at the Council of Trent during 1547 and 1563 is R. Lettmann, *Die Diskussion über die klandestinen Ehen und die Einführung einer zur Gültigkeit verpflichtenden Eheschließungsform auf dem Konzil von Trient* (Münster, 1966).

18.   The *theologi minores* were theologians who accompanied the prelates as personal assistants or were appointed to the council by the pope or the emperor. They had no vote at the council. They were so called to distinguish them from those prelates (always a minority) who were qualified in theology. The legates sometimes commissioned them to prepare the ground by discussing problematic points.

19.   The prelates agreed to suspend the Bolognese proceedings at a general congregation on September 14, 1547 (CT 6. 1:460–64), although some of them continued to deliberate through January, 1548. Pope Paul III gave the remaining bishops leave to return home on September 17, 1549. See J. W. O'Malley, *Trent: What Happened at the Council* (Cambridge, Mass., 2013), 137–38.

contracted *in facie ecclesiae?*[20] Preparatory proceedings on the sacrament of marriage began in February when the *theologi minores* met to discuss several erroneous articles on marriage, including one on clandestine marriages. The prelates, who were then preoccupied with the sacrament of orders, were encouraged to attend these meetings as auditors during the mornings.[21] The prelates themselves began to vote on the first of the four successive drafts of decrees on marriage on June 24 of 1563.

Many arguments and counterarguments emerged in the course of the proceedings, but for convenience one may divide the prelates into two main parties: the majority of proponents, who advocated invalidation, and the substantive minority of opponents. The ratio of proponents to opponents was roughly 5:2 throughout the proceedings and at the final vote (Session XXIV). Opinions were not divided consistently along regional or provincial lines, but most of the French and Spanish prelates were proponents, whereas roughly half of the Italian prelates were opponents, making up the majority of this contingent. The opponents considered the proposal to be at best rash and perhaps even impossible, reasoning that the essential conditions of any sacrament were inalterable. Among the proponents, a small contingent maintained that marriage, like every other sacrament, was essentially a religious rite, requiring the sacred ministry of a priest who joined and blessed the spouses. Those in the main stream emphasized the church's power to make positive law, the duty of children to obey their parents, the civic harm done by clandestine marriages, and the need to subordinate individual choice to the public good.

Three main strands of argument emerged from the votes of these mainstream proponents: that the church must have the power to do whatever is "expedient" (i.e., needful, necessary for well-being);[22] that the church in a *res publica christiana* has the power to invalidate the civil contract that the sacrament presupposes, without "touching" the sacrament *per se* by

---

20.   CT 8: 378–79.

21.   CT 9: 375–76: "Deinde ut theologi disputarent de his articulis, qui pertinent ad sacramentum matrimonii...."

22.   This argument emerged during discussion of the second draft: see especially Iustinpolitanus, CT 9: 706; Sulmonensis, 707; Leriensis, 713; Vulturariensis, 714; Montis Morani, 715. The argument is not always distinguishable from impatience with the proceedings!

altering its conditions;[23] and that the church has the power to "inhabili-
tate" (disqualify) the contractants. According to the theory of *inhabilitatio*,
which had emerged at Bologna, the church would not invalidate the manner (*modus*) of contracting marriage but rather would disqualify the partners from contracting marriage. This theory arose because the most obvious precedent for invalidation was the unquestioned right of the church
to add and subtract diriment impediments of relationship, such as those
of consanguinity.[24] Although the theory of *inhabilitatio* never gained wide
support during the proceedings, there is a trace of it in the decree *Tametsi*,
according to which the church now renders those who attempt to marry clandestinely "entirely incapable [*inhabiles*] of contracting," so that such
contracts will henceforth be null and void.[25]

Guerrero explains his own intentions concisely at the beginning of
the treatise:

> Among many matters that were subjects of inquiry and controversy
> when the Council of Trent under Pius IV deliberated over the sac-
> rament of marriage, the question of clandestine marriages and of the
> marriages of minors [*filii familias*] that occur without the consent of
> their parents was debated for a long time, and it greatly vexed the
> fathers of the council. Did the church have the power to render them
> null and void, whether by making the persons illegitimate and ren-
> dering them incapable [*inhabiles*] of contracting marriage, or by an-
> nulling their consent, or in some other way? Also, was it expedient
> for the church to do so?[26]

Guerrero was an advocate of the *inhabilitatio* theory at the council,[27]
but here he seems to avoid committing himself to it. Guerrero does not
invoke the theory in the treatise: a prudent policy, for it was arguably a

---

23. Bracarensis, CT 9: 650, 697; Lancianensis, 651; Sagiensis, 654; Clugiensis, 655;
Brugnatensis, 656; Auriensis, 663; Gebennensis, 663; Cotronensis, 665; Uxentinus, 667;
Civitatensis, 668; Namurcensis, 670; Lucensis, 974; Monopolitanus, 675; Naxiensis, 700;
Aquinatensis, 714.

24. E.g., Card. Lotharingus, CT 9: 642; Leriensis, 661; Auriensis, 663.

25. In N. Tanner, ed., *Decrees of the Ecumenical Councils* (London, 1990), 756/15–20.

26. Guerrero, *De matrimonio*, f. 346r (ed. López Martín, 155).

27. CT 9: 690/3–7, 781/3–4.

contrived legal fiction. The distinction between possibility and expedience that he invokes here was a persistent theme of the proceedings, and it is a crucial theme of his treatise.[28] Both the proponents and the opponents questioned whether possibility and expedience could be disentangled, but the questions were logically separate: Does the church have the power to invalidate clandestine marriages? And would invalidation be beneficial to pastoral and civil life?

Guerrero explains that some of the *theologi minores* discussed these questions first, and that only two of them denied that the church had the power to invalidate clandestine marriages. Moreover, only a few doubted that invalidation would be expedient, and even these were prepared to leave the matter to the prelates.[29] This account is broadly consistent with what we know from the *acta*.[30] When the prelates considered the question, Guerrero continues, 137 held that the church both could and should invalidate clandestine marriages henceforth, whereas 57 contradicted them, maintaining either that the church did not have the power to invalidate or that invalidation would not be expedient. But very few of them, Guerrero adds, dared to say that the church lacked the power. We do not know whence Guerrero came by these numbers or how he calculated them. Unlike modern minutes, the *acta* do not record numbers *pro* and *contra*. Moreover, the prelates were voting not on single issues but on a complicated document with many parts, including matters both of dogma and of discipline. They could and often did say *"placet"* to one part and *"non placet"* to another, but their decisions were often qualified and sometimes hedged or equivocal, and there were several possible reasons for opposing the decree on clandestinity. The exact count is a matter for interpretation, therefore, but the ratio entailed by Guerrero's numbers is close to what one finds in the recorded *acta*.[31]

28. Guerrero uses the verb *posse* to denote both active potency (the ability of an agent to do something) and neutral potency (the possibility that something may happen).

29. 346r (155). A "class" of fifteen theologians considered from February 9 through 16 whether marriage was truly a sacrament instituted by God and whether clandestine marriages should be rendered null and void.

30. The two members of the class who opposed invalidation were Antonius Coquier, a French secular cleric (CT 9: 397–98), and Antonius de Gragnano, an Italian conventual Fransciscan (CT 9: 407–409).

31. By my own count, the numbers for and against invalidation in the voting on the four drafts and in the final vote of Session XXIV respectively are as follows: 125:51,

That said, Guerrero oversimplifies the division of opinion, and his use verb "to dare" (*audere*) points to what actually happened. Most of the opponents reasoned on theological albeit largely intuitive grounds that the only parties to the contract were the two spouses and God, who joined them together, and that no one else had any right to intervene. No human being can separate those whom God has joined together (Mark 10:9). But because the proponents increasingly emphasized the church's God-given power to do whatever was needful for pastoral and civic well-being, the opponents were forced to concede that invalidation was theoretically possible while maintaining that it would be rash and repugnant to tradition, as well as counterproductive in practice.

The question that Guerrero addresses in the treatise, he explains, is twofold: first, whether the church is able to raise the level of prohibition from simple prohibition to invalidation; second, whether it is now expedient to do so. Guerrero emphasizes that the church already prohibits the marriages in question and penalizes them in one way or another. What is in question, therefore, is not a new prohibition but an enhancement of the existing prohibition.[32] Guerrero maintains that in any legal system, whether secular or ecclesiastical, there will be both prohibitive impediments and diriment impediments, and that there is a natural progression from simple prohibition to invalidation. When a contract or other voluntary institution is harmful, the relevant authority first tries to prevent it through simple prohibition, without invalidating it *post factum*. If that proves ineffective, the authority raises the level of prohibition to invalidation.[33]

Throughout the treatise, as in the opening passage quoted above, Guerrero couples clandestine marriages in the proper sense—i.e., marriages contracted secretly (*clam*)—with the marriages of minors (*filii familias*) contracted without parental consent. The two categories are loosely included under the general heading of clandestinity, but Guerrero neither conflates nor separates them. He seems to assume that the two errors stand or fall together, so that an argument for invalidating one is implicitly an

---

159:73, 134:60, 125:51, 134:55. A few prelates (never more than a dozen) abstained from committing themselves at each stage.

32. 346v (155).

33. Guerrero states this principle briefly as premise 6 (5), 348r–349r (159–60). He develops it extensively in the twelfth objection, 376v–378r (206–08).

argument for invalidating the other, presumably because he considered the second error to be the chief hazard of the first. The early drafts of the decree on clandestine marriages at the council took the same approach.

Guerrero explains what the term "clandestine marriage" means. In general terms, a marriage is clandestine when it is contracted without whatever formalities (*solemnitates*) the church normally requires, and without a dispensation from observing them (which would be granted in cases of parental coercion, for example). More precisely, marriages may be contracted clandestinely in any of three circumstances, which constitute a descending scale of clandestinity: (i) when there are no witnesses at all, and consequently no proof that the spouses are married if they choose to deny it; (ii) when there are witnesses present but no priest; and (iii) when there are witnesses and a priest, but not the "proper" priest, that is, the contractants' parish priest or his appointed ordinary. In addition, the marriages of minors without parental consent are customarily said to be clandestine even if they are not contracted clandestinely—indeed, even if the partners plight their troth *in facie ecclesiae*.[34]

Whereas the couplet of errors is conjunctive, another couplet that occurs throughout the treatise is disjunctive: that of "natural or divine law" (*lex naturalis aut divina*). This couplet comprehends the unchangeable givens of law in contrast to the positive laws introduced by human agents, which are rescindable and generally capable of dispensation. Guerrero uses another inclusive disjunction to characterize laws of the latter sort: that of ecclesiastical or human laws. This deliberate circumvention of distinctions is resolved in the appendix.

There was much discussion during the proceedings as to whether the issue should be handled only as a matter of discipline or as a matter both of doctrine and of discipline. A doctrinal decree typically consisted of a general declaration—either a brief introduction or a detailed statement in several chapters—followed by several canons expressing particular dogmas by anathematizing anyone who denied them. When pronouncements of both sorts were issued on a given topic, the doctrinal definitions came first. Since doctrinal edicts were statements of truth and were presumed to be infallible, the force of such definitions applied always and everywhere. Dis-

34. Premise 2, 346v–347r (156).

ciplinary edicts, on the contrary, could be rescinded if they proved counterproductive, and they would apply only in those regions or provinces where
they were promulgated: an important consideration in regard to marriage
law. But there were deeper issues at stake. The first draft of the decrees on
marriage included two pronouncements on clandestine marriage: a doctrinal canon and a corresponding disciplinary decree. The former anath-
ematized those who denied that clandestine marriages freely contracted
through the mutual consent of the partners were true and settled (*vera et
rata*), as well as those who said that the parents had for that reason the
power to determine whether such marriages were valid or invalid.[35] The
disciplinary decree ruled that clandestine marriages and the marriage of
minors without parental consent would henceforth be null and void. The
apparent incongruity between the two edicts troubled some of the proponents, and in subsequent drafts there was no doctrinal canon, although
several prelates called for it to be restored. Instead, the church's existing
condemnation of the Protestant heresy was described in the preamble to
the disciplinary decree. But the opponents maintained that although invalidation itself would be a matter of discipline, whether invalidation was even
possible was a theological question. And the proponents countered that
on that basis every disciplinary edict would presuppose a corresponding
doctrine regarding its possibility, which was absurd.

Guerrero handles this problem judiciously in the treatise, recognizing that it is a serious issue and shunning flippant rebuttal. Moreover,
he articulates a concern that does not emerge in the *acta*: that a doctrinal edict would require something close to unanimity. A vote of 137 to 57
would suffice for a disciplinary edict but not for a definition of doctrine
or an anathema.[36] A decree invalidating the marriages in question would
in itself be a *de facto* and not a *de iure* matter, Guerrero says: a matter not
of doctrine but of discipline. If a *de facto* edict turns out to be counterproductive, the pope can easily rescind it.[37] Guerrero concedes, nevertheless,
that such a decree presupposes a doctrine, which if true is necessarily true,
and if false is necessarily false. But he points out that this truth is affirmed
only indirectly and by implication. There is a great difference between (a)

35.   Canon 3, CT 9: 640.
36.   Objection 3, 367r (191).
37.   364r (187).

declaring dogmatically that the church has the power to do something and anathematizing those who deny this, and (b) tacitly presupposing that the church has this power by making a decree of reform. What Guerrero and the other proponents are proposing is an action of the second kind. The church already dispenses from certain impediments without condemning those, such as Thomas Aquinas, who considered them to be indispensible. Moreover, it is not the case that there are as many presupposed doctrines of possibility as there are impediments, for all the impediments of ecclesiastical law presuppose one and the same legislative power. Besides, even if one grants that a decree of invalidation would presuppose a particular implied doctrine, the problem would not be fatal. Very few of the prelates and only two of *theologi minores*, as Guerrero has explained, denied that the church had the power to invalidate. Many argued that invalidation would not be expedient, but that is a matter not of dogma but of fact (*res facti*), and a simple majority (*maior pars*) rather than something close to unanimity is sufficient for a matter of fact.[38]

Although Guerrero's way of organizing and presenting his material is not at all scholastic, his conceptual methods are thoroughly scholastic. In particular, Guerrero likes to parse and to subdivide and to posit intermediate categories. As well as condemning the marriages in question as perilous and subversive, Guerrero identifies the precise category of moral evil to which they belong. Some actions are intrinsically indifferent but may be bad or good according to circumstances, such as picking up a stick.[39] Other actions are intrinsically good or intrinsically evil (*de se*). But one must make two further distinctions. Some intrinsically evil actions are necessarily and always evil, whereas others are usually evil but are good in rare circumstances. Likewise, some intrinsically good actions are necessarily and always good, whereas others are usually good but are evil in rare circumstances. Clandestine marriages and marriages without parental consent are intrinsically evil in the sense that they are usually evil but are good in rare circumstances.[40] Guerrero presents this observation as one of his initial

---

38.   368r (193).

39.   This is standard scholastic example. Cf. Thomas Aquinas, *Summa theologiae* I-II.18.8, resp. (817b). For the *Summa theologiae*, I cite the edition of Ottawa (1941–1945).

40.   Premise 7 (6), 359r–v (160–61). Cf. Granatensis, CT 9: 689/25–26: "Item matrimonia clandestina de se sunt mala, et similiter contrahere absque licentia parentum...."

premises. Although he does not explicitly use it in what follows, it reflects a disputed point that arose during the proceedings. Some of the opponents objected that it was sometimes expedient for persons to marry secretly or without knowledge of their parents—to avoid scandals, for example, or to escape coercion or unreasonable parental resistance—for it is always better to marry than to burn (1 Cor 7:9). The proponents countered, as Guerrero does in the treatise, that all human laws are beneficial only in the majority of cases, and that special dispensations can be made in exceptional circumstances. Every new law, Guerrero points out, is disadvantageous to a few persons. When necessary, a bishop can oversee the marriage contract and take the place of the bride's father by giving her away.[41]

GUERRERO'S FIVE-STEP ARGUMENT

Guerrero's central, five-step argument presupposes that one may construe any marriage solely as a contract, even when that marriage happens also to be a sacrament in the proper sense.[42] The argument also presupposes two mutually implicative metaphysical axioms.

Guerrero assumes that one may regard even a Christian marriage solely in respect of its contractuality (*ratio contractus*), which is the subject of natural and civil law, and without regard to its sacramentality (*ratio sacramenti*), which is exclusively subject to inalterable divine law. But that would not be possible if the distinction were merely conceptual. There must be a "real distinction," Guerrero reasons, which one can establish by showing that the contract can be separated in reality from the sacrament.[43] To that end, it suffices to show that marrying is sometimes a non-sacramental contract, especially if that separation occurs among God's people (including

---

Granatensis, 781/7–8: "Probavit, quod clandestina sunt de se mala, cum ut in pluribus sint mala; ergo, convenienter irritantur."

    41.   Objections 5–7 (4–6), 369r–370r (194–96).

    42.   Guerrero introduces the distinction between contract and sacrament as the third premise, 156–57 (347r), and their real separability as the fourth premise (347v, 157–58).

    43.   Clodiensis, CT 9: 704, argued that the distinction was real and not merely conceptual, as some were arguing. In scholastic usage the terms "sacrament" and "contract" denoted the transitory event of marrying primarily, and only secondarily denoted the state of being married.

the Jews of the Old Covenant), and above all when it occurs among Christians. The issue of the "separability" of the contract from the sacrament had been the subject of much debate since the fourteenth century, and it was especially prominent at Trent.[44] Guerrero reviews several circumstances in which marriage is only a contract and not a sacrament in the proper sense, although in some of these it is a sacrament in the broad sense: a sign instituted to signify a sacred reality (*signum sacrae rei*). Marriage would have been a contract but not a sacrament in the proper sense if, counterfactually, human beings had remained in the original, sinless condition. In the real world, all marriages before Christ, even among God's people, were merely contractual, as are all marriages after Christ between two non-Christians or between a Christian and a non-Christian. Protestants who marry intending not to receive the sacrament, which they deny, receive only the contract, as do Catholics who marry intending only to receive some temporal benefit, even if they do not intend *not* to receive the sacrament.[45]

Guerrero asks his readers initially to put the sacramentality of marriage out of mind, therefore, and to consider marriage only as a contract. He claims that his chief argument is not theological but "physical," or a matter of moral philosophy.[46] He reintroduces the sacramentality of marriage at the third step of his argument, but he does so only negatively, to show that it is not an obstacle to invalidation of the contract.

The two axioms, which together comprise "a certain and Catholic dogma," are as follows:
1. God is not deficient in necessary things.
2. God is not abundant in superfluous things.[47]
As Guerrero indicates, the second axiom is version of a familiar scholastic principle: that God and nature do nothing in vain.[48] It follows from this axiom that if the church has the power to do something, exercising it "can sometimes be expedient" (*potest expedire quandoque*). It follows from

44.   A. Duval, "Contrat et sacrement de mariage au concile de Trente," *La Maison-Dieu* 127 (1976): 34–63.

45.   347v (157–58).

46.   349v–350r (161–62).

47.   Conclusion 4, 363v (186). Guerrero also states the first of the two axioms at the beginning of the treatise, immediately after the introductory statement translated above.

48.   363v/19–20: "Deus autem et natura nihil faciunt frustra."

the two axioms respectively, Guerrero argues, that the following two arguments are equally sound:

a. Excercise of the power can sometimes be expedient. Therefore, there is
such a power in the church, otherwise the church would not be provided
for sufficiently.

b. The church has been given such a power. Therefore, the exercise of that
power can sometimes be expedient.[49]

Guerrero uses both lines of argument: the first to show that the church
has the power to invalidate marriage, and the second to show that exercising
that power can sometimes be expedient. Whether he can use both without committing a fallacy of circular argument is a question that I shall not
pursue here. The modal proposition that something "can sometimes be appropriate" is hard to interpret, but Guerrero seems to construe this neutral
potency in a statistical manner. Whereas what is necessary always occurs,
and what is impossible never occurs, what is possible sometimes occurs.

The argument then proceeds in five steps, or *conclusiones*, as follows.
First, every republic or its ruler (*princeps*) has the power preemptively to
render clandestine marriage contracts and the marriage contracts of minors
without parental consent null and void, unless a superior law or judicial
authority prohibited invalidation. Second, the church, too, must possess
that essentially civil, temporal power. Third, the sacramentality of marriage does not detract from that power. Fourth, the exercising of the power
"can sometimes be expedient." Fifth, the exercise of that power is expedient
now. I shall attempt to reconstruct Guerrero's argument for each step.

(i) **Every republic or its ruler has the power to render clandestine
marriage contracts and the marriages of minors contracted without parental consent null and void, unless prohibited by a superior law or judicial authority:**[50] The crux of Guerrero's argument is that *every res publica*,
as the term itself implies, has the power to do whatever is expedient for the
common good, to which all particular, private goods are subordinate.[51] The

---

49.   363v/220–25: "Quare sicut valet argumentum potest expedire quandoque,
ergo iam est talis potestas in ecclesia (alias enim non sufficienter esset provisum) ita valet,
est potestas iam data, ergo et quandoque potest expedire illa uti, ex illo dogmate certo et
catholico, quod Deus neque deficit in necessariis neque abundat in superfluis."

50.   Conclusion 1, 350r–353r (162–168).

51.   351v (164–65).

power to regulate such contracts, therefore, belongs naturally to the republic, and it is a right bestowed by God. No one doubts that this power includes the right to regulate other civil contracts, ranging from bequests and sales to voluntary servitude, by determining certain conditions for validity, such as a minimum age or a certain number of witnesses.[52] If this is true of other contracts, why should it not be true of marriage?[53] Unlike the conjugal act, Guerrero argues, marrying is public by its very nature. Among all the peoples of the world, no event is more public, more celebrated, more witnessed, and more surrounded by formalities and solemnities. Marriages are contracted publicly in every well-governed republic, for people need to know who has legitimately begotten whom.[54]

Guerrero discusses at length the manner in which positive human law determines (i.e., specifies) what is either indifferent or not fully determined in natural or divine law. What the superior law concedes or permits, the inferior law may prohibit or command. Only when the superior law commands or prohibits is the inferior law prevented from making a determination of this sort. Guerrero illustrates this legal principle with similes from physics and logic. The influence of one and the same universal cause, such as the sun or the heavens, is indeterminate until it is determined through diverse secondary causes to result in diverse specific effects: generating another human being through a human parent, for example, or a fire through a fire. In logic, one and the same major premise can yield diverse conclusions through diverse minor premises. The opponents, Guerrero argues, fail to appreciate the flexibility of human laws in relation to natural or divine law.

The flow of determination is not arbitrary. Here, Guerrero invokes the first axiom: God is not deficient in necessary things. It follows that God will always provide the republic with whatever is expedient for its welfare.[55] One must concede that the republic has the power to invalidate the marriages in question, therefore, *unless* one can show that such invalidation

52.   350v (163).
53.   352r (165–66).
54.   Objection II, 373r (200).
55.   Conclusion I, 351v/2–4 (164): "...cum non sit potestas haec supernaturalis, nec supervacanea sed potius expediens et necessaria in ipsa republica. Et Deus numquam deficiat in necessariis et valde expedientibus."

is repugnant to natural or divine law. Now, everyone concedes that such marriages have always been and are prohibited, although at least during recent times the prohibition has not been diriment. If simple prohibition is not repugnant to the superior law, then neither is invalidation.[56] For similar reasons, the burden of proof is with the opponents of invalidation, and not with the proponents. Unless they can show that invalidation is repugnant to natural or divine law by using proofs based on reason or Scripture, then one must assume that invalidation is possible.[57]

(ii) **The church, too, must have the civil power to render clandestine marriage contracts null and void:**[58] Guerrero's proof of the second conclusion is brief because he has already established the basic principles elsewhere. Republics have the natural right to regulate contracts *unless* they are prohibited from so doing by a superior republic or authority, for example, by the removal of cases or by the annulling of judgments. Guerrero assumes that the church is the plenary authority, and that the secular republic is subordinate to it. If an emperor has the right to suppress the marriages in question by imposing grave penalties, then he also has the right to invalidate them "unless the church has removed such power from him." As a "son of the church," the emperor would cheerfully cede the right of invalidation to the church because marriage is a sacrament.[59] The reason why the church assumes legislation and jurisdictional authority over a civil contract in this case is that marriage is also a sacrament, but Guerrero puts no limitations of principle on the church's superior authority: "If a republic has the power to do something," Guerrero claims, "so also does the church."[60] The church has assumed this essentially civil, republican power

56. 351v (164).

57. Premise 1, 346v (156). Cf. Granatensis, CT 9: 781/2–6: It is difficult to prove that the church is unable to invalidate clandestine marriages because it is difficult to prove a negative. Those who claim that the church is not able must prove that invalidation is contrary to divine or natural law.

58. Conclusion 2, 353v (168).

59. Conclusion 1, 353r (167).

60. Conclusion 2, 353v/6–7 (168): "si enim respublica quaecumque potest, ergo et ecclesia." Cf. Granatensis, CT 9: 644/18–19: "Princeps saecularis posset irritare matrimonia clandestina, ergo a fortiori ecclesia." The following prelates argued at Trent that the church in a *res publica christiana* assumed the civil power to invalidate the marriage contract: Leriensis, CT 9: 661; Legionensis, 665; Lancianensis, 699; Clodiensis, 704; Iustinopolitanus, 706; Bracarensis, 697.

over the validity of marriage contracts. Contrariwise, whatever contractual regulations the church has imposed, such as impediments, a republic would also have the right to impose if it were left to exercise its authority independently.

The claim that the church has plenary power over the republic or its prince makes sense only if one assumes that Guerrero's political theology tended rather to the hierocratic model than to the dualistic, Gelasian model. According the dualistic model, ecclesiastical and secular rulers have separate domains and should not intrude upon each other's domain, although the ecclesiastical domain has greater dignity because it pertains to eternal, heavenly welfare, whereas the prince's domain pertains to temporal, civic welfare. According to the hierocratic model, which Hugh of Saint-Victor was the first to articulate clearly, the prince's royal power is in some sense delegated to him by the church, which holds plenary power.[61]

(iii) **The sacramentality of marriage does not detract from the church's power to annul clandestine marriage contracts:**[62] The opponents held that invalidation was impossible because the church had no power to alter whatever was essential to any sacrament, such as its matter and form, for this had been instituted by Jesus Christ. Guerrero accepts that premise, but he argues that the church has exactly the same power over the validity of the sacrament of marriage as it has over that of the contract, and for the same reasons. The church has the same power over the sacrament as the church or the republic would have had over the contract if marriage were not a sacrament. The reason is that the Gospel of Jesus Christ did not take away anything from the natural order, for grace perfects and does not destroy nature.[63] The contractuality of marriage remains intact and is naturally subject to the same conditions, just as the water of baptism is still water.[64] The proposal is to invalidate marriage qua contract, and not qua sacrament, but if there is no contract there is no sacrament, "for marriage considered as a contract is prior both in reality and conceptually to the sac-

---

61. See J. A. Watt, "Spiritual and Temporal Powers," in J. H. Burns, ed., *Cambridge History of Medieval Political Thought, c. 350–c. 1450* (Cambridge, 1988), 367–423.

62. Conclusion 3, 353v–363v (168–86).

63. Cf. Granatensis, CT 9: 644/26–27: "Nec his contrariatur, quod dicitur matrimonium esse sacramentum, quia gratia non destruit, sed perficit naturam."

64. Premise 4, 347v–348r (158). Conclusion 3, 353v–354v (168–69).

rament, which presupposes it. Thus, whatever power the church has over marriage as a contract, it also has in consequence over marriage as a sacrament."[65] To illustrate this point, Guerrero asks the reader to reflect on two imaginary scenarios. Suppose that some other secular contract, such as a sale or a donation, were raised to the level of a sacrament. Again, suppose that someone prevented the sacrament of eucharist from taking place by intervening and turning the bread and wine into some other stuff.[66] Guerrero assumes, with Thomas Aquinas, that the sacramentality of marriage is related to the contract as form is to matter, and as the sacrament of baptism is to external ablution with water.[67]

To corroborate the third conclusion, Guerrero reviews the history of the impediments of relationship.[68] The church has extended and reduced the impediments of consanguinity, and the church has added some entirely made-up impediments, such as those of spiritual relationship, legal relationship, crime, and public honesty. These new impediments did not exist in the natural law or in the divine law of the Leviticus code.[69] Whenever the church introduced an impediment of relationship, it rendered persons illegitimate or incapable (*inhabiles*) of marriage who were previously legitimate and capable, and it prevented marriages that would have been sacraments hitherto.[70]

Some object that the impediments of relationship are not apposite precedents because they entail some quality that inheres in the persons, such as their being first cousins, and because they exist before the contracting of marriage. The defect of clandestinity, on the contrary, pertains to how marriage is contracted and entails no inherent quality. Some of the opponents at Trent, most notably the archbishop of Rossano, used this ar-

---

65. Conclusion 3, 354r/14–17 (169): "Matrimonium enim in ratione contractus est prius re aut ratione ipso sacramento et illi praesupponitur, quare quaecumque potest ecclesia super matrimonium, ut est contractus, ex consequenti potest ut est sacramentum."
66. 354v (169).
67. Thomas Aquinas, *IV Sent.* 27.1.2, quᵃ 1, resp. (*Opera omnia*, Vivès edition [Paris, 1871–1880], 11:83a–b); *IV Sent.* 27.1.2, quᵃ 2, resp. (83b).
68. Cf. Granatensis, CT 9: 644/21–25.
69. 354v–355r (170–71).
70. 354r (169).

gument to refute the theory of *inhabilitatio*.[71] Guerrero replies that the objection exaggerates the difference. What inherent quality comes between the spouses in the more remote degrees of blood relationship, or in spiritual or legal relationship, or in public honesty?[72] Moreover, such impediments are imposed not because of anything that exists prior to the contract but in view of the consequences of the contract, especially the goods that accrue from exogamy. Clandestine marriages and the marriages of minors without parental consent, too, are prohibited because of the consequences of the contract.[73] Just as the purpose of the impediments of relationship is to extend friendship and prevent enmity through exogamy, so the purpose of prohibiting the marriages in question is to prevent scandals and enmity.[74]

(iv) **The exercising of that power can sometimes be expedient** (*"potest expedire quandoque"*): Here, Guerrero applies the second metaphysical axiom. Since the church has the power to invalidate the marriages in question, the exercise of that power can sometimes be expedient. "Such a power would be in vain if its use and execution were not sometimes permitted and expedient," for "God and nature do nothing in vain."[75]

If Guerrero can show that invalidation is expedient now, as he does at the fifth and final step, why does he need to show first that it *can sometimes* be expedient? Guerrero seems to use the argument to establish a metaphysical basis for the empirical case that he will make next. It amounts to affirming that if God has given the church this power, he must have done so for a purpose. Consequently, the church should not shy away from exercising it. In contrast, the opponents, having been backed into a corner, conceded that the church had the power while maintaining as a matter

71. Rossanensis, CT 9: 644/51–53, 647/23–28, 690/23–25. Likewise, Rhegensis, 651; Dertusensis, 671.

72. Lancianensis, CT 9: 699/10–14, countered that a spiritual relationship (acquired through sponsoring a baptism) comes to exist in the persons not from nature but only through the church's institution. Likewise, Iustinopolitanus, 706/29–31, countered that *cognatio legalis* (acquired through adoption) has no enduring inherent cause in the persons. Cf. Granatensis, CT 9: 690/3–7: If one who contracts marriage with a blood relation is *inhabilis* because the consanguinity remains in him, how much more *inhabilis* is the one who has within himself the disorder of wishing only to follow his lust without obeying either the church or his parents?

73. 355v–357r (171–74).

74. 399v (178).

75. 346r (155).

of principle that the church should never use it, regardless of the perils of clandestinity.

(v) **The exercising of that power is expedient now:** Guerrero's argument for the fifth step is twofold. First, the marriages in question are extremely harmful, and simple prohibition has proved ineffective. Invalidation is the only remedy. Second, only a general council can raise the level of prohibition to invalidation, because of its universality, the broad range of expertise that it represents, and its special authority. If invalidation is expedient, therefore, it is urgently expedient to enact the law now.

The errors in question undermine all the goods and goals of marriage, Guerrero claims. Consider Augustine's three goods of marriage: faith, offspring, and sacrament. As a result of clandestinity or lack of parental consent, the offspring are illegitimate, fidelity is missing, and the sacrament is profaned by sacrilege. Marriage is supposed to reconcile families and to extend peace, but these marriages cause disputation, dissent, and enmity, especially among noble families. People are murdered, witnesses perjure themselves, and fathers die from grief. Moreover, such marriages often turn out badly, leading to mutual hatred or adultery. Elsewhere, Guerrero cites covert adultery as the most serious hazard of clandestine marriage: when someone marries one person clandestinely, in the private forum, but then marries a second person publicly, in the public forum. There is no remedy in such cases, and invalidation is the only way to prevent the abuse.[76] This was the classic example of the dangers of clandestinity, which Hugh of Saint-Victor had expounded at length in the 1130s,[77] and it was the only hazard cited in the decree *Tametsi*. (It appeared in all the drafts as well as in the final version.) There was no remedy because the church could make judgments only on the basis of evidence in the public forum.

GUERRERO'S THEORY OF LAWS

Guerrero's theory of laws is broadly Thomistic, and he cites Thomas to substantiate several of the key points of his argument. No other schoolman gets more than one or two citations in the treatise, but Guerrero cites fifteen texts from Thomas explicitly: two from the *Summa theologiae* and the

76.   359v–360r (178–79).
77.   *De sacramentis christianae fidei* II.11.6, PL 176:488C–490D.

others from Thomas's *Scriptum* on Book IV of Peter Lombard's *Sentences*. Guerrero could have found the latter in the posthumous *Supplementum* to the *Summa*, but in fact he provides references to the *Scriptum* itself.

Most of the passages from Thomas that Guerrero cites pertain to the rightful power of human authorities, whether secular or ecclesiastical, to make positive laws. Thomas's early *Scriptum* is a richer source of reflection on the positivity of law than his *Summa theologiae*,[78] and Thomas develops this aspect of his thought in the former work mainly in relation to marriage law. Two texts from Thomas that Guerrero cites, taken together, seem in retrospect to contain the germ of Guerrero's own theory. In one, from a discussion of nonage, Thomas says that since marrying is a species of contract, it is "subject to the ordination of positive law, as are other contracts."[79] In the other, Thomas considers a complex objection to the church's ability to introduce impediments, one strand of which is that no impediments can be introduced because marriage is a divinely instituted sacrament. In his reply, Thomas points out that marriage, unlike the other sacraments, is not *only* a sacrament, and that positive human law must adapt to the changing circumstances of human kind.[80] Guerrero deduces from these texts that human law may prohibit what natural or divine law concedes or permits.[81]

Following Aristotle, Thomas held that positive law introduced precepts of right and wrong where the natural law was indifferent, and that the citizens' obligation to obey such laws began in the will of the legislator and could not be traced back to the natural law or discovered through reason.[82] But Thomas held that the purpose of positive law (or of human law, as he calls it in the *Summa theologiae*) is to embody and to realize the natural law. Some positive laws that are close to the natural law are derived from it in a quasi-deductive manner, but most positive laws arise through a process of "determination," whereby the extremely general principles of the natural law

78. J. Finnis, "The Truth in Legal Positivism," in R. P. George, ed., *The Autonomy of Law: Essays on Legal Positivism* (Oxford, 1996), 195–214, is a good introduction, although it misses some of the ground that Thomas covers in the *Scriptum*.

79. *IV Sent.* 36.un.5, resp. (185a).

80. *IV Sent.*, 34.un.1, ad 4 (164b).

81. Objection 11, 374r–v (201).

82. Aristotle, *Nicomachean Ethics* V.7, 1134b18–35. Thomas Aquinas, *Sententia libri Ethicorum* V, lect. 12, on 1134b18–19 (*Opera omnia*, Leonine edition, 47.2: 304–05); *III Sent.* 37.un.3, ad 2 (ed. Moos [Paris, 1947], 3: 1245).

are applied to particular situations and circumstances in a particular community.[83] The more remote the laws are in relation to the first principles of the
natural law, the more they are prone to exceptions. Positive laws are beneficial
only in the majority of cases, therefore, and they are capable of dispensation.[84]

Guerrero, too, emphasizes that the church's laws must adapt to current exigencies. Only natural or divine laws are perpetual, whereas human
laws, even those of the church, are and must be changeable.[85] Some of the
opponents at Trent objected that by invalidating the marriages in question
the church would be agreeing with the Protestant heretics and implicitly
committing the same heresy. Guerrero argued in response that whereas the
Protestants claimed that the natural law invalidated clandestine marriages, the council was proposing that the *church* should invalidate clandestine
marriages. This policy would emphasize what the Protestants deny: the
power of the church over marriage.[86] In the treatise, Guerrero refutes the
arguments used at Trent to show that the necessary conditions of marriage
are unchanging, and he ridicules the opponents of invalidation for using
them. They argue, for example, that if the church were able to invalidate
marriages in question, it would have done so before,[87] and that marriage is
a natural rather than a civil contract.[88] Guerrero marvels that they cannot
grasp how weak such arguments are.[89] Everything that the church does or
teaches changes and evolves over time, according to the circumstances of
each place and each era. Even the truth about God is revealed and made
explicit only gradually and partially, at appropriate times and places, under
the providential guidance of the Holy Spirit.[90]

83.   *IV Sent.* 26.2.2, ad 1 (Vivès edition, 11: 73a) and 36.un.1, ad 3 (181a)

84.   *IV Sent.* 15.3.2, qu³ 1, resp. (ed. Moos, 712, §423).

85.   Objection 2, 366v–367r (190–92). Cf. Granatensis, CT 9: 644/28–29: "Re-
spondit ad id, quod dicitur, numquam id fuisse factum in ecclesia: quia nihil fieret de novo,
si semper attenderetur ad ea tantum, quae facta sunt."

86.   Granatensis, CT 9: 781/11–15.

87.   Objection 1, 365r–366r (188–90). Guerrero develops this argument at Objection 12, 376r–v (205–207).

88.   Objection 10, 371r (197).

89.   Ibid., 371v (198): "Mirum est, quod hii homines non intelligant suarum ratio-
num fragilitatem."

90.   Objection 1, 366v/17–20 (190): "Sic Spiritus sanctus docet ecclesiam omnem
veritatem suis locis et temporibus prout ipsi expedit scire, non omnia simul, sed ordinate
et quando necessarium est...."

Guerrero is especially interested in the determination of human or ecclesiastical laws in relation to foundations in natural or divine law. Human or ecclesiastical law has the power to prohibit or command what natural or divine law concedes or permits. In developing the first of his five conclusions, as we have seen, Guerrero argues that the proposed decree would determine natural or divine law by changing concession into prohibition. He likens that determination to what happens when a universal cause, such as the sun or the heavens, works through a secondary cause, such as a parent or a fire.[91] Guerrero extends this simile later in the treatise to illuminate the natural progression from simple prohibition to invalidation. When a universal cause prohibits something, it may concur with a secondary cause that causes what is prohibited, or it may prevent that outcome. For example, although God prohibits evil acts, he usually concurs with their secondary causes, but he sometimes intervenes miraculously, as when he prevented the three men from being consumed in the fiery furnace (Dan 3:19–27). In the same way, the church formerly concurred with the marriage contracts that it prohibited, but there is nothing to stop the church from preventing them now. But God also bestows something akin to his universal power on the republic or on the church, to which the actions of individuals are subordinated. Whether in the workings of nature or of grace, therefore, and whether in the universe as a whole or in the body politic as a whole, God disposes everything sweetly and everything is coordinated, just as a hand or other member of the human body does not act without the subject's consent and concurrence.[92]

Guerrero pursues a different but not incompatible approach in developing the third of the five theses. The proposed law invalidating clandestine marriages and marriages without parental consent determines natural or divine law, but the superior law is not merely indifferent. There are three possibilities to be considered. Natural or divine law may (1) concede or permit people to marry thus, or (2) command them to so do, or (3) prohibit them from doing so. Obviously, the superior law does not command, for then even the church's current prohibition would be iniquitous. Nor can the higher law concede or permit, for in that case the church would have

91. Conclusion 1, 350r–351r (162–64).
92. Objection 4, 368v–369r (193–94).

the power to *command* people to marry clandestinely or without parental consent, by determining at the lower level what is indefinite at the higher level. The only possibility that remains, therefore, is that natural or divine law *prohibits* the marriages in question, albeit without invalidating them. That being so, what is to prevent the church from determining the superior law by raising the level of prohibition to invalidation?[93]

Until the appendix, as we have seen, Guerrero treats natural and divine law as an unanalyzed inclusive disjunction, and he treats human law and ecclesiastical law in the same way. Guerrero resolves this lack of definition at the end of the treatise, when he explains the multiple senses of the term "divine law." Now it becomes clear that both natural law and what he calls positive divine law are branches of divine law,[94] and that both civil law and ecclesiastical law are branches of human law. Guerrero explains that a species or branch of law gets its name from the legislator: human laws are made by human beings, whereas divine laws are made by God.[95] This is a departure from Thomas in the *Summa theologiae*, who defines the branches teleologically: Human law leads to the natural, temporal perfection of human beings as human beings, whereas divine law leads to eternal beatitude.[96]

In the order of created reality, Guerrero explains, everything is the work of God in a broad sense, but some things are more properly said to be God's work than others, for God works on three levels. First, God makes some things without working with or through secondary, created causes. God makes the angels, the heavens, the four elements, and human souls in this way, and he justifies souls in the same unmediated manner. Second, God also works with or through creatures to achieve things that are beyond their powers. In some cases, as in the miracle of the fiery furnace, the power that God supra-naturally bestows is natural *per se*. In others, as with the sacraments, God bestows supernatural powers on created things.[97] Third,

93.   Conclusion 3, 359v–361r (178–80).

94.   381v/18–19 (215): "Est etiam ius divinum duplex, naturale scilicet sive naturae, et positivum, quod vocatur ut condistinguatur naturali." Medieval theologians usually reserve the term "positive" for human law in contradistinction to natural law.

95.   Objection 12, 381r–v (215).

96.   *Summa theologiae* I-II.91.4 (1212a).

97.   Guerrero is presupposing the theory that the sacraments are physical instrumental causes, which the Dominicans espoused. The Franciscans preferred the theory of covenantal or moral causality.

God works through secondary natural causes in a natural way, using the innate powers that he instilled in them by creating them. Such are the mundane physical motions of generation and corruption. These, too, are works of God, but they are less properly so called than works of the first and second kinds.[98]

Similarly, all law is divine law in the broadest sense, but some branches of law are more properly called divine than others. First, God promulgates some laws directly, without using human mediators. Such is the Decalogue and the natural law: both the law that human beings share with all animals and the *ius gentium*. Such, too, are the laws that God reveals directly to angels, prophets, and holy persons, inasmuch as he reveals them thus. Second, God uses human beings as messengers (*nuncii, praecones*), who announce his laws to the people. Then an angel or a prophet begins by saying, "Thus says the Lord." And that is why St. Paul says, "The Lord says, not I" (1 Cor 7:10). Such laws are properly called laws of God (*leges Dei*) and divine laws (*iura divina*). Third, God appoints human beings to make laws and gives them the power to do so: not as messengers but as legislators. That is why St. Paul says, "I say, not the Lord" (1 Cor 7:12). Moses, too, promulgated precepts in his own name (*suo nomine*). Kings and other secular legislators have this role, as well as prophets and apostles, for all regulatory power comes from God (Rom 13:1–7). These human laws, too, are divine, but in a secondary sense. Moreover, some of them deserve the term "divine" more than others. Canon law is more properly called divine than civil or political law because it is more closely related to the supernatural law revealed in Scripture, and because it is more immediately directed to the supernatural end of human beings. Within the field of ecclesiastical law, laws that regulate more spiritual matters or that are more arduous, such as those regarding fasting and almsgiving, are more properly called divine than the other ecclesiastical laws.[99]

Just as civil laws determine and are subordinate to the law of nature, Guerrero claims, so ecclesiastical laws determine and are subordinate to divine law. "Ecclesiastical or canon laws," he writes, "are related to the super-

---

98.   382r–v (216–17).
99.   382v–383r (217–19).

natural law of God as civil laws are to the law of nature."[100] It seems, then, that in his view canon law is not simply a mixture of temporal and spiritual laws (as, I think, most scholastic theologians assumed). Rather, it is a determination of positive divine law, just as civil law is a determination of the natural law and the *ius gentium*. Whether this conclusion is consistent with Guerrero's claim that the church has plenary power over the republic is a question that I shall not pursue here.

---

100.   383v/1–2 (219): "Habent enim se ecclesiastica seu canonica iura ad legem Dei supernaturalem, ut civilia ad legem naturae...."

Some Elizabethan Marriage Cases

Sir John Baker

For many centuries, and until comparatively recently, the law of property leaned heavily on the law of marriage. Upon the death of a landowner most real property, subject to the rights of a surviving spouse (usually interests for life), devolved upon the heir, whose identity was determined by the automatic operation of fixed canons of descent. This was the position not only in the case of a fee simple at common law but also where there was a gift in tail or a family settlement effected through a trust. In all these cases the passing of property depended on the existence of a valid marriage, either of the spouse or of the heir's parents or ancestors. Usually this gave rise to no legal difficulty. When it did, the basic legal principle was clear. Although any litigation over real property belonged exclusively to the royal courts, questions of marriage and bastardy belonged exclusively to the ecclesiastical courts. In accordance with this principle, if issue was joined in a common-law court on bastardy, or upon the plea "never joined in lawful matrimony," a writ went to the bishop of the appropriate diocese to determine the question, and his certificate was conclusive.[1] The break with Rome did not affect this regime, since the bishop of Rome had never been

---

1.   If, however, the facts were not pleaded but found by a special verdict, a common-law court could decide whether they disclosed a valid marriage: *Holliday v. Hethe* (1585) Cambridge University Library [CUL] MS Ii. 5. 38, fol. 12v (private marriage ceremony performed before Lord Hunsdon and his chaplain); below, n. 19.

a bishop with whom the king's judges were in procedural communion.[2] It was in any case of the essence of the Elizabethan Church of England that it was still part of the catholic church, the *ecclesia anglicana* of Magna Carta,[3] even though appeals to the pope were no longer allowed. According to the now prevailing common-law position, the discontinuance of such appeals was not a fundamental innovation, since the king had always been supreme head of the Church for the purposes of English law. This position was argued with much common-law learning in the widely circulated preface to Richard Gynes's reading in the Inner Temple (on tithes) during Lent 1568, which has received little or no attention from modern scholars.[4] It was revisited at some length in James Morice's reading in the Middle Temple in 1578,[5] and was also the subject of an argument in court by Serjeant Fletewoode in 1583, citing biblical authorities.[6] It followed from this continuity that the medieval canon law, including the papal decretals, remained of au-

---

2.   The royal judges could not send a writ to the pope: YB Mich. 8 Hen. VI, fol. 3, pl. 8, *per* Chauntrell serjeant; YB Mich. 12 Edw. IV, fol. 15, pl. 18; *Sonde v. Pekham* (1484–9) Public Record Office [PRO], KB 27/909, m. 76; YB Mich. 2 Ric. III, fol. 4, pl. 8; YB Trin. 4 Hen. VII, fol. 13, pl. 12; J. Baker, *Oxford History of the Laws of England*, VI (Oxford, 2003), 238.

3.   The apostolic succession was achieved via three former diocesans who had been deprived of their sees under Mary I, and one suffragan, a circumstance which caused some temporary qualms about the formal requirements for consecration: see J. H. Baker, *Reports from the Lost Notebooks of Sir James Dyer*, I, Selden Society 109 (1994), introduction, lxviii–lxix.

4.   British Library [BL] MS Harley 813, fols. 111–118v; MS Add. 11405, fols. 5–13v; MS Add. 28607, fols. 3–11; Lincoln's Inn [LI], MS Hale 80, fols. 188–197; Exeter College, Oxford, MS 101, fols. 7–13; Folger Shakespeare Library, Washington, D.C., MS V. b. 74, fols. 227v–237.

5.   BL MS Egerton 2376, at fols. 46–60, in the polished redaction prepared at the instance of Lord Burghley. Morice's principal subtext, as a Puritan lawyer, was that the royal supremacy was a matter of common law, so that the royal judges had a general superintendency over the legal activities of the Church, and in particular had the power to restrain abuses by the High Commission of the oath *ex officio*.

6.   *Bishop of Salisbury v. Pytchaver* (1583), BL MS Harley 4988, fols. 14v–16v, *per* Fletewoode serjeant ("Le pape ne unques avoyt aucthorytye in temporal ou spiritual causes in Engleterre. Primerment il prove per scripture que le roy est supreme teste in spiritual et temporal causes deins son realme. Et il dit que il ne forsque voile voucher ces comen places descripture a prover ceo queux fueront vouche per les sage judges de cest realme in 26 H. 8 quant Cromwel per comandment le roy assemblea les judges et les expertes homes de cest realme darguer cest matter...").

thority. Indeed, both temporal and spiritual courts were required by statute to allow and follow the old canon law in so far as it was not contrariant
or repugnant to the laws and customs of the realm.[7] Professor Helmholz
has demonstrated how immune that learning was to successive changes of
ecclesiastical regime.[8]

The clear division of responsibility between the two jurisdictions
should have been impervious to legal maneuvering, or so one might have
thought. Moreover, the law of marriage was a minefield into which common lawyers might well have feared to tread.[9] A group of cases from the
Elizabethan courts of King's Bench[10] and Common Pleas shows that the
reality was not quite so straightforward. If enough turned upon the outcome, questions of marriage law could be aired in the temporal courts, and
if necessary doctors of Civil law might be brought in to assist, or sometimes
to confuse.

THE FORMATION OF MARRIAGE

Perhaps the most important Elizabethan case concerning the formation of
marriage occurred in the first few years of the reign. Though of immense
significance to the future of the monarchy, it rested on fact rather than
law. Lady Katherine Grey,[11] sister of Lady Jane Grey and claimant to the
throne under the terms of Henry VIII's will, had lain with Edward Seymour, the young earl of Hertford, and become pregnant. They were both
committed to the Tower, where they had managed to gain further access
to each other and Katherine had become pregnant again. Their supporters
believed the truth of the matter to be that they had contracted to marry
per sponsalia de futuro, and had gone through a secret ceremony of marriage

---

7.   25 Hen. VIII, c. 19, the final proviso. The statute is still in force.

8.   R. H. Helmholz, *Roman Canon Law in Reformation England* (Cambridge,
1990).

9.   Ibid. 76–7.

10.   We have Sir Edward Coke's authority for so referring to the court during the
reign of a queen. On the other hand, Sir John Popham and Sir Thomas Egerton, as law
officers, said it became the Queen's Bench: CUL MS Dd. 11. 64, fol. 48.

11.   She had been previously married, at the age of twelve, to Henry Herbert, but
that marriage had been annulled.

in the presence of a priest (who could not subsequently be traced), though to avoid incurring the queen's displeasure it had been done in private, with no other witnesses, and kept secret. Since the canon law required two witnesses, this seemed to fall into the awkward category of a valid marriage which was incapable of legal proof.[12] The parties could be required by law to live apart, even though they were morally obliged in conscience to live together. This was not a question which could safely be left to an ordinary ecclesiastical court, and so it was referred in January 1562 to a commission of delegates consisting of divines and Civilians, together with the Master of the Rolls (Sir William Cordell) and Mr. Justice Weston, presided over by Archbishop Parker. Their conclusion, embodied in a formal decree on 12 May, was that there was no marriage and that the parties had therefore committed fornication.[13] Some considered this decision an affront to good conscience as well as natural justice.[14] The earl's supporters procured John Hales, clerk of the hanaper, to frame a case (omitting the real names) for submission to law faculties in Italy and Germany, following the precedent of Henry VIII's divorce case, and also to write a treatise on the succession; for this effrontery Hales spent two or three years in the Tower.[15] In so far as there was any point of law in the original case, it perhaps lay in the underlying assumption that those in the immediate line of succession to the crown needed royal consent to marry, although the omission to obtain such consent was only a punishable offence rather than an impediment.[16] But the decision on the facts, however dubious, was momentous in ensuring

12.   See R. H. Helmholz, *Marriage Litigation in Medieval England* (Cambridge, 1974), 62–4.

13.   *The Earl of Hertford's Case* (1562–3), Baker, *Reports from the Lost Notebooks of Sir James Dyer*, I, 81. There are contemporary accounts of the proceedings in BL Cotton MS Vitellius C. XVI, part ii, fols. 459–462 (including a copy of the decree); MS Add. 33749.

14.   It was alleged that witnesses had been heard in the absence of the parties, the latter "havinge noe proctour nor counsell" (Cotton MS).

15.   *Hales' Case* (1564), Baker, *Reports from the Lost Notebooks of Sir James Dyer*, I, 92, 94. There are references there to further literature. Hales' principal offence was contempt of the delegates, in saying that they had given an unjust sentence contrary to their consciences. See also the entries on John Hales and Catherine and Edward Seymour in *ODNB*.

16.   It was made an impediment by the Royal Marriages Act 1772 (12 Geo. III, c. 11), recently amended by the Succession to the Crown Act 2013 (c. 20).

the later succession of the House of Stuart. The earl survived into the next reign, having been passed over as a possible heir to the throne, and in 1604 thought the time might be ripe to seek a reversal of the 1562 decree. That, however, could not be allowed. The matter was still too dangerous, since Katherine's son was still living.[17]

CAPACITY

The law of marriage was untouched, of course, by the Tridentine reforms in the Roman Church.[18] A marriage in private, though irregular, was still valid. The validity of private marriages was confirmed by the King's Bench in the 1580s,[19] although it had been doubted about fifteen years earlier.[20] Edward Coke was awkwardly reminded of the consequences of irregularity when attorney-general, after marrying the young Lady Hatton privately and at night in Hatton House in 1598. His somewhat disingenuous defense that he was ignorant of ecclesiastical law may have softened the penalty imposed by Archbishop Whitgift;[21] but fate was to arrange that his real punishment would be the marriage itself.

Although there was no reform from without, the law relating to the formation of marriage had nevertheless been altered in two or three ways in 1540. The previous canon law had recognized as impediments to marriage a

---

17.   Some of the cause papers are in BL Cotton MS Vitellius C. XVI, part ii, fols. 413–421, 463–471, 516–517, 622. A commission was appointed on 28 Feb. 1604/5, consisting of Sir Julius Caesar, Dr. Dunne, Sir Richard Swale and Sir John Bennett. The son was styled Viscount Beaumont, as if he were legitimate, but in the event he predeceased his father.

18.   See Helmholz, *Roman Canon Law in Reformation England*, 69–73.

19.   See *Holliday v. Hethe* (1585), above, n. 1; also reported in BL MS Lansdowne 1104, fol. 89v (1586). The question, raised by a special verdict in ejectment, was whether a marriage conducted in a chamber at Somerset House by a minister, in the presence of Lord Hunsdon, was valid.

20.   Ibid.: "...Et Wray [C.J.] dit que devant, in dower port per Serjeant Manwood [1567/72] pur un fem, Bendlos voile aver demurr sur ceo quia le fem esteant marie in un chamber ne unques fuit accouple in loial matrimony."

21.   R. B. Outhwaite, *Clandestine Marriage in England 1500–1850* (London, 1995), 23. The case was cited by Dr. Andrews in *Middleton v. Croft* (1734) Cas. t. Hard. 57 at 58, from Archbishop Whitgift's register.

precontract to marry another, even if not consummated by carnal copulation, and also various relationships through kindred or affinity beyond those mentioned in the Book of Leviticus. Parliament asserted in 1540, with some semblance of fair comment,[22] that these impediments had been devised by the Roman Curia in order to make money from dispensations, and that their consequence was sometimes to invalidate marriages of long standing "and many just marriages brought in doubt and danger of undoing." It was therefore enacted that no marriage which had been solemnized in church, and consummated, should be impeached unless it was contrary to God's law.[23] The statute was repealed in respect of the impediment of precontract in 1548 and in its entirety between 1554 and 1558.[24] The law of precontract, having thus been rescued from permanent extinction, came to be discussed in *Dr Julio's Case* in the 1570s. The queen's physician, Dr. Giulio Borgarucci (commonly known as Dr. Julio), after eighteen years of marriage to Alice Nosworthy, decided that the marriage was void for precontract and married another woman. Although he eventually obtained a formal divorce, despite strenuous opposition from the archbishop of Canterbury and his official principal,[25] the sentence was not given until 1577, after the second marriage had taken place.[26] The common-law judges held that the second marriage was nevertheless valid, without any new solemnization, because the first was void *ab initio*.[27] Here

22.   Whether dispensations were in practice very common is debatable: Helmholz, *Marriage Litigation in Medieval England*, 85. But cf. ibid. 64 ("There was no preference in the canon law for the settled marriage as against a mere contract by words of present consent").

23.   32 Hen. VIII, c. 38.

24.   2 & 3 Edw. VI, c. 23; 2 & 3 Ph. & Mar., c. 8; 1 Eliz. I, c. 1. For a discussion by a contemporary canonist of the effect of this legislation on marriage by cousins german see BL Cotton MS Vitellius C. XVI, fols. 216–223.

25.   Thomas Yale, LL.D. (Cantab.), official principal and judge of the Court of Audience, who died in Nov. 1577. He was dean of the Arches 1567–73.

26.   Camden reported a contemporary rumor that the business was the principal factor contributing to Grindal's disgrace and suspension by the queen in that year. See BL Cotton MS Titus B. VII, fol. 36 (letter from Borgarucci to Leicester, 4 Dec. 1576), printed in *Leicester's Commonwealth*, ed. D. C. Peck (Athens, Ohio, 1985), 275 (with commentary at 274–6); P. Collinson, *The Elizabethan Puritan Movement* (Oxford, 1967), 198; *Archbishop Grindal 1519–1583* (Berkeley, 1979), 254–5; *Godly People* (London, 1983), 378.

27.   *Dr Julio's Case* (1577 or later) BL MS Add. 35951, fol. 111v. The report occurs in the manuscript as an appendix to *Bury's Case* (1598), to be considered below. The doctor died in 1581.

a divorce decree was apparently unnecessary.[28] The logic of nullity was that the parties could "divorce" themselves, since the issue in any subsequent proceedings concerning their marital status would not be whether they should have obtained a judicial decree but whether the first marriage was in fact void. Automatic nullity could also be raised after the parties' deaths: that had been King Richard III's case in seeking a posthumous declaratory annulment of Edward IV's marriage. Although the logic had been temporarily superseded by the statute of 1540, it had returned with the restoration of the impediment.[29] Self-help divorce was, nevertheless, precarious unless the divorcing party had evidence which would satisfy an ecclesiastical court in case of subsequent dispute; and, in the absence of depositions, this would require any witnesses to remain alive. That may have been one of the reasons why Henry VIII had thought it necessary or desirable to obtain formal divorces from his own wives; the descent of the crown could not be left in evidential doubt. A more difficult question arose in 1591: what if there *was* a judicial divorce, but the marriage had not contravened the law of God? A man had married his deceased wife's sister's daughter and the High Commission had decreed a divorce, even though such marriages were not within the Levitical injunctions. The King's Bench at first took the view that such a marriage was odious and that its validity was a matter for the spiritual court to decide.[30] The following term, however, it was held that the court could grant a prohibition, by reason of the Henrician legislation. In the immediate case it declined

28. For "self-divorce" in an earlier period see Helmholz, *Marriage Litigation in Medieval England*, 59–64.

29. See *Bunting v. Leppingwell* (1585), below, 197–99. Cf. *Riddlesden v. Wogan* (1601) Cro. Eliz. 858, where in debt on a bond the defendant pleaded that at the time of the bond she was married to John Inglebert and so it was not her deed. The plaintiff replied that after the bond was made there was a suit in the spiritual court and the marriage was declared void because Inglebert had another wife living. The defendant demurred in law on the ground that this decree was made after the bond, and until the decree there was a marriage de facto; but the plaintiff had judgment. The divorce decree was merely declaratory of what had always been the case, and no sentence was needed to make it so.

30. *Anon.* (Hilary term, 1591) BL MS Harley 2036, fol. 30v: "Mes touts les justices contra et que fuit trop odious, et pur ceo consultation fuit grant, car an soit encontre le Leviticall ley ou nemy covient destre adjudge per lespirituall judge et nemy in cest court per le comon ley." Presumably this is the same case as that in the following footnote.

to do so because the application was made in general terms when it should have been special;[31] but such prohibitions are found in the following century.[32]

Another new question considered by the judges was whether the children of priests were legitimate. The lawfulness of priests' marriages had been confirmed by Parliament in 1548, and the statute was retrospective except in cases where a divorce had formally been decreed.[33] This legislation was, however, repealed in the time of Mary I and not revived until the reign of James I.[34] It is said that Elizabeth I did not like priests to be married. This may explain why the Common Pleas was asked as late as 1572 whether the issue of a priest was capable of inheriting land.[35] Chief Justice Dyer said that the very point had been argued at the bar recently by doctors of law and that he was still in doubt whether the issue were legitimate. But the other justices thought it clear that they were. For one thing, the marriage of priests had already been rendered lawful before 1548 by the statute of 1540,[36] since it was not against the law of God. Dyer said, "he well remembered that Dr. Redman, one of the aforesaid doctors, said that English priests did not vow chastity, unless silently, whereas all other priests did so."[37] Perhaps more decisively, the common law had always regarded such a marriage as voidable rather than void, so that if one of the parties died before any divorce was sought the issue were legitimate. That had been settled by all the judges of England in the Exchequer Chamber in the last quarter of the fifteenth century.[38]

---

31.   *Man's Case* (Easter term, 1591) Cro. Eliz. 228; 4 Leon. 16; Moo. K.B. 907 (says the prohibition was granted).

32.   Helmholz, *Roman Canon Law in Reformation England*, 74–6.

33.   2 & 3 Edw. VI, c 21; reinforced by 5 Edw. VI, c. 12.

34.   1 Mar. I, st. 2, c. 2. The legislation is discussed in 2 Co. Inst. 686–7.

35.   *Anon.* (1572) LI MS Maynard 77, fol. 94 ("Gawdy serjant mova cest case pur estre advise per le court..."). The report does not say when the marriage took place.

36.   32 Hen. VIII, c. 38; above, at n. 23.

37.   Ibid. ("Dyer dit que il bien remember que Doctor Redman, un de les doctours avandites, disoit quod sacerdotes Anglicani non voverunt castitatem nisi silencio sed quod alii sacerdotes voverunt expressement et affirmaverunt"). The identity of Dr. Redman is elusive. The only advocate of this name in Squibb's list is Robert Redman, who took his LL.D. at Cambridge in 1586 and was admitted in 1590: G. D. Squibb, *Doctors' Commons* (Oxford, 1977), 205 (mistakenly says Oxford). (Biographical information about other doctors mentioned below is taken from Squibb.)

38.   Pas. 19 Hen. VII, Fitz. Abr., *Bastardy*, pl. 33; reprinted in YB Mich. 21 Hen. VII, fol. 39, pl. 53. Fitzherbert was reporting what Frowyk C.J. and Vavasour J. told him in

The more legally interesting cases in the law reports, to which we now turn, concerned the practice of infant marriage. Heirs and heiresses to landed estates were commonly married by their guardians while under the notional age of puberty, which was fixed by law as twelve for girls and fourteen for boys. Such a marriage was a good marriage *de facto*, but did not constitute full lawful matrimony and when the parties arrived at the age of puberty they could disagree to it. In the event of disagreement the marriage became a nullity retrospectively and the parties were free to marry again.[39] On the other hand, if they agreed to remain married, either expressly or by implication, for instance by cohabitation and consummation, the marriage became permanent.[40] This was the background to *Mynne's Case*, which occupied the courts for eight years in the 1570s.

MARRIAGE BELOW THE AGE OF DISCRETION: MYNNE'S CASE (1572–80)[41]

Elizabeth, daughter of Robert Drury of Hawstead, Suffolk, on 18 March 1566 married the sickly eleven year-old Thomas de Grey (1555–66), only son

---

1504, but the case had been reserved at Warwick assizes by Fairfax J. (d. 1495) and Vavasour J. It concerned the marriage of a deacon, but the point of law was the same. Monks and nuns were, however, in a different position since they were *civiliter mortui*.

39. A disagreement before the appointed age had no legal effect: *Bannester's Case* (1582–3) 4 Co. Rep. 17; Coke's notebook, BL MS Harley 6686, fol. 404. Each party retained the right to disagree until they were *both* over the appointed age: *Babington v. Warner* (1600) MS Harley 6686, fol. 404 ("Mes nota si le home soit 14 et la fem infra annos nubiles, ou si fem soit ouster 12 et le home deins 14, uncore le home ou feme que soit supra annos nubiles poet disagree auxi quant lauter vient al age de consent"); BL MS Add. 48186, fol. 245 (citing Pas. 41 Eliz., rot. 668); Moo. K.B. 575; 3 Co. Inst. 89. Dr. Crompton said in this case that a party only had three days to disagree before or after reaching the age of discretion.

40. In *Anon.* (1582) BL MS Lansdowne 1104, fol. 52v, Serjeant Fletewoode argued that the assent ought to be recorded in a spiritual court, and that this had been decided in the Duchy [Council] in the time of Queen Mary. The King's Bench judges do not seem to have agreed with him.

41. *Mynne's* (or *Myn's*) *Case* (1572–80) Dyer 305, 313, 368; Dyer's notebook, J. H. Baker, ed., *Reports from the Lost Notebooks of Sir James Dyer*, II, Selden Society 110 (1995), 379; Dal. 79; BL MS Hargrave 9, fols. 44–45; MS Add. 35942, fols. 8–9; Bodleian Lib., Oxford, MS Rawlinson C. 728, fols. 207v–208v (copy writs and certificates); CUL MS Mm. 4. 31, fol. 3; LI MS Misc. 487, fols. 6v–8.

and heir of Thomas de Grey (d. 1562)[42] of Merton, Norfolk, by arrangement with his guardian. The boy died shortly afterwards in the same year and the inheritance went to his uncle Robert.[43] Elizabeth then married Nicholas Mynne (or Myn) of Little Walsingham, Norfolk. Mynne is an obscure figure, the obscurity resulting in part from the number of namesakes. Canon Augustus Jessopp wrote, in evident exasperation, that he "belonged to a malignant family who christened their sons Nicholas again and again with no other object than to puzzle genealogists."[44] He has nevertheless been identified on convincing grounds as a servant of the duke of Norfolk who served as a member of Parliament for various constituencies belonging to the duke between 1558 and 1572. The *History of Parliament* says that nothing is known about him after 1572, the year of the duke's fall.[45] But that is to ignore the celebrated dower suit which he and Elizabeth brought against uncle Robert. This was commenced in 1571 and rumbled on for the rest of the decade. The action was met by a plea of "never joined in lawful matrimony," and a writ was duly sent on 30 October to the bishop of Norwich, John Parkhurst, to determine the question. It has been credibly asserted that Parkhurst wanted to help the Mynnes,[46] though he seems at first sight to have done so in an inept way. A simple certificate that the marriage with Thomas had been valid would have given Elizabeth her dower without further debate. But that, as we now know from extrinsic sources, is just what

42. Of Gray's Inn, son of Edmund de Grey (d. 1547), bencher of Gray's Inn, and Elizabeth Spelman.

43. Robert took the precaution of making Thomas suffer a recovery in his favor shortly before his death: Norfolk Record Office, WLS/IV/1/407 x 6. His patent of livery is no. 2 in the same bundle.

44. *The Visitation of Norfolk in the Year 1563*, ed. Brig.-Gen. [L.] Bulwer, II (Norwich, 1895), at 212.

45. *The History of Parliament: the House of Commons 1558–1603*, ed. P. W. Hasler (London, 1981), III, 117; cf. earlier namesakes in J. Baker, *The Men of Court 1440 to 1550*, Selden Society Supplementary Series 18 (London, 2012), II, 1142. He was dead before 1596, when his widow Elizabeth was lady of the manor of Hillington, Warwickshire, by survivorship: Shakespeare Centre, Stratford-upon-Avon, Warwickshire, DR 10/2369.

46. Jessopp, cited in the *Visitation of Norfolk*, ed. Bulwer, n. 44 above. This is almost certainly true, since the bishop wrote in 1572 that he was "willing to pleasure the gentlewoman in this case (law and conscience not offended)...": *The Letter Book of John Parkhurst, Bishop of Norwich, Compiled During the Years 1571–5*, ed. R. A. Houlbrooke, Norfolk Record Society 43 (Norwich, 1974), 123.

he was advised not to do, on the ground that the espousals did not amount under the canon law to "lawful matrimony."[47] In order to avoid this difficulty Parkhurst certified the facts, namely that the couple entered into a contract *per verba de praesenti* when the husband was "around 12" and the wife 16, and procured it to be solemnized in Baconthorpe church, Norfolk. The Court of Common Pleas rejected this as unsatisfactory, since it did not expressly find whether the marriage was valid or not, and ordered a writ *de melius certiorando*. The bishop complained to the chancellor of his diocese, William Maister, LL.D. (Cantab.), who advised him that, although he was inclined to favor Mynne, the certificate must state simply whether the marriage was lawful or not, and that on the facts it must state that it was not. The following day the bishop received a letter from Dr. Thomas Wilson, another Cambridge LL.D., strongly urging the contrary; the parties had been married *in facie ecclesiae* by the bishop's license, and "as all men know, *consensus non concubitus facit matrimonium*." This seems a disingenuous argument, since the true question was whether the consent was vitiated by infancy.[48] The bishop replied that he found himself in a quandary, that he had asked Chief Justice Dyer for more time, and had advised Mynne "to procure me the judgment of some of the Arches, under their handes, wherein also I wish you be one; so that I may be sufficiently defended in that I shold certefye...and that cheifelye because I wold in the tyme have my chauncellor somewhat satisfied." The bishop himself subsequently selected three doctors of the Arches (Doctors Gibbon, Dale and Huick), who advised him in March that he should state the husband's age exactly (instead of "around 12")[49] and state more directly that the parties had lawfully solemnized the marriage (instead of saying that they "procured the solemnization"), "and soe declare the facte as it was in trothe, leaving the judge-

47. The following information is from *The Letter Book of John Parkhurst*, 101 (writ from the Common Pleas), 105 (letter from Dr. Maister, 19 Jan. 1572), 107 (letter from Dr. Wilson, 20 Jan. 1572, with reply), 110 (bishop's letter to Dyer C.J., 26 Jan. 1572), 111 (bishop's letter to Dr. Wilson), 122–3 (letter seeking the opinion of three doctors), 123–4 (their opinions, dated 28 March 1571, *recte* 1572), 124 (form of Latin certificate recommended to be used, and an opinion of Dr. Drury), 125–6 (opinion of four Civilians), 126–7 (advice from Serjeants Manwood and Mead), 225 (letter from Burghley).
48. Cf. Coke's argument, below, 195.
49. The next certificate gave the husband's age precisely as 11 years, 10 months and 20 days.

ment upon this declaration of the facte to the courte, which we take to be the most aggreable to lawe, equitie and conscience." This equitable course was adopted, and the result was that the bishop was fined £20 for another bad return.[50] The bishop then sent a third certificate, finding the facts as before but adding the conclusion "and so were joined in lawful matrimony." Whether this was a good return occasioned another full argument in the Common Pleas.[51] Serjeants Rhodes and Gawdy argued against it, since the conclusion was contrary to the premises; the facts returned showed that it was not *legitimum matrimonium*, and although a woman was said to be entitled to dower from the age of nine, that was only true if the marriage was not repudiated at full age. In any case, the bishop ought to have certified his own judgment rather than the supporting reasons. Serjeant Anderson, against him, argued that the marriage was not void but defeasible, and therefore it was good unless there was disagreement at the age of consent, which was no longer possible. The court was at this time inclined to treat the bishop's recital as surplusage and accept his conclusion, but judgment was nevertheless withheld. No doubt the court's difficulties were increased by the opinion of fourteen doctors of law, procured by the defendant, that the bishop's certificate was repugnant in itself and insufficient.[52] In 1576, the year after Bishop Parkhurst's death, the matter was raised in Parliament.[53] The queen herself intervened to order expedition, and in November 1579 it was at last resolved in Chief Justice Dyer's chambers that the third return was indeed insufficient. A fourth writ was thereupon sent to the bishop of Norwich, now Edmund Freke, who was less troubled by the scruples of

---

50.   Dyer 305. This is entered under Michaelmas term 1571 but the correspondence shows that it must relate to the following Hilary term. On 12 June 1572 the bishop was still being urged (by Lord Burghley) to make a certain return: *The Letter Book of John Parkhurst*, 225, no. 201. The third certificate was dated 16 June 1572: Bodleian MS Rawlinson C. 728, fol. 208.

51.   LI, MS Misc. 487, fols. 6v–8; CUL MS Mm. 4. 31, fol. 3 (same report). Neither report is dated, but the form of the return shows that it related to this stage of the case.

52.   Cf. the opinion of four doctors (Drs. Yale, Johnes, Harvye and Hammond), dated 13 April 1572, to the same effect: *The Letter Book of John Parkhurst* 125–6, no. 82. The first two also subscribed the 1576 opinion. In Michaelmas term 1572 Gray told a reporter he had "use les advises de plusours des mieulx doctors del civill ley" and showed him an opinion subscribed by Dr. Hammond: BL MS Harley 443, fol. 57v. The opinion was not favorable to Gray.

53.   Dyer 313.

his predecessor and certified on 27 April 1580 that he had caused diligent inquiry to be made and discovered that the parties were joined in lawful matrimony at Baconthorpe. This certificate the court finally accepted in Trinity term 1580. Judgment was presumably given accordingly, and on 18 May 1582 the parties reached an agreement under which Nicholas and Elizabeth Mynne accepted the manor of Hillington, Warwickshire, in extinguishment of all the dower which Elizabeth had in the Norfolk manors of Merton, Thompson and Beachamwell.[54]

The underlying reason for all the difficulty was that in strictness of canon law the marriage of 1566 amounted only to *sponsalia* which, by reason of Thomas's death aged 11, had never become a full marriage.[55] It had nevertheless eventually been accepted by a substantial body of doctors of law that such a marriage was sufficient for the purposes of dower.[56] This would have brought the English ecclesiastical law into line with the common law,[57] which seems to have been Bishop Parkhurst's intention. Far from being obtuse, Parkhurst had hoped to avoid the conflict of opinion among the doctors of law by finding the facts specially and referring the question to the judges who administered the law of dower. Indeed, he had been advised to do that by learned counsel. It was the judges who frustrated the compromise.[58]

Six years later, in *Anne Bedingfield's Case* (1586),[59] upon the issue "never joined in lawful matrimony" in a writ of dower, another bishop of Norwich made a general return, in common form, which was conclusive. Coke pointedly observed, "to which certificate, being short and to the point, no exception was ever taken." This does not square easily with his manuscript notebook, in which he says that the case was argued by doctors and counsel

54. Norfolk Record Office, WLS/IV/5/407 x 6.

55. See YB Mich. 7 Hen. VI, fol. 11, pl. 36, where it was argued by a bachelor of laws that there could be *sponsalia* below the age of consent but not *matrimonium*.

56. See the further "solution" of fifteen doctors (six of whom had signed the earlier opinion) in Dyer 369. This presumably dated from 1580.

57. For the latter see 12 Ric. II, Fitz. Abr., *Dower*, pl. 54; identified as *Moryn v. Moryn* (1388), YB Pas. 12 Ric. II (Ames Foundation), 154, pl. 6.

58. It was said in 1572 that Lord Burghley had taken the opposite approach in *Shingleton's Case* in the Court of Wards: *The Letter Book of John Parkhurst*, 107, no. 455.

59. 9 Co. Rep. 15 at 19v.

learned in the common law.[60] Perhaps he meant only that the certificate was not challenged in point of form. At any rate, it is clear that he was intending to make an unsympathetic contrast with the troublesome certificate in Mynne's case. For whatever reason, the common lawyers, including Coke, showed themselves not merely content but positively eager to keep the question of lawful matrimony firmly within the exclusive jurisdiction of the Church.

OTHER CASES CONCERNING UNDER-AGE MARRIAGE

The status of infant marriage was again considered in *Leigh v. Hanmer* (1587) in the Mayor's Court, London.[61] The wardship of Elizabeth Leigh had been granted to John Hanmer, who covenanted that Thomas Hanmer (his heir apparent) should marry Elizabeth before either party reached the age of 14. They did marry, John being only 13 and Elizabeth 9, but when Thomas reached the age of 14 in 1580 he disagreed and renounced the marriage. The question was, whether this was a performance of the covenant. This was really a question of interpretation: what was meant by "marry."[62] Counsel for the plaintiff relied on Justinian's definition of marriage and said there was no marriage in this case because the parties were not old enough to make the contract. There were *sponsalia* but no *nuptiae*. On the other side the solicitor-general, Thomas Egerton, argued successfully that the marriage was to be "considered according to the reason of the common law and not according to the rules and grounds of the canon or civil law, not as a marriage in right but as a marriage in possession." Marriage in possession was triable by the country and not by the bishop's certificate. Numerous year-book authorities were cited on this point. Moreover, it was

---

60.   BL MS Harley 6687D, fol. 720, clearly referring back to the report on fol. 719v. He did not report the arguments but promised a later report which is not to be found.

61.   1 Leon. 52 (debt on a statute staple in London, attachment, and *scire facias*).

62.   Cf. *Stokes v. Somershall* (1558), Dyer's circuit notebook, Baker, ed., *Reports from the Lost Notebooks of Sir James Dyer*, II, 418. A feoffment was made to the use of Marmion and his wife Margaret, who had been espoused when she was under the age of consent, in tail; she disagreed (and also obtained a divorce), but survived Marmion and continued in possession under the settlement. The court was doubtful whether the entail was determined immediately by the divorce. They encouraged the parties to settle, which they would not, and the case was decided on a technicality of pleading.

only required under the covenant that the parties "marry," not that they should remain married.

Finally, on the same subject, we may notice *Sir Arthur Gorges' Case* (1598–1600).[63] This was an information in the Court of Wards against Sir Arthur for withholding the body of his daughter Ambrosia Gorges, whose wardship belonged to the queen as heir to her grandfather Henry Howard, Viscount Bindon. The agreed facts were that Viscount Bindon had issue Douglas ("Duglasse" or "Dowglass"), his daughter and heir,[64] who married Sir Arthur, and they had issue Ambrosia. Sir Arthur had married off Ambrosia between the ages of 8 and 9 to Francis Gorges, son of Sir Thomas Gorges, who was over 14, but he had died when she was still under 11. One of the points was whether such a marriage was defeated *ab initio* if one of the parties died before the time for agreement or disagreement. Coke argued that it was not *matrimonium* in the canonical sense, but only *sponsalia*, because (in the words of *Bracton*) *consensus non concubitus facit matrimonium*, and there was no valid consent below the age of confirmation; for that reason, if a man was espoused to a girl who died under the age of 12, he could lawfully marry her sister.[65] On the other hand, it was clearly established as common law that a wife under age did not lose dower if the husband died before her age of agreement or disagreement. In the end it was decreed, after "conference with the Civilians," and on the advice of the chief justices, that the wardship belonged to the queen, on the ground that "it was no complete marriage."[66]

---

63. 6 Co. Rep. 22; 2 And. 207; Moo. K.B. 737; BL MS Add. 35951, fols. 108–110; Coke's notebook, MS Harley 6686, fols. 316v–317v, 382.

64. Douglas died in 1590, aged 20, and was buried in Westminster Abbey.

65. It was a standard provision in marriage settlements that, if the intended bride should die, the groom should take her next eldest sister. For a boy married to three sisters consecutively in the 1530s and 1540s see the case of Francis Warren, below, 201.

66. Cf. *Edward Hampden's Case* (1587) 2 Co. Inst. 93; Coke's notebook, BL MS Harley 6687D, fol. 731 (Court of Wards). Hampden's only daughter and heir was contracted at the age of 12 to William Fitton (MS) or Ditton (Inst.) and then while still under 13 married John Croker (MS) or Croke (Inst.), but a few years later (aged 16) she was divorced from Croker by reason of precontract. The question was whether the queen should have the value of the marriage. It was argued that this depended on whether the queen could at any time have tendered marriage, but the question was avoided when the chief justices held that the queen was entitled anyway.

JUDICIAL DIVORCE

No change had been made in the law of divorce since the break with Rome,
though there had been considerable discussion of widening the grounds
for divorce *a vinculo*, for which there was biblical authority.[67] In particular there was a growing popular misapprehension that divorce for adultery enabled the parties to remarry, even though in law it was still only
a separation *a mensa et thoro* and not a dissolution (*a vinculo*). This false
belief nevertheless had considerable theological support,[68] and had doubt-
less been encouraged by the publication of the *Reformatio Legum* in 1571. In
the following year Sir James Dyer, while on his Lent circuit, was asked to
take the acknowledgment of a fine by Martin Harburgh and his wife Alice.
Alice protested that she was not his wife but had obtained a divorce on the
grounds of his adultery. On investigation it appeared that Harburgh had
married another woman since the decree of divorce, saying that he had the
authority of the archbishop of Canterbury for doing so. The chief justice,
evidently puzzled, later took the question up with the archbishop, who
firmly disclaimed responsibility ("qui inde allocutus negavit constanter mi-
hi").[69] But it was no isolated aberration. As late as 1598 it was argued by a
serjeant at law in the Common Pleas that the innocent party to a divorce
for adultery could marry again.[70] And before the Star Chamber reaffirmed
in 1602 that a divorce for adultery did not entitle the innocent party to

---

67.   For the context see Helmholz, *Roman Canon Law in Reformation England*,
73–4.

68.   E.g. BL MS Add. 48030 (formerly Yelverton MS 34) (a mid-sixteenth century
treatise, perhaps as early as the time of Henry VIII, in favour of remarriage, with a refutation in the same hand); Cotton MS Vitellius C. XVI, fols. 2–72 (a long "discourse" in favor
of remarriage, c. 1590, aimed chiefly against Bellarmine; on fol. 33v it alludes to the defeat
of the Spanish armada as recent); *The Minor Works of Lancelot Andrewes*, ed. J. P. Wilson
and J. Bliss (Oxford, 1854), 106–10 (treatise against remarriage by Andrewes, dated 1601,
which survives in numerous manuscript copies).

69.   Dyer's notebook, Baker, ed., *Reports from the Lost Notebooks of Sir James Dyer*,
II, 299, pl. 391 (Northampton assizes).

70.   *Berrie's Case* (1598) BL MS Lansdowne 1074, fol. 291, *per* Harris serjeant ("A
woeman divorced *causa adulterii* she shall never marry againe, because the fault sprung in
her selfe, but the man may").

remarry, Archbishop Whitgift was sufficiently troubled by the question to feel the need to consult divines and Civilians before judgment was given.[71]

Now we may turn to the two leading Elizabethan cases in the secular courts on the law of divorce. These raised different questions which were in no way contingent upon recent developments. One concerned procedural justice and the other the question of whether frigidity could be selective.

IRREGULAR DIVORCES: *BUNTING V. LEPPINGWELL* (1585)[72]

The first arose from an action of trespass in the King's Bench to try the title to a copyhold tenement in Gaines Colne, Essex. The facts as found specially by the jury were that John Bunting[73] contracted an informal marriage *per verba de praesenti* with Agnes Adingshall, "intending to marry" (as Coke put it), but then she left him and in 1555 married one Thomas Twede[74] solemnly in church. This second marriage was annulled by the Court of Audience in 1556 and Agnes was ordered to solemnize the marriage with Bunting, which she did, and they had issue Charles Bunting (the plaintiff) while Twede was still living. The plaintiff now claimed the copyhold as heir to John Bunting,[75] and the question was whether he was legitimate or whether his mother's second marriage was valid (notwithstanding the

71. *Rye v. Fuljambe* (1602) Moo. K.B. 683; Noy 100. Possibly this was the occasion of Lancelot Andrewes's treatise of 1601 (above, n. 68); Andrewes, master of Pembroke Hall, Cambridge, was also chaplain to Archbishop Whitgift.

72. *Bunting v. Leppingwell* (1585) 4 Co. Rep. 29; Coke's notebook, BL MS Harley 6687D, fol. 710; Co. Litt. 634; 2 Co. Inst. 684; Moo. K.B. 169 (dated Pas. 1581, though no entry could be found this term in PRO, KB 27/1277); CUL MS Ii. 5. 26, fols. 91v–92 (a version of Moore); BL MS Add. 35951, fol. 110v (another); MS Harley 4562, fols. 33–34 (another).

73. An obscure figure. He was bailiff in Essex for the dean and chapter of St. Paul's in 1585–1600: Essex Record Office [ERO], Q/SR 94/12 to 128/4; Public Record Office [PRO], ASS 35/42/1. One of this name was a weaver of Colne Engaine in 1584: ERO, Q/SR 88/89.

74. The printed version of Moore gives the name as Twine, and in MS Add. 35951 it is Troy, though it is correctly spelt in the Harleian MS. Twede was a local name. A Thomas Twede of Fordham, yeoman, was indicted for an assault in the porch of Earls Colne parish church in 1566: ERO, Q/SR 20/22. He appears on a coroner's jury at Harwich in 1570: Public Record Office [PRO], ASS 35/12/4.

75. The nominal defendant Leppingwell was merely the servant of the real defendant. He was of Earls Colne, Essex, and died c. 1592: will in ERO, D/ACW 2/41.

divorce) and his father's marriage void. The grounds of the divorce were commonplace (except between 1540 and 1548), but it was objected that the decree had been made without joining Twede as a party. It was therefore contrary to common-law procedural standards, known today as the principles of natural justice. Since the line between an engagement to marry *per verba de futuro* and espousals *per verba de praesenti* was in practice notoriously indistinct, and Twede might have been able to adduce evidence to disprove Agnes's claim, an *ex parte* divorce was grossly irregular. But could the King's Bench concern itself with that? Coke clearly thought not. His printed report of the case, deploying the technique familiar to us from *Slade's Case* in the same volume, presented his own successful arguments for the plaintiff as the judgment of the court.[76] Since cognizance of the right of marriage belonged to the ecclesiastical court, and the same court had given sentence in this case, the judges of "our law" ought to give credit to their proceedings, "even though it be against the reason of our law."[77] Francis Moore's report adds a little more detail. For the defendant it was argued, firstly, that at common law espousals in church were so strong that they could not be defeated without a divorce and without conventing both parties to say what they could. Secondly, precontract did not make a marriage automatically void, but voidable, and therefore both parties had to be convented before a divorce was decreed. This was, of course, contrary to the decision in Dr. Julio's case, but that was not cited. On the other side, the plaintiff was represented by William Goldingham, LL.D. (Cantab.).[78] Dr. Goldingham argued, firstly, that Agnes was in "Civil ley" a wife by the first marriage and was not liable to punishment for adultery or fornication but only for contempt against the edict of the Church which prohibited carnal copulation before espousals *in facie ecclesiae*. Solemnization in church, he

---

76. Coke did not mention in the printed report that he was involved as counsel, though it is mentioned in his manuscript notebook: next note.

77. Cf. the contemporary version in the notebook: "Et del auter part fuit argue per moy que intant que les droites des espousels sont destre decide per le ecclesiasticall ley, et tielx mariages queux sont avoidables sont destre avoide per mesme le ley, serra dure pur les judges de nostre ley de appeler in question le reason et course ou le mannour et forme de lour sentences. Mes les judges de nostre ley soient a doner credit a lour sentences, come lour judges sont a crediter judgmentes done in les courtes le roy."

78. Misspelt in BL MS Add. 35951 as "Goulding." None of the versions of Moore mentions Coke.

contended, was introduced by Pope Innocent III, but before that the husband went to the wife's house and brought her back—whence the expression *ducere in uxorem*—and that was the whole ceremony. Ceremony was never of the essence. Agnes was thus disabled from marrying anyone else, the espousals with Twede were "quasi nuls," and no divorce was needed.[79] Second, John Bunting was not driven to take notice of the second espousals but only to convent Agnes before the spiritual judge to know why she would not marry him; and that is what he did. Third, inasmuch as the sentence was given by the Court of Audience it must be presumed that all those who needed to be convented were in fact convented. This was the gist of Coke's argument as well, and the court agreed. No judicial reasons are reported, but later in the term the judges held Charles to be legitimate, and his action therefore succeeded. According to a manuscript version of Moore's report, in a passage which is not in the printed version, Chief Justice Wray in announcing the decision said he had conferred with Dr. Dale and Dr. Aubrey and that in their view it was clear that the conventing of Twede was unnecessary.[80]

The decision was followed at the end of the reign, with different consequences, in *Kenn's Case* in the Court of Wards.[81] Christopher Kenn in 1545 married Elizabeth Stowell and they had issue Martha, the plaintiff's mother; but in 1554 the Court of Audience, at Kenn's instance, declared the marriage void because the parties were under age, thereby bastardizing Martha. Christopher thereupon married Elizabeth Beckwith,[82] who in

79. This seems to be the gist of Coke's argument that the sentence was only declaratory. In his notebook, however, this is given as part of his opponent's argument.

80. MS Harley 4562, fol. 34: "Et puis en cest terme fuit adjudge que Charles fuit legittimat. Car Wray chief justice dit que il ad conferre ove Doctour Dale et Doctour Abry, civilians, que tient assettes cleere que convention del Tweede ne fuit necessarie, et le precontract fist le mariadge voide quant le sentence est pronounce vers le feme."

81. *Williams v. Stallenge* (c. 1594–1606) 7 Co. Rep. 43; Cro. Jac. 186; BL Cotton MS Vitellius C. XVI, fols. 174–175, 404–405v (apparently from Coke). The precise date is uncertain. It must have begun after Christopher Kenn's death in Jan. 1594, but it was still pending when Sir Nicholas Stallenge died (on 10 Jan. 1605/6: monumental inscription at Kenn, Somerset). Martha died pending the suit, which was revived by her daughter Elizabeth Robertson

82. Daughter of Sir Roger Cholmleley (d. 1565), chief justice of the King's Bench, and widow of Sir Leonard Beckwith. Cf. *The Men of Court*, i. 290, where there may be some confusion between namesakes.

1563 sued for divorce before the ecclesiastical commissioners on the grounds
that her husband was already married. The commissioners pronounced the
former marriage void and Elizabeth's marriage valid. Elizabeth then died,
and Christopher married Florence, the defendant, with whom he had issue
a daughter Elizabeth. After Christopher's death in 1594 the inquisition *post
mortem* found this last daughter, aged 10 months at the time of his death,[83]
to be the heir, and her wardship was granted to Florence's second husband, Sir Nicholas Stallenge. This was the occasion for a suit by Martha
in the Wards, joining with her husband Silvanus Williams,[84] in which she
claimed to be her father's heir on the ground that her parents were in fact
of the age of consent when they married and had cohabited for nine or ten
years before the supposed divorce. The plaintiffs contended that, since the
ages of consent were recognized by and part of the common law, this question of fact was triable at law. But the Court of Wards held, following *Bunting's Case* (amongst others), that the divorce was binding and conclusive
even if founded on a falsehood.[85] The common-law position was essentially
based on comity between courts and issue estoppel.[86] But it is also observ-
able that these disputes commonly arose in the next generation after the
decree, and it would not have been sensible to reopen the very difficult factual evidence surrounding consent after several decades had passed. This
was well illustrated by another case in the Wards, which incidentally shows
the confusions caused by consecutive infant marriages.[87] Francis Warren

83.   Elizabeth, who was born in 1593 and died in 1663, married (1) John, 1st Baron
Poulet, (2) John Ashburnham.

84.   One of this name was buried in St. Michael Cornhill, London, in 1594, having
hanged himself.

85.   Cf. *Boules v. Bacon* (1594) BL MS Harley 443, fol. 228v. In an action for slandering the title of his wife's inheritance, the defendant pleaded that she was not his wife
but the wife of X; the plaintiff replied that she had been married to X but was divorced,
to which the defendant rejoined that the divorce was obtained by fraud and collusion. The
court held the rejoinder bad, because the sentence of divorce was a binding judgment.

86.   Cf. *Boules v. Bacon* (1594) BL MS Harley 443, fol. 228v. In an action for slandering the title of his wife's inheritance, the defendant pleaded that she was not his wife
but the wife of X; the plaintiff replied that she had been married to X but was divorced,
to which the defendant rejoined that the divorce was obtained by fraud and collusion. The
court held the rejoinder bad, because the sentence of divorce was a binding judgment.

87.   *R v. Francis Englefield* (1604) BL Cotton MS Vitellius C. XVI, fol. 165 (an
information for intrusion). The dispute seems to have arisen after the death of Francis's

married Dorothy Fitton, when he was about the age of 4 and she was 3, in 1537; she died soon afterwards and he married Dorothy's sister Mary; he later obtained a divorce from Mary on grounds of infancy and married the third sister Margaret Fitton, aged 9, in 1546; Margaret then divorced him on grounds of infancy and want of consent and married John Englefield (d. 1567). Now, half a century later, it was suggested that the last marriage was invalid, because Margaret had consented to the Warren marriage before her disagreement, and that their son Francis Englefield (created baronet in 1611) was therefore illegitimate. Francis protested that the crown was relying on the depositions of beggars, outlaws, excommunicates and common strumpets, taken before biased commissioners, to prove facts which had occurred over fifty years earlier. The outcome is not at present known.

Selective Frigidity: Bury's Case (1560–99)

The most remarkable of all the Elizabethan marriage cases occupied the courts for forty years, in various ways, and was still a matter of debate in the reign of James I. The accepted facts were that John Bury of Colaton, Devon,[88] married Wilmot, daughter and heir of John Gifford, on 20 November 1553. On 26 June 1561 he was divorced *a vinculo matrimonii* on grounds of impotency, at the suit of his wife, in the Canterbury Court of Audience.[89] The definitive sentence, pronounced by Dr. Thomas Yale in the chancel of St. Faith's beneath St. Paul's, London, found that they had solemnized the marriage, had cohabited for two or three years, and had slept in the same bed desiring to have children, but had never become of one flesh ("nunquam per carnalem copulam fuerunt una caro"), and that Wilmot remained a virgin by reason of her husband's impotency, a problem of which they were unaware at the time of marriage. The husband's condition was said to be one which neither medical science nor the passage of time could remove ("nulla unquam medicorum arte aut temporis cursu corrigi vel tolli

---

uncle Sir Francis Englefield in 1596.

88.   Formerly spelt Collaton or Colleton. The *History of Parliament* (below, n. 90) seems to be in error in saying he was of Colyton. John Bury was the son of Richard Bury (d. 1543) and grandson of John Bury (d. 1533) of Colaton and Lyon's Inn, whose eldest son Anthony Bury (d. 1555) was a bencher of the Middle Temple: *The Men of Court*, I, 406–7.

89.   The sentence is recited in the special verdict, from a sealed testimonial copy dated 26 Feb. 1584.

potuit aut potest"), and this had been proved both by *medici* and by experienced *matronae*. Wilmot remarried and had four children, all of whom were to die without issue.[90] More remarkably, and this was the cause of all the legal difficulty to come, John also remarried (in 1562) and two years later his new wife gave birth to Humphrey Bury.[91] This obviously threw doubt on the validity of the divorce, inasmuch as the Court of Audience appeared to have been mistaken as to the facts.[92]

The difficulty was first raised in court in the 1560s, when a motion was made to stay the engrossing of a fine in the Common Pleas by John and his wife.[93] The court took the opinion of doctors of law, who held that the original parties should now be compelled to commune and cohabit as man and wife because it was apparent that the Church had been deceived in its judgment. This may have been the occasion for John Bury's second wife to leave him and remarry.[94] But the judges, contrary to a command from Lord Keeper Bacon, nevertheless ordered the fine to be engrossed. No reasons are reported, and it was later suggested that the printed report was defective.[95] This little tangle, however, was only the beginning of a long saga.

90. The husband was Sir George Carey (d. 1616) of the Inner Temple, recorder of Totnes, sometime lord deputy of Ireland: *The Visitation of the County of Devon in the Year 1620*, ed. F. T. Colby, Harleian Society 6 (London, 1872), 49, 51; *History of Parliament: The House of Commons 1558–1603*, ed. Hasler, i. 546.

91. His second wife was Philippa, daughter of "Mangey" or Mongey (Mountjoye in the special verdict): *Visitation of Devon 1620*, ed. Colby, 42. By what seems to be merely a coincidence of names which ran in the families, one Philippa, "relict of Mountjoy," married Giles Risden and had a son Thomas (the bencher of the Inner Temple) who married Wilmot, daughter of Thomas Gifford: *Visitation of Devon 1620*, ed. Colby, 241.

92. No suggestion was made in any of the proceedings that the son might have been born out of wedlock. This may seem an obvious factual possibility, but the courts were precluded from considering it. So long as the parents' marriage was valid, legitimacy was irrebuttably presumed.

93. *Bury's Case* (c. 1565?) Dyer 179. The dating is a puzzle, since Dyer reported the case as an addendum to one of 1560, saying that it was in that year or the year after. But there must have been time for the second wife to conceive and have issue. Indeed, according to the special verdict of 1598 (below), Humphrey was born in 1564.

94. According to the special verdict she married one John Langdon while John Bury was still living.

95. *Morrys v. Webber* (1587), below, as reported in BL MS Lansdowne 1087, fol. 255: "mes limpression est faux en ceo, car si les judges la avoient tenus le ley destre que le divorce ne fuit perpetuel ils ne voilent aver accept le fyne."

The matter arose again a quarter of a century later, after John Bury's death, when the inheritance was disputed between John's son Humphrey and his brother Hugh, and it was first litigated in an action of ejectment commenced in the Common Pleas in 1586 by Humphrey's lessee against Hugh's lessee.[96] The action was tried at Exeter assizes on 18 July 1586 before Chief Justice Anderson and Mr. Baron Gent, and the relevant facts were found by a special verdict. The following term, according to Chief Justice Anderson, it was "argue per serjeants, mes petite a le purpose; car le point et matter del case voile depend sur le Canon ley." The court therefore invited the parties to choose two doctors of law each, who were not retained of counsel, to hear arguments and come to a resolution. But this seems to be a foreshortening of events by Anderson, since there are reported versions of oral arguments by Civilians in the Common Pleas prior to the certificate by the four doctors.

The arguments of the serjeants in Trinity and Michaelmas terms 1587, even if "little to the purpose," were reported by Moore and Leonard.[97] Serjeants Shuttleworth and Walmsley, for the plaintiff, argued that a perpetual sentence of divorce should stand so long as it was not reversed by another sentence obtained after summoning both parties ("convocatis partibus"). The temporal courts in such matters deferred to the spiritual, and did not concern themselves with the cause of the divorce. Moreover, the common law did not allow issue to be bastardized after the death of their parents. Counsel relied not only on year-book cases but on the report in Dyer concerning the same divorce. Serjeant Fenner, for the defendant, argued that since it appeared from the birth of Humphrey that

> The cause and matter upon which the divorce was grounded was an offence of the time and not of nature, for he is now recovered,[98] and

96. *Morrys v. Webber*, alias *Turnor* (1586–8) Moo. K.B. 225; 2 Leon. 169; 1 And. 185; Noy 72; BL MS Lansdowne 1087, fols. 255–257; sub nom. *Buries Case* (1588) BL MS Lansdowne 1104, fols. 104–105. The record is PRO, CP 40/1461, m. 1711. Dr. Susanne Jenks kindly provided the writer with digital photographs of the lengthy record of this case and of the 1598 sequel.

97. Quotations are from 2 Leon. 169–73 unless otherwise stated. This report confusingly calls John Bury "Henry."

98. Cf. MS Lansdowne 1087, fol. 255: "sil recover son naturell heate enapres issint que il nest frigidus uncore le sentence serra determine."

inasmuch as the Church hath erred in the sentence of this divorce, which error is now apparent, this court shall adjudge according to the truth of the matter as the spiritual law *ought* to have adjudged, and not as they *have* adjudged.

Serjeant Gawdy, on the same side, referred to the opinion of the doctors in the previous case. Chief Justice Anderson said the question was whether a definitive sentence of divorce could be treated as *ipso facto* void, without being reversed by the spiritual court. He had consulted "many learned in the canon law," including Dr. Dale,[99] who were of that opinion, and invited the parties to retain one doctor each to argue the point.

Both Moore and Leonard reported the ensuing argument of the doctors. The plaintiff was represented by Dr. Goldingham, followed in Hilary term 1588 by Dr. Creake, and the defendant by Dr. Steward.[100] One of the manuscript reports of their arguments is in Latin, and it seems possible that they were allowed to make their submissions in that tongue.[101] Dr. Goldingham followed the serjeants in arguing that by the sentence the whole matter was determined by judgment (*transit in rem judicatam*) and so the facts could not be reopened while the sentence was in force. Dr. Steward suggested that that was not true if the soul was in danger, as where the Church was deceived by a probable error, for then the parties would be compelled to continue in adultery unless and until the sentence was annulled. He then introduced a new point: when a man is divorced *causa frigiditatis* he may not marry again, and if he does so he is in the canon law perjured and an adulterer. To this purpose he "cited divers authorities of the canon law," but the report does not indicate whether they were predicated upon the divorce having been at the suit of the man. Dr. Golding-

---

99.   Valentine Dale, D.C.L. (Oxon.), judge of the Court of Admiralty. He died in 1585, before the present action was commenced. Cf. above, n. 80.

100.   Nicholas Steward and Thomas Creake were both Cambridge LL.D.s. For Goldingham see above, at n. 78.

101.   BL MS Lansdowne 1104, fols. 104–105. Cf. YB Mich. 7 Hen. VI, fol. 11, pl. 36, where "Huls bachalarius utriusque juris argua moult in Latin" in the Common Pleas on a question of marriage law; *Rowley's Case* (1589) Yale University, Law School MS GR 29.6, fol. 63 (argument of Dr. Foorde [Forthe] reported in Latin). The practice of hearing Civilians argue on questions of ecclesiastical law is discussed in J. H. Baker, "Ascertainment of Foreign Law," *International and Comparative Law Quarterly* 28 (1979): 141 at 143–4.

ham responded that the sentence was not properly a divorce, for there was never properly a marriage, as in cases of precontract, but was "a sentence of the Church upon the error of the parties." The following term, Dr. Creake added a new argument for the plaintiff. The canon law recognized that a man might be impotent temporarily or with respect only to one person. Impotency was either natural, as in the case of frigidity, dryness (*siccitas*) or *carnositas*, or it was "accidental," as in the case of witchcraft (*maleficium*). In this case it did not appear from the sentence which kind of impotence it was, and therefore it was possible that the Church was not deceived. Even if the divorce was bad, it remained effective until annulled by a declaratory sentence after proceedings in which the second wife and child were represented. Dr. Steward had little difficulty disposing of the new point. The sentence referred to perpetual impotency, and also to the evidence of medical doctors, neither of which was consistent with witchcraft: *maleficium non curatur per medicos sed per orationes.*[102] In any case, there was a special form of libel *in casu maleficii*, with a prescribed procedure providing for an attempt to remove the witch's spell, and this had not been used in the present case. As to the procedural argument, there was no need for a declaratory sentence if a divorce was proved to be void, because the sentence could only declare what was already the case. The parties who remarried would be guilty of adultery even if there was no sentence. To this Dr. Creake replied that that was only so if the parties were morally guilty. Moreover, even if a man married his cousin or aunt he could not leave her when he pleased, without a sentence, but must seek a divorce. According to Moore, the judges were persuaded by Dr. Steward's argument that the divorce was not *ex maleficio*, but they remained greatly in doubt about the validity of the divorce. This seems to be the point at which the panel of doctors of law was asked to report.[103] They reported that the plaintiff was legitimate, the divorce remaining unrepealed, and the impediment not extending to prevent marriage with a subsequent wife. The Common Pleas gave judgment accordingly, in Michaelmas term 1588.

102. BL MS Lansdowne 1104, fol. 104v, meaning "witchcraft is not cured by doctors but by prayers."
103. 2 And. 186; BL MS Add. 25194, fol. 53 ("per que adjornatur destre argue arere per auters doctours et devant auters doctours indifferent que serront come judges, sur loppinion de queux les justices voilent resolver").

The matter arose for a third time seven years later, between different parties, on a plea of bastardy. Little is known of this case save that the
Civilians gave it as their opinion that whoever was fit for one woman was
fit for another, and therefore the first marriage must have been valid ("qui
aptus est ad unam aptus est ad aliam, et quando potentia reducitur ad ac-
tum debet ire ad primas nuptias").[104] This opinion, being contrary to the
previous resolution, may have given further encouragement to Hugh Bury
in resisting the claims of Humphrey's heirs. At any rate, in 1598 another
ejectment in the Common Pleas was launched against him, in respect of
different lands.[105] This was tried at Exeter Castle on 6 March 1598, before
Justices Walmsley and Fenner, and this time the lengthy process and all
the examinations of the witnesses in the Court of Audience, some of them
in English,[106] were made part of the special verdict in order to show that
the impotency was perpetual. Chief Justice Anderson in 1588 had been
squeamish about the medical evidence, which he said was "not suitable to
be reported,"[107] but the Common Pleas was no longer to be spared. The
evidence, none of which was challenged, was returned in minute detail. It
can only be summarized briefly here. The parties had both been aged 12
at the time of the marriage and had lived apart for a few years, but after
reaching the age of puberty they had slept together on numerous occasions
without achieving sexual congress. Eight "matrons," led by Margaret, Lady
Dennys, and the wives of three local esquires, gave corroborative evidence
as to the various periods of bed-sharing—the couple seem not to have had

---

104. *Stafford v. Mongy* (Hil. 1595) in Treby's note to Dyer (1688 edn), 179 citing
Thomas Tempest's manuscript. This appears to relate to the same facts. Mongy (*alias*
Mountjoy) was the maiden name of Bury's wife.

105. *Webber v. Bury* (1586–98) 5 Co. Rep. 98; Coke's notebook, BL MS Harley 6686,
fol. 318v; MS Lansdowne 1074, fols. 290v, 291; MS Lansdowne 1076, fol. 170. The lengthy
record is PRO, CP 40/1602, m. 360. The lands in suit were in Burrington, whereas the previous suit was for lands in Winkleigh. The defendant Hugh Bury was stated in the special
verdict to be the servant of Hugh Bury, brother of John.

106. They were certified in a testimonial copy dated 2 Aug. 1595.

107. 1 And. 185 ("le quel libel contein auxint plusors parols nient convenient de estre
reports," 186 ("ils [*the doctors of law*] monstrent a moy auters causes, queux fuerunt reason-
ables de ground lour opinion come devant, queux examples ne so[nt] convenients de estre
cytes"); 2 Leon. 169, *per* Anderson C.J. ("sufficient matter did appear to the said Ecclesiasticall Judges, (which for modesty sake ought not to be entred of Record)").

a marital home of their own—and as to Wilmot's continued virginity.[108] John's great-uncle Robert Pollard recounted the occasion when John had revealed to him his grief concerning his "desease"; the door of the room was locked, "the saide Berrey undid his coddpeece and theare this deponent did handle the seid Berrey his coddes,[109] and theare was but on little stone about the bignesse of a beane." Lewis Hatch deposed that he was told the condition resulted from Bury's being kicked by a horse ("ex concussione cujusdam equi circa testiculos"), and that Bury had obtained medicines and medical advice without effect. Dr. Richard Argentyn, prebendary of Exeter and a doctor of medicine,[110] had examined Bury and found that he had only one small and defective testicle which was incapable of generating semen ("testiculum non integrum set diminutum et conquassatum et contritum et ex quo semen gignitivum emitti ad prolem generandam minus poterit nec valet"), to which another medical man, Dr. Ambrose Storie, added that he was not capable of arousal ("nullo veneris stimulo agitatus fuit"). Bury's own explanation was that "when he was younge he fortuned to have a stripe of a horse upon his coddes and was then so soare brused that sythence that tyme [he] was never well in that place." He accepted that he had been unable to have intercourse with Wilmot. There was thus ample and uncontested testimony that Bury's impotency was incurable.

This testimony not only tended to support the sentence of divorce but also cast considerable doubt on the possibility of relative frigidity in Bury's case. Mr. Justice Walmsley nevertheless recalled that in the former suit, in which he had been of counsel, "the opinion of the wisest doctors and of others who were in judicial places was had, and it was then resolved that the second issue was legitimate, and that one may be frigid as to one and warm as to another, and the sentence that he has a perpetual frigidity is only between the two parties and does not extend to others."[111] Counsel went over

---

108. This was considered to be proved by her solemn oath to some of them.

109. I.e. scrotum.

110. He was formerly an Ipswich schoolmaster and is remembered chiefly as a troublesome controversialist: *ODNB*, s. v. Richard Argentine.

111. MS Lansdowne 1076, fol. 170: "In largument del case Walm. dit quant il fuit serjeant in cest courte cest case fuit, et donques loppinion del sagest doctours et de ascuns que fueront in judiciall liews fuit ewe et donques resolve que le second yssue fuit legittimate et que poit estre frigidus a un et callidus a auter, et le sentence que il ad un perpetuall frigiditie nest forsque inter eux deux et nextend al auters."

the same ground as before, and Serjeant Hele asserted that one could be
"*frigidus quoad unam et callidus quoad alteram* per cannons civill." This drew
from Serjeant Harris the memorable quip that "he which is *frigidus quoad
unam et calidus quoad alteram* is like to prove *callidus nebulo*."[112] According to
Harris's argument, those who were incapable by nature (*inhabiles ab initio*)
could not remarry, though it was otherwise of incapacity *per accidens*.[113] The
judges this time decided the matter more expeditiously than before, and in
Michaelmas term 1598 they again gave judgment for the plaintiff in support
of Humphrey's legitimacy.[114] The divorce *a vinculo* freed both parties to remarry; and, even if the second marriage was voidable, if it was not in fact
avoided by a divorce in the lifetime of the parties the issue was legitimate. A
writ of error was brought in the King's Bench, but "after many arguments
and great deliberation" the judgment was affirmed.[115]

That was the end of the matter. But two interesting sidelights on the
case may be obtained from evidence beyond the law reports. The first is an
account by the Devonshire antiquary William Pole (1561–1635) of the Inner
Temple, son of William Pole (d. 1587) of Colyton, Devon, a bencher of the
same inn. He and his father were well placed, as neighbors and as lawyers,
to know the facts recounted. According to Pole, John Bury was a simpleton
of whom advantage was taken by his younger brother Hugh. Hugh kept
him as a prisoner, enjoyed the profits of his land, "and wastefully consumed,
and sold the land."[116] John, however, managed to steal away from his brother, secretly remarried, and brought up the son Humphrey without Hugh's
knowledge of his existence. It was when Humphrey came of age that he
took the matter to law, "and after much trouble concerninge the validyty

112.   This is a pun on *calidus* (warm) and *callidus* (crafty): *callidus nebulo* means
crafty knave.
113.   Cf. Serjeant Fenner's argument in the earlier case, MS Lansdowne 1087, fol.
255, that in such cases only the wife was allowed to remarry, "car le baron est allowe daver
ancillam mes nemy pur marry."
114.   The costs this time amounted to £40. 12s, 8d. In 1588 they had been £19. 10s.
4d.
115.   There is a very full report of these final proceedings in *Berrye v. Webber* (1599–
1600) BL MS Add. 25203, fols. 102–104v, 149. The judgment on the writ of error was given
in Hilary term 1600.
116.   In the Devon Record Office (3799M-0/T/4/1) there is an exemplification of a
deed of 1571 settling the manor of Colaton and other lands, of the inheritance of Richard
Bury, which were John Bury's, on his brother Hugh Bury and his heirs.

of the divorce betwixt his father and his first wief, at length recovered back all the land which was sold by his unkle Hugh."[117] This certainly fits the chronology, since Humphrey would have been 22 when the first ejectment was commenced. But can all the depositions have been untrue?

The second revelation comes from the infamous divorce case of Lady Catherine Howard and the earl of Essex in 1613.[118] This depended on the concept of frigidity *quoad unam*, for which the only relevant English precedent was that of John Bury. The archbishop of Canterbury, George Abbot, was anxious to distinguish the case and caused research to be carried out, as a result of which he discovered an opinion in Bury's case signed by seven doctors of law. This revealed that "it was proved by divers witnesses, of which two were physicians, that the said *Bury* had but one little stone, and that no bigger than a bean."[119] The sentence, therefore, was that the first marriage was void *propter defectum et vitium testiculorum*.[120] So much for all the learned arguments about *maleficium*. As a contemporary bishop observed, "maleficiation is the very garbage of popery."[121] The Church had not been deceived after all. Abbot's discovery might certainly have appeared decisive to anyone who had not seen the special verdict of 1598. The archbishop seems to have been unaware, or failed to mention, that the evidence from the ecclesiastical court had in fact been considered by the two principal common-law courts before the final decision had been reached in 1598. The opinion of the seven Civilians, however, was directly opposed to that of the judges. Their conclusion was that the issue of the second marriage must have been illegitimate on either view of the case.[122] For if the cause of the divorce was true, as must be presumed until the contrary was deter-

117. W. Pole, *Collections towards a Description of Devon* (London, 1791), ed. J. W. de la Pole, 433. His account errs in describing John's first wife as Thomasine Yeo.

118. Numerous opinions written in this case by canonists, mostly in Latin, and many of them badly damaged by fire, are in BL Cotton MS Vitellius C. XVI (confusedly bound up with other papers concerning marriage).

119. "The Speech intended to be delivered at Lambeth, Sep. 25, by George, Archbishop of Canterbury" in *Case of the Countess of Essex* (1613) 2 St. Tr. 785 at 849.

120. These words do not, however, appear in the sentence as set out in the special verdict.

121. Quoted by Abbot, 2 St. Tr. at 847.

122. The opinion is undated but the doctors who signed it were John Loyde, Henry Jones, John Hone, Nicolas Stuard, Edward Crompton, Robert Fourth, William Farrand. William Farrand was admitted an advocate of the Arches in 1580, and Henry Jones (or

mined by a competent court, the second marriage was invalidated by the same perpetual impediment.[123] And if the cause was untrue, so that the Church was deceived, the first marriage was good and the second void on that ground instead. But that is not how the case had been presented to the courts of law, and Abbot's argument—which he did not have the opportunity to present orally—was ineffective in 1613 as well. A finding of frigidity as between two parties to a divorce did not work an estoppel in relation to other parties.

CONCLUSION

The evidence of the common-law reports confirms, from the other side of the jurisdictional divide, the picture of "business as usual" which has been so convincingly painted by Professor Helmholz. There was no inclination on the part of the Tudor royal judges to take over or modify the law of marriage. The unusual number of marriage cases coming before the highest lay courts in the later sixteenth century has no obvious explanation, but nearly all of them seem to have been cases which could have arisen before the sixteenth century and were not symptomatic of new attitudes to marriage or of jurisdictional conflict. What is new about the early-modern period, from the historian's point of view, is that so much more can be found out about the parties to litigation and the background to their cases. This extrajudicial evidence prevents us from making unwarranted speculations about great social or intellectual changes in this area. The cases typically arose from family disputes, often protracted and intergenerational, in which Civilian advocates as well as common lawyers were ranged on both sides. It is noteworthy that the common lawyers, both counsel and judges, were fully prepared to deal with the Civil lawyers on their own terms and in their own language, displaying a competent familiarity with what had traditionally been called "their law," if not with all their chapter and verse. Nevertheless, whatever might have happened if a new statutory code of ec-

---

Johns) died in 1592. It seems therefore to relate to the proceedings in 1587–8 and to contradict the opinion on which the court then acted.

    123. This argument assumes that impotence makes a marriage void *ab initio* rather than voidable. This does not seem correct, since it was permissible for a wife to waive the defect and accept the marriage.

clesiastical law had materialized, what we see in Elizabethan England is an accommodation between the two legal systems which allowed the Church and its lawyers to remain in control of the law of marriage for another 300 years.

The Arguments in *Calvin's Case* (1608)

David Ibbetson[1]

No scholar has done more than Dick Helmholz to illuminate the relationship between the continental European *ius commune* and the English common law in the medieval and early modern periods. It is not easy, and perhaps it is impossible, to pin down the precise level of continental influence on English law, but we would certainly no longer say that after an initial dalliance with the learned laws "English law flourished in noble isolation from Europe."[2] It is possible to trace injections of substantive rules or principles from Roman law or the *ius commune* into English law in the late-sixteenth and early-seventeenth centuries, but they are elusive. A more clearly visible point of connection, or influence, at this time is the nature of legal method, where both continental works on legal dialectic and rules of reasoning derived from Roman law can be shown to have been at work. A *locus classicus* of this is *Calvin's Case*, decided in 1608.

Calvin's Case was one of the most important constitutional cases decided early in the reign of James VI and I. The question was a simple one, whether those born in Scotland after the union of the crowns of England and Scotland, the so-called *post-nati*, should be treated as natural-born subjects so far as the law of England was concerned.

---

1.   I am grateful to the participants in legal history seminars in the University of Aberdeen and the University of Cambridge, and especially to Mr. David Foster. The usual disclaimer applies.

2.   J. H. Baker, *An Introduction to English Legal History*, 3rd ed. (London, 1990), 35.

The issue had been dealt with as a political matter at the beginning of James's reign as King of England. A commission had been set up to consider it, and its conclusions had been debated in parliament. Parliament took the advice of the judges, all but one of whom concurred in saying that the *post-nati* were indeed natural-born subjects by the law of England, though the members of the House of Commons disagreed with this.[3] But this was not to be the end of the matter. It was then raised as a purely legal question in a test case brought in the King's Bench by Robert Calvin (or Colville), an infant born in Scotland after 1603, who claimed to have been disseised of land in Shoreditch in East London. The defendants pleaded his alien status, that he was born in Scotland "out of the allegiance of the king of his kingdom of England," as a result of which he could not have been seised of the land in London since aliens lacked the capacity to hold property rights at common law, and hence he could not in law have been disseised of it. A parallel case raising the identical point, though involving a different parcel of land, was brought in the Chancery, and both cases were referred to the Exchequer Chamber for debate by all the judges of England and the Lord Chancellor. As a matter of English law, were those born in Scotland after 1603 natural-born subjects in England or aliens?[4]

The substance of the arguments has been examined by others,[5] and there is no necessity to spend time on it. The central issue was whether allegiance was owed to the king personally, in which case Calvin should be regarded as natural-born since he owed allegiance to James; or to the king as a political entity, as king of England or king of Scotland, in which case Calvin owed allegiance to the king of Scotland and was an alien by the law of England. That the king had a natural body and a political body was a commonplace, but the issue was which of these two bodies was relevant when it came to examining the question of the subject's allegiance. The

3.   B. Galloway, *The Union of England and Scotland* (Edinburgh, 1986), 148–157. See too B. P. Levack, "The Proposed Union of English Law and Scots Law in the Seventeenth Century," *Juridical Review* n.s. 20 (1975), 97; L. A. Knafla, *Law and Politics in Jacobean England* (Cambridge, 1977), *passim*; P. J. Price, "Natural Law and Birthright Citizenship in *Calvin's Case* (1608)," *Yale Journal of Law and the Humanities* 9 (1997), 73.

4.   Although the case was argued on the basis of English law, parallel arguments could be found elsewhere: Price, "Natural Law and Birthright Citizenship," 128–135.

5.   Galloway, *Union of England and Scotland*, 151–55; K. Kim, "*Calvin's Case* (1608) and the Law of Alien Status," *Journal of Legal History* 17 (1996), 155.

question was recognized as a hugely important one, if technically buried beneath a very small question whether Robert Calvin could have been unjustly disseised of his free tenement; but, given the near-unanimity of the judges in giving advice to parliament, it was perhaps not surprising that the near-unanimous opinion was reached that allegiance was personal and that Calvin was not an alien.

The focus of the present paper is not on the result, nor on the reasons for the result, but on the way in which the case was argued. As well as notes of the different arguments taken by those who were present,[6] we have three very substantial texts which we can treat as the polished versions made by their authors: the argument of Francis Bacon, the Solicitor-General; the report of the case published by Edward Coke; and the argument of the Lord Chancellor, Lord Ellesmere, technically his reasoned decision on the Chancery suit.[7] Since these were polished texts produced by their authors, we cannot be sure that they are accurate representations of what was actually said. Coke's report, in particular, claimed to be a redaction of the arguments of all the judges. Comparison of his report with notes taken by others of his speech suggests that it does indeed contain points which he did not himself argue, but overall the structure of the printed report looks to be very similar to the structure of the argument which he is elsewhere reported to have made. In the preface to his published speech, Ellesmere tells that he had reconstructed his argument from his "scribbled and broken papers" and reproduced as nearly as he could the words which he had spoken.[8] Both Hawarde's report and the notes of the argument in

---

6. W. P. Baildon, ed., *Les Reportes del Cases in Camera Stellata 1593 to 1609, from the Original MS. of John Hawarde* (Privately Printed, 1894), 349–366 (hereafter Hawarde); Cambridge University Library MS Dd 11.53, fols. 4v–25; Public Record Office SP 14/34 fols. 11–23v; SP 14/32 fols. 64–71 (argument of Yelverton J.).

7. *The Argument of Sir Francis Bacon, His Majesties Sollicitor Generall, in the Case of the Post-Nati of Scotland*, in *Three Speeches of the Right Honorable, Sir Francis Bacon Knight* (London, 1641); 7 Co. Rep. 1; *The Speech of the Lord Chancellor Of England, in the Eschequer Chamber, Touching the Post-Nati* (London, 1609), edited in L. A. Knafla, *Law and Politics in Jacobean England* (Cambridge, 1977), 202. All three of these are reproduced in W. Cobbett, *Complete Collection of State Trials* (London, 1809), available online through google books (hereafter Cobbett). Bacon's argument begins at col. 575, Coke's at col. 607, Ellesmere's at col. 659.

8. "To the Readers" (unpaginated); Cobbett, 660.

the Cambridge manuscript fit well with the printed text,[9] so there is little reason to doubt this; such minor points of divergence as can be identified are consistent with his having had to reconstruct the argument in places.[10] The summary we have in the State Papers is similarly very close to what we read in the printed speech, and it may well be that the note of his argument was originally based on a prepared text which was later to be put in print. At one stage in the State Papers report the writer has noted in the margin "not urged,"[11] which seems clearly to indicate that there was a source of his argument separate from the oral speech, seemingly an earlier version of what was to be published,[12] but also that the content of that version was in general a true reflection of what had actually been said. We do not have an equivalent check for Bacon's published argument, but there seems no reason to doubt that it bears a reasonable relationship to what was said. In any event, even if the published arguments are in truth different from what was actually said at the time, at the very least they must represent what their authors saw as proper arguments, fit to be written at length, and in the case of Coke's and Ellesmere's put by them into the public domain. Moreover, since they flow directly from the pens of their authors we are able to read them without having to go through the intermediary of a reporter who was present in court, who might have misheard what was said or misunderstood it, who would inevitably have abbreviated what was said, who might have jotted down things which he found interesting himself even if they had not been stressed by the speaker, and who might have got confused in transcribing his notes into a neat report—as John Hawarde admitted he had done when reporting the argument of Coke CJ.[13]

The first thing that needs to be said about the three arguments is that they have very different characters. Bacon's is well structured, beginning with observations on the nature of law and then with the different

---

9.   Hawarde, 363; MS Dd 11.53, fol. 23v.

10.   See for example the beginning the speech as reported in MS Dd 10.53, fol. 24, which points to his having stressed that the case should be judged by law rather than equity, something that does not appear in the printed text.

11.   PRO SP 14/34, fol. 26.

12.   The section marked "not urged" does not appear in the printed text, which also contains references to the arguments of some of the other judges, showing that it had been edited before printing.

13.   Hawarde, 357.

types of personal status recognized at common law. This is followed by a refutation of the arguments that the *post-nati* had alien status and the positive arguments why they should be treated as natural-born subjects; all of this lightly larded with references to cases and statutes. Coke's began with definitions of the relevant terms, followed by consideration of a mass of previous cases, consistent with his argument that the answer was to be found in previous cases or by analogy with them. Finally, Ellesmere's reads almost like a disquisition on legal method, with relatively little discussion of the case in hand and rather more by way of interesting asides, with the result popping out almost by magic at the end.

More importantly, though, the three texts give us an insight into the ways in which lawyers approached law in the early seventeenth century. They allow us to look at styles of argumentation at this period, the time at which English legal argumentation was coming to take something like its modern form of case-law, though as yet without the rigid doctrine of *stare decisis* which was to become characteristic of legal thinking in the nineteenth century. A second feature at which we should look is the function of natural law as a regulator of common law, something more normally treated through the study of *Doctor Bonham's Case* decided a few years later.[14] And thirdly, I shall consider the way in which Roman law, or more generally the civil law, might be relevant in English legal argument.

PRECEDENT AND AUTHORITY

I have put forward elsewhere a number of arguments about legal reasoning before and after 1600.[15] Three of these are relevant to the present discussion. First of all, in the sixteenth century the argument from authority was a straightforward instance of the medieval dialecticians' argument *ab auctoritate*, that is to say an argument flowing from statements made by others. The authority might be necessary, as where it was based on the scriptures, or it might be probable. In the latter case the starting point was not necessarily true, and consequently neither was the conclusion; but as a general rule the person who was expert in his art was to be believed. In the former case the starting point was unquestionably true, so the conclusion was also

14. (1610) 8 Co. Rep. 114.
15. "Authority and Precedent" (forthcoming).

true provided that the argument based on it was sound. Secondly, when sixteenth-century lawyers based themselves on precedents, they were referring in particular to formal writings: precedents of charters, precedents of forms of pleading and the like, including enrolled judgments. Thirdly, as we move into the early seventeenth century, and particularly in the writings of Edward Coke, these ideas of authority and precedent began to run together, giving especial weight to the judicial decision. These were the ideal type of precedents, and it could be said not only that they were authorities but that they had authority. All of these elements appear in the arguments in *Calvin's Case*.

First, we see arguments based on authorities, in the broad sense of materials, mostly non-legal materials such as events from history, which could be used as a starting point to reach provisional conclusions. So Francis Bacon pointed to parallels with the Spartan king Lycurgus and the biblical king David, joining them with references to Aristotle and Xenophon in drawing the analogy between the king and the father of a family or a shepherd with his sheep.[16] That there were kings before there were laws was shown by Bacon by reference to Sparta, Greece and Rome as well as to Saxon England,[17] while Coke used the book of Genesis and Aristotle to prove the same thing, adding to them Virgil's *Aeneid* and the historical account of Roman law preserved by Pomponius in Justinian's Digest.[18] And that there was originally a state of equality of men, without there being kings and subjects, was demonstrated by Bacon from the book of Genesis.[19] This broad sweep of materials to give color to an argument was wholly typical of the argument *ab auctoritate* found in all sorts of writing in England at the time, and which had been found all over Europe for centuries.

More self-consciously, though, Coke signaled his reliance on the medieval tradition of arguing from authority, probably known to him through one of the sixteenth-century Dutch works on legal reasoning such as Nicolas Everard's *Loci Legales*. Hence he cited explicitly the opening section of Aristotle's *Topics* which underlay the understanding of the argument from authority in the sixteenth century and before, quoting the rule that the

16.   Bacon, 5–6; Cobbett, 578–79.
17.   Bacon, 9–10; Cobbett, 581.
18.   7 Co. Rep. 13; Cobbett, 630.
19.   Bacon, 35; Cobbett, 594–95.

expert ought to be believed in his own art.[20] Similarly, Ellesmere may have been picking up on the terminology of the dialectical tradition when he said that the absence of examples of a particular form of pleading might *probably* show that it was not permitted, a linguistic cue to the distinction between necessary and probable arguments.[21] As with any argument of authority, the validity of conclusions depended on the evaluation of the starting points. So, unlike Bacon and Coke, he refused to rely on earlier writers to show that kings preceded laws, in particular rejecting Plato and Aristotle as proof of this since they wrote at a different time and place, before Christ had brought direct knowledge of God to humanity.[22] In other words, they were only probably authority, and it was possible and permissible to show reasons why they should not be regarded as determinative. He preferred to rely on an express text from the Book of Proverbs to show that kings received their power from God and were therefore constituted by a law, though the law of God rather than that of man.[23]

Secondly, we see the reliance on precedents in the sense that the term was used in the sixteenth century. "Show me a precedent of a pleading [in a certain form],"[24] said Bacon, arguing that the lack of any such precedent counted in favor of his argument; and, as has been seen, Ellesmere argued that the lack of a precedent of pleading in a particular form was a probable reason for holding that it was not permitted.[25] Ancient records and precedents were used to show the legal status of those born in Ireland, of Gascony, and of France when the crowns of the two kingdoms were joined in the fourteenth century.[26] All of this is utterly typical of sixteenth-century usage.

Coke referred to precedents, but in a rather different way from this. For him, when he talked of precedents he seems to have been talking of decided cases. Hence, that as a matter of English law allegiance was due to the king in his natural person rather than to his office was proved by "in-

---

20. 7 Co. Rep. 19; Cobbett, 641.
21. Ellesmere, 89; Cobbett, 687.
22. Ellesmere, 105; Cobbett, 692.
23. Ellesmere, 105; Cobbett, 692.
24. Bacon, 33; Cobbett, 588.
25. Ellesmere, 89; Cobbett, 687. Cf. Yelverton, PRO SP 14/32, fol. 67v.
26. Bacon, 30; Cobbett, 592.

finite precedents and book-cases."[27] In determining the law, recourse was to be had primarily to "examples and precedents in like cases,"[28] with the focus therefore on the decided case rather than simply on formal exemplars. In the absence of this it might be necessary to resort to reason, but here it was not so, since there were many "examples, precedents, judgments and resolutions in the laws of England" which, according to his argument, were enough to resolve the issue.[29] These were the "authorities of law" which he cited in his report to justify his conclusion that Calvin was not an alien so far as English law was concerned.[30] His focus, unlike that of Bacon and Ellesmere, was strongly on the decided case, very much what we see elsewhere in his writings in the first decade of the seventeenth century.

These three well-crafted arguments in *Calvin's Case*, then, reflect what seems to be happening more generally in English law at this time. Arguments from authority and precedents are found in their traditional forms, but in Coke's formulation we find a real sharpening of focus onto the judicial decision as the core idea of the precedent that had authority. It is not that Coke was doing anything new in relying on case-law, for English lawyers had for centuries relied on previous cases, and once law reports began to be printed it was absolutely commonplace to put weight on previous decisions. Exactly the same happened in continental Europe, Ellesmere pointed out.[31] What was different with Coke was that he was theorizing this reliance on previous decisions within the different traditions of reasoning from authority and from precedent, generating a system within which decisions had probable rather than necessary authority, thereby enabling the growth of a system of case-law within which previous decisions were guides for later courts but not absolutely determinative. Coke's focus on the judicial *decision* as the source of later law contrasts with Ellesmere's focus on the judicial *opinion*, so that he could put weight on the near-unanimous opinion of the judges expressed to parliament four years earlier[32] whereas Coke might have found difficulty in doing so.

27.   7 Co. Rep. 11; Cobbett, 626.
28.   7 Co. Rep. 18b; Cobbett, 641.
29.   7 Co. Rep. 19; Cobbett, 641.
30.   7 Co. Rep. 25b; Cobbett, 654.
31.   Ellesmere, 55; Cobbett, 677.
32.   Ellesmere, 18; Cobbett, 665.

Whilst it is in Coke's report that we see most clearly the relationship between authority and precedent in the treatment of judicial discussions, others were concerned to justify the reliance on previous cases. As we shall see, Chancellor Ellesmere and Justice George Croke did so by treating judicial opinions as the equivalent of the Roman lawyers' *responsa prudentium*, which had the authority of the emperor: they were, therefore, not merely evidence of what the unwritten law was, but had authority.[33] Similarly, notes of the speech of Baron James Altham show that he began "in legibus sita est judicis authoritas," the authority of the judge is grounded in the laws.[34] The presence of this observation at the start of his argument, apparently not connected to anything else he is reported to have said, points to his having been concerned to identify what might constitute acceptable bases for legal reasoning, against the background in particular of the Roman rule that one should judge according to *lex* rather than *exempla*. If the authority of judges was founded on *lex*, as he argued, then it would be possible to justify reliance on previous decisions as being recognized by *lex*.

NATURAL LAW AND THE NATURE OF THE COMMON LAW[35]

Legal philosophers today disagree trenchantly about the nature of law. It is not surprising therefore to find that there were similar levels of disagreement in the early seventeenth century.

Francis Bacon's speech reveals two antinomies, first between the law of nature and positive human law, and secondly between reason and authority. The core of his reasoning on the relationship between natural and positive law is found in his discussion of the character of the obligation of allegiance to a king. Since, for him, the institution of kingship, and the respective rights and duties of king and subjects, predated the existence of law, it followed that the subject's obligation of allegiance was not something that came into existence as a matter of positive law but as a matter of nature, only later formalized by law. Equally, the fact that there were

---

33. Below, 228.
34. SP 14/34. fol. 14v; MS Dd 11.53, fol. 7.
35. On this, see in particular Kim, "*Calvin's Case*," 156–60 and R. H. Helmholz, "Natural Law and Human Rights in English Law: From Bracton to Blackstone," *Ave Maria Law Review* 3 (2005), 1.

legal rules designating the king and defining the details of his powers did not supersede the underlying basis of the nature of kingship. The situation was the same as with the Romans' *patriapotestas*, which arose as a matter of nature though was given shape by law: the obligation owed by the son to his father was no less natural because it had come to have a legal form. The duty of allegiance was confirmed by positive law, but at root it belonged to the law of nature.

There may be a logical, and not merely a factual, point behind this. Given that the king was a constitutive part of the law-making sovereign, his powers could not have been derived from the very law which he made. The same argument has been made today, that parliament (or the government) cannot have untrammeled powers to alter constitutional arrangements when it is a part of those arrangements.[36] It is not absolutely clear that Bacon was actually saying this, but it seems likely that he was. The argument that the natural obligation precedes the legal needs more underpinning than that, as a matter of historical observation, there were kings before there was law. To focus on the obligation of allegiance of Robert Calvin to King James, it is not easy to see how the fact that there might have been kings in Saxon England, or Greece or Sparta or Rome, before there were formalized laws actually determines this question.

But there is more subtlety than this, or perhaps more confusion, in Bacon's position. Although the obligation of allegiance was rooted in the law of nature, it did not follow that the law of nature took precedence over positive law as a source of enforceable obligations. English law, it was said, was grounded on the law of nature, and human laws should therefore be taken strictly since they operated to abridge the law of nature.[37] There was an order of worthiness, with natural law prevailing over common law and common law over statutes,[38] but this reversed the order of authority, where statute prevailed over common law and common law over the law of nature.

Bacon's second, related, antinomy was between reason and authority. Here he looked not so much at what the rules were, but at the nature of legal argument. Reason, for Bacon, was undoubtedly important, but it did not in itself prevail over authority. Rather, he said, it gave dignity to the

36.   T. R. S. Allan, *The Sovereignty of Law* (Oxford, 2013), 133–67, esp. at 140–41.
37.   Bacon, 36; Cobbett, 595.
38.   Bacon, 10; Cobbett, 581.

authority of laws.[39] Hence, there was an argument that where two rights or capacities were joined together in a single person the two capacities remained distinct,[40] and it was one of the central questions in the case whether, and if so how, this applied to the facts in issue. This was a maxim derived from Roman law, and was described by Bacon as a rule of reason. But what was really important for Bacon, it seems, was that it had been received into all laws,[41] and was hence accepted as being a part of the common law.

Coke too refers both to natural law and to reason, though he says less about both than does Bacon. However, what he does say is pregnant with meaning. We may look first at natural law. This Coke identified with the moral law or the eternal law, infused into the heart of man at his creation.[42] Following Aristotle, and we might say many others both in the classical world and in medieval England, this was seen as something absolute. It was indelible and immutable, and could not be changed by any human law.[43] This is very different from Bacon's positivism, where natural law was something that gave greater worth to the common law but could be abridged and regulated by it. It is, perhaps, very revealing of Coke's approach to the law. On the one hand, we know him to have been a staunch, perhaps even obsessive, defender of the common law against encroachment from all other courts; so we might expect him to have given primacy to the common law against even the law of nature. On the other hand, his defense of the common law was based on something like a belief in its *objective* validity as a system, though accepting that individual rules might be changed without compromising that validity; hence, we might think, his apparent commitment to its indeterminate antiquity. Though this belief in its objective validity does not necessitate a commitment to any sort of natural law theory, there are very clear parallels. Just as individuals could be given rights by the natural law, so too they could be given rights by the ancient common law.

It is, of course, possible that what we are seeing in Coke's report of the arguments is a genuine redaction of what some other lawyer had said, for he does say that he is not reproducing the arguments of any one of the

39. Bacon, 4; Cobbett, 578.
40. Bacon, 25; Cobbett, 589.
41. Bacon, 15; Cobbett, 584.
42. 7 Co. Rep. 1, 12b; Cobbett, 629.
43. 7 Co. Rep. 1, 13b; Cobbett, 630.

judges.[44] However, two lapidary notes of Coke's own argument suggest that he did make this point, as he is reported to have said in one that "Nature writes the law of government in the heart of man for his preservation,"[45] and in the other "Ius naturae nullo iure civili deleri potest," the law of nature cannot be destroyed by any civil law.[46] It seems likely, therefore, that it does represent Coke's own argument.

Perhaps more surprising is a related point which appears in a note of Coke's argument but is not found in his printed report, that the king's natural prerogative cannot be limited by any act of parliament.[47] This is rather at odds with his view as expressed in the *Case of Proclamations* in 1610, that the king has no prerogative except that which is allowed to him by the law of the land.[48] Since it unlikely that the report of his speech records something that was not said, all the more so when it fits with his argument that allegiance is owed to the king as a natural person, we can only conclude that this was a point which was redacted out when the printed version of the speech was prepared.

The second point about the nature of law to derive from Coke's report is the role of reason, *ratio*. In the absence of express texts, or examples and precedents in similar cases, he says, it is necessary to decide by natural reason.[49] But this statement required careful unpacking. The reason concerned was not just the reason of a wise man, not even the reason of the wisest man if he did not profess the laws of England. Rather it was the reason of those who were learned in the laws of the realm as a result of diligent study and long experience and observation. Although this was justified with maxims more normally found explaining the relevance of reasoning from authority, in particular that the person expert in his art was to be believed, its underlying sense was rather different. If the reasoning of the wisest of men did not suffice, then the relevant reason was something internal to the law. The experienced lawyer's skill was directed towards identifying this inner logic, what we might call the *ratio legis*; it need have nothing to do with reason

---

44. 7 Co. Rep. 1, 4; Cobbett, 613.
45. Hawarde, 358.
46. SP 14/34, fol. 21v.
47. SP 14/34, fol. 21v.
48. 12 Co. Rep. 74, 75.
49. 7 Co. Rep. 1, 18b; Cobbett, 641.

in the sense that it was used by Bacon, as a criterion of argumentation, nor need it be related to reasoning processes at all. Coke's argument here is wholly consistent with the position he is recorded to have taken in the *Case of Prohibitions del Roy* a few months earlier, that the king could not himself decide any case at law, for even if the law was based on reason it was not on natural reason but on the artificial reason of the lawyers.[50]

Ellesmere's speech contains very little about the relationship between human and natural law. He says that the common law is grounded on the law of God, which extends to the law of nature and also the universal law of nations,[51] the *ius gentium* and *ius naturale* which had been described by some of the Roman lawyers. We may suspect that his position was like that of Bacon, that behind the common law there was God's law, something that gave it extra quality and weight, rather than Coke's position that this natural law or eternal law was something that could not be changed and therefore prevailed over any inconsistent positive law. But from his few remarks in the case it is difficult to be sure.

More interesting is his treatment of reason, *ratio*, though what he says is not easy to interpret. It is clear that, unlike for Coke, reason or *ratio* was not something internal to the law, to be identified by a proper understanding of it. In the absence of law, he said, the judge should look to custom, and in the absence of custom he should have recourse to reason.[52] So, we can say, reason is something that comes into play when law and custom fail. An alternative line is to begin with direct laws, by which he means written statutes. These need to be interpreted, and he says something about the way in which this should be done. But if, once interpreted, they give no answer, then recourse must be had to reason and to judicial decisions.[53] Of these, judicial decisions applied by analogy carry the greater weight; but since the first precedent, when it was decided, could itself have had no precedent, it follows that in some situations reason must come into play independent of precedent. Again, it is something existing beyond the law. Indeed, for him, law is the height of reason,[54] by which he seems to be meaning that the law

50. 12 Co. Rep. 63, 64–65.
51. Ellesmere, 32; Cobbett, 670. Cf. PRO SP 14/32, fol. 64v (Yelverton).
52. Ellesmere, 41–42; Cobbett, 672–73.
53. Ellesmere, 45; Cobbett, 674.
54. Ellesmere, 84; Cobbett, 685: *lex est ratio summa* (Cicero, *De Legibus*, 1.18).

is a normative system generated by the truest exercise of reason. It must be deep reason, he says, "not the light and shallow distempered reasons of common discoursers walking in Powles, or at ordinaries, in their feasting and drinking, drowned with drinke, or blowne away with a whiffe of tobacco."[55] How different is this from Coke, seeking out the reason within the law and giving no weight at all to the reasoning of the wisest man who is not a lawyer! All that Ellesmere is excluding is the so-called reason of the unwise or of those sated by food, drink or tobacco. Perhaps, too, it is different from Bacon's approach, where reason relates particularly to types of argument rather than to the application of wisdom to reasoning from first principles.

We can probably not draw any wholly satisfactory conclusion from all of this, except that three of the leading lawyers of the early seventeenth century seem to have had radically different views of the intellectual underpinnings of the common law at the time. But maybe that would have been true of common lawyers at all times. At the very least it should warn us, when looking at cases like *Doctor Bonham's Case*[56] and trying to discern from that whether the courts have power to regulate or annul parliamentary legislation, that there would in all probability have been a multiplicity of different views at the time. We may say rather the same about reason. Although all three of Bacon, Coke and Ellesmere gave weight to reason as something within the common law, it is clear that they meant rather different things by it, perhaps very different things. The same word was— and is—capable of encapsulating, or concealing, a range of very different theoretical positions.

COMMON LAW AND CIVIL LAW

The most telling difference between the arguments of Bacon and Coke on the one hand and Ellesmere on the other is that the latter makes enormous use of techniques of argumentation drawn from the civil law whereas the former do not. Coke makes a trivial nod in the direction of the civil law when he says that we should not draw distinctions which are not drawn by

55. Ellesmere, 84; Cobbett, 686.
56. (1610) 8 Co. Rep. 114; see I. S. Williams, "Dr *Bonham's Case* and 'Void' Statutes," *Journal of Legal History* 27 (2006), 111, with further references.

the law,[57] but the point is an obvious one and we should not see it as anything more than an example of the use of authority in its broad old-fashioned sense. And civilian ideas might have weight not because they were Roman in origin but because they had been received into common law. When Bacon refers to the civilian maxim that when two rights concur in one person it is as if they are distinct persons, he describes it not merely as a maxim of the civil law, but as a part of the domestic law of all nations.[58] Similarly, Coke referred to Skene's *De Expositione Verborum*, which had earlier been cited by Walmsley J., but only to say that Scots law happened to be the same as English Law.[59]

Contrast this with Ellesmere. Right from the start, he made clear that he was arguing from rules and reasons both of common law and of civil law,[60] and his speech is everywhere shot through with civilian learning. We might suppose from this that he was assuming that the Roman civil law had as much weight in England as it did in continental Europe. It is indeed possible that he was assuming this, but only on the basis that even in France and Spain it only lay behind the national law rather than being directly applicable within it.[61] However, when we examine the use he makes of civil law reasoning, we see that it is not substantive law that he is borrowing so much as the techniques of argumentation and the understanding of legal authority.

His main concern was the justification for grounding rules on prior judicial opinions, an issue of considerable importance at a time when English law was coming to treat this as the dominant source of legal argument. We might read his argument as if it were directed at a person trained in the civil law, following the express Roman rule that one should judge according to *lex* rather than *exempla*. To this we may understand him as making two responses. First was that continental lawyers, in the civilian

---

57. 7 Co. Rep. 1, 5b; Cobbett, 615. The maxim *ubi lex non distinguit nec nos distinguere debemus* is not found in Roman law, but was used by Cuias in commenting on D. 40.14.4: *Opera* (Prato, 1838), 4.1496.

58. Above, 223.

59. 7 Co. Rep. 1, 5; Cobbett, 614; cf. Hawarde, 350.

60. Ellesmere, 7; Cobbett, 662.

61. Cf. Ellesmere, 43; Cobbett, 673; Hawarde, 365; MS Dd.10.53, fol. 24v. Contrast Yelverton's express statement that common law was different from the civil law which applied elsewhere: SP 14/34, fol. 70.

tradition, based their arguments on previous decisions just as much as did English lawyers. They collected "arrests," *arrêts*, and were guided by these. *Sententia facit ius*, the decision makes law. *Res judicata pro veritate accipitur*, a matter that has been adjudged is taken for truth. *Legis interpretatio legis vim obtinet*, the interpretation of a law has the force of a law.[62] Secondly, he was arguing that in truth this was consistent with Roman law. The decisions of judges were the equivalent of the Romans' *responsa prudentium*, the answers of the learned, which were treated by the Romans as having the force of law.[63] Moreover, this was not inconsistent with imperial authority, since according to a text in the Code of Justinian the Roman jurists were given the power to create law by the Emperor. So too in England, it was said that the judicial opinions were received, allowed and put in practice and execution by the king's authority. Now, as a matter of legal reality we may doubt whether judicial decisions were genuinely given the royal stamp of approval, but that was not really the point. What was important, seemingly, was that the justification found in the Roman texts could be used to explain or defend the English practice. It is as if there was a set of meta-rules relating to legal argument and authority, independent of the rules of any particular system.

There are other hints in Ellesmere's speech of civilian parallels in legal reasoning. Weight should be given to what lawyers agreed the law to be, just as the civilians relied on the writings of learned professors and rightly followed the *communis opinio* as representing the law itself.[64] Courts had their own sets of rules and practices, what civilians would refer to as the *cursus curiae*, the course of the court;[65] and this too could be treated as representing law. The provision in chapter 24 of the statute of Westminster II that the clerks of Chancery could create new writs by analogy with existing ones was treated as the same as the civilian rule that one should proceed by analogy, *de similibus ad similia*.[66] And in determining how written laws should be interpreted, he borrowed expressly from the Dutch writer Joa-

---

62. Ellesmere, 55; Cobbett, 677.

63. Ellesmere, 47; Cobbett, 674. The same point, he said, had been made by Croke
J.

64. Ellesmere, 56; Cobbett, 677.

65. Ellesmere, 38; Cobbett, 671.

66. Ellesmere, 41; Cobbett, 672.

chim Hoppers,[67] whose works we know to have been read and used by other lawyers in England in the late sixteenth and early seventeenth centuries.

But all of these hints go to the same point, that the civilian approach to legal authority and interpretation could be used in common law reasoning. There was no sense at all, even in Ellesmere's romanized argument, that substantive rules of Roman or continental law should be applied in England.

CONCLUSIONS

This is not a paper that gives itself to radical conclusions, but there are three important things that I think come out of it. First is that the three arguments analyzed here are very different from each other. That Coke's report was different may be explicable on the basis that it was a reworked report prepared for publication, though we may guess that it was not vastly different from his own argument in the Exchequer Chamber. But the differences between Bacon's argument and Ellesmere's are so great that we have to recognize that at this time legal arguments could be structured in very different ways. There was no canonical form for the shaping of legal arguments at this time. *Calvin's Case* might have been extreme, in so far as it raised a question as much of interest to political theorists as to common lawyers, but such a variation in the form of argumentation would not have been untypical at the time.

Secondly, what is common to all three arguments is their recognition of the authority of case law. They approach the point in different ways, Coke simply assuming it and using previous decisions to justify his conclusion, Bacon integrating it into a more reasoned argument, and Ellesmere spending a good deal of time trying to explain why it was authoritative. But it fits with what we know from elsewhere, or at least with what has been argued elsewhere, that the dominant role given to the authority of judicial precedent was probably the most noteworthy feature of English legal reasoning in the early seventeenth century.

Thirdly, and finally, we can see that, for all the apparent insularity of the common law, in the first decade of the seventeenth century argu-

---

67. Ellesmere, 85; Cobbett, 686.

ments based on the texts of Roman law or on continental European practice could still be made at the highest level of legal discourse, in particular when discussing the meta-question of legal dialectic, the way in which legal argument could be structured, rather than the substantive law which was being argued about. It is perhaps here that we can see the clearest point of influence of continental legal thinking on the common law in the early modern period.

Hugo Grotius and the Natural Law of Marriage: A Case Study of Harmonizing Confessional Differences in Early Modern Europe

John Witte, Jr.

In a series of writings spanning more than four decades, Professor R. H. Helmholz has brought to brilliant light and life the deep legal learning of the *ius commune* in medieval and early modern times. His methodology is legendary. He offers probing case studies of early court records,[1] incisive analysis of the development of sundry legal doctrines,[2] arresting profiles

---

1. See, e.g., R. H. Helmholz, *Marriage Litigation in Medieval England* (Cambridge, 1974); idem, *Select Cases on Defamation to 1600*, Selden Society 101 (1985).
2. See, e.g., R. H. Helmholz et al., *The Privilege Against Self-Incrimination: Its Origins and Development* (Chicago, 1997); R. H. Helmholz and Reinhard Zimmermann, ed., *Itinera Fiduciae: Trust and Treuhand in Historical Perspective* (Berlin, 1998); idem, "Baptism in the Medieval Canon Law," *Rechtsgeschichte* 21 (2013), 118; idem, "Judicial Review and the Law of Nature," *Ohio Northern University Law Review* 39 (2013), 417; "The Law of Slavery and the European *Ius Commune*," in *The Legal Understanding of Slavery: From the Historical to the Contemporary*, ed. Jean Allain (Oxford, 2012), 17; idem, "Religion and Succession in the History of English Law," in *Der Einfluss religiöser Vorstellungen auf die Entwicklung des Erbrechts*, ed. R. Zimmermann (Tübingen, 2012), 103; idem, "Human Rights in the Canon Law," in *Christianity and Human Rights: An Introduction*, ed. John Witte, Jr. and Frank Alexander (Cambridge, 2010), 99; idem, "*Scandalum* in the Medieval Canon Law and in the English Ecclesiastical Courts," *Zeitschrift der Savigny-Stiftung für Rechtsgeschichte* 127, Kan. Abt. 96 (2010), 258; idem, "Children's Rights and the Canon Law: Law and Practice in Later Medieval England," *Jurist* 67 (2007),

of leading jurists and judges,[3] close attention to the power and patterns of
legal education and learning,[4] all of which are marshaled into authoritative
longer studies of the history of canon law.[5] The main themes and aims of his

39; idem, "Marriage Agreements in Medieval England," in *To Have and To Hold: Marrying
and its Documentation in Western Christendom, 400–1600*, ed. Philip L. Reynolds and John
Witte, Jr. (Cambridge, 2007), 260; idem, "Der *Usus modernus Pandectarum* und die Ur-
sprünge des eigenhändigen Testaments in England," *Zeitschrift für Europäisches Privatrecht*
4 (1995), 769; idem, "Excommunication in Twelfth Century England, *Journal of Law and
Religion* 11 (1994), 235; idem, "The Origin of Holographic Wills in English Law," *Journal
of Legal History* 15 (1994), 97; idem, "Contracts and the Canon Law," in *Towards a General
Law of Contract*, ed. John Barton (Berlin, 1990), 49; idem, "Damages in Actions for Slander
at Common Law," *Law Quarterly Review* 103 (1987), 624; idem, "Usury and the Medieval English Church Courts," *Speculum* 61 (1986), 364; idem, "Early Enforcement of Uses,"
Columbia Law Review 79 (1979), 1503; idem, "Roman Law of Guardianship in England,
1300–1600," *Tulane Law Review* 52 (1978), 223; idem, "Support Orders, Church Courts, and
the Rule of *Filius Nullius*: A Reassessment of the Common Law," *Virginia Law Review* 63
(1977), 431; idem, "Abjuration *sub pena nubendi*," *The Jurist* 32 (1972), 80; idem, "Canonical
Defamation in Medieval England," *American Journal of Legal History* 15 (1971), 255.

   3.   See, e.g., R. H. Helmholz, *Three Civilian Notebooks, 1580–1640*, Selden Society 127 (2011); idem, "Sir Daniel Dun (c. 1545–1617)," *Ecclesiastical Law Journal* 16 (2014),
205; idem, "Richard Zouche (1590–1661)," *Ecclesiastical Law Journal* 15 (2013), 204; idem,
"Roger, Bishop of Worcester (c. 1134–1179)," *Ecclesiastical Law Journal* 15 (2013), 75; idem,
"Natural Law and the Trial of Thomas More," in *Thomas More's Trial by Jury*, ed. H. A.
Kelly (Woodbridge, 2011), 53; idem, "Alberico Gentili e il Rinascimento. La formazione
giuridica in Inghilterra," in *Alberico Gentili: Atti dei convegni nel quarto centenario della
morte* (Milan, 2010), 311; idem, "Thomas More and the Canon Law," in *Medieval Church
Law and the Origins of the Western Legal Tradition: A Tribute to Kenneth Pennington*, ed.
Wolfgang Müller and Mary Sommar, (Washington, D.C., 2006), 375; idem, "Christopher
St German and the Law of Custom," *University of Chicago Law Review* 70 (2003), 129; idem,
"Richard Hooker and the European *ius commune*," *Ecclesiastical Law Journal* 6 (2001), 4;
idem, "Brian Simpson in the United States," in *Human Rights and Legal History: Essays in
Honour of Brian Simpson* (Oxford, 2000); "Harold Berman's Accomplishment as a Legal
Historian," *Emory Law Journal* 42 (1993), 475.

   4.   R. H. Helmholz, "University Education and English Ecclesiastical Lawyers
1400–1650," *Ecclesiastical Law Journal* 13 (2011), 132; idem, "The Education of English Proctors, 1600–1640," in *Learning the Law: Teaching and the Transmission of Law in England
1150–1900*, ed. Jonathan Bush and Alain Wijffels (London 1999); idem, "Ethical Standards
for Advocates and Proctors in Theory and Practice," in *Proceedings of the Fourth International Congress of Medieval Canon Law*, ed. S. Kuttner (Vatican City, 1976), 283.

   5.   See, e.g., R. H. Helmholz, *The Canon Law and Ecclesiastical Jurisdiction from
597 to the 1640s* (Oxford, 2004); idem, *The Spirit of the Classical Canon Law* (Athens, Ga.,
1996).

work are equally legendary: Helmholz has documented and demonstrated better than anyone the remarkable doctrinal and procedural continuities across common law, civil law, and canon law,[6] the many sturdy bridges between the legal teachings and cultures of England and the Continent,[7] and the enduring resilience of the late medieval canon law even in early modern Protestant lands on both sides of the Atlantic.[8] For anyone interested in seeing the interdisciplinary, ecumenical, and transnational power of law

---

6.   See, e.g., R. H. Helmholz, "*Scandalum* in the Medieval Canon Law and in the English Ecclesiastical Courts"; idem, "Citations and the Construction of Procedural law in the *Ius Commune*," in *The Creation of the* Ius Commune: *From* Casus *to* Regula, ed. J. W. Cairns and Paul du Plessis (Edinburgh 2010), 247, idem, "The *Ratio decidendi* in England—Evidence from the Civilian Tradition," in *Ratio Decidendi: Guiding Principles of Judicial Decisions*, ed. W. Hamilton Bryson and Serge Dauchy (Berlin, 2006), 73; idem, "The *Ius Commune* and Sanctuary for Insolvent Debtors in England," in *Panta Rei: Studi dedicati a Manlio Bellomo*, ed. Orazio Condorelli (Rome, 2004), 2.581; idem, "Canonical 'Juries' in Medieval England," in *Ins Wasser geworfen und Ozeane durchquert: Festschrift für Knut Wolfgang Nörr*, ed. Mario Ascheri et al. (Köln, 2003); idem, "The *litis contestatio*: Its Survival in the Medieval *ius commune* and Beyond," in *Lex et Romanitas: Essays for Alan Watson*, ed. Michael Hoeflich (Berkeley, 2000); idem, "Scandinavian Law and English Law: An Historical Sketch and a Present Opportunity," in *Family, Marriage and Property Devolution in the Middle Ages*, ed. Lars Ivan Hansen (Tromsø, 2000), 17; idem, "Magna Carta and the *ius commune*," *University of Chicago Law Review* 66 (1999), 297; idem, "Spanish and English Ecclesiastical Courts (1300–1500)," *Studia Gratiana* 28 (1998), 415; idem, "The Learned Laws in 'Pollock and Maitland'," *Proceedings of the British Academy* 89 (1996), 145; idem, "The Transmission of Legal Institutions: English Law, Roman Law, and Handwritten Wills," *Syracuse Journal of International Law & Commerce* 20 (1994), 147; idem, "Use of the Civil Law in Post-Revolutionary American Jurisprudence," *Tulane Law Review* 66 (1992), 1649; idem, "The English Law of Wills and the *ius commune*," in *Marriage, Property and Succession*, ed. Lloyd Bonfield (Berlin, 1992), 309; idem, "Conflicts between Religious and Secular Law: Common Themes in the English Experience, 1250–1640," *Cardozo Law Review* 12 (1991), 707; idem, "Continental Law and Common Law: Historical Strangers or Companions?" *Duke Law Journal* (1990), 1207; idem, "Support Orders, Church Courts, and the Rule of *Filius Nullius*: A Reassessment of the Common Law."

7.   R. H. Helmholz and Vito Pierviovanni, ed., *Relations Between the Ius Commune and English Law* (Genoa, 2009); R. H. Helmholz, *La Magna Carta del 1215: Alle origine del costituzionalismo inglese ed europo*, trans. Dolores Freda (Rome, 2012); idem, *The Ius Commune in England: Four Studies* (Oxford, 2001); idem, *Canon Law and the Law of England* (London, 1987).

8.   R. H. Helmholz, *Roman Canon Law in Reformation England* (Cambridge, 1990); idem, *Canon Law and English Common Law* (London, 1987); idem, ed., *Canon Law in Protestant Lands* (Berlin, 1992).

in the West, Helmholz's work is indispensable. This is comparative legal history, and law and religion scholarship, at its very best.

One important source of this legal connectivity and continuity across time, space, and legal cultures in the West, Helmholz has shown, was the Bible. From the fourth to the eighteenth century, Christianity was the established religion of the West, and a common commitment to basic biblical teachings usually transcended tribal, feudal, political, economic, and linguistic differences. The Bible was no comprehensive legal textbook of course, but it provided a number of the legal and moral posts, even foundations, on which the Western legal tradition was built.[9] A second important source of legal connectivity and continuity was the Roman law. This vast legal system—developed over 1200 years and distilled in Justinian's sixth-century *Corpus Iuris Civilis*—was the anchor text for Western jurists after it was rediscovered in the later eleventh century. The Continental civil law tradition was most obviously dependent on the Roman law, but Helmholz has shown the ample uses of Roman law by the canonists and common lawyers as well, forming a growing *ius commune* for the West.[10] A third important source was the teaching of natural law, natural rights, and natural justice. All these terms were variously defined in the Western legal tradition, but the common starting point was the idea of a "law written on the hearts of all men" and known through reason, conscience, intuition, custom, and more. Western jurists and judges alike, Helmholz shows, made ready use of these natural sources in constructing their legal systems and doctrines, in crafting their statutes and consilia, and in resolving hard cases of law and equity that came before them.[11]

9.   Though this theme is notable in his work, see notably R. H. Helmholz, "The Bible in the Service of the Canon Law," *Chicago-Kent Law Review* 70 (1995), 1557.

10.   See sources in notes 7 and 8.

11.   See R. H. Helmholz, *Natural Law in Court: A History of Legal Theory in Practice* (Cambridge, Mass., 2015 [forthcoming]); For earlier work, see R. H. Helmholz, "Natural Law and Religion: Evidence from the Case Law," in *Law and Religion: The Legal Teachings of the Protestant and Catholic Reformations*, ed. Wim Decock et al. (Göttingen, 2014), 91; idem, "Natural Law and the Trial of Thomas More"; "Natural Law and Human Rights in English Law: From Bracton to Blackstone," *Ave Maria Law Review* 3 (2005), 1; idem, "Natural Human Rights: The Perspective of the *Ius Commune*," *Catholic University Law Review* 52 (2003), 301; idem, "Bonham's Case, the Law of Nature, and Judicial Review," *Journal of Legal Analysis* 1 (2009), 324.

In this article—dedicated to Professor Helmholz in admiration, appreciation, and affection—I would like to illustrate the use of natural law theory to build toward a universal law of marriage and the family in post-Reformation Europe. Marriage and marital jurisdiction were heated topics of controversy in the sixteenth-century Reformation era, and a source of sharp confessional differences between and among Catholics and Protestants in early modern times. One of the important contributions of seventeenth- and eighteenth-century natural law theorists was to show the natural foundations and common norms of sex, marriage and family life that Catholics and Protestants—and even Christians and non-Christians—shared with each other, and with the earlier civilizations of the West. Many seventeenth-century natural law theorists pressed this argument of continuity and connectivity. One of the earliest and most effective was the Dutch jurist and theologian, Hugo Grotius, who will be my main focus.

I choose this topic because it illustrates the power of Helmholz's insights into legal continuity and connectivity in the Western legal tradition. I also choose it because marriage and family life have long been important topics for Helmholz—indeed the subject of his first article and his first book.[12] Marriage, he has shown, was among the classic *res mixta* of the West, alongside education and charity on which he has also written at length.[13] Marriage is an institution with spiritual and temporal dimensions and with overlapping jurisdictional claims of church and state. It's a topic where the Bible, Roman law, and natural law all have had important insights. And it's a topic where civil law, canon law, and common law alike have developed important overlapping insights.

In what follows, I first show some of the sharp confessional differences over sex, marriage, and family life that emerged during the Reformation era. I then show how Grotius was in the vanguard of early modern jurists who used natural law theory to create a common framework of sex, mar-

---

12.   Helmholz, *Marriage Litigation*; R. H. Helmholz, "Bastardy Litigation in Medieval England," *American Journal of Legal History* 13 (1969), 360.

13.   R. H. Helmholz, "The Law of Charity and the English Ecclesiastical Courts," in *Foundations of Medieval Ecclesiastical History: Studies Presented to David Smith*, ed. Philippa Hoskin et al. (Woodbridge 2005), 111.

riage, and family norms that transcended the strained religious, political, and national divisions of his day.

MARRIAGE AND CONFESSIONALIZATION
IN THE REFORMATION ERA

Sex, marriage, and family life were one of the hotly contested issues of the sixteenth-century Protestant Reformation and one of the first institutions to be reformed. The leading Protestant theologians of the sixteenth century—Martin Luther (1483–1546) and Philip Melanchthon (1497–1560), John Calvin (1509–1564) and Martin Bucer (1491–1551), Thomas Cranmer (1489–1556) and Heinrich Bullinger (1504–1575)—all prepared lengthy tracts on the subject in their first years of reform. Scores of leading jurists took up legal questions of marriage in their *consilia* and commentaries, often working under the direct inspiration of Protestant theology and theologians. Virtually every city and territory on the Continent that converted to the Protestant cause in the first half of the sixteenth century had new marriage laws on the books within a decade after accepting the Reformation. And, in England, it was Henry VIII's "great marriage affair" with Catherine that prompted the English break with Rome.

The Protestant reformers' early preoccupation with marriage was partly driven by their reaction to the prevailing Catholic sacramental theology and canon law of marriage that had dominated the West for the prior half millennium. The medieval Catholic Church's jurisdiction over marriage was, for the reformers, a particularly flagrant example of the church's usurpation of the state's authority. The Catholic sacramental concept of marriage on which the church predicated its jurisdiction was, for the reformers, a self-serving theological fiction. The canonical prohibition on marriage of clergy and monastics ignored the Bible's teachings on sexual sin and the Christian vocation as the reformers understood them. The church's intricate regulations of sexual feelings and practices, even within marriage, were seen a gratuitous insult to God's remedial gift of marital love for Christian believers and an unnecessary intrusion on private life and Christian conscience. The canon law's long roll of impediments to engagement and marriage together with its prohibitions against complete divorce and remarriage stood in considerable tension with the Protestant understanding of the natural and biblical right and duty of each fit adult to marry and remarry.

Many Protestant theological leaders acted on this critique of the Catholic canon law tradition. Most of these early Protestant clergy were ex-priests or ex-monastics who had forsaken their orders and vows, and married shortly thereafter. New Protestant converts followed their examples by marrying, divorcing, and remarrying in open contempt of canon law rules. As Catholic Church courts and their secular counterparts began punishing these canon law offenses with growing severity, Protestant theologians and jurists rose to the defense of their coreligionists—producing a welter of new writings that denounced traditional norms and pronounced a new Protestant gospel of sex, marriage, and family life.

Protestant political leaders rapidly translated this new gospel into new civil laws. Taken together, these new Protestant marriage laws (1) shifted marital jurisdiction from the church to the state; (2) abolished monasteries and convents; (3) commended, if not commanded, the marriage of clergy; (4) rejected the sacramentality of marriage and the religious tests and spiritual impediments traditionally imposed on Christian unions; (5) banned secret or private marriages and required the participation of parents, peers, priests, and political officials in the process of marriage formation; (6) sharply curtailed the number of impediments to engagements and marriages that abridged the right to marry or remarry; and (7) introduced fault-based complete divorce with a subsequent right for divorcees to remarry.[14]

These new family norms became a permanent point of confessional conflict between Catholics and Protestants—particularly after the Council of Trent declared its anathemas on these Protestant reforms in the decree *Tametsi* of 1563.[15] But confessional differences over family norms were also dividing Protestants by this point. Lutherans propounded a social model of marriage that gave principal marital jurisdiction to the state and allowed for quite liberal marital formation and dissolution rules. Calvinists propounded a covenantal model of marriage, with strict formation and dis-

---

14.   See detailed primary and secondary sources in my *From Sacrament to Contract: Marriage, Religion, and Law in the Western Tradition*, 2nd ed. (Louisville, Ky., 2012).

15.   Reprinted in H. J. Schroeder, *Councils and Decrees of the Council of Trent* (St. Louis, 1941), 180 ff.

solution rules, and with church and state sharing jurisdiction. Anglicans, despite the early promise of reform, ultimately returned to much of the medieval canon law of sex, marriage, and family life, including the use of church courts in administering its family laws. In the early modern period, when Anglicans, Lutherans, Calvinists, and Catholics were slaughtering and slandering each other with a vengeance, these differences over marriage and family life and its governance were sharp flashpoints of confessional contestation.[16]

In the seventeenth century and thereafter, a number of theologians and jurists sought to bridge these confessional differences by building a common natural law account of the main features of marriage and family life that prevailed in all Christian and sometimes non-Christian communities alike. These natural law theorists used various methods to make their case. Some drew increasingly sophisticated inferences from pair-bonding patterns and reproductive strategies among animals, building on Aristotelian-Thomistic insights. Some uncovered the common forms and norms of marriage that were shared by Jews and Christians, sometimes even by "pagans," "heathens," and "exotic" religions from Asia, Africa, and the Americas—all of which they took as evidence of a common natural law at work in the hearts and consciences of all men. Some developed a practical, prudential, and even utilitarian logic of what worked best for husbands and wives, parents and children to exercise and enjoy their natural rights and duties in the household. Orthodox theologians often decried these efforts, especially as some of their philosophical brethren moved toward ever more exclusive rationalist formulations. But most natural law theorists on marriage saw their efforts as a complement to, even a confirmation of, the work of the theologians.[17]

---

16.   See *From Sacrament to Contract*, chapters 5–7 which set out these three Protestant models of marriage.

17.   See generally on early modern Protestant natural law, and the controversies it occasioned within some Protestant circles, Luigi Lombardi Vallauri and Gerhard Dilcher, eds., *Christentum, Säkularisation, und modernes Recht*, 2 vols. (Baden-Baden, 1981); Christoph Strohm, *Calvinismus und Recht: Weltanschauliche-konfessionale im Werk reformierter Juristen in der frühen Neuzeit* (Tübingen, 2008); David VanDrunen, *Natural Law and the Two Kingdoms: A Study in the Development of Reformed Social Thought* (Grand Rapids, Mich., 2010).

Part of this early modern natural law theory was its own alternative theological exercise—to show the existence of a common natural theology of marriage that Protestants shared with Catholics and that Christians shared with the many other religions being discovered in the new age of world trade, mission, and colonization. Part of it was a philosophical exercise—to prove the existence, if not the truth, of traditional marital forms and norms, much like others sought to prove the existence of God against the growing ranks of skeptics and atheists. Part of it was an historical exercise—to retrieve and reconstruct some of the rational core of marriage and family life developed by classical writers, neo-classical and reception of Roman law movements being highly fashionable in the day. And part of this was a jurisprudential exercise—to create a common law of marriage that would form part of a universal law of nations that could transcend, if not pacify, the many European nations that had become locked in bloody religious warfare.

HUGO GROTIUS AND THE NATURAL LAWS OF MARRIAGE AND THE FAMILY

In light of this last point, it is not so surprising that it was Hugo Grotius (1583–1645), the so-called "father of international law," who was among the first to press for a strong natural law of marriage and family life as part of his broader theory of international law. Among legal historians, Grotius is famous for his path-breaking writings on the laws of war and peace and on the laws of prize and the sea which became so critical to the development of modern international law.[18] Among church historians, Grotius is infamous for defending his fellow Dutchman, Jacob Arminius, against charges of "Pelagianism," an act which won him a prison sentence for heresy. What is forgotten by some legal historians is that Grotius was also an avid student of the neo-Thomist writings of the Spanish school of Salamanca and that he drew (with ample attribution) many of his cardinal legal ideas directly

18.   Hugo Grotius, *De Jure Belli ac Pacis*, trans. Francis W. Kelsey (Oxford, 1925), with alternative translation as idem, *The Rights of War and Peace*, trans. Jean Barbeyrac, ed. Richard Tuck (Indianapolis, 2005); idem, *Commentary on the Law of Prize and Booty*, trans. and ed. Martine Julia van Ittersum (Indianapolis, 2006); idem, *The Free Sea*, trans. Richard Hakluyt, ed. David Armitage (Indianapolis, 2004).

from such Catholic luminaries as Francisco Vitoria who wrote in the century before him. Indeed, a number of historians now call Vitoria, rather than Grotius, the father of international law.[19] What is forgotten by some church historians is that Grotius was a rather distinguished theologian in his own right and not just an amateur layman seduced by free-will liberals. Grotius wrote several commentaries on the New Testament, a learned tract on church-state relations and ecclesiastical law, several pamphlets of Christian devotion, and a richly textured work of Christian apologetics.[20] Drawing on diverse Catholic, Protestant, and classical sources, and using the tools of theology, jurisprudence, and natural philosophy alike, Grotius set upon a life-long quest for religious and political peace.[21]

Crafting a common legal understanding of marriage was an important part of this effort. "The union of the sexes, whereby the human species is continued, is a subject well worthy of the highest legal consideration," Grotius wrote. For, as Aristotle taught us, marriage is the "seedbed of the republic," the first natural association, and "the first school" of morality, virtue and good citizenship. To get this institution right was essential to creating coherent national communities, which needed internal stability before they could work toward any kind of international legal harmony. Grotius also regarded marriage as a "natural right" of all men and women, echoing the views of Vitoria and other jurists in Salamanca. Even slaves and captives should be granted this right, Grotius insisted contrary to

19.   James Brown Scott, *The Spanish Origins of International Law, I, Francisco de Vitoria and his Law of Nations* (Oxford, 1934). For a good sampling see Antonio Truyol Serra, ed., *The Principles of Political and International Law in the Work of Francisco de Vitoria* (Madrid, 1946).

20.   See Hugo Grotius, *Opera omnia theologica*, 3 vols. (London, 1679); idem, *Explicatio trium utilissimorum locorum N. Testamenti* (Amsterdam, 1640); idem, *De imperio summarum potestatum circa sacra*, 4th ed. (The Hague, 1661); idem, *De veritate religionis Christianae* (Oxford, 1662), translated as *Hugo Grotius on the Truth of Christianity*, trans. Spencer Madan (London, 1782).

21.   Among many studies, see recently with ample bibliographies, Florian Mühlegger, *Hugo Grotius, ein christlicher Humanist in politischer Verantwortung* (Berlin, 2007); J. P. Heering, *Hugo Grotius as Apologist for the Christian Religion* (Leiden, 2004). On his theory of marriage, which is understudied, see Hubert Rinkens, "Die Ehe und die Auffassung von der Natur des Menschen im Naturrecht bei Hugo Grotius (1583–1648), Samuel Pufendorf (1632–1694), und Christian Thomasius (1655–1728)" (Ph.D. Diss., Frankfurt am Main, 1971).

civil law precedents, given that marriage is "the most natural association" known to mankind. He regarded celibacy as an option for those few with unique abilities or disabilities, but thought that celibacy was "repugnant to the nature of most men" and women and that its mandatory imposition on the clergy was a source of "grave sin."[22]

Both in his legal and in his theological writings, Grotius showed full command of and respect for biblical norms and conventional Christian principles of sex, marriage and family life. He adverted repeatedly to the axial biblical texts on marriage in Genesis 1 and 2, Matthew 19, I Corinthians 7, and Ephesians 5, some of which he further glossed in his New Testament commentaries. He pored over the Mosaic laws of marriage and the Pauline household codes. He cited frequently to the marital writings of Augustine, Aquinas, Vitoria, and hundreds of other classical and Christian authorities. "Christianity is by far the most excellent of all possible religious systems," he wrote proudly, in no small part because "Christians are commanded to preserve indissoluble the sacred obligations of the marriage vow, by mutual concessions and mutual forbearance" of husband and wife, each "bearing an equal part in all the duties of the marital estate."[23]

But to build his natural law framework, Grotius was more interested in what the law of nature itself could teach us about sex, marriage and family life independent of biblical norms and divine revelation. That was in part the challenge he set for himself by uttering his "impious hypothesis:" that natural law would exist even if "we should concede that which cannot be conceded without the utmost wickedness, that there is no God, or that the affairs of men are of no concern to him."[24] It was the further challenge he set by his definition of natural law whose contents and commandments were to be rationally self-evident:

> The law of nature is a dictate of right reason, which points out that
> an act, according as it is or is not in conformity with rational nature,

22. Grotius, *Truth*, 108–09; Grotius, *War and Peace*, 2.4.21, 2.5.8

23. Grotius, *Truth*, 327–29; Grotius, *Explicatio trium utilissimorum locurum N. Testamenti*, ad loc. Matt. 19:1–9, Ephesians 5:32; and distillation of his fuller theological views in the lengthy notes by Jean Barbeyrac in Grotius, *War and Peace*, 2.5.9, n. 7 and repeated citations to Scripture and Christian authorities in ibid., 2.5.1–23. A full list of his sources is in Grotius, *De Jure Belli ac Pacis*, 889–930.

24. Grotius, *De Iure Belli ac Pacis*, Prolegomena, 11.

has in it a quality of moral baseness or moral necessity; and that, in consequence, such an act is either forbidden or enjoined by the author of nature, God.

The acts in regard to which such a dictate exists are, in themselves, either obligatory or not permissible, and so it is understood that necessarily they are enjoined or forbidden by God. In this characteristic the law of nature differs not only from human law, but also from volitional divine law.[25]

When deliberated purely rationally, without the aid of the Bible or divine authorities, Grotius concluded, natural law confirms a number of traditional Christian teachings of sex, marriage, and family, but not all of them and not altogether clearly. Grotius insisted that the Bible does not prescribe or proscribe anything "which is not agreeable to natural decorum." But he further insisted that the "laws of Christ do oblige us" to conduct that goes well beyond "what the law of nature already requires of us." Those who believe that Scripture and nature command exactly the same conduct are fooling themselves, Grotius observed. They will be "strangely embarrassed" when they try "to prove that certain things which are forbidden by the Gospel, such as concubinage, divorce, and polygamy are likewise condemned by the natural law." While "reason itself informs us that it is decent to refrain" from such deviations from faithful monogamous marriage, natural law does not necessarily prohibit them outright; that usually requires religious sanction and command.[26]

With these distinctions in mind, Grotius began to sort through what features of traditional Christian marriage "are necessary to marriage according to the law of nature" and what are required "only according to the Gospel."[27] He sometimes was content simply to show the overlaps between Christian and "heathen" marital practices, evidently thinking this was proof enough of the natural qualities of these practices. "The instances are numerous," he wrote,

25. Ibid., 1.1.10.
26. Grotius, *War and Peace*, 1.2.2–3, 1.2.6.
27. Ibid., 2.5.9.

Wherein heathens are observed to have inculcated, severally, the very same principles and duties which are collectively enjoined by our [Christian] religion: they teach us, for example, that…the intentional adulterer is guilty of the actual sin of adultery; …that a man should be the husband of one wife; that the marriage covenant should be inviolable.[28]

Grotius sometimes combined the common patterns of animals with the common customs of advanced civilizations to demonstrate what he thought was natural. For example, he condemned "the promiscuous en-joyment of all women in common," which some ancients and "savage" peo-ples practiced and which even Plato had commended in his *Republic*. Such practices would reduce the state to "a common brothel," Grotius concluded. "Even some of the brute animals" observe natural law far better, for "they are seen to observe a sort of conjugal obligation" at least in their produc-tion of offspring. "Far more just and reasonable it is, therefore, that man, the most excellent and most distinguished of all animals, should not be suffered to derive his origin from casual and uncertain parents, to the total extinction of those mutual ties, the filial and the parental affections." Ob-serving the natural law, humans have thus learned "to ensure the certainty of the bond between parents and children" by tying procreation to endur-ing monogamous marriages so "that confusion of offspring may not arise." And because of the long period of human infantile dependency, humans have further learned to treat monogamous marriage as a "real friendship," "a perpetual and indissoluble union," "a full participation and mutual con-nection both of body and soul."

The superior advantage of this institution, in respect to the proper education of children, is a truth as obvious as undeniable. Monogamy was even the established custom of some particular pagan nations; among the Germans, for example, and the Romans: and herein the Christians also follow their example, on a principle of justice, in re-paying, on the part of the husband, the entire and undivided affec-tion of the wife; while, at the same time, the regulations of domestic economy may be better preserved under one head and mistress of the

28. Grotius, *Truth*, 221–22.

family; and all those dissensions avoided which a diversity of mothers must create among the children.

Genesis 1 and 2 further confirms this natural preference for monogamous marriage, said Grotius. Because "God gave to one man one woman only, it sufficiently appears what is best" for the marriages of the human race.[29]

Grotius's argument for monogamy was a textbook restatement of the natural law configuration of marriage expounded by Thomas Aquinas and the Spanish neo-Thomists. In his *Summa Contra Gentiles*—a tract that used natural law and natural observation to try to prove truths of Christianity to Jews, Muslims, and other peoples ("*Gentiles*")—Thomas had argued as follows: First, unlike most other animals, humans crave sex all the time, especially when they are young and most fertile. They don't have a short rutting or mating season, followed by a long period of sexual quietude. Second, unlike most other animals, human babies are born weak, fragile, and utterly dependent for many years. They are not ready to run, swim, or fly away upon birth or shortly thereafter. They need food, shelter, clothing, and education. Most human mothers have a hard time caring fully for their children on their own, especially if they already have several others. They need help, especially from the fathers and his kin networks. Third, most fathers will bond and help with a child only if they are certain of their paternity. Put a baby cradle on a road, and most women will stop out of natural empathy. Most men will walk by, unless they are unusually charitable. Once assured of their paternity, however, most men will bond deeply with their children, help with their care and support, and defend them at great sacrifice. For they will see their children as a continuation and extension of themselves, of their name, property, and teachings, of their own bodies and beings—of their genes, we now say. Fourth, unlike virtually all other animals, humans have the freedom and the capacity to engage in species-destructive behavior in pursuit of their own sexual gratification. Given the lower risks and costs to them, men have historically been more prone to extramarital sex than women, exploiting prostitutes, concubines, and servant girls in so doing and yielding a perennial underclass of "bastards" who have rarely fared well in any culture. Given these four factors, said Thomas,

---

29.   Ibid., 109–11; Grotius, *War and Peace*, 2.5.8–10.

nature has strongly inclined rational human persons to develop enduring and exclusive sexual relationships, called marriages, as the best form and forum of sexual bonding and reproductive success. Faithful and healthy monogamous marriages are designed to provide for the sexual needs and desires of a husband and wife. They ensure that both fathers and mothers are certain that a baby born to them is theirs. They ensure that husband and wife will together care for, nurture, and educate their children until they mature. And they deter both spouses from destructive sexual behavior outside the home.[30]

Grotius accepted this argument, and repeated it several times to condemn extramarital sex, adultery, prostitution, and unilateral divorce without cause, all of which violated this basic natural configuration of enduring and exclusive marriage. But while monogamy is the naturally preferred form of marriage and forum for sex, he continued, he could not say that polygamy was automatically rendered "void by the law of nature only." After all, a number of animals, from chickens and cattle to lions and wolves, are polygamous and fare quite well. A number of successful biblical patriarchs and kings were polygamous, and no Old Testament law explicitly forbade them. A number of advanced civilizations like Muslims are polygamous, and they are strong. Grotius thought that polygamy was a "reprehensible" exploitation of women and an indulgence of a man's "brutal appetite." And he praised the institution of monogamous marriage taught by Christianity. But he concluded that it takes "the law of Christ" to "condemn polygamy outright."[31] Some Protestant writers like Samuel von Pufendorf and Chris-

---

30. See Thomas Aquinas, *Summa Contra Gentiles*, trans. Vernon J. Bourke, 4 vols. (Notre Dame, 1975), III-II.122–124. See also *Summa Theologica: Complete English Edition in Five Volumes*, trans. Fathers of the English Dominican Province (New York, 1947–48), vol. 5, qq. 41, 65–67. Grotius knew this argument largely through reading Francisco de Vitoria, "Relectio de matrimonio," in idem, *Relectiones theologicae XII* (Louvain, 1557), with modern Spanish-Latin version *Relecciones Teológicas del Maestro Fray Francisco de Vitoria*, ed. Luis G. Alonso Geton (Madrid, 1933), 1:420–452, 2:439–504. See also Francisco de Vitoria, *Comentarios a la Secunda Secundae de santo Tomás*, ed. Vincente B. de Heredi (Salamanca, 1932–1952), excerpted in Francisco de Vitoria, "On Law: Lectures on ST I-II, 90–105," in idem, *Political Writings*, ed. Anthony Pagden and Jeremy Lawrance (Cambridge, 1991), 153–204; Francisco de Vitoria, *Commentariorum ac disputationum in tertiam partem Divi Thomae* (Mogvntiae, 1599); See discussion in Gerhard Otte, *Das Privatrecht bei Francisco de Vitoria* (Cologne, 1964), 23–40, 121–32.

31. Grotius, *Truth*, 109–10, 328; Grotius, *War and Peace*, 2.5.9–10.

tian Thomasius agreed with Grotius, but later Protestants developed powerful natural law and natural rights arguments against polygamy, which they used to support the continued criminalization of polygamy by both civil law and common law authorities.[32]

Grotius had less trouble condemning polyandry—one woman with multiple husbands—as contrary to natural law. But he did so with a heavy-handed patriarchal argument that went beyond even the patriarchal conventions of his day. A marriage "contracted with a woman, who already has a husband, is void by the law of nature, unless her first husband has divorced her; for till then his property in her continues." "In its natural state," Grotius explained, a marriage "puts the woman, as it were, under the immediate inspection and guard of the man: for we see, even among some beasts, such a sort of society exists between the male and female." In human marriages, too, "the authority is not equal; the husband is the head of the wife in all conjugal and family affairs; for the wife becomes part of the husband's family, and it is but reasonable that the husband should have the rule and disposal of his own home."[33]

The gist of Grotius's argument was that polyandry was unnatural because the natural law gives a man exclusive dominion over his wife's person, property, and contracts—what common lawyers call the doctrine of "coverture," but now cast in natural law terms. This argument not only contradicted Grotius's starting premise that men and women have an equal and natural right to marry, but it also made little sense. Men by nature share property and power all the time—else no civilization could ever emerge from the state of nature. Moreover, bees, ants, and other animals sometimes operate successfully with matriarchies: why should they count any less than a herd of cattle in describing the contents of natural law, especially since the orderliness of beehives served Grotius's later arguments about the natural legal order. Thomas Aquinas had rejected polyandry as unnatural and unjust, especially to children. Later Protestant writers, beginning with John Locke, rejected Grotius's argument about polyandry, instead condemning this practice with more egalitarian natural law rationales.[34]

    32.   See detailed sources in my *Why Two in One Flesh? The Western Case for Monogamy over Polygamy* (Oxford, 2015), chapter 10.
    33.   Grotius, *War and Peace*, 2.5.8, 2.5.11.
    34.   Ibid., 2.5.5

Grotius was considerably more nuanced and convincing in his treatment of what he called a "difficult, if not impossible, question": whether the natural law outlaws incest—sex with or marriage to a party related by blood or family ties. Biblical law and Roman law firmly outlawed incest, and both Catholics and Protestants wrote endlessly on this topic in their discussions of the impediments of consanguinity and affinity. There is a strong natural law argument against incest, too, said Grotius, which supports at least some of these traditional legal prohibitions. It's the argument from "natural revulsion." "Brute animals," who operate by "natural instinct" alone, simply avoid sexual relations between parents and children, brothers and sisters—no matter how desperate their urge to mate. They are by nature repelled by such sexual connections. Among humans, reason translates this natural "aversion" to sex with close relatives into stronger terms of "moral abhorrence" as well. "Unless they have been corrupted by an evil education," or are simply "crazy," Grotius wrote, most people have an automatic and visceral "revulsion" against such close sexual unions. They see them as "contrary to human nature"—not only "impure" and "immodest" but an outright "corruption" and "defilement" of their rational nature. Moreover, such close relations confuse natural family roles. How can a father marry his daughter, or a mother her son, when they already have a complete, and life-long relationship of parent and child? How can a child who must always remain subordinate to the parent, become that parent's spouse, or even her head, through marriage? Also, to allow parents and children and brothers and sisters who daily share the same household to have sex together will "pave the way to unchastity and adultery, if such loves could be cemented in marriage." Sex or marriage between close relatives is contrary to human nature and contrary to the laws of nature that govern humans. This insight anticipated what modern scientists call the "revulsion reflex" against incest, which humans evidently share with other higher primates.[35]

Most civilizations, Grotius showed, used similar logic to extend the category of incest to ban sexual and marital relations with other near rel-

35.   Ibid., 2.5.12–14. See Frans B. M. de Waal and Amy S. Pollick, "The Biology of Family Values: Reproductive Strategies of our Fellow Primates," in *Family Transformed: Religion, Values, and Society in American Life,* ed. Steven M. Tipton and John Witte, Jr. (Washington, D.C., 2005), 34–51.

atives as well, even if "these prohibitions do not come from the pure law of nature" alone. While "brute animals" couple with more distant relatives, "rational humans" do not. The Mosaic layers of consanguinity and affinity that define the crime of incest, Grotius argued, have parallels in many other legal cultures, both before and after the time of Moses. Grotius adduced dozens of Jewish, Greek, Roman, and Christian writers who condemned incest, even if they differed on exactly where to draw the line between distant relatives. Incest prohibitions and aversions are so commonplace among men, Grotius concluded, "it follows that some law of nature" must be driving this—whether "given by God to man in Paradise," or customarily "insinuated...in the minds of men" over time, or "forbidden by natural reason without a formulated law."[36]

Grotius's natural law argument against incest became a standard among later Protestant natural law theorists. Many of them cited "natural repugnance" and "inherent revulsion" as the strongest indicators that incest of some sort was against the natural law. Others added utilitarian arguments about "bettering the breed of mankind" by "mixing blood lines" and about "enlarging friendships in the world, by alliances" formed by marriages between unrelated parties. Most Protestant writers agreed with the eighteenth-century Anglican clergyman and judge, Richard Cumberland, who said that "all the laws in Scripture against incest are not absolutely, but in a degree and measure, greater or lesser, laws of nature, or branches of the law of nature...[for] doing otherwise is ordinarily, in the nature of the thing, an incongruity."[37] But most also agreed with French philosopher, Baron Montesquieu, who wrote that, with incest and other sexual offenses, "it is a thing extremely delicate to fix exactly the point at which the laws of nature stop, and where the civil laws begin."[38]

Defining more clearly the point at which the natural laws of marriage start and stop was one challenge Grotius left for later Protestant and Enlightenment natural law theorists. Defining more fully what else nature teaches about many other features of traditional norms of sex, marriage,

---

36.   Grotius, *De Jure Belli ac Pacis*, 2.5.14; idem, *The Free Sea*, 105.

37.   Richard Cumberland, *A Treatise on the Laws of Nature*, trans. John Maxwell, ed. Jon Parkin (Indianapolis, 2005), Appendix 2, sect. 11, 854–55.

38.   Montesquieu, *The Spirit of Laws*, 26.14, in *The Complete Works of Montesquieu* (London, 1777), 2:218.

and family life not treated fully by Grotius was a further challenge. But he helped to unleash a large wave of Protestant natural law writing about sex, marriage, and the family, often as part of broader theories of natural law (*ius naturale*) and the law of nations (*ius gentium*). Among English Protestants, the best and most original such natural law reflections on marriage came from the Puritan legal historian, John Selden, the Anglo-Puritan philosopher and theologian, John Locke, the Anglican philosopher and cleric, William Paley, and the Cambridge jurist, Thomas Rutherforth. Among Lutherans, the most prolific natural law writers on marriage were Samuel von Pufendorf (whose work together with that of Grotius was popularized in Europe and America by the Genevan jurist, Jean Jacques Burlamaqui) as well as the German jurists, Johannes Wolfgang Textor and Christian Thomasius. Among Calvinists, the most interesting writings came from the many Presbyterians associated with the Scottish Enlightenment, most notably Gershon Carmichael, David Fordyce, Frances Hutcheson, Adam Smith, and Henry Home. All these Protestants stood alongside and drew in part on the formidable natural law writings on sex, marriage, and family life developed among early modern Catholics, both before and after the Council of Trent. While early modern Catholic natural law theory on marriage and the family is well known, a solid intellectual history and analysis of the parallel Protestant natural law writings on marriage remains to be written. It will be a large treatise if done comprehensively.

The Work of the English Ecclesiastical Courts, 1725–1745

Troy L. Harris

One of Richard Helmholz's most important scholarly contributions has been to demonstrate the significance of the records of the ecclesiastical courts for understanding English legal history, particularly from the medieval period through the seventeenth century. It seems a fitting tribute, therefore, to carry Professor Helmholz's story of continuity and change a bit further, into the terra incognita of the early eighteenth century. Although a relatively neglected period of English legal history, the eighteenth century has, fortuitously, become a battleground for political and religious historians.[1] Thus, solid evidence of what the ecclesiastical courts were doing may be of interest to those scholars as well.

What the records reveal is that, as in earlier periods, the ecclesiastical courts were remarkably busy. This evidence stands in stark contrast to the conclusions reached by earlier historians, who have generally adopted narrative of "decline." This essay first surveys the historiography of the eighteenth-century ecclesiastical courts—such as it is. It then surveys the number and types of causes heard between 1725 and 1745 in five different fora, the High Court of Delegates, the Court of Arches, the York Chancery

---

1. See, e.g., J. C. D. Clark, *English Society, 1660–1832: Religion, Ideology and Politics During the Ancien Regime* (Cambridge, 2000); John Walsh, Colin Haydon, and Stephen Taylor, eds. *The Church of England, c. 1689–c. 1833: From Toleration to Tractarianism* (Cambridge, 1993).

Court, and the consistory courts of Lichfield and Durham. The litigation
rates demonstrate both continuities with and changes from the courts'
work in earlier periods.

The first full-length study of the eighteenth-century ecclesiastical
courts was B. D. Till's unpublished 1963 work, "The Ecclesiastical Courts
of York, 1660–1883: A Study in Decline." Despite its promising title, however, the bulk of the work focused upon the period 1660–1712, with only
one chapter devoted to "The Eighteenth and Nineteenth Centuries—An
Epilogue." Till used the court records themselves, but his sampling of new
causes begun in the York Consistory and Chancery courts during the eighteenth century do not reveal any clear "decline."[2] Till drew heavily upon
Sykes's courts-in-decline story of *From Sheldon to Secker*,[3] and it may be that
Till felt obliged to make his interpretation accord with Sykes's. Similarly,
Robert Rodes has found that, at least with respect to discipline of the laity,

2.   B. D. Till, "The Administrative System of the Ecclesiastical Courts in the Diocese and Province of York: Part III: 1660–1883: A Study in Decline," (University of York,
Borthwick Institute of Historical Research, 1963, photocopy), 250. To be sure, there was
a large drop in the total number of causes coming before the York Chancery court after
1720–1, but this was because the Chancery ceased to hear defamation cases (which accounted for 119 out of 157 causes begun in 1720–1) by mid-century. Till, "Decline," 247–50.
Till also argued that the eighteenth century saw a drop in Consistory and Chancery business from late seventeenth-century levels. Till, "Decline," 61–2. Again, however, the drop
in the number of new causes may tell less of a story of "decline" than Till supposes. While
the drop in total number of cases in the Consistory court from the late seventeenth to
the early eighteenth centuries is indeed impressive, Till fails to consider what effect two
Parliamentary statutes may have had on this drop. Specifically, An Act for the More Easy
Recovery of Small Tithes, 7 & 8 W. III, c. 6, gave the justices of the peace concurrent
jurisdiction with the ecclesiastical courts over tithe disputes under forty shillings. Under
An Act that the Solemn Affirmation and Declaration of the People Called Quakers, shall
be Accepted Instead of an Oath in the Usual Form, 7 & 8 W. III, c. 34, the justices of the
peace had jurisdiction over amounts in controversy of up to £10 if the defendant was a
Quaker. According to Till's own figures, the single largest category of business in the Consistory court before 1700 was typically tithe litigation. Till, "Decline," 71. Thus, the drop
in number of new causes may be attributable to the passage of the two foregoing statutes.
Till's failure to itemize the causes in the Chancery court make it impossible to critically
examine his figures for that court.
        3.   Norman Sykes, *From Sheldon to Secker: Aspects of English Church History*,
1660–1768 (Cambridge, 1959); see, e.g., Till, "Decline," 10, 18, 58, 151, 171–6, 212.

"the élan had gone out of the system by the 1670s, and it was scarcely possible to take it seriously beyond the early eighteenth century."[4]

Other historians have dissented from the declension model of the eighteenth-century church courts. Anne Ashley, in an article on the Isle of Man,[5] argued that the courts were alive and well into the eighteenth century. However, the peculiar legal system of the Isle of Man (e.g., the Canons of 1603 did not apply there)[6] makes generalizations from the Manx courts to other ecclesiastical courts hazardous. More promising, at first blush, is Jan Albers's work on the courts of the archdeacons of Chester and Richmond.[7] Rejecting what she termed "the myth of the demise of Church discipline,"[8] Albers concluded that the work of the ecclesiastical courts in Lancashire showed the continued vitality of Anglicanism throughout the eighteenth century.[9] Albers's conclusions in this regard are compromised, however, because they are premised upon the assumption that participation in the disciplinary processes of the archidiaconal courts was wholly voluntary: "the Church could do nothing to force the individual to comply, for it had no right to extort a fine or imprison the guilty."[10] While it is true that excommunication was the most severe sanction an ecclesiastical judge could impose, excommunication could become the basis for imprisonment via the writ *de excommunicato capiendo*. Indeed, Chancery issued some 83 *significavits* between 1738 and 1745.[11] Perhaps more important, from a practical standpoint, were the disabilities visited upon the excommunicate, "For an excommunicated person can neither be plaintiff in a civil, nor an ac-

4.   Robert E. Rodes, Jr., *Law and Modernization in the Church of England: Charles II to the Welfare State* (Notre Dame, Ind., 1991), 23.

5.   Anne Ashley, "The Spiritual Courts of the Isle of Man, Especially in the Seventeenth and Eighteenth Centuries," *English Historical Review* 72 (1957), 31–59.

6.   Ashley, "Spiritual Courts," 38.

7.   Jan Albers, "Seeds of Contention: Society, Politics, and the Church of England in Lancashire, 1689–1790" (Ph.D. diss., Yale University, 1988).

8.   Albers, "Seeds of Contention," 215, citing Roy Porter, *English Society in the Eighteenth Century* (Harmondsworth, Middlesex, 1982), 188; Robert W. Malcolmson, *Life and Labour in England, 1700–1780* (New York, 1981), 85; and Keith Thomas, *Religion and the Decline of Magic* (New York, 1971), 263.

9.   Albers, "Seeds of Contention," 274–8.

10.   Albers, "Seeds of Contention," 220.

11.   C207.

cuser in a criminal cause."[12] In a society as litigious as eighteenth-century England, these disabilities were not insignificant, particularly given that many of those involved in proceedings in the ecclesiastical courts were also parties to related litigation in the temporal courts. Appearance in the archdeacons' courts is, thus, a poor measure of Anglican devotion.

Echoing Albers's conclusions is Mary Kinnear's article on the disciplinary court in Carlisle.[13] Although Kinnear limited her investigation to the prosecution of morals offenses, her data showed that the reports of the death of the post-Restoration ecclesiastical courts have been greatly exaggerated. Specifically, Kinnear showed that presentments for morals offenses (e.g. fornication and clandestine marriage) remained relatively constant for the period 1704–1756, with a veritable surge in the 1730s.[14] Among other interesting conclusions, she stated that the frequency of prosecutions for antenuptial fornication cast doubt on "several historians' verdict that an invariable motive in prosecuting sexual incontinence was economic."[15] More importantly for present purposes, however, is Kinnear's overall conclusion that the ecclesiastical courts fulfilled important functions at the local level.[16]

To much the same effect is Anne Tarver's detailed examination of the diocese of Lichfield during the long eighteenth century.[17] According to Tarver, "Many historians have dismissed the church courts as in terminal decline, or insignificant by 1700. In Lichfield they continued to serve an important and substantial role in the community for another century."[18] As we shall see below, it appears that much of what Kinnear and Tarver found with respect to the dioceses of Carlisle and Lichfield, respectively, can be generalized to include most of England in the early eighteenth century.

12. Ayliffe, "Of Excommunication," in *Parergon Juris* (London, 1726), 257. See also Richard Burn, "Excommunication," in *Ecclesiastical Law*, 2nd ed. (1767), II, 204–205; Hill, *Society and Puritanism* (New York, 1964), 357.

13. Mary Kinnear, "The Correction Court in the Diocese of Carlisle, 1704–1756," *Church History* 59 (1990), 191–206.

14. Kinnear, "Diocese of Carlisle," 196.

15. Kinnear, "Diocese of Carlisle," 196 (footnote omitted).

16. Kinnear, "Diocese of Carlisle," 205.

17. Anne Tarver, "The Consistory Court of the Diocese of Lichfield and Coventry and its work, 1680–1830" (Ph.D. diss., University of Warwick, 1998).

18. Tarver, "Lichfield and Coventry," 422–3.

What kinds of business actually went on in the ecclesiastical courts? Holdsworth noted in his survey of local law that one of the salient features of eighteenth-century governmental institutions was the diversity of customs and practices,[19] and his generalization holds true in important respects when applied to the ecclesiastical courts. Despite much similarity in types of causes heard and modes of proceeding, each jurisdiction turns out to have had its own character, with some jurisdictions more litigious than others and some types of causes more prevalent in certain jurisdictions than in others. I have chosen to focus upon the work of five courts during the period 1725 to 1745, the High Court of Delegates, the Court of Arches, the York Chancery Court, the Consistory Court of the Bishop of Lichfield and Coventry, and the Consistory Court of the Bishop of Durham. Thus, I have examined the national court of final appeal in ecclesiastical causes, the two intermediate, provincial courts of appeal, and one diocesan trial court in each province. The best source for this quantitative type of information is the act books for the various courts, which record the actions taken by the court in each cause it heard on each court day. Because the act books do not always reflect the type of cause, however, cross-referencing to the cause papers (e.g., citations, depositions, articles, personal answers), if any, in a given case is sometimes necessary. I have chosen to include the three appellate courts as a way of providing at least some comparative information about each jurisdiction in the country. Although the picture that emerges illustrates the need for further research into individual dioceses, it also confirms the accuracy of the common perception that styles of governance varied significantly from one place to the next.[20]

COURT OF DELEGATES

Tables 1 and 2 summarize the causes heard by the High Court of Delegates in the period 1725 to 1745. Table 1 shows the court of origin of each of the 304 appeals lodged with the Delegates, while Table 2 focuses more specifically upon the appeals from English ecclesiastical courts of general jurisdiction. Each Table reveals a number of interesting points. Table 1

19.   Holdsworth, *History of English Law* 10 (London, 1938), 126–339.
20.   A short note describing my sources and methods appears at the end of this essay.

shows that, from a purely numerical standpoint, the vast bulk of the Delegates' work consisted of appeals in ecclesiastical causes, the remainder of its work consisting of admiralty and other civil law matters. Fully 78% of appeals to the Delegates came from ecclesiastical courts in the provinces of Canterbury and York. Moreover, as between the two, Canterbury plainly dominated, and the testamentary work of the Prerogative Court of Canterbury was the single most fertile source of appeals. These facts are not especially surprising, because the Court of Delegates, as the institutional expression of the principle of Royal Supremacy over the Church, was created to hear appeals in ecclesiastical causes. What is more curious is that, in so maritime a nation as Britain, admiralty appeals should be swamped by appeals in ecclesiastical causes. Of course, as Holdsworth pointed out, the

Table 1. Appeals to the High Court of Delegates

	1725–1731	1732–1738	1739–1745	Total
Province of Canterbury				
Court of Arches	39	30	27	96
Prerogative Court of Canterbury	59	38	38	135
Province of York				
York Consistory Court	5	10	1	16
York Chancery Court	1	2	0	3
Exchequer & Prerogative Court of York	4	1	1	6
Ireland				
Ireland	11	10	9	30
Dublin Consistory	3	0	0	3
Prerogative Court of Ireland	2	0	2	4
Delegates of Ireland	1	0	0	1
Tuam Consistory	1	0	0	1
Military & Chivlary	0	2	1	3
Convocation of Oxford	1	0	0	1
Commission of Review	2	0	1	3
Unknown	1	0	1	2
Total	**130**	**93**	**81**	**304**

Source: Del. 8/73.

common law courts had succeeded in taking away much business from the admiralty courts in the late seventeenth century,[21] which may account for the relative scarcity of admiralty appeals. Until we have more quantitative data for the work of the temporal courts in this period, it is impossible to draw firm conclusions about the relative significance of the various bodies of law. What is clear is that there was relatively little fluctuation in the total number of appeals coming to the Delegates each year from the various courts under its jurisdiction.

Table 2 reveals three interesting facts about the types of appeals brought to the Delegates from the ecclesiastical courts. First, it shows that testamentary appeals from the courts of general jurisdiction were particularly frequent. Adding those appeals to Table 1's figures for appeals from courts having jurisdiction over testamentary matters alone (e.g., the Prerogative Courts of Canterbury and York) highlights just how important the Delegates' appellate testamentary jurisdiction was. Second, Table 2 shows that, after the Delegates' testamentary business, disciplinary and matrimonial appeals were the next most frequent type of appeal from the English ecclesiastical courts. As we shall see, such appeals to the Delegates were quite out of proportion to their frequency at the trial-court level, which suggests that the will to fight to the bitter end may have been stronger in disciplinary and matrimonial causes than in other types of suits. Finally, although disciplinary causes were the single most frequently occurring type of appeal from the English ecclesiastical courts of general jurisdiction, none involved a doctrinal dispute. According to H. C. Rothery's 1868 report to the House of Commons regarding appeals to the Court of Delegates in causes of doctrine or discipline, the only doctrinal cause between 1704 and 1759 was the prosecution in 1713 of the Arian William Whiston, which was eventually dropped.[22]

---

21. Holdsworth, *History of English Law*, 12: 692.
22. Quoted in Great Britain, Royal Commission on Ecclesiastical Courts, "Report of the Commissioners Appointed to Inquire into the Constitution and Working of the Ecclesiastical Courts," *House of Commons Reports and Papers, 1883*, Historical Appendix IX, 1: 188.

Table 2. Types of Ecclesiastical Appeals to Court of Delegates

	1725–1731	1732–1738	1739–1745	Total
Court of Arches				
Testamentary	6	6	6	18
Defamation	1	0	0	1
Tithe	0	0	1	1
Church Rate	6	1	0	7
Discipline	18	4	7	29
Faculty, Pew	4	0	0	4
Churchwardens	1	0	1	2
Matrimonial	2	18	6	26
Misc./Unknown	1	1	6	8
Total	**39**	**30**	**27**	**96**
York Consistory Court				
Testamentary	1	3	1	5
Defamation	0	0	0	0
Tithe	1	1	0	2
Church Rate	0	0	0	0
Discipline	1	0	0	1
Faculty, Pew	1	1	0	2
Churchwardens	0	0	0	0
Matrimonial	1	1	0	2
Misc./Unknown	0	4	0	4
Total	**5**	**10**	**1**	**16**
York Chancery Court				
Testamentary	0	0	0	0
Defamation	0	0	0	0
Tithe	0	0	0	0
Church Rate	0	1	0	1
Discipline	1	0	0	1
Faculty, Pew	0	0	0	0
Churchwardens	0	0	0	0
Matrimonial	0	0	0	0
Misc./Unknown	0	1	0	1
Total	**1**	**2**	**0**	**3**

Source: Del. 8/73.

CANTERBURY AND YORK

Tables 3 to 6 summarize the work of the two provincial appellate courts, the Court of Arches and the York Chancery Court. Perhaps the most striking difference between the provincial courts of appeal is simply the disparity in the number of causes each heard. Even allowing for the fact that the province of Canterbury was much larger and more populated than York, it is still somewhat surprising to find the Court of Arches hearing over 600 appeals to the York Chancery Court's 130. To some extent one may account for this difference by reference to the fact that appeals from the consistory court for the diocese of York itself went directly to the Court of Delegates, but as Tables 1 and 2 showed, there were only sixteen such appeals in the period 1725 to 1745.

Surveying the appellate work of the Court of Arches reveals a number of interesting points. The total number of appeals coming before the court remained fairly steady, as shown in Table 3, but when examined in terms of the courts from which the causes were appealed, it becomes obvious that some courts sent more appeals than others. As one might expect, given its sheer population, the diocese of London accounted for the largest number of appeals (92), although other dioceses in the southern province were well represented too. Consistory courts in the dioceses of Bath and Wells, Exeter, Hereford, Lichfield, Lincoln, and Norwich all sent a steady stream of appeals to London. On the other hand, very few appeals were taken from some dioceses (e.g., Oxford and Ely). Two observations regarding this discrepancy are appropriate. First, the number of appeals coming from a court is, at best, an imperfect guide to the trial work of that court. As we shall see, the consistory court at Durham handled over 1400 causes during the period 1725–1745, but only 18 of them were appealed to the York Chancery Court. Second, although the ecclesiastical courts were *an* essential instrument of ecclesiastical jurisdiction, they were not the *only* such institution. For example, the courts of the universities may well have been the fora of choice for those in the dioceses of Oxford and Ely. If so, the small number of appeals to the Court of Arches from those dioceses becomes more understandable. Until we know much more than we do at present about how much and what kinds of business the courts were hearing in the various dioceses, the significance of the absence of appeals must remain an open question.

Table 3. Appeals to the Court of Arches

	1725–1731	1732–1738	1739–1745	Total
Bangor	3	4	2	9
Bath and Wells	7	14	19	40
Bristol	0	8	2	10
Canterbury	0	2	1	3
Chichester	4	2	4	10
Ely	1	2	0	3
Exeter	24	26	9	59
Gloucester	2	0	4	6
Hereford	15	11	8	34
Lichfield	21	24	11	56
Lincoln	22	12	4	38
Llandaff	21	21	2	44
London	41	34	17	92
Norwich	8	15	14	37
Oxford	1	0	1	2
Peterborough	2	13	4	19
Rochester	0	1	0	1
St. Asaph	4	2	4	10
St. David	7	1	2	10
Salisbury	5	1	3	9
Winchester	7	13	3	23
Worcester	2	14	5	21
Unknown	14	22	29	65
Total	**211**	**242**	**148**	**601**

Source: A27–32; Aa32–35.

Examination of Table 4's breakdown of the Arches' appellate business yields three important conclusions. First, there was great diversity among the dioceses, not only with respect to the number of appeals coming from each but also with respect to the type of causes appealed. For example, appeals from the diocese London in matrimonial causes were much more frequent (over 30% of the London total) than such appeals from the diocese of Exeter (roughly 5% of the Exeter total). Second, like the Court of Delegates, the Court of Arches relied upon testamentary and disciplinary appeals for much of its business. Third, the Court of Arches heard a substantial number of appeals in categories that were hardly represented at all in the Court of Delegates (e.g., defamation and tithe).

Table 4. Types of Appeals to Court of Arches[23]

	1725–1731	1732–1738	1739–1745	Total
Bangor				
Testamentary	1	2	1	4
Defamation	1	0	1	2
Tithe	0	0	0	0
Church Rate	0	0	0	0
Discipline	0	0	0	0
Faculty, Pew	0	0	0	0
Churchwardens	1	1	0	2
Matrimonial	0	1	0	1
Misc./Unknown	0	0	0	0
Bangor total	**3**	**4**	**2**	**9**
Bath and Wells				
Testamentary	0	2	4	6
Defamation	3	0	3	6
Tithe	1	0	2	3
Church Rate	1	2	1	4
Discipline	0	1	0	1
Faculty, Pew	0	1	1	2
Churchwardens	0	0	0	0
Matrimonial	1	0	3	4
Misc./Unknown	1	8	5	14
Bath and Wells total	**7**	**14**	**19**	**40**
Bristol				
Testamentary	0	2	0	2
Defamation	0	0	0	0

23.   Source: A27–32; Aa32–35.

	1725–1731	1732–1738	1739–1745	Total
Tithe	0	4	1	5
Church Rate	0	0	0	0
Discipline	0	1	0	1
Faculty, Pew	0	0	0	0
Churchwardens	0	0	1	1
Matrimonial	0	1	0	1
Misc./Unknown	0	0	0	0
Bristol total	**0**	**8**	**2**	**10**
Canterbury				
Testamentary	0	1	0	1
Defamation	0	0	0	0
Tithe	0	0	0	0
Church Rate	0	0	0	0
Discipline	0	1	0	1
Faculty, Pew	0	0	0	0
Churchwardens	0	0	1	1
Matrimonial	0	0	0	0
Misc./Unknown	0	0	0	0
Canterbury total	**0**	**2**	**1**	**3**
Chichester				
Testamentary	2	1	1	4
Defamation	1	0	0	1
Tithe	1	0	0	1
Church Rate	0	0	1	1
Discipline	0	0	0	0
Faculty, Pew	0	1	0	1
Churchwardens	0	0	2	2
Matrimonial	0	0	0	0
Misc./Unknown	0	0	0	0
Chichester total	**4**	**2**	**4**	**10**
Ely				
Testamentary	0	0	0	0
Defamation	0	0	0	0
Tithe	0	1	0	1
Church Rate	0	0	0	0

	1725–1731	1732–1738	1739–1745	Total
Discipline	1	0	0	1
Faculty, Pew	0	0	0	0
Churchwardens	0	0	0	0
Matrimonial	0	0	0	0
Misc./Unknown	0	1	0	1
Ely total	**1**	**2**	**0**	**3**
Exeter				
Testamentary	5	7	4	16
Defamation	1	0	1	2
Tithe	1	7	1	9
Church Rate	3	0	0	3
Discipline	5	4	0	9
Faculty, Pew	1	1	2	4
Churchwardens	4	1	0	5
Matrimonial	2	0	1	3
Misc./Unknown	2	6	0	8
Exeter total	**24**	**26**	**9**	**59**
Gloucester				
Testamentary	0	0	0	0
Defamation	1	0	0	1
Tithe	0	0	1	1
Church Rate	0	0	0	0
Discipline	0	0	1	1
Faculty, Pew	0	0	0	0
Churchwardens	0	0	1	1
Matrimonial	1	0	1	2
Misc./Unknown	0	0	0	0
Gloucester total	**2**	**0**	**4**	**6**
Hereford				
Testamentary	2	5	2	9
Defamation	1	0	0	1
Tithe	5	1	3	9
Church Rate	1	0	0	1
Discipline	0	2	0	2
Faculty, Pew	0	3	2	5

	1725–1731	1732–1738	1739–1745	Total
Churchwardens	0	0	0	0
Matrimonial	3	0	0	3
Misc./Unknown	3	0	1	4
Hereford total	**15**	**11**	**8**	**34**

Lichfield

	1725–1731	1732–1738	1739–1745	Total
Testamentary	9	3	3	15
Defamation	1	0	1	2
Tithe	0	11	0	11
Church Rate	0	1	0	1
Discipline	9	5	1	15
Faculty, Pew	2	0	3	5
Churchwardens	0	2	2	4
Matrimonial	0	0	1	1
Misc./Unknown	0	2	0	2
Lichfield total	**21**	**24**	**11**	**56**

Lincoln

	1725–1731	1732–1738	1739–1745	Total
Testamentary	0	5	0	5
Defamation	3	0	1	4
Tithe	4	1	0	5
Church Rate	0	0	0	0
Discipline	8	2	0	10
Faculty, Pew	1	3	1	5
Churchwardens	3	0	1	4
Matrimonial	0	0	0	0
Misc./Unknown	3	1	1	5
Lincoln total	**22**	**12**	**4**	**38**

Llandaff

	1725–1731	1732–1738	1739–1745	Total
Testamentary	6	2	0	8
Defamation	8	7	0	15
Tithe	1	9	0	10
Church Rate	1	0	1	2
Discipline	2	0	0	2
Faculty, Pew	2	0	0	2
Churchwardens	0	2	1	3
Matrimonial	0	0	0	0

	1725–1731	1732–1738	1739–1745	Total
Misc./Unknown	I	I	O	2
Llandaff total	21	21	2	44

London

	1725–1731	1732–1738	1739–1745	Total
Testamentary	6	I	3	10
Defamation	4	2	O	6
Tithe	O	I	O	I
Church Rate	I	9	O	10
Discipline	9	I	7	17
Faculty, Pew	3	O	I	4
Churchwardens	5	6	O	11
Matrimonial	11	12	5	28
Misc./Unknown	2	2	I	5
London total	41	34	17	92

Norwich

	1725–1731	1732–1738	1739–1745	Total
Testamentary	2	5	O	7
Defamation	O	4	I	5
Tithe	O	O	2	2
Church Rate	2	I	I	4
Discipline	4	2	3	9
Faculty, Pew	O	2	2	4
Churchwardens	O	O	3	3
Matrimonial	O	I	O	I
Misc./Unknown	O	O	2	2
Norwich total	8	15	14	37

Oxford

	1725–1731	1732–1738	1739–1745	Total
Testamentary	O	O	I	I
Defamation	O	O	O	O
Tithe	O	O	O	O
Church Rate	I	O	O	I
Discipline	O	O	O	O
Faculty, Pew	O	O	O	O
Churchwardens	O	O	O	O
Matrimonial	O	O	O	O
Misc./Unknown	O	O	O	O
Oxford total	I	O	I	2

	1725–1731	1732–1738	1739–1745	Total
Peterborough				
Testamentary	0	4	1	5
Defamation	0	0	0	0
Tithe	1	1	0	2
Church Rate	0	2	1	3
Discipline	1	4	1	6
Faculty, Pew	0	1	0	1
Churchwardens	0	0	0	0
Matrimonial	0	1	0	1
Misc./Unknown	0	0	1	1
Peterborough total	**2**	**13**	**4**	**19**
Rochester				
Testamentary	0	0	0	0
Defamation	0	0	0	0
Tithe	0	0	0	0
Church Rate	0	0	0	0
Discipline	0	0	0	0
Faculty, Pew	0	0	0	0
Churchwardens	0	0	0	0
Matrimonial	0	1	0	1
Misc./Unknown	0	0	0	0
Rochester total	**0**	**1**	**0**	**1**
St. Asaph				
Testamentary	1	2	4	7
Defamation	1	0	0	1
Tithe	1	0	0	1
Church Rate	0	0	0	0
Discipline	0	0	0	0
Faculty, Pew	1	0	0	1
Churchwardens	0	0	0	0
Matrimonial	0	0	0	0
Misc./Unknown	0	0	0	0
St. Asaph total	**4**	**2**	**4**	**10**
St. David				
Testamentary	1	1	1	3

	1725–1731	1732–1738	1739–1745	Total
Defamation	1	0	0	1
Tithe	0	0	0	0
Church Rate	0	0	0	0
Discipline	2	0	0	2
Faculty, Pew	0	0	1	1
Churchwardens	0	0	0	0
Matrimonial	1	0	0	1
Misc./Unknown	2	0	0	2
St. David total	7	1	2	10
Salisbury				
Testamentary	0	0	1	1
Defamation	0	0	1	1
Tithe	0	0	0	0
Church Rate	0	0	0	0
Discipline	1	0	1	2
Faculty, Pew	1	0	0	1
Churchwardens	1	0	0	1
Matrimonial	0	1	0	1
Misc./Unknown	2	0	0	2
Salisbury total	5	1	3	9
Winchester				
Testamentary	0	3	0	3
Defamation	1	0	0	1
Tithe	0	0	0	0
Church Rate	0	0	0	0
Discipline	2	2	2	6
Faculty, Pew	1	4	0	5
Churchwardens	1	1	0	2
Matrimonial	0	1	1	2
Misc./Unknown	2	2	0	4
Winchester total	7	13	3	23
Worcester				
Testamentary	1	3	1	5
Defamation	1	2	2	5
Tithe	0	2	1	3

	1725–1731	1732–1738	1739–1745	Total
Church Rate	0	4	0	4
Discipline	0	0	1	1
Faculty, Pew	0	0	0	0
Churchwardens	0	2	0	2
Matrimonial	0	0	0	0
Misc./Unknown	0	1	0	1
Worcester total	**2**	**14**	**5**	**21**
Unknown				
Testamentary	3	2	3	8
Defamation	0	0	0	0
Tithe	0	1	0	1
Church Rate	0	0	0	0
Discipline	0	0	0	0
Faculty, Pew	0	0	0	0
Churchwardens	0	0	0	0
Matrimonial	0	0	1	1
Misc./Unknown	11	19	25	55
Unknown total	**14**	**22**	**29**	**65**

	Total by Type
Testamentary	120
Defamation	54
Tithe	65
Church Rate	34
Discipline	86
Faculty, Pew	41
Churchwardens	42
Matrimonial	51
Misc./Unknown	108
Total	**601**

Table 5 shows that, like the Court of Delegates and the Court of Arches, the York Chancery Court heard a relatively constant, if smaller, number of appeals each year between 1725 and 1745. Interestingly enough, well over half of the appeals (85) came from the diocese of Chester, either by way of the consistory court of Chester (57) or the Richmond Archdeaconry (28). Table 6 demonstrates that testamentary and disciplinary business again figured largely among the appeals, but disputes over faculties and pews were proportionately more significant in the York Chancery Court (19 appeals out of 130, or over 14%) than the Court of Arches (41 appeals out of 604, or less than 7%). Most interesting of all is the fact that, if one excludes appeals from the diocese of London, appeals in matrimonial causes were just under 4% of the total heard by the York Chancery Court (5 appeals out of 130) and just over 4% of the total heard by the Court of Arches (23 appeals out of 512). At the same time, appeals in matrimonial causes from the diocese of London accounted for a prodigious 30% (28 appeals out of 92) of the total number of appeals coming from that diocese to the Court of Arches. While there are many factors that affect overall rates of litigation, it is surely significant that the most urban diocese in the country had a rate of marriage-related appeals that was roughly seven times higher than the average.

Table 5. Appeals to the York Chancery Court

	1725–1731	1732–1738	1739–1745	Total
Alme and Tollerton	0	1	0	1
Carlisle Consistory	3	4	0	7
Chester Consistory	31	18	8	57
Durham Consistory	9	5	4	18
Howden	0	1	0	1
Nottingham Archdeaconry	1	4	1	6
Richmond Archdeaconry	20	5	3	28
Sodor and Man	0	0	1	1
Dean of York	0	1	0	1
Dean and Chapter of York	2	2	1	5
Unknown	1	3	1	5
Total	67	44	19	130

Source: Chanc. AB/45–48.

Table 6. Types of Appeals to York Chancery Court[24]

	1725–1731	1732–1738	1739–1745	Total
Alme and Tollerton				
Testamentary	0	0	0	0
Defamation	0	0	0	0
Tithe	0	0	0	0
Church Rate	0	0	0	0
Discipline	0	0	0	0
Faculty, Pew	0	0	0	0
Churchwardens	0	0	0	0
Matrimonial	0	0	0	0
Misc./Unknown	0	1	0	1
Alme and Tollerton total	**0**	**1**	**0**	**1**
Carlisle Consistory				
Testamentary	1	1	0	2
Defamation	0	0	0	0
Tithe	0	1	0	1
Church Rate	1	0	0	1
Discipline	0	0	0	0
Faculty, Pew	0	1	0	1
Churchwardens	0	0	0	0
Matrimonial	1	0	0	1
Misc./Unknown	0	1	0	1
Carlisle total	**3**	**4**	**0**	**7**
Chester Consistory				
Testamentary	5	7	3	15
Defamation	3	2	1	6
Tithe	1	0	0	1
Church Rate	3	0	0	3
Discipline	1	0	0	1
Faculty, Pew	6	3	2	11
Churchwardens	0	1	0	1
Matrimonial	0	1	0	1
Misc./Unknown	12	4	2	18
Chester total	**31**	**18**	**8**	**57**

24. Source: Chanc. AB/45–48.

	1725–1731	1732–1738	1739–1745	Total
Durham Consistory				
Testamentary	1	0	0	1
Defamation	1	1	0	2
Tithe	3	2	1	6
Church Rate	0	0	0	0
Discipline	0	1	1	2
Faculty, Pew	0	0	1	1
Churchwardens	0	0	0	0
Matrimonial	1	1	1	3
Misc./Unknown	3	0	0	3
Durham total	**9**	**5**	**4**	**18**
Howden				
Testamentary	0	0	0	0
Defamation	0	0	0	0
Tithe	0	0	0	0
Church Rate	0	0	0	0
Discipline	0	1	0	1
Faculty, Pew	0	0	0	0
Churchwardens	0	0	0	0
Matrimonial	0	0	0	0
Misc./Unknown	0	0	0	0
Howden total	**0**	**1**	**0**	**1**
Nottingham Archdeaconry				
Testamentary	0	0	0	0
Defamation	0	0	0	0
Tithe	0	1	0	1
Church Rate	1	0	0	1
Discipline	0	2	0	2
Faculty, Pew	0	1	1	2
Churchwardens	0	0	0	0
Matrimonial	0	0	0	0
Misc./Unknown	0	0	0	0
Nottingham total	**1**	**4**	**1**	**6**
Richmond Archdeaconry				
Testamentary	2	4	2	8

	1725–1731	1732–1738	1739–1745	Total
Defamation	0	0	0	0
Tithe	1	0	0	1
Church Rate	3	0	0	3
Discipline	6	0	0	6
Faculty, Pew	3	0	0	3
Churchwardens	0	0	0	0
Matrimonial	0	0	0	0
Misc./Unknown	5	1	1	7
Richmond total	**20**	**5**	**3**	**28**
Sodor and Man				
Testamentary	0	0	0	0
Defamation	0	0	0	0
Tithe	0	0	0	0
Church Rate	0	0	0	0
Discipline	0	0	0	0
Faculty, Pew	0	0	0	0
Churchwardens	0	0	0	0
Matrimonial	0	0	0	0
Misc./Unknown	0	0	1	1
Sodor and Man total	**0**	**0**	**1**	**1**
Dean of York				
Testamentary	0	0	0	0
Defamation	0	1	0	1
Tithe	0	0	0	0
Church Rate	0	0	0	0
Discipline	0	0	0	0
Faculty, Pew	0	0	0	0
Churchwardens	0	0	0	0
Matrimonial	0	0	0	0
Misc./Unknown	0	0	0	0
Dean of York total	**0**	**1**	**0**	**1**
Dean and Chapter of York				
Testamentary	1	1	0	2
Defamation	0	0	0	0
Tithe	0	0	0	0

	1725–1731	1732–1738	1739–1745	Total
Church Rate	0	0	0	0
Discipline	0	0	0	0
Faculty, Pew	0	1	0	1
Churchwardens	0	0	0	0
Matrimonial	0	0	0	0
Misc./Unknown	1	0	1	2
Dean and Chapter total	**2**	**2**	**1**	**5**
Unknown				
Testamentary	0	0	0	0
Defamation	0	0	0	0
Tithe	0	0	0	0
Church Rate	0	0	0	0
Discipline	0	0	0	0
Faculty, Pew	0	0	0	0
Churchwardens	0	0	0	0
Matrimonial	0	0	0	0
Misc./Unknown	1	3	1	5
Unknown total	**1**	**3**	**1**	**5**

	Total by Type
Testamentary	28
Defamation	9
Tithe	10
Church Rate	8
Discipline	12
Faculty, Pew	19
Churchwardens	1
Matrimonial	5
Misc./Unknown	38
Total	**130**

LICHFIELD AND DURHAM

Tables 7 and 8 summarize the business of the consistory courts of the dioceses of Lichfield and Coventry and Durham. Perhaps the most important fact revealed by these tables is that a tremendous number of causes were begun that never resulted in an appeal to the provincial courts. Indeed, between 1725 and 1745 a total of 2100 causes were begun in the Lichfield consistory court and 1458 in the Durham consistory court. We have seen that, during the same period, the Court of Arches received only 56 appeals from Lichfield (Table 3) while the York Chancery Court received only 18 appeals from Durham (Table 5). The significance of these facts lies, in part, in their methodological implications: to understand the importance of the ecclesiastical court system in English society one must look at the work of the trial courts, because that is where the vast majority of the work was taking place, not in the appellate courts. Table 7 shows that, between 1725 and 1745, a fairly steady number of causes was begun in the Lichfield consistory court and that testamentary, defamation, tithe, and disciplinary disputes were the most common types. Faculty and Church rate causes represented a significant proportion of business as well, while matrimonial litigation accounted for just 1% of the court's business (21 causes out of 2100). Table 8 shows that, like the other jurisdictions, the Durham consistory court heard roughly the same number of causes each year, with testamentary, defamation, tithe, and faculty causes representing the bulk of the business. The analysis for Durham is less complete, owing to the higher number of causes of unknown subject-matter. If one assumes that each year brought approximately the same mix of new causes to the court, then most of the causes classed as "misc./unknown" were probably testamentary, defamation, tithe, or faculty causes.

Perhaps the most important conclusion to emerge from this survey of litigation rates in the ecclesiastical courts is that the courts were, in fact, quite busy. Far from being moribund relics of the medieval period, the ecclesiastical courts were very much alive and well in the early eighteenth century, particularly in the provinces. There seems to be little reason to doubt that, within the metropolis, the King's Bench, Common Pleas, Exchequer, and Chancery had much more business than the Court of Arches or the Consistory Court of London. But, of course, those temporal courts had nation-wide jurisdiction, whereas the Court of Arches and the Consistory Court of London had much more limited original jurisdiction, and a relatively small percentage of causes begun elsewhere were ever appealed to the Arches. Thus, if the legal landscape one considers extends no farther than

Table 7. Causes Begun in Lichfield Consistory Court

	1725–1731	1732–1738	1739–1745	Total
Testamentary	266	185	222	673
Defamation	173	140	122	435
Tithe	149	178	108	435
Church Rate	50	34	11	95
Discipline	35	44	52	131
Faculty, Pew	39	25	23	87
Churchwardens	12	10	7	29
Matrimonial	8	3	10	21
Misc./Unknown	94	49	51	194
Total	**826**	**668**	**606**	**2100**

Source: B/C/2/95–102.

Table 8. Causes Begun in Durham Consistory Court

	1725–1731	1732–1738	1739–1745	Total
Testamentary	12	68	96	176
Defamation	45	209	113	367
Tithe	44	52	33	129
Church Rate	2	1	1	4
Discipline	18	10	9	37
Faculty, Pew	35	40	38	113
Churchwardens	0	0	1	1
Matrimonial	6	2	14	22
Misc./Unknown	427	99	83	609
Total	**589**	**481**	**388**	**1458**

Source: DDR III/22–25.

the capital, it is hardly surprising that the ecclesiastical courts should suffer by comparison with the temporal courts. But the foregoing litigation figures show that the administration of justice in eighteenth-century England was not only (and perhaps not even primarily) a London affair. On the contrary, much more attention must be paid to litigation at the ecclesiastical courts, quarter sessions, and assizes before an adequate history of the subject can be written. Indeed, there is good reason to believe that the relevant context for understanding the eighteenth-century ecclesiastical courts is as much the eighteenth-century legal system as the eighteenth-century Church of England. As we saw in Table 3, for example, appeals to the Court of Arches fell in the early 1740s. While the conventional wisdom would ascribe this drop to general religious malaise and indifference, it appears that the early eighteenth century saw a downturn in the volume of litigation heard by the temporal courts as well. Indeed, C. W. Brooks found that, from 1640 to 1750, the courts at Westminster experienced a "spectacular" decline in business.[25] Given that much of the ecclesiastical courts' business was, in substance, "temporal" (e.g., tithe disputes and testamentary litigation), the concurrent drop may have had common causes, such as low unemployment, high real wages, agricultural depression, and urbanization.[26]

A second conclusion that can be drawn from the above litigation survey is that a significant source of public knowledge about the ecclesiastical courts—perhaps more significant than theoretical treatises—was experience, either directly or through family, friends, or acquaintances.

Finally, although much of the business in the Church's courts directly affected the Church, much had only an historical connection with the Church. In the first category one can count litigation involving discipline of the clergy and laity, suits by clerics for unpaid tithes, and disputes over faculties to alter parochial church fabric. Tithe suits brought by laymen and defamation and testamentary litigation affected the Church less directly.

The foregoing litigation statistics admittedly do little to give one a sense of what the early eighteenth-century English ecclesiastical courts meant to real people. Mining the court records and other sources for qualitative information about the significance of their work is another task for another day. What the statistics do permit one to conclude is that facile generalizations the courts were in decline are not to be trusted.

25. C. W. Brooks, "Interpersonal Conflict and Social Tension: Civil Litigation in England, 1640–1830," in *The First Modern Society: Essays in Honour of Lawrence Stone*, ed. A. L. Beier, David Cannadine, and James M. Rosenheim (Cambridge, 1989), 360–363.

26. Brooks, "Interpersonal Conflict," 369–371.

Note on Sources and Methods

Manuscript Sources

A. Public Record Office (London)
High Court of Delegates
    Del. 8/73   Repertory Book, 1701–1789

Chancery, Cursitors' Records (Petty Bag Office)
    C207   Significations, Elizabeth I to Victoria

B. Lambeth Palace Library (London)
Court of Arches
    A27–32   Act Books, 1727–1753
    Aa32–35   Acts of Court, 1725–1728

C. Borthwick Institute of Historical Research (York)
York Chancery Court
    Chanc. AB/44–48   Act Books, 1722–1756

D. Lichfield Joint Record Office (Lichfield)
Lichfield Consistory Court
    B/C/2/95–102   Act Books, 1723–1746

E. Durham Archives and Special Collections (Durham)
Durham Consistory Court
    DDR III/22–25   Act Books, 1711–1759

There is no completely satisfactory way to count the number of causes begun each year in the ecclesiastical courts. I counted only those contested causes that progressed sufficiently far to appear in the act books. This method of counting causes had the effect of understating the total activity of the courts for two reasons. First, many matters the courts dealt with were really administrative matters, such as the appointment of guardians or the granting of unopposed petitions for faculties. Second, many more citations were issued than ever resulted in court proceedings. I regarded both the administrative matters and the "saber-rattling" of procuring a citation that was never enforced as sufficiently far from my main concern of discovering the role of the ecclesiastical courts in the administration of justice to justify disregarding them.

In counting the causes I followed the treatment of the act books. Thus, if they treated a matter with one plaintiff and three defendants as one cause, then so did I. On the other hand, if they treated it as three separate causes, then so did I. This method may, at first, seem somewhat arbitrary, but there were generally substantive reasons for the registers (and everyone else) to treat the causes as they did. For example, a suit for a faculty to erect a pew might elicit numerous formal objections and cause various individuals to intervene to assert their alleged interests in the matter; but only one decision would ultimately be arrived at—the faculty would be granted, in whole or in part, or not. Accordingly, the registers gave this kind of cause one entry in the act books. By contrast, one vicar or tithe-farmer might sue a dozen or more people for subtraction of tithes, and each could be liable for different amounts or nothing at all. Thus, the registers gave each separate cause a separate entry in the act books.[27] Likewise, I followed the act books in treating subsequent appeals to the same court in the same cause as a separate cause, and I counted appeals from interlocutory orders of lower courts the same as appeals from definitive sentences.

Because the nine categories into which I have placed the causes are not mutually exclusive, a word about what each label covers is in order. In general I have tried to classify each cause according to what seemed to me to be the underlying dispute. Thus, "Testamentary" causes include (criminal) articles against a defendant for allegedly suppressing a decedent's will and maladministration of estates, in addition to causes such as withholding legacies and contested grants of administration. "Unknown/Miscellaneous" includes suits over disputed jurisdiction, suits by proctors against former clients for failure to pay fees, suits for dilapidations, sequestrations, non-payment of ecclesiastical fees, and disputed licensing of preachers, curates, parish clerks, and school teachers. "Churchwardens" covers contested elections, disputed accounts, and official misconduct. "Faculties" includes those causes where ownership of a seat or pew in a church was contested, as

27. This substantive difference among causes seems to be lost on Till, who counted multiple tithe suits brought by the same plaintiff as one cause. See Till, "Decline," 250.

well as contested suits for permission to build up or tear down a structure. "Church Rate" causes encompass proceedings to confirm a rate levied by the parish authorities and suits to enforce payment of the same. "Marriage" includes suits for restitution of conjugal rights, jactitation (boasting) of marriage, and divorces *a mensa et thoro*. "Defamation" includes defamation of clergy. Besides morals offenses, "Discipline" includes brawling in church-yards and suits for contracting or solemnizing clandestine marriages.

Because specifying the peculiars from which appeals went to the Court of Arches would have further lengthened an already long Table 4, I classified such appeals by reference to the diocese in which the peculiar was located, regardless of the actual location of the court rendering the decision appealed from. Thus, for example, I classified an appeal to the Arches from Isleham, a peculiar of the bishop of Rochester, under "Ely," because that is the diocese in which Isleham was located. Such appeals counted for fewer than a dozen of the total cases appealed to the Arches. Because the number of dioceses and peculiars from which appeals were taken to the York Chancery Court was considerably smaller, I have stated specifically the court from which the appeal came.

Testamentary Proceedings in Spanish East Florida, 1783–1821

M. C. Mirow

The East Florida Papers in the Library of Congress reveal a great deal about law, legal institutions, legal practice, and legality in colonial Florida during the second Spanish period from 1783 to 1821.[1] This contribution provides an initial study of the testamentary proceedings recorded in these papers. It describes these cases and discusses the dossier of one case to illustrate the administrative and legal work done by Spanish officials to distribute a decedent's property. It concludes that these documents merit further study for what they tell us about wills and succession in Spanish East Florida and about the legal history of the region.

THE ORIGIN AND CONTENT OF THE EAST FLORIDA PAPERS

The East Florida Papers in the Manuscript Division of the Library of Congress have been used rarely by legal historians.[2] This lack of study by legal

---

1.   East Florida Papers, Manuscript Division, Library of Congress, Washington, D.C. (hereinafter "EFP").

2.   There are two studies related to the promulgation of the Constitution of Cádiz in East Florida that make use of these papers. M. C. Mirow, "The Constitution of Cádiz in Florida," *Florida Journal of International Law* 24 (2012), 271–329; Alejandro Quiroga Fernández de Soto, "Military Liberalism on the East Florida 'Frontier': Implementation of the 1812 Constitution," *Florida Historical Quarterly* 79 (2001), 441–468. For a brief study of the civil causes found in the East Florida Papers see M. C. Mirow, "Causas civiles en la

historians can be explained by this collection's location and the difficulties of accessing the microfilms that were made in the 1960s. First, the Library of Congress is somewhat off the beaten path for those working in Spanish and Latin American materials. Second, the nature of these papers would only attract the attention of a small subset of historians scouring materials in the Library of Congress. And third, it is only in the past 25 years that historians in the United States have begun to explore and to consider in detail what is known as the second Spanish period in Florida from 1783 to 1821.[3] Legal scholars have only begun to scratch the surface of this period of Florida as it relates to Spanish colonial imperial history.[4]

The East Florida Papers were microfilmed by the Library of Congress in 1964 and 1965 and contain 175 reels. Covering almost every conceivable aspect of Spanish government and administration in East Florida from 1783 to 1821, the East Florida Papers have an unusual provenance. Spain transferred East Florida to the United States in 1821 under the terms of the Adams-Onís Treaty of 1819. The Spanish records were supposed to be shipped to Cuba but were seized by the United States which maintained their overall Spanish organization in bundles.[5] In 1849, the Florida surveyor-general in Tallahassee, Florida, gained control of the papers for the newly created General Land Office of the United States Department of

---

Florida Oriental, 1783–1821," in *Estudios en Homenaje al Profesor Doctor Don Abelardo Levaggi*, ed. Agustín Parise and Ricardo Rabinovich-Berkman (Buenos Aires, forthcoming). I have also used these papers to investigate the deputy for Florida to the Spanish Cortes of 1813: M. C. Mirow, "Gonzalo Herrera y las Floridas frente a las Cortes de Cádiz," in *Actas del XVIII Congreso del Instituto Internacional de Historia del Derecho Indiano* (Córdoba, Argentina, forthcoming).

3.   William S. Coker and Susan R. Parker, "The Second Spanish Period in the Two Floridas," in *The New History of Florida*, ed. Michael Gannon (Gainesville, 2012), 150–166; Sherry Johnson, "The Spanish St. Augustine Community, 1784–1795: A Reevaluation," *Florida Historical Quarterly* 68 (1989), 27–54; David J. Weber, *The Spanish Frontier in North America* (New Haven, 1992), 276–278.

4.   Comparisons with legal practices in other North American Spanish colonies must wait until more is known about Spanish East Florida. Charles R. Cutter, *The Legal Culture of Northern New Spain, 1700–1810* (Albuquerque, 1995) (areas of colonial New Mexico and Texas).

5.   Laura J. Kells, *East Florida: A Register of Its Records in the Library of Congress (A Finding Aid to the Collection in the Library of Congress)* (Washington, D.C: Library of Congress, 2011), 2–4: http://hdl.loc.gov/loc.mss/eadmss.ms005002.

the Interior, although it appears that the physical location of the papers continued to be St. Augustine, Florida.[6] In the late 1860s, the papers were transferred to Tallahassee when several regional land offices, including the office in St. Augustine, were consolidated.[7] Although this control was briefly disrupted during the Civil War, the papers stayed with the General Land Office until 1905 when, excluding papers relevant to land grants, they were transferred to the Library of Congress. In this journey, the East Florida Papers gained the addition of some related documents from after 1821, but these are not particularly relevant for our purposes.[8]

The collection is divided into 100 series of different topics that fortunately maintain the original structure of Spanish administration.[9] It has approximately 65,000 folios arranged in 372 bundles.[10] These include all manner of correspondence and official documents related to the colonial administration of St. Augustine and its surrounding province. The collection contains files of correspondence at all governmental levels. Subjects covered in the papers include taxation, military matters, ecclesiastical matters, the Royal Hospital, civil engineering, smaller municipalities, census returns, marriage licenses, shipwrecks and captures, notarized instruments, relations with indigenous communities, relations with the United States, and city council proceedings, among others.[11] Testamentary Proceedings comprise 18 bundles of documents that range in date from 1756

6.   Irene A. Wright, "The Odyssey of the Spanish Archives of Florida," in *Hispanic American Essays*, ed. A. Curtis Wilgus (Chapel Hill, 1942), 188.

7.   Ibid., 194–195.

8.   Kells, *East Florida*, 4. A brief description of the papers may be found at Mabel M. Manning, "The East Florida Papers in the Library of Congress," *Hispanic American Historical Review* 10 (1930), 392–397. For a detailed history of the provenance of these records see Wright, "The Odyssey," 169–207. A searchable index to the East Florida Papers may be found at http://web.uflib.ufl.edu/spec/pkyonge/eflapap.html.

9.   A complete list of the series topics can be found at Kells, *East Florida*, 4–20.

10.   Library of Congress, *Handbook of Manuscripts in the Library of Congress* (Washington, D.C., 1918), 121; Library of Congress, *Report of the Librarian of Congress* (Washington, D.C., 1905), 50.

11.   Kells, *East Florida*, 4–10.

to 1821 with only two documents from before 1783.[12] These cases are the subject of this study.[13]

THE PROVINCE OF EAST FLORIDA
AND ST. AUGUSTINE, 1783–1821

An examination of these papers reveals the rather unusual border society that existed in East Florida during the second Spanish period. The attributes of this city and province are equally reflected in the estate documents and proceedings studied here. The Spanish fort, the Castillo de San Marco, was constructed in 1672 and after the British rule from 1763 to 1783, served as the hub for St. Augustine and the territorially ill-defined province of East Florida. British, U.S., Spanish and Native American interests abutted and interacted in the region where trading, warring, invading, rebelling, raiding, and smuggling were frequent activities.[14]

East Florida was a linguistically and racially diverse society with Spaniards, Minorcans, other Europeans, Anglos, Anglo-Americans, Scots, Irish, Native Americans, indentured workers, free blacks, and slaves who filled various roles in the economic, maritime, and military activities of the city and region.[15] Important commercial activities included trade with Native Americans, shipping, agriculture, land speculation, and slave deal-

12.   Ibid., 45–48.
13.   There are other series of the papers that may also contain a significant number of legal cases or documents. These include 12 bundles dealing with criminal causes (1785–1821), one bundle concerning the Royal Court of the District (1800–1821), 13 bundles entitled Miscellaneous Legal Instruments and Proceedings (1784–1821), three bundles of Courts-Martial (1785–1821), two bundles of Criminal Proceedings related to the Rebellion of 1795, three bundles of Treasury Accounts (1790–1821), one of the Discharge of State Prisoners, two of Exchequer Proceedings (1787–1818), 17 bundles of notarized instruments and volumes of Notarized Instruments from Fernandina, and Records of Title to Slaves. Kells, *East Florida*, 19, 21, 33, 39–45, 54–55.
14.   Mirow, "The Constitution of Cádiz in Florida," 274–278. See James G. Cusick, *The Other War of 1812: The Patriot War and the American Invasion of Spanish East Florida* (Gainesville: University Press of Florida, 2003); Sherry Johnson, "The St. Augustine Hurricane of 1811: Disaster and the Question of Political Unrest of the Florida Frontier," *Florida Historical Quarterly* 84 (2005), 28–56; Rembert W. Patrick, *Florida Fiasco: Rampant Rebels on the Georgia-Florida Border, 1810–1815* (Athens, Ga., 1954).
15.   Mirow, "The Constitution of Cádiz in Florida," 274–278.

ing.[16] The fort and its garrison required continuous provisions of food and wares which were often supplied locally. The records of civil litigation from this period reveal this mix of population and economic activities. While many cases concerned small amounts and local parties, other cases involved transnational commercial transactions and significant sums. The court often needed documents in English translated into Spanish for its work and public interpreters were employed to handle this task and, on occasion, to translate Native American languages.[17]

The province was politically in flux even during the Spanish period studied here. From 1783 to 1812 the city was under the military jurisdiction and the Spanish crown. The Governor of St. Augustine reported to the Captaincy General of Cuba and the Two Floridas in Havana, Cuba, which, in turn, reported to the central government in Cádiz or Madrid, depending on the period under examination.[18] This structure did not change with the promulgation of the Constitution of Cádiz of 1812, but the Constitution brought new local and regional structures including a Constitutional Mayor, and Constitutional City Council, both in St. Augustine, and a Provincial Deputation in Havana with authority over St. Augustine. These all reported to the Cortes in Cádiz, in the south of Spain.[19] From 1812 to early 1815, St. Augustine was under and complied with the provisions of the Constitution of Cádiz.[20] When Fernando VII returned to the throne in 1814, he rejected the Constitution that established a constitutional monarchy in his name and announced that he would rule with absolute power. This change in political structure reached St. Augustine in late 1814 and the last meeting of the Constitutional City Council was in January, 1815.[21] Fernando VII was later forced to acquiesce to the Constitution in 1820, and St. Augustine and East Florida returned to a constitutional regime under the Constitution

16. William S. Coker and Thomas D. Watson, *Indian Traders of the Southeastern Spanish Borderlands: Panton Leslie & Company and John Forbes & Company, 1783–1847* (Gainesville, 1986).

17. M. C. Mirow, "Causas civiles en la Florida Oriental."

18. Quiroga, "Military Liberalism," 444. See also Duvon Clough Corbitt, "The Administrative System in the Floridas, 1783–1821, II," *Tequesta* 3 (1943), 57.

19. Quiroga, "Military Liberalism," 445.

20. Mirow, "The Constitution of Cádiz in Florida," 279–302.

21. Ibid., 302–309.

of Cádiz until their transfer to the United States on July 10, 1821.[22] These changes in institutions had little effect on the judicial function of the governor as the judge who heard civil causes and as the judge for testamentary proceedings.

RECORDS OF TESTAMENTARY PROCEEDINGS

The index of records of testamentary proceedings contains 372 separate entries dated from May 18, 1756 to June 18, 1821.[23] Only two entries are dated from before the beginning of the second Spanish period in 1783; one was not concluded until 1803 but the other appears to have been resolved by

22. Ibid., 309–327.

23. Pedro de Espinosa testamentary proceedings (hereafter only the decedent's name is used), May 18, 1756, EFP, Reel 134, Item 1756–16; and Jorge Later, June 18, 1821, EFP, Reel 145, Item 1821–24. The final document for the Jorge Later proceedings is dated June 26, 1821, when the Spanish government was already well into preparing the transfer of the territory to the United States which occurred on July 10, 1821. Mirow, "The Constitution of Cádiz in Florida," 322–327.

Although the records are almost entirely in Spanish, I have adopted the title in English assigned by the *Index to the East Florida Papers*, George A. Smathers Library, University of Florida. http://web.uflib.ufl.edu/spec/pkyonge/eflapap.html. I have also removed the phrase "testamentary proceedings" that follows almost every entry listed in the index. Reel numbers in this index are often off by one or two digits, perhaps because of the existence of Reel 134A, a continuation of Reel 134. Where possible, I have used the corrected reel number, instead of the reel numbers as found in the *Index*.

A typescript description in English of many of these documents was prepared by Emily L. Wilson and is found microfilmed on Reel 134 and Reel 134A. Wilson's references to the documents do not coincide with the Library of Congress references. Nonetheless, Wilson's notes may be useful in a fuller study of these documents. Notes by Emily L. Wilson on Testamentary Proceedings, Florida, 1783–1821, EFP, Reel 134.

It would be useful to study the testate proceedings and their wills in light of the wills recorded in the notarial records for the same period (Escrituras, 1784–1821, EFP, Reels 167–173). Wills were deposited in these archives. There is a finding list of wills from this collection of documents from 1784 to 1816, and several of the testate estates found in the records studied here have an entry for a will in the notarial records in this finding list. Nonetheless, because the time periods are different, no attempt has been made to draw any conclusions about the presence of a will in a testamentary proceeding and its existence in the notarial records. See Emily L. Wilson, *Spanish Wills, East Florida, 1784–1816*, in Escrituras (St. Augustine Historical Society, n.d.). Wilson identified 102 wills in the notarial records for the period she examined. Twenty five of these wills apparently were used in the testamentary proceedings studied here.

1763.[24] The 372 proceedings relate to 168 decedents, with a rough estimate of about 60% of the decedents with Spanish surnames and about 40% with Anglo or other European surnames.[25] Twenty-seven (approximately 15%) of the decedents were women. The index of these proceedings indicate that of these 168 decedents, 72 (approximately 43%) died testate. Of these 72 testate estates, about one-half can be associated with Spanish surnames and about one-half with Anglo or other European surnames. Testatrices accounted for only 11 of the 72 wills, or approximately 15%, again in the same rough proportion they bear to the decedent population as a whole found in these records. Thus, will making seems to have been spread quite evenly across the Spanish and non-Spanish residents with women accounting for a much smaller slice of the will-making population.

The courts' power to supervise this activity in the Americas was set out in the general collection of laws for the Spanish colonies, the *Recopilación de leyes de los reynos de las Indias* (1681).[26] In large cities with central royal courts (*audiencias*), one member of the court was appointed a judge of the goods of the deceased (*juez de bienes de difuntos*) who served for two years.[27] In smaller cities without a central royal court, such as St. Augustine, the governor was to appoint a judge.[28] It appears that the practice in St. Augustine was for the governor to act in this capacity. These judges supervised the inventory and safeguarding of the decedent's property, the accounts and activities of executors (*albaceas*), the accounts to royal officials, the retrieval of wills from public archives and scribes, the payment of

24. Joseph Escalona, January 18, 1763, EFP, Reel 134, Item 1763-1.

25. A trove of information concerning the national origin of East Florida's population awaits analysis in Oaths of Allegiance, 1790–1821, EFP, Reels 163–164, which contain oaths and detailed lists of resident non-Spaniards who swore allegiance to the king to remain in St. Augustine and the province of East Florida. The lists associated with the oaths contain information on the country or state of origin, religion, and the resident's family members, cattle, goods, and slaves. The nationality of non-Spanish decedents might be found through these records.

26. *Recopilación de leyes de los reynos de las Indias* (Madrid, 1681; facsimile edition Mexico City, 1987), Tit. 32, Lib. 2. (hereinafter "R.I.").

27. *R.I.*, Ley 1, Tit. 32, Lib. 2.

28. *R.I.*, Ley 19, Tit. 32, Lib. 2.

claims against the decedent, and the distribution of property.[29] They exercised jurisdiction in testate and intestate estates.[30]

A well-developed Castilian law of succession appears to have been applied in the Americas. Although subject to variation, the general principles were that under the *legítima*, legitimate male and female descendants of were entitled to four fifths of the decedent's property divided equally. Adopted, assumed, natural, and spurious children generally did not receive a forced share, but might take from the testator's share subject to devise under a will or might take a portion by intestacy. Furthermore, rights of support of natural children were recognized under Castilian law and in the Americas, and in turn, these rights were recognized to create a smaller shares for these children. Through the *mejora*, the testator could supplement a devise to benefit certain family members, providing some limited testamentary freedom over this fraction of the property. The portion not allocated through forced heirship or for other obligations was subject to the testator's testamentary freedom and often left for pious purposes. Entails (*mayorazagos*) were known in the Americas, but I have not yet observed any reference to them in these records.[31]

For the thirty-eight year span from 1784 to 1821, the court accepted on average approximately 10 proceedings each year, with a low of only one in 1789 and a high of 30 in 1815. Figure 1 shows the breakdown of the number of cases by five-year periods.

Entries represent a group of documents that range from a couple to several hundred pages. An entry may contain a claim for debt against an estate, a will, a petition to the court, or a full assortment of estate documents including petitions, wills, claims against the estate, determinations of children, settlements between interested parties, and final orders. Some estates were complex and produced substantial records. For example, the estate of Jesse Fish, with 41 separate entries, takes up over ten percent of

29. R.I., Leyes 17–56, Tit. 32, Lib. 2.

30. R.I., Ley 42, Tit. 32, Lib. 2.

31. M. C. Mirow, *Latin American Law: A History of Private Law and Institutions in Spanish America* (Austin, 2004), 64–65, 67–68. See, generally, Humberto Gutiérrez Sarmiento, *El derecho civil en la confrmación de América* (Bogotá, 1992), 95–123; Francisco Luis Pacheco Caballero, "El acto *mortis causa* en los derecho hispanicos durante la edad moderna (notas sobre sucesión testamentaria)," *Recueils del la Société Jean Bodin pour l'Histoire Comparative des Institutions* 60 (1993), 225–256.

Figure 1. Testamentary Proceedings in East Florida.
Number of Cases, 1784–1821

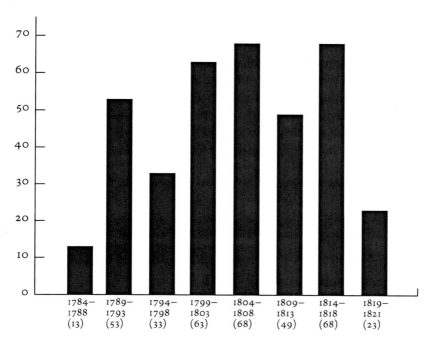

the all entries combined. Just one stage of the litigation surrounding this estate produced over 550 pages of materials.[32] Although a study of this estate is beyond the scope of this contribution, these materials appear to be a highly fruitful area for further work, especially considering the complexity, wealth, and historical importance of the testator in this case. It is particularly worthy of exploration because Fish apparently attempted to hold lands in trust for "old Floridanos," Spaniards from the first Spanish period that ended with England's possession of East Florida from 1763 to 1783. When the territory was ceded back to Spain, many of these landholders or their heirs returned to reclaim their property from Fish, and subsequently Fish's estate, raising the nature of his holding of the property and the va-

32.   Jesse Fish: meeting of creditors, October 9, 1790, EFP, Reel 134, Item 1790-14.

lidity of these secret arrangements to foil English claims against the real property held.[33]

Jesse Fish is not the only decedent of interest in these documents. Of particular importance for Haitian history, the proceedings of Jorge Biassou, the Haitian revolutionary general, are found among these papers.[34] Other decedents of historical importance found in these materials include Governor Enrique White and Maria Evans, a wealthy trader and shopkeeper.[35]

I have attempted to characterize the proceedings into categories in figure 2. The largest category is separate individual claims of debts owed by the estate, usually to individual creditors. These records often have a petition to the court stating the nature of the debt and requesting payment.

Figure 2. Nature of Testamentary Proceedings in East Florida, 1756–1821

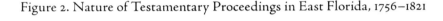

---

33. "Fish reputedly made money as an *hacendado*, land dealer, slaver, smuggler, usurer and cunning crook…Fish's name conjures up lucid images of money, land, and commercial enterprise. In such imagery, he becomes a successful but unscrupulous businessman, a swindler of St. Augustine property, and Florida's first orange exporter," Robert L. Gold, "That Infamous Floridian, Jesse Fish," *Florida Historical Quarterly* 52 (1973), 1. See also, Robert. L. Gold, "Politics and Property during the Transfer of Florida from Spanish to English Rule, 1763–1764," *Florida Historical Quarterly* 42 (1963), 16–34. Jesse Fish has a Wikipedia page, http://en.wikipedia.org/wiki/Jesse_Fish.

34. Jorge Biassou, July 15, 1801, EFP, Reel 138, Item 1801-2 (193 pages).

35. Enrique White, April 17, 1811, EFP, Reel 142, Item 1811-2; Maria Evans, October 17, 1792, EFP, Reel 135, Item 1792-8.

They are often accompanied with written instruments setting out the debt which was frequently recorded on small scraps of paper signed by the decedent. Such separate individual claims are often covered in ten to twenty pages of documents.[36]

I have called the second largest category "administration of estate." These proceedings usually contain some or all of the following stages of administration: a petition to the court for the administration of the estate by the executor, the will, an inventory of the assets of the decedent, claims of creditors, some plan or process of distribution of the property under the will, final orders of the court, and notations by the scribe that notice has been delivered to the interested parties at each stage of the proceedings. Such documents often run several hundred pages.[37]

Other petitions or documents reveal the many topics addressed by the court. These included petitions, for example, for the appointment or re-

---

36. E.g., Tomas Carballo: claim of Antonio Llambias, May 21, 1792, EFP, Reel 135, Item 1793-33 (suit for payment for bed built for decedent with the record containing the receipt for payment, 16 pages); Tomas Carballo: claim of July Boby, January 18, 1793, EFP, Reel 135, Item 1793-39 (suit for back rent owed by Carballo, again with receipt, 16 pages).

37. Estates with the largest dossiers are: Father Pedro Camps, May 19, 1790, EFP, Reel 134, Item 1790-12 (167 pages); Maria Evans, October 17, 1792, EFP, Reel 135, Item 1792-8 (469 pages); Jacobo Wiggins, January 26, 1797, EFP, Reel 136, Item 1797-14 (283 pages); Estevan Divor, June 8, 1797, EFP, Reel 136, Item 1797-15 (222 pages); Miguel Iznardy, April 13, 1803, EFP, Reel 139, Item 1803-1 (541 pages); Miguel Iznardy, April 13, 1803, EFP, Reel 139, Item 1803-8 (second entry, 340 pages); Mateo Guadarrama, September 6, 1804, EFP, Reel 139, Item 1804-10 (255 pages); Isabel Mayar, March 7, 1805, Reel 139, Item 1805-3 (306 pages); Buenaventura Boix, September 20, 1806, EFP, Reel 140, Item 1806-9 (348 pages); John McQueen, October 12, 1807, EFP, Reel 140, Item 1807-2 (380 pages); Francisco Xavier Sanchez, October 31, 1807, EFP, Reel 140, Item 1807-1 (363 pages); Jose Maria de la Torre, December 7, 1807, EFP, Reel 141, Item 1807-10 (208 pages); Antonio Matanza, December 12, 1807, EFP, Reel 140, Item 1807-6 (278 pages); Juan Lauren, July 17, 1809, EFP, Reel 142, Item 1809-5 (393 pages); Juan Bautista Ferriera and Elizabeth Nixon, August 23, 1810, EFP, Reel 142, Item 1810-13 (409 pages); Enrique White, April 17, 1811, EFP, Reel 143, Item 1811-2 (269 pages); Maria de la Carmen Hill, August 31, 1813, EFP, Reel 143, Item 1813-2 (289 pages); Manuel Fernandez Bendicho and Maria Rafaela Rodriguez, August 11, 1814, EFP, Reel 144, Item 1814-18 (218 pages); Juan Jose Bousquet, January 2, 1815, EFP, Reel 144, Item 1815-7 (429 pages); and Juan McClure, December 29, 1815, EFP, Reel 144, Item 1815-6 (391 pages).

appointment of executors,[38] to pay bequests or legacies,[39] to transfer a legacy,[40] to resolve claims of multiple creditors,[41] to annul the sale of a church as ecclesiastical property,[42] to collect debts owed the estate,[43] to verify debts,[44] to return a dowry,[45] to return a widow's separate property,[46] to determine the number of children of the decedent,[47] to account,[48] to collect taxes owed,[49] and to correct an inventory.[50] Parties appeared to have been willing to assert their various concerns related to these proceedings to the court.

An important yet relatively small number of petitions relate to the devise or manumission of slaves who appear in inventories and were counted among the assets of an estate when assessing the estate's ability to pay creditors and distribute assets to devisees and heirs. For example, James

38. E.g., Jose Sanchez, December 22, 1787, EFP, Reel 134, Item 1787-3; Mariana de Garro, November 10, 1791, EFP, Reel 135, Item 1791-9.

39. E.g., Maria Evans: claim of Antonio Palma, January 9, 1794, EFP, Reel 136, Item 1794-18; Maria Evans: claim of Manuel Marshall, January 9, 1794, EFP, Reel 136, Item 1794-15; Elisabeth Leslie, August 11, 1806, EFP, Reel 139, Item 1806-12; Father Miguel O'Reilly: claim of the Junta de Caridad, August 19, 1813, EFP, Reel 144, Item 1813-15 (petition by president of the Junta de Caridad for legacy left by the decedent).

40. E.g., Andrew Dewees: suit of Jose Joaneda against Catalina Cliken, October 29, 1794, EFP, Reel 136, Item 1974-26.

41. E.g., Jesse Fish: meeting of creditors, October 9, 1790, EFP, Reel 134, Item 1790-14;

42. Jesse Fish: annulment of the sale of the Torre de Tolomato, April 27, 1792, EFP, Reel 135, Item 1792-12.

43. E.g., Maria Evans, May 12, 1795, EFP, Reel 136, Item 1795-5; Miguel Ceballos: debt of Julian Pani, December 16, 1800, EFP, Reel 138, Item 1801-8; Maria Evens, June 26, 1809, Reel 141, Item 1809-9.

44. E.g., Miguel Iznardy: claim of Bartolome de Castro y Ferrer, October 4, 1806, EFP, Reel 141, Item 1808-4.

45. E.g., Buenaventura Boix: claim of Josefa Meneses, May 23, 1807, EFP, Reel 142, Item 1807-15.

46. E.g., Martin Crosby: claim of Maria George, May 17, 1814, EFP, Reel 143, Item 1814-24 (for property brought to the marriage).

47. E.g., Antonio Matanza, November 18, 1807, EFP, Reel 141, Item 1807-20 (intestacy).

48. E.g., Perrachu, Feburary 8, 1808, EFP, Reel 141, Item 1808-22 (account of sale of French barber who disappeared).

49. E.g., Maria Evans: claim of Ministros de Real Hacienda, February 12, 1819, EFP, Reel 145, Item 1819-11.

50. E.g., Juan McClure: claim of James English, April 20, 1816, EFP, Reel 145, Item 1816-41.

Wilson's records include the auction of 19 slaves, the claim of a creditor for transporting 29 slaves, and a claim for debts resulting from a slaving expedition to Angola with a contract the decedent entered into with two other slavers.[51] Similarly, the cost of transporting six slaves from St. Mary's, Georgia, to Fernandina, north of St. Augustine and within its jurisdiction, was asserted as a claim against an estate in 1815.[52]

Numerous petitions sought the disposition, transfer, and manumission of slaves. Slaves might be sold to satisfy the debts of the decedent or expenses of the estate.[53] Some petitions sought the return of slaves from an estate so they would not be subject to creditors' claims.[54] Others sought manumission of a slave on payment of money to the estate.[55] When slaves purchased their freedom from an estate, the executor might petition the court for permission to purchase another slave to replace the freed individual.[56] Claims of manumission on the death of the decedent were made on the past declarations of the decedent.[57] Still other petitions requested the court effect a transfer of slaves to devisees or heirs or to permit their sale.[58]

51.   James Wilson, October 28, 1811, EFP, Reel 143, Item 1811-4; James Wilson: claim of Fernando de la Maza Arredondo, January 28, 1812, Reel 143, Item 1812-12.

52.   Maria del Carmen Hill: claim of Simeon Sanchez, October 25, 1815, EFP, Reel 144, Item 1815-18.

53.   E.g, Maria del Carmen Hill, July 6, 1815, EFP, Reel 144, Item 1815-23; Redin Blunt (Reddin Blunt), December 13, 1815, EFP, Reel 144, Item 1815-29 (petition to sell decedent's only asset, the slave Cloe, to cover costs to prosecute decedent's murderers).

54.   Jesse Fish: claim of Jesse Fish, Jr., April 16, 1793, EFP, Reel 135, Item 1793-16.

55.   E.g., Maria Evans: request of Isabel, June 27, 1793, EFP, Reel 135, Item 1793-15; Maria Evans: request of Sambo, November 6, 1793, EFP, Reel 135, Item 1793-19;

56.   Juan Saunders, September 14, 1803, EFP, Reel 139, Item 1803-18. Saunders' estate included at least 17 slaves who were distributed to his heirs. Juan Sanders [*sic*], October 10, 1804, EFP, Reel 139, Item 1804-13.

57.   John Forester: request of Pedro Sivelly, July 27, 1808, EFP, Reel 141, Item 1808-21.

58.   E.g., Elizabeth Leslie: claim of John Forrester, January 30, 1806, EFP, Reel 139, Item 1806-13; Elizabeth Leslie: claim of Thomas Travers, Febrary 5, 1806, Reel 139, Item 1806-14; Elizabeth Leslie: claim of Maria Fortune, February 7, 1806, EFP, Reel 139, Item 1806-11; Property of the minor Francisco Milles: request of Robert McHardy, January 17, 1818, EFP, Reel 145, Item 1816-6; Hepworth Carter: request of Horatio Dexter, December 18, 1818, EFP, Reel 145, Item 1818-9.

Other proceedings addressed general questions of status and ownership of slaves left by a decedent.[59]

Another category of petitions requested the court's permission to deal with the decedent's property other than slaves. For example, in 1790, the executors of Jesse Fish's estate, John Leslie and Thomas Travers sought the governor's permission to rent Fish's famous hacienda "La Vergel" to Enrique White.[60] Similarly, in 1815, a widow sought permission before selling a house.[61]

Several other petitions contained a request to investigate the nature of the decedent's death.[62] A maritime community, St. Augustine experienced deaths through shipwreck and drowning.[63] Other investigations revealed the hazards of daily life. For example, in the mid-1790s, an inebriated Alexander MacDonell fell from an upper story window in John Leslie's house and died.[64] In 1810, Juan Dary died from an overdose of laudanum.[65] There were also suicides and murders.[66] These investigations usually led to some form of administration of the property of the decedent after the determination of the cause of death.

59.   E.g., John Forrester: suit of Philip Robert Yonge and Company, July 27, 1808, EFP, Reel 141, Item 1808-14; Juan O'Reilly: suit of the estate of Father Miguel O'Reilly, August 6, 1813, EFP, Reel 143, Item 1813-6; Margarita McClean, August 5, 1814, EFP, Reel 144, Item 1814-23 (claim by former owner of slaves against decedent for slaves removed to the United States by the decedent's widower).

60.   Jesse Fish, February 15, 1790, EFP, Reel 134, Item 1790-15.

61.   Sebastian Olivera, April 12, 1815, EFP, Reel 144, Item 1815-1. See also, Jose Pons, November 27, 1818, EFP, Reel 145, Item 1818-33.

62.   E.g. Robert Caldwell, November 12, 1804, Reel 139, Item 1804-11; Bryan Connor, February 15, 1808, EFP, Reel 142, Item 1808-12.

63.   Antonio Reguertas, May 23, 1790, EFP, Reel 136, Item 1794-3 (shipwreck); Pedro Casaly, October 3, 1799, EFP, Reel 137, Item 1799-14 (drowning); Manuel Lopez, March 18, 1814, EFP, Reel 143, Item 1814-19 (shipwreck); Jose Huis, April 26, 1814, EFP, Reel 143, Item 1814-17 (drowning); Manel Fernandez Bendicho and Maria Rafaela Rodriguez, August 11, 1814, DFP, Reel 144, Item 1814-18 (death of both in shipwreck); Joaquin Navarro, February 19, 1816, EFP, Reel 145, Item 1816-29 (river wreck).

64.   Alexander MacDonell, June 11, 1795, EFP, Reel 136, Item 1795-2.

65.   Juan Darcy, July 18, 1810, EFP, Reel 142, Item 1810-19.

66.   Valentin Pinzon, April 1, 1800, EFP, Reel 137, Item 1800-17 (suicide after killing a man in Charleston); James McEnery, December 16, 1801, EFP, Reel 138, Item 1801-1 (decedent murdered); Cuthbert Riggs, May 16, 1803, EFP, Reel 138, Item 1803-2 (suicide aboard ship); Manuel Tobar, March 11, 1809, EFP, Reel 141, Item 1809-1 (decedent murdered).

The records also illuminate will making in this border city. There are petitions related to the existence, production, opening, or returning wills.[67] Some petitions requested the production of a sealed will left in the custody of scribe or notary.[68] A petition in 1795 requested that the will be sent to Georgia for the benefit of the heirs of the decedent's sole heir.[69] Another petition, in 1799, requested the return of a sealed will deposited with the scribe.[70] There is also one mention of a joint will of a couple who died together in a shipwreck.[71]

These proceedings also provide a window into family life and structure. Widows and legitimate and illegitimate children claimed shares. Baptismal records were presented to determine parentage. Minors and orphans sought protection through the court. Adopted children might claim a portion from the estate.[72] Another set of estate papers indicate that the natural children a wealthy Spanish decedent had with a free black woman, Beatriz de Piedra, took a share of the estate in addition to shares for his widow, Maria del Carmen Hill, and his legitimate children. The baptismal records of both the legitimate and natural children were included in the proceedings, and shares were assigned to both kinds of children.[73] In 1816, an individual petitioned the court to be named a *curador* for the decedent's children who were mistreated by their stepfather and ignored by their mother.[74] Similarly, in 1818, an individual petitioned to protect the property of a minor orphan.[75]

Thus a wide variety of documents were produced as the court instructed executors, examined debts and competing claims to decedents' property, and often verified and considered documents from elsewhere

67. John Thorp, November 15, 1808, Reel 141, Item 1808-10 (petition to open will); Jorge Sibbald, February 10, 1810, EFP, Reel 143, Item 1810-12 (widow's petition to open will).

68. Francisco Xavier Sanchez, May 12, 1795, EFP, Reel 136, Item 1795-3.

69. Allan Keegan, December 14, 1795, EFP, Reel 136, Item 1795-1.

70. Petition of Owen Sheridan, November 29, 1799, EFP, Reel 138, Item 1799-15.

71. Manuel Fernandez Bendicho and Maria Rafaela Rodriguez, August 11, 1814, EFP, Reel 144, Item 1814-18.

72. Estevan Divor, June 8, 1797, EFP, Reel 136, Item 1797-15.

73. Francisco Xavier Sanchez, October 31, 1807, EFP, Reel 140, Item 1807-1.

74. Juan Triac: suit of Pedro Rodriguez de Cala, December 3, 1816, EFP, Reel 145, Item 1817-2. See also, Roque Leonardy, January 5, 1819, EFP, Reel 145, Item 1818-15.

75. Property of the minor Penelope Lee, March 14, 1818, EFP, Reel 145, Item 1818-7.

in the Spanish world and from the United States, England, and Ireland among other countries. Documents were frequently in English and were translated for the court.

AN EXAMPLE: PEDRO DIMARACHE
TESTAMENTARY PROCEEDINGS

To give a general sense of the kind of documents and issues found in these proceedings, the materials associated with the estate of Pedro Dimarache, a Corsican carpenter resident in St. Augustine, may serve as an illustration.[76] My main reasons for the selection of this estate as an example were the quality and clarity of the documents, the relatively short length of the dossier as a whole, and my desire to present a testate estate. Many usual elements are missing in this estate, such as slaves or real property as part of the decedent's property. Nonetheless, it provides a sense of the issues that these documents present and of their promise for additional research.

The document contains 31 numbered folios written in legible late-eighteenth century hand in Spanish. The title page of the document states, "No. 43, Florida, Año de 1792, Testamentaria por muerte de Pedro Dimarache."[77] The first document, is a petition to the governor from Pedro Cocifacio stating that Cocifacio was named the executor (*alvacea tetestamentario*) and the decedent's son-in-law, Miguel Acosta, was named the guardian of the property in Dimarache's will.[78] Cocifacio requested that because he had many things to attend to, Acosta should handle everything. The governor replied that the request should be presented with the inventory.[79] The public scribe then certified the signature of the governor and separately certified notice of the governor's decision to Cocifacio.[80] Such notices were typical and were repeated throughout the document after every stage.

---

76. Wilson, *Spanish Wills*, 2.

77. Pedro Dimarache, August 27, 1792, EFP, Reel 135, Item 1792-43.

78. A guardian (*tenedor de bienes* or *curador*) was necessary because Dimarache left a minor son. Gutiérrez Sarmiento, *El derecho civil*, 109–110. The *tenedor* is also mentioned in *R.I.*, Ley 54, Tit. 32, Lib. 2.

79. Pedro Dimarache, August 27, 1792, EFP, Reel 135, Item 1792-43, fol. 1.

80. Ibid., fol. 1v.

About a week later, the public scribe reported to the governor (now styled the "tribunal," *el tribunal*), executor, and heirs that after a diligent search of the records (*el archivo*) he was unable to find an inventory of the estate and awaited the instruction of the court.[81] The governor then ordered information concerning the decedent's testamentary dispositions.[82]

The next entry is a copy of Dimarache's will, apparently taken from the copy deposited in the notarial records in December, 1791.[83] The last will and testament (*testamento ultima y postrera voluntad*) begins with common Roman Catholic invocations, "In the name of Almighty God, and of his Blessed Mother, my Lady the Virgin Mary, conceived without original sin. Amen."[84] He stated that he was a natural of a city in Corsica, the son of Nicolas and Maria, a widower, and that he was in grave sickness from an accident that God had occasioned on him.[85] A substantial recitation of Catholic doctrine follows.[86]

The following description paraphrases the will's dispositive provisions. First, the testator commended his soul to God, his body to the earth to be buried in holy ground after having been wrapped in white cloth. He gave instructions for a modest funeral and burial according to the wishes of his executor. Second, he provided for three Masses for his soul.[87] Third, he stated that he was a member (*hermano* or brother) of the Cofradía of the Blessed Souls (*Cofradía de las Benditas Aminas*) which should pay for his funeral, with any excess due paid from his goods. Fourth, he allocated 21 pesos from his goods for Masses. Fifth, he stated that from his marriage he has a married daughter, Maria, who was 16 years old and a son, Nicolas, who was 13 years old. Sixth, he had 250 pesos in a strong box, a note against the Royal Treasury for nine pesos, a canoe in possession of his son-in-law, furniture, clothes, and carpenter's tools. Seventh, he recognized a few small debts and recorded a few carpentry projects that had not been paid. Master Carpenter Martín Hernández should bill for these projects for payment to

81.   Ibid., fols. 1v–2.

82.   Ibid., fols. 2–2v.

83.   Wilson, *Spanish Wills*, 2; Pedro Dimarache, August 27, 1792, EFP, Reel 135, Item 1792-43, fol. 8v.

84.   Ibid., fol. 3.

85.   Ibid., fol. 3.

86.   Ibid., fols. 3–4.

87.   Ibid., fol. 4.

the executor. He noted that the King owed him for 21 days of service and wood he supplied for pavilions constructed for the battalion.[88] Eighth, he listed more debts owed him. Ninth, he stated that he owed no one, but if a creditor appeared with a legitimate instrument of debt, it should be paid. Tenth, he made a legacy from his goods of 8 pesos to his Cofradía, here called the Blessed Souls of Purgatory. Eleventh, he wished to benefit his son Nicolas with 50 pesos (*dexar mejorado en cinquenta pesos a mi hijo Nicolas*).[89] Twelfth, he left his tools to Alberto Rayes in thanks for his kindnesses. Thirteenth, the rest of his goods, debts, rights, and actions that belong to him he instituted and named his children Maria and Nicolas as his heirs to divide everything equally, except for his clothes which were to go to his son and the other clothes divided as the children agree.[90] Fourteenth, he named his son-in-law Miguel Acosta as "tutor" of his son Nicolas and as the guardian of his goods to provide for the son's food and education. He named Pedro Cocifacio his executor (*albacea testamentario y fideicomiso*), and Bernardo Segui as substitute to carry out his last dispositions.[91] He revoked and annulled any prior testaments, powers, and codicils except the present one dated December 24, 1791, as presented to Fernando de la Puente, Lieutenant of the Infantry Regiment, as commissioned by the governor for these purposes because there was not an official scribe in the city.[92] The will was not signed by the testator because he stated he did not know how to write but was witnessed by five witnesses, the "said commissioned judge," and four other "provisional witnesses."[93]

An order of the court followed on September 12, 1792. It first expressed concern that the will lacked the requisite recitations of obligations to constitute Miguel Acosta as Nicolas's testamentary tutor and that Acosta did not make an account to the court as required by law. The court also stated that the lack of an inventory made Acosta somewhat suspect in the position.[94] It observed that Cocifacio, as executor, should be fined for not

---

88. Ibid., fols. 5–6.
89. This indicates the usual possibility of the *mejora*.
90. Pedro Dimarache, August 27, 1792, EFP, Reel 135, Item 1792-43, fols. 6v–7.
91. Ibid., fols. 7–7v.
92. Ibid., fol. 8.
93. Ibid., fol. 8v.
94. Ibid., fol. 9.

making an inventory. The heirs were ordered to account and not to embezzle (*desfalcar*) anything from the pupil. The executor was informed that he could not presently renounce his duties and that he should make an account and inventory of all the goods under his authority and collect the debts owed the decedent. The order required that burial should be entered for the participation of the "Vicar Priest and Ecclesiastical Judge of the Parochial Church of this city." The governor noted that the executor and tutor had until now not done anything wrong, had always been respected, trustworthy, and law-abiding men, and did not fraudulently omit the accounts and inventory. Additionally, the order noted that the city lacked the personnel to give them proper instruction. Considering these factors, the governor waived the fines while warning Cocifacio and Acosta to conduct their affairs in the matter consistent with the prescribed laws.[95]

Certifying the decedent's death, the next document is a copy from the parochial archive citing the location of the original in the archive. The document states that on December 25, 1791, Pedro Dimarache, a forty-two year old in communion with the Church, died having received the holy sacraments and not giving his testament. Dimarache's body was buried in the cemetery of the church the day after his death by Thomas Hapott, vicar priest and ecclesiastical judge of the parish.[96]

Cocifacio and Acosta responded to the governor's order by asserting that the assets of the estate were so few that they would be consumed in preparing the documents required by the court. They requested that the court instead accept their sworn statement concerning the disposition of the goods and the division of the property between the heirs.[97] The governor responded with the reasoning of his legal advisor (*asesor general*) Licenciado Ortega that the requirements of the earlier order should be fulfilled.[98] On May 29, 1793, Cocifacio responded that after inquiring with Dimarache's relatives, he found that there were no other assets than those mentioned in the will and that they had been distributed according to the terms of the will.[99] This report appeared to have been acceptable to the governor and

95. Ibid., fols. 9–10.
96. Ibid., fol. 11.
97. Ibid., fol. 12.
98. Ibid., fols. 12v–13v.
99. Ibid., fols. 13v–14.

the *asesor general* who approved the statement on May 31, 1793.[100] A detailed financial account (inventory) and sworn statement of the administration of the estate dated September 3, 1793, followed in the record.[101] Assets were listed first, each accompanied with a descriptions such as "ten pesos and three reales charged to Alberto Rayes and which are mentioned in the seventh clause of the testament."[102] Expenses were then listed with receipts attached. Receipt number 5 lists the costs of the burial and funeral, including the burial itself, particular clerical vestments (*capa de coro*), a vigil of three readings, bells, incense, another entry for burial, and five accompanying priests totaling 21 pesos, 1 real.[103] After payment of expenses, approximately 400 pesos remained for division between the heirs.[104]

The court approved the document and forwarded it to Miguel Acosta as tutor of the minor child.[105] Miguel Acosta responded through the public attorney (*procurador público*), Rafael Saavedra de Espinosa, that he had no objection to the account and requested that Cocifacio be released from his duties as executor and that the assets be distributed to the heirs.[106] On March 12, 1794, the governor and *asesor general* agreed.[107] The following day, the court issued another order stating that the interested parties to the estate had agreed on the accounts and that their consent was approved and ordered to be done. This concluded the proceedings concerning the parties, and the court ordered an extrajudicial divisions of the property with the provision that no objection of rights arose that may cause doubt with respect to the testament or hinder the rights of Nicolas, the minor.[108] The following pages reflected court costs for signatures of the governor, *asesor general*, *procurador publico*, and scribe amounting to 190 reales.[109] The proceedings were closed on March 18, 1794, by a certification from the scribe that the extrajudicial distribution of property to the heirs had been com-

---

100. Ibid., fols. 14–15.
101. Ibid., fols. 16–18.
102. Ibid., fol. 16.
103. Ibid., fol. 22v.
104. Ibid., fol. 17v.
105. Ibid., fol. 27
106. Ibid., fols. 28–28v.
107. Ibid., fol. 28v.
108. Ibid., fols. 29–30.
109. Ibid., fols. 30–30v.

pleted. Notations in the margin indicated a summary of the distribution mentioned in the text, including the legacy of 50 pesos to the minor son.[110]

CONCLUSION

This relatively simple estate of a Corsican carpenter in St. Augustine reveals a wealth of information about testamentary dispositions in St. Augustine, East Florida, in the late eighteenth century. Care was taken to follow procedural requirements even in small estates and the governor, probably through his *asesor general*, read wills with care to determine the validity of their provisions. The interests of beneficiaries were closely protected by the court indicating a high level of official oversight. In addition to the obvious richness of these materials for social and family history, they offer a great deal of unexplored material for legal historians.

The level of legal compliance and legality in a northern border military city is also particularly noteworthy. These records may lead the way to constructing and to reassessing the place of law as in daily colonial life, on one hand, and the maintenance of empire, on the other, during this period. I was unable to survey the materials for citations to legal authority from *derecho indiano* and the *ius commune*. Having quickly swept through the pages of these proceedings, I did not notice heavy reliance on such materials, but a closer reading, particularly where legal opinions might have been obtained in large cases, will likely reveal more to the trained eye and patient reader. Work conducted on constitutional law and civil proceedings in this region of the Spanish empire during the same period indicates a complex, and at times sophisticated, legal world.[111] Closer examination of the testamentary proceedings will add to our knowledge of the legal history of this relatively neglected part of North America in the eighteenth and early nineteenth centuries.

110. Ibid., fols. 30v–31.
111. Mirow, "The Constitution of Cádiz in Florida;" idem, "Causas civiles."

The Durability of Maxims in Canon Law: From *regulae iuris* to Canonical Principles

Norman Doe and Simon Pulleyn

Frederic William Maitland claimed in 1898: "When in any century, from the thirteenth to the nineteenth, an English lawyer indulges in a Latin maxim, he is generally, though of this he may be profoundly ignorant, quoting from the Sext" (a canon law text of 1298).[1] Richard Helmholz and others (notably Roscoe Pound and Peter Stein) have done much to make sense of this claim in the medieval and Reformation periods. This paper seeks to extend a little the knowledge these scholars have given us. It describes the enduring appeal of juridical axioms to church lawyers across almost one thousand years of canonical history; it evaluates the influence of juridical axioms in the practice of the English common law courts; and, from the age of Enlightenment to the present, it proposes both the domestication of juridical axioms in the ecclesiastical law and canonical jurisprudence of England, and their novel deployment today in the juridical life of the world-wide Anglican Communion and, more recently, in the wider ecumenical context. Whilst there is continuity across the centuries in the spirit of juridical axioms, there has also been change—not least in the terms used to signify them, in the abandonment of many axioms of the classical canon law, and in the creation of new axioms to meet the needs of ecclesial life.

---

1. F. Pollock and F. W. Maitland, *The History of English Law before the Time of Edward I*, 2nd ed. (Cambridge, 1898; repr. Indianapolis, 2010), I, 231.

BROCARDS AND REGULAE IURIS IN MEDIEVAL CANON LAW

Roman law is the starting point for the medieval development of *regulae iuris* in the canon law of the Latin Church.[2] The last title of Justinian's Digest (50.17) is *De diversis regulis iuris antiqui*.[3] Its *regulae* are modelled on popular and literary proverbs, formulated under the influence of techniques in Greek philosophy, and represented "traditional authority" often associated with the work of particular jurists.[4] A *regula* is "a brief exposition of an existing state of affairs: not of such a nature that the law is derived from the rule, but the rule is established by the existing law"; *regulae* are like *causae coniectio* (the outline of a case presented to a judge at trial) and a *regula* "ceases to function when it is vitiated in any way."[5] *Regulae iuris* are: cited as generally recognized truths or maxims; formulated to express a point concisely (for practitioners and perhaps students); applied and interpreted as rules of law (similar to statutory rules today); understood sometimes as propositions of natural law; and deployed to interpret legislation and legal transactions.[6] Examples include: in testaments we interpret the will of the testator liberally; in penal causes the milder interpretation is to be made; and, if there are different possible interpretations, the more intrinsically meritorious is to be adopted.[7] Whilst *regulae* may represent one of the first theoretical formulations of law, many became merely "high-sounding generalities"; for instance: "One who remains silent certainly does not speak: but nevertheless it is true that he does not deny"; "Ignorance of law will not help those seeking to acquire, but will not be prejudicial to those who are

2.   For the use by canonists of Roman law sources generally, see R. H. Helmholz, *The Spirit of Classical Canon Law* (Athens, Ga., 1996), Chapter 1.
3.   P. Stein, *Regulae Iuris: From Juristic Rules to Legal Maxims* (Edinburgh, 1966), 1–2.
4.   R. Pound, "The maxims of equity—I: of maxims generally," *Harvard Law Review* 34 (1921), 809, 809–810: maxims "bridge the gap between customary moral rules and ethical principles."
5.   Stein, op. cit., 67 (citing Paul, *lib.* xvi *ad Plautium*, D. 50.17.1).
6.   Pound, op. cit., 816.
7.   Ibid., 813 ff.; testator: D. 50.17.12; penal causes: D. 50.17.155.2; interpretation: D. 1.3.19.

seeking their own"; and: "No one is held to act wrongfully who makes use of his own right."[8]

Medieval civil lawyers glossed the Roman *regulae iuris*. There was debate, for example, as to whether a *regula* was derived from law or else was itself law, and whether an exception constituted a separate *regula* or was implicit in the *regula* in question. Bulgarus (died c. 1166) considers that "a *regula* is formed from pre-existing law" as "a kind of joining together of single instances"; also, the rule "what is no-one's property is conceded to the occupant" suggests that "divine things belong to the occupant" but, as this contradicts the proposition "divine things are no-one's property," he reformulates a separate *regula* as an exception: "what is no-one's property, *if that property is suited to human use*, is conceded to the occupant." By way of contrast, according to Placentinus (died c. 1192), exceptions are implicit in the rule, or, *de regula*: e.g. "anyone who disobeys the order of a magistrate is guilty of bad faith," he qualifies with "unless in matters contrary to God and the Gospel and nature." Azo (died c. 1220), repeats the idea of a *regula* as a conjunction of causes, understands *causa* to be *ratio*, and maintains that if a *regula* is vitiated on proof of an exception, almost all rules must be declared false; also, *regulae* are principles (*principia*) and roots (*radices*) of law. Accursius (died 1263) proposes that in cases already decided, a *regula* does not make law, though for new and similar cases, the *regula* does make law; he also recognizes that no rule can cover all cases, but that too many exceptions undermine the value of the rules.[9] The first civilian collections of *brocards* (pegs upon which to hang a legal argument) appear around 1180, and by the time of Azo there was little difference between a *brocard* and a *regula*.[10]

The interest of the medieval canon lawyers of the Latin Church in *regulae* reflects their tendency "to abstract and generalise the decision found in

---

8.   Pound, op. cit., 814–815; silence: D. 50.17.142; ignorance: D. 22.6.6; rights: D. 50.17.55.

9.   Stein, op. cit., 133, 138, 139, 143, 147.

10.   According to Baldus de Ubaldis (c. 1327–1400), Pillius Medicinensis (c. 1185) was the first civil lawyer to collect brocards: Stein, op. cit., 145, discussing Azo: "There came to be little difference between a *generale* (or brocard) and *a regula*, except that a *regula* was normally found stated in the authoritative texts, while a *generale* was manufactured out of materials found in the texts."

the Roman legal texts and to make explicit their relation with each other."[11] In the twelfth century, this occurs in their formulation, use and discussion of *brocards* (*brocardica*). Canonists often use *brocards* as a synonym for *generalia*, freestanding axioms or propositions (*loci communes*), presented in legal argument and counter-argument, which may be reconciled in the form of a solution. Damasus (a professor at Bologna around 1220) compiled his *Brocarda sive regulae canonicae* (c. 1230) with 125 maxims which, after 1234, was revised by Bartholomew of Brescia in his *Brocardica iuris canonici*.[12]

The etymology of the word *brocard(a)* has called forth some ingenious, but not entirely persuasive, etymologies. It is not easy to tell whether it originated in Latin or French, although the suffix, not really at home in Latin, appears to point to the word having been built originally in French. That said, it would appear to have been adopted pretty much immediately into Latin. Kantorowicz and Kuttner suggested that it was derived from the Latin words *pro et contra*, indicating a derivation from the practice of lawyers citing established rules first in favor of, then against, a particular position.[13] They give no linguistic motivation for the mutation of the initial voiceless stop into a voiced one, which is hard to understand given that both Latin and French have plenty of words beginning with "pr-,"[14] and they say nothing about the suffix.[15] Spargo, apparently in all seriousness, put forward the view that the word was related to the Old English *brock* and the Greek *phorkos* and apparently denoted something of a gray or variegated hue, the quality he associated with what he saw as the often heterogeneous and shadowy character of *brocards* themselves.[16] This etymology is, at best,

---

11.   Stein, op. cit., 131: they did not confine *regulae* to maxims described as *regulae* in the texts or in the title *de regulis*—any brief rule of law could be a *regula*.

12.   G. Evans, *Law and Theology in the Middle Ages* (London, 2002) 75; Stein, op. cit., 131.

13.   H. Kantorowicz, "The *Quaestiones disputatae* of the Glossators," *Tijdschrift voor Rechtsgeschiedenis* 16 (1935), 4; S. Kuttner, "Réflexions sur les Brocards des Glossateurs," *Mélanges Joseph de Ghellinck, S.J.* (Gembloux, 1951), 767 ff.

14.   Voicing is not unknown in borrowings into French, but its motivation in a case such as this remains obscure. See further M. K. Pope, *From Latin to Modern French* (Manchester, 1934; repr. 1973), 229, 232.

15.   This may be assumed to be the pejorative suffix seen in *froussard, canard, bâtard*, etc.

16.   J. W. Spargo, "The Etymology and Early Evolution of Brocard," *Speculum* 23 (1948), 472–476.

fanciful and need not detain us. The same may be said of the widespread notion that *brocard* derives (with internal metathesis) from the name of Burchard of Worms. This has all the air of a bookish and picaresque etymology, of the kind that sees *La Infanta de Castilla* behind the Elephant and Castle. The most plausible etymology is put forward by Spitzer, who looks to the Latin adjective *broccus* (used of the projecting teeth of animals such as horses),[17] and the Old French *broche* (a needle). The thought would be that *brocards* have the same sharp and pithy quality as a nicely turned barb or shaft of wit.[18]

Reflection by canon lawyers on the *regulae* often mirrors that amongst the civilians, including debate about the relationship of *regulae* to law and that about exceptions. Initially, canonists understood *regulae iuris* not as maxims but as specific rules of law. Gratian explains in his *Decretum* (c. 1140) that "'Canon' is Greek for what is called 'rule' (*regula*) in Latin": "It is called a rule because it leads one aright and never takes one astray. But others say that it is called a rule because it rules, presents a norm for living rightly, or sets aright what is twisted or bent"; and the rule itself may admit its own exceptions.[19] Bernard of Pavia (d. 1213) included in his *Compilatio Prima* (1187–1191), a collection of decretals issued after Gratian's *Decretum*, a title *de regulis iuris*, and his later *Summa Decretalium* might be the canonists' first full discussion of *regulae*. Influenced by the civilians, he defined a *regula* variously as a maxim as well as *constitutio canonica* (e.g. a monastic rule of life); and all *regulae* have exceptions. Again, Bertram Bishop of Metz (1181–1212) in his commentary *de regulis*, citing Bulgarus and Placentinus, sees a *regula* as a "universal proposition" and *regulae* as *causae cum causa coniunctio* ("the joining of one principle with another"); and for him *causa* means a principle or *ratio*. The distinction between *regulae* and *brocards* was also becoming blurred.[20]

Two landmarks in the development of canonical *regulae* were the *Liber Extra* (or *Gregorian Decretals*), which consists of five books produced

17. Varro, *De re rustica* 2.7.3, 2.9.3; cf. Lucilius fr. 117 (ed. Marx).

18. L. Spitzer, "Latin médiéval *brocard(ic)a* > français *brocard*," *Modern Language Notes* 70 (1955), 501–506. See also T. E. Hope, *Lexical Borrowing in the Romance Languages* (Oxford, 1971), I, 168.

19. Gratian, *Decretum*, Dist. III, Part 1, c. 1 and c. 2.

20. Stein, op. cit., 144, 147.

at the direction of Pope Gregory IX (1227–41),[21] and the *Liber Sextus*, also five books, compiled at the direction of Pope Boniface VIII (1294–1303) and promulgated in 1298.[22] There are eleven *regulae iuris* at the end of the fifth book of the *Liber Extra* and eighty-eight in the last title of the *Liber Sextus* (which itself may be the work of Dinus Mugellanus).[23] Scholars are in broad agreement about the nature and purposes of these *regulae*. First, they are, variously: "moral proverbs";[24] "judicial maxims";[25] "fundamental laws in the form of axioms"; "an exposition of several laws on the same subject, conclusions or deductions, rather than principles of law drawn from constitutions or decisions"; "general rules or principles serving chiefly for the interpretation of laws";[26] and "common sense."[27] Secondly, a *regula* may be descriptive (rooted in previous cases) or prescriptive (designed to resolve new cases).[28] Thirdly, some *regulae* apply to specific matters (e.g. benefices), others generally (e.g. "No one can be held to the impossible"; "Time does not heal what was invalid from the beginning"; and "What one is not permitted to do in his own name, he may not do through another");[29] and many derive from the Digest, other parts of Roman law, the *generalia* or *brocards*.[30]

21.   J. Brundage, *Medieval Canon Law* (London, 1995), 196–7: it was the work of Raymond de Penyafort (d. 1275); Stein, op. cit., 145: Gregory based it on the Compilation of Bernard of Pavia and others; "Like Bernard, he concluded the work with a title of *regulis* (5.41)…an odd bundle…which shows signs of being put together without much thought."

22.   Brundage, op. cit., 197–8; the title *regulae* is in VI 5.13; it was compiled by a committee of canonists.

23.   Stein, op. cit., 149 (Sext, hereafter VI): the number 88 "glowed with…symbolism"; duplicating "8 represented the Pope's double power, spiritual and temporal," and "being 2 to the power of 3, it could suggest the two natures of Christ…with the three persons of God."

24.   Stein, op. cit., 145, e.g. X 5.41 reg. jur. 3: it is better to allow scandal than to abandon truth.

25.   R. H. Helmholz, *The Canon Law and Ecclesiastical Jurisdiction from 597 to the 1640s*, *The Oxford History of the Laws of England*, 1 (Oxford, 2004), 154.

26.   A. Meehan, "Regulae iuris," *The Catholic Encyclopedia*, Vol. 12 (New York, 1911).

27.   Evans, op. cit., 76.

28.   M. B. Carosi, "Some notes on the problem of *regulae iuris* in the history of law," *Annuario di emeneutica giuridica* 10 (2005), 305–312.

29.   VI 5.13.1 (benefices), 6 (impossibility), 18 (time), 47 (doing in one's own name).

30.   Stein, op. cit., 145: e.g. X 5.41.1: "by whatever means anything comes into being, by the same means it is dissolved," a version of D. 50.17.35; 149: e.g. VI 5.13.65, from D.

Particular use was made of *regulae* in teaching canon law, both to sum up the law and to resolve contradictions.[31] Several maxims were also used to determine when a narrow or a wide interpretation of law was appropriate; for example: "It is fitting that odious things be restricted and favorable ones extended"; "A general concession does not include those particular items which one would not likely have included"; "In obscure matters, the least severe solution is to be followed."[32] The work of the English canonist William Lyndwood also includes maxims which have a home-spun flavor: "Let him who has not been punished in his pocket be punished in his body."[33] In sum, as Pound puts it, the canonical maxims "help to lead the jurist from a body of hard and fast rules, authoritatively imposed, above question and subject only to interpretation, to a conception of principles of reason, discoverable by juristic theory and philosophy, of which particular positive rules were but declaratory."[34]

The *regulae iuris* of Roman civil law and canon law also made their way into the medieval English common law,[35] which itself consists of "rules."[36] Explicit reference is made to "maxims," by counsel in argument and by judges to justify decisions,[37] and general propositions are seen as rooted in juridical "erudition."[38] The commentators also equate "maxim"

50.17.126, 154; VI 5.13.29 (*quod omnes tangit debet ab omnibus approbari*), from Code 5.59.5.2; Pound, op. cit., 818–819: e.g. VI 5.13.6, D. 50.17.185; VI 5.13.33, D. 50.17.73; VI 5.13.44, D. 50.17.142; VI 5.13.48, D. 50.17.206; VI 5.13.55, D. 50.17.10.

31.   Pound, op. cit., 817. See also D. M. Owen, *The Medieval Canon Law: Teaching, Literature and Transmission* (Cambridge, 1990), 7: in 1424 a Cambridge library lists Dinus Mugellanus' *regulae*.

32.   Brundage, op. cit., 169–170: VI 5.13.15; 81; 30; 34 (borrowed from D. 50.17. 80).

33.   *Provinciale*, 321: *qui non luit in bursa, luet in corpore.*

34.   Pound, op. cit., 819.

35.   The *Leges Henrici Primi* of the twelfth century have maxim-like propositions, e.g. "No one is to be judged in his absence" (5.3). Also, proverbs appear in earlier Anglo-Saxon legal texts, e.g. the Exeter Book (late tenth-century) states: "For the wound there must be a bandage; for the hard man, vengeance."

36.   N. Doe, *Fundamental Authority in Late Medieval English Law* (Cambridge, 1990) 36.

37.   YB 2 Edw. II, 106b (1308–9), Selden Society 19 (1905), 17: Bereford, J: "*Vostre masime est trop large*"; P 18 Hen. VI, 6,6 at 7, Newton CJCP: "it is an ancient maxim in law, *volenti non fit injuria.*"

38.   J. H. Baker, ed., *Reports of Cases by John Caryll, Part I, 1485–1499*, Selden Society 115 (1998), 26: *Anon* (1490) at 27: "*Yaxley*: I have always taken it [as] a maxim (*pur*

with "principle" and classify *regulae iuris* as such.[39] Sometimes propositions function as determinants in cases, without being classified as maxims or principles, on the basis that they were consistent with "reason,"[40] and the preference to ensure legal consistency over possible injustice in a case was summed up in the home-grown maxim: "a mischief will be suffered sooner than an inconvenience."[41] In turn, reference was made for example to maxims from the Sext, such as *volenti non fit injuria*,[42] *nemo obligatur ad impossibile*,[43] *melior est condicio possidentis*,[44] and *ratihabitio retrotrahitur et mandato comparatur*;[45] and *quod omnes tangit* was famously used by counsel in 1440 arguing that "the territory of Ireland is separate from the kingdom of England, for if a tenth or fifteenth be granted here, it shall not bind the people of Ireland unless they will to approve of this in their own parliament, even though the king under his great seal send the same statute to Ireland."[46]

---

erudition)...Browne: Do not swear to it. You...have heard it...as a distinction but not *pur erudition*."

39.   Fortescue (d. c. 1476), *De Laudibus*, c. 8: "principles (*principia*)...are no other than...*universalia*" which "the learned in the law...call maxims (*maximas*); in rhetoric... *paradoxa*, [and] the civilians call them *regulae iuris*"; Littleton (d. 1481) interchanges "maxim" and "principle" for rules of law: Co. Lit., 343a: "That which our author here calleth a principle, Sect. 3 & 90, he calleth a maxime."

40.   Doe, op. cit., 123: Mich. 6 Ed. IV, 7, 18: "where a man has *damnum absque injuria*, in this case he shall have no action, for if he has [suffered] no wrong it is not reason that he will recover damages."

41.   Doe, op. cit., 155–174.

42.   E.g. YB Trin. 6 Edw. II, 2 (1313), Selden Society 36 (1918), 4, 9; VI 5.13.27: "To the one who knows and approves" etc.

43.   YB Mich. 4 Edw. II, 38 (1311), Selden Society 22 (1907), 199, 200; VI 5.13.6: "No-one is obliged to do the impossible."

44.   YB Mich. 30 Edw. I (1302); Hil. 4 Edw. II, 36 (1310–11), Selden Society 26 (1911), 68; VI 5.13.45: "In obscure cases, consideration is given to that which is most probable or which happens most often."

45.   Cornish Iter. 30 Edw. I (1302) Horwood, 129; from VI 5.13.10: "Ratification has a retroactive effect and may certainly be compared to a procuration."

46.   Mich. 20 Hen. VI, 8, 17 (Doe, 19); from VI 5.13.29.

Maxims in Canon and Ecclesiastical
Law: The Reformation

The continental civilians and canonists of the sixteenth and seventeenth centuries continued to use *regulae iuris*.[47] This "axiomatization" of law has been understood to express a quest both for a purer and earlier under-standing of law, and for simplicity of method in applying and in learning the law—law students at most major European universities studied the Digest *regulae* as part of their formal training.[48] There are commentaries on the *regulae* of canon law,[49] studies on individual *regulae*,[50] compilations for laymen,[51] as well as collections of *brocards*, sometimes presented as "axioms" (*axiomata*).[52] Once more, there were various understandings of *regulae*. According to Nicolaus Everardus (d. 1532), all statements in civil and canon law which are preceded by the words *plerumque* (generally) or *semper* (always) are to be regarded as *regulae*.[53] For Sebastiano Medicis (in 1586): "A *regula* is a general and brief definition and statement, whereby, in a succinct communication, many similar cases are summarized, not to give expression

47. For maxims in the jurisprudence of the Reformers, see J. Witte, *Law and Prot-estantism: The Legal Teachings of the Lutheran Reformation* (Cambridge, 2002), 164–165: "the magistrates are ministers, that is, servants of the laws" (Oldendorp); for Luther, the ruler "who does not know how to dissemble does not know how to rule" and "equity will weigh for and against."

48. D. van der Merwe, "*Regulae iuris* and the Axiomatisation of the Law in the Sixteenth and Early Seventeenth Centuries," *Tydskrif vir die Suid-Afrikaanse Reg* (1987), 286 at 288; see e.g. Decius, *In titulis Digestis de regulis iuris* (1568); 290: Dinus Mugellanus had at least five new editions in the sixteenth century.

49. E.g. Petrus Peckius (1529–1589), *Ad regulas iuris canonici commentaria elabora-tissima* (1570).

50. E.g. Diego Covarruvius (1512–1577), *Regulae, Peccatum. De regulis iuris libro sex-to relectio* (1558), a commentary on the rule *peccatum non dimittitur, nisi restituatur ablatum* ("a sin is not forgiven unless what has been taken away is restored") (VI 5.13.4).

51. Stein, op. cit., 162; e.g. Thomas Murner (1475–c. 1534), *Utriusque iuris tituli et regulae* (1518); satirized by Rabelais (c. 1493–1553) in his *Third Book* (1546), 3 39: judge Brid-legoose dispensed justice by the throw of dice and found authority for his methods in the *regulae iuris* of civil and canon law.

52. E.g. Augustinho Barbaros (d. 1649), *Axiomatum iuris usufrequentiorum exposi-tio* (1631).

53. *Topica legalia* (1516)–in the 1581 edition, under the title *Loci argumentorum le-gales*, at 72.

to a special law, but to convey the *ratio* of those cases."[54] Some jurists compared *regulae* with other legal forms; for example: *lex*, derived from factual situations, has "incontrovertible authority," whereas a *regula*, derived from law, has "probable authority," i.e. as "a formulation of the accumulated wisdom of jurists explaining and commenting upon the law."[55] Commentators also draw a parallel between *regulae* and *prima principia iuris* or *axiomata*.[56]

It is in the sixteenth century that we first see reflection on "maxims" by commentators on the common law and equity in England.[57] Christopher St. German uses "maxim" and "principle" synonymously: the six "grounds of the law of England" are the law of reason, the law of God, customs used throughout the realm, local customs, statutes, and "divers principles, that be called in the law maxims, the which have always been taken for law in this realm, so that it is not lawful for any that is learned in the law to deny them; for every one of those maxims is sufficient for itself."[58] Some such maxims are said to be "of the same strength and effect in law as statutes"; with others it is unclear whether they be "only maxims of the law or...grounded upon the law of reason" (e.g. "the accessory shall not be put to answer before the principal"); as with the latter, some echo canonical *regulae* (e.g. "for that law seems not reasonable that binds a man to an impossibility"); several seem native to English law (e.g. "escuage uncertain makes knight's service"; "escuage certain makes socage"; and: "There is an old maxim in the law that a mischief shall be rather suffered than an inconvenience."[59]

54. *Tractatus de regulis iuris* in his II *Tractatuum* (1586), 2 par. 10.

55. E.g. Vigelius, *Methodus regularum utriusque iuris* (1584), 9–10; Giphanius (1534–1604) *Tractatus de diversis regulis iuris antique utilissimus* (1607), 12–13.

56. van der Merwe, op. cit., 297–298.

57. G. Behrens, "Equity in the Commentaries of Edmund Plowden," *Journal of Legal History* 20 (1999), 25: equity involved upholding the legislator's intent, which seems to echo VI 5.13.88: "Those who comply with the letter of the law but against the intention of the law are really against the law."

58. *Dialogue between a Doctor of Divinity and a Student of the Common Law* (published in Latin, 1523, English, 1532) I, c. 8 (1523); equity relaxes law if in conflict with divine law or the law of reason.

59. Pound, op. cit., 830; *Dialogue* II, c. 5 (impossibility); c. 36 (mischief and inconvenience); see also VI 5.13.42: "That which is accessory ought to follow the condition of the principal."

This theoretical discussion of maxims in St. German echoes their continued use by the common lawyers in court. A "maxim" is a "ground" of the law, and the words are often used synonymously;[60] examples include: a mischief will be suffered sooner than an inconvenience; statutory words are understood by their antecedents; a person may not give himself an action; and the law does not concern itself with trivialities.[61] Many maxims either mirror or resemble those in the Sext (and some have the appearance of propositions of logic or reason); for example: an action dies with the person;[62] whoever breaches faith with a party is not entitled to ask that party to be faithful;[63] everything of greater worth draws to itself everything of lesser worth;[64] he who acts through another is deemed to act himself;[65] a man may alienate such things as he may lawfully alienate;[66] a man may not take advantage of his own wrong;[67] regard must be had to the intention and not to the result;[68] no-one is bound to betray himself;[69] consent does

---

60. J. H. Baker, ed., *Reports of Cases from the Time of King Henry VIII*, vol. I, Selden Society 120 (2003), 103, 221, 240; vol. II, Selden Society 121 (2004), 241, 298, 304, 307, 324, 343, 349.

61. Selden Society 121 (2004), 293 (mischief), 298 (antecedents), 379 (action); J. H. Baker, ed., *The Reports of Cases by John Caryll*, vol. I, Selden Society 115 (1998), 45 (trivialities).

62. Selden Society 121 (2004), 209, 241; VI 5.13.7: "A personal privilege follows a person and ceases with him."

63. Selden Society 121 (2004), 462 at 467; perhaps VI 5.13.75: "He who breaches faith toward his partner, is not entitled to ask him to be faithful."

64. Selden Society 121 (2004), 433; VI 5.13.35: "That which is greater always contains that which it lesser."

65. Selden Society 121 (2004), 434; VI 5.13.72: "A person who acts through another is (sc. in the same position) as if he acted by himself."

66. Selden Society 115 (1998), 138; VI 5.13.79: "No one can transfer to another more rights than he possesses."

67. J. H. Baker, ed., *The Reports of William Dalison: 1552–1558*, Selden Society 124 (2007), 58; VI 5.13.48.

68. J. H. Baker, ed. *Reports from the Lost Notebooks of Sir James Dyer*, vol. I, Selden Society 109 (1993), 73; VI 5.13.23: "Who is not culpable should not be punished."

69. Selden Society 109 (1993), xxx n. 82, lxvii, lxxix n. 56, p. 144 (*Thomas Lee's Case* (1568); perhaps VI 5.13.20.

not constitute injury;[70] and penal law must be construed strictly.[71] Other canonical *regulae* may be conceived as implicit in "maxims" at common law and coincident with "good reason."[72] Reference is also made to "principles of law,"[73] "common sayings,"[74] and proverbs,[75] e.g. to be human is to err,[76] or, acknowledgment of the sin is the beginning of health.[77] Also, in equity: an impossible term in a lease is ignored;[78] if land in dispute is alienated, an injunction for possession is not granted;[79] and a plea engrossed on parchment cannot be withdrawn.[80] Indeed, some practitioners confidently attributed to maxims the authority of reason; in a case of 1551 counsel stated: "There are two principal things from which arguments may be drawn...our maxims, and reason which is the mother of all laws"; that is: "maxims are the foundations of the law, and the conclusions of reason"; also, they may be

70.   J. H. Baker, ed., *The Reports of Cases by John Caryll*, vol. II, Selden Society 116 (1999), 621; VI 5.13.27.

71.   J. H. Baker, *Reports from the Lost Notebooks of Sir James Dyer*, Vol. II, Selden Society 110 (1994), 390: Jesuits were not in breach of a statute of 25 Edw. III "because a penal law must be construed strictly"; VI 5.13.49: "In matters of penalty a more benign interpretation is the right one."

72.   Selden Society 121 (2004), 298: "it is a maxim (*grounde*) that if I give land to someone, reserving one acre...this is void, in as much as it is part of the thing given": VI 5.13.61: "Whatever is given for the benefit of another should not be turned to his disadvantage"; VI 5.13.80: "No doubt, the part is contained in the whole."

73.   Selden Society 116 (1999), 621: *Scrope v. Hyk* (1511) p. 618: "*Car est un principal en le ley*" that "no one may have a freehold without livery, or something tantamount."

74.   Selden Society 116 (1999), 572: *Anon* (1507): "every statute which is penal and goes in derogation of the common law shall be taken strictly. That is a common saying (*common dit*)."

75.   J. H. Baker, *The Notebook of Sir John Port* (d. 1540), Selden Society 102 (1986), 105: a good huntsman in his youth will be a good gamekeeper; p. 125: a man is more bound to help the king than his own father.

76.   Selden Society 109 (1993), 187: *Att-Gen. v. Blanchard* (1570).

77.   Selden Society 109 (1993), 134: *Att-Gen v. Appleyard* (1567), at 135 (a saying of Epicurus).

78.   W. H. Bryson, *Cases Concerning Equity and the Courts of Equity 1550–1660*, Selden Society 117 (2001), 96, Case 6 (*Anon.*, 1567): this equates with VI 5.13.6: "No-one can be obliged to the impossible."

79.   Selden Society 117 (2001), 112, Case No. 30 (*Anon.*, 1582); this mirrors VI 5.13.3: "No prescription without possession."

80.   Selden Society 117 (2001), 131, Case No. 57 (*Att-Gen, ex rel. Robinson v. Robinson*, 1589); this mirrors VI 5.13.21: "What was approved once cannot be disapproved later."

compared but "do not vary," so "that a thing is nearer to one maxim than to another, or placed between two maxims"; yet: "they ought never to be impeached or impugned, but always observed and held as firm principles and authorities of themselves."[81]

The termination of papal jurisdiction and the establishment of the Church of England meant neither the demise of civilian learning nor the abandonment of *regulae iuris* in the sixteenth and seventeenth centuries.[82] Church court practice abounds in the use of maxims, such as, statutes in derogation of the canonical *ius commune* are to be interpreted strictly, and suit must be brought in the forum of the defendant.[83] They are also common in the civilian notebooks; for example, in that of Sir Julius Caesar: where there is a profit to be made, ignorance of the action of a deceased is not presumed;[84] a person who succeeds to the rights of another is reckoned to have a just cause for his ignorance;[85] a sentence that is a nullity is without effect if no appeal is made from it;[86] and it is fraudulent to sue for something one has an obligation to restore to another;[87] moreover, in that of Sir Thomas Eden (c. 1610): prescription does not begin without possession; no matter how long the period, prescription does not obtain for possession in bad faith; an offence is not forgiven if reparation is not made; and one

81. *Colthirst v. Bejushin*, Serjeant Morgan: I Plowden 21, 27 (1551). See Pound, 831 and Stein, 160–1.

82. Richard Hooker's *Of the Laws of Ecclesiastical Polity* (1594) contains citations to the *Liber Sextus* and he makes use e.g. of the *quod omnes tangit* principle (VI 5.13.29): see R. H. Helmholz, "Richard Hooker and the European *ius commune*," *Ecclesiastical Law Journal* 6 (2001), 4 at 5 and 9.

83. Helmholz, *The Canon Law and Ecclesiastical Jurisdiction*, 280 (statute); see also 509–10, *Actor forum rei sequitur* ("The claimant must follow the forum of the thing in dispute"), X 2.2.10; 532: *Nemo allegans turpitudinem suam est audiendus* ("No man is to be heard pleading his own wrongdoing"); 632: the "maxim *inclusio unius exclusio alterius*" ("The inclusion of one thing excludes the other"); VI 5.13.35: *Plus semper in se continent quod est minus* ("The greater includes the lesser"). See also Selden Society 116 (1999), 683 (*Dr Standish's Case* (1515)) at 684: "Therefore, since the [papal] decree was never received (*resceive*) here in England, for that reason it does not bind."

84. R. H. Helmholz, *Three Civilian Notebooks: 1580–1640*, Selden Society 127 (2010), *Notebook of Sir Julius Caesar*, at 24; VI 5.13.13 (citing Dinus and Peckius).

85. Ibid., 16: VI 5.13.14 (citing Peckius).

86. Ibid., 18: VI 5.13.52 (citing Peckius).

87. Ibid., 25: VI 5.13.59 (citing Dinus).

cannot grant a privilege he does not himself hold.[88] Indeed, Eden (d. 1645) wrote a commentary on the Digest with a title *De regulis iuris* (1633), working through those of the Sext "stating their meaning, providing examples, limitations, extensions, exceptions, and...citing learned authorities" (notably Philippus Decius (d. 1536/7)).[89] Likewise, John Godolphin's *Repertorium Canonicum or Abridgement of the Ecclesiastical Laws of this Realm* (1678),[90] in which "material points...are succinctly treated," includes as "rules of canon law": a vacant benefice must be filled within six months; a metropolitan shall never collate for a lapse;[91] an archdeacon must carry out a visitation in person;[92] when the cause ceases, the effect ceases;[93] *Apud eum debet fieri Renunciatio, apud quem pertinere dignoscitur Confirmatio;*[94] and: the "Rule in Law, *Qui non facit quod debet, non recipit quod oportet.*"[95]

There is little to distinguish these seventeenth-century Civilian uses of the *regulae iuris* and the contemporary common lawyers' use of "maxims." For Edward Coke (1551–1633) a maxim is "a proposition to be of all men confessed and granted without proof, argument or discourse," "a conclusion of reason, so called *quia maxima est eius dignitas et certissima authoritas, atque quod maxime omnibus probetur* ["because its worth is very great and its authority most sure, and because it is greatly approved by all"]—so sure...that they ought not to be questioned"; these maxims he presents var-

---

88.   Ibid., 95, VI 5.13.2–4 (citing Diego Covarrivias); see also 93, VI 5.13.79 (citing Peckius).

89.   R. H. Helmholz, *Roman Canon Law in Reformation England* (Cambridge, 1990), 136–137.

90.   For John Godolphin see J. H. Baker, *Monuments of Endlesse Labours: English Canonists and their Work 1300–1900* (London, 1998), 77.

91.   *Repertorium Canonicum*, 39: "the Rule of the Canon Law" (vacancy); 268: "a Rule" (lapse).

92.   Ibid., Chapter IX: (5): "And it is a Rule in the *Canon Law, Quod nulla est adversus Procurationem praescriptio*" (citing e.g. Lyndwood).

93.   Ibid., Chapter IX (11): "And so the Rule of *Cessante causa cessat effectus* doth not hold in this case."

94.   Ibid., Chapter XXV (3): resignation renders a benefice void: "for it is a Rule in the *Canon Law, Apud eum debet fieri Renunciatio, apud quem pertinere dignoscitur Confirmatio*" ("A resignation may only be made before him to whom the right of accepting it specifically belongs").

95.   "He who does not do what he must does not receive what he ought": ibid., p. 509 (14): a husband is not obliged to pay alimony to a deserting wife; see also p. 108: *regula.*

iously as detailed rules, proverbs, propositions and principles;[96] and some equate with the canonical maxims; e.g. ignorance of the law which everybody is supposed to know does not afford excuse.[97] However, Francis Bacon (1561–1626) combines the common law maxim (as a ground of the law) and the civilian *regula iuris* (as derived from law); his twenty-five *Maxims of the Law* (1630), a collection of "the rules and grounds dispersed throughout the body of the laws," is designed: to assist "in new cases and such wherein there is no direct authority, to sound into the true conceit of law by depth of reason"; "to confirm the law...in cases wherein the authorities do square and vary"; and "in cases wherein the law is cleared by authority...to see more profoundly into the reason of such judgments and ruled cases" (Preface); his maxims are in Latin (for brevity and ease of memory) and his commentary in English lists situations in which they do and do not apply.[98] Henry Finch (d. 1625), in *Law or a Discourse Thereon* (1627), organizes rules on the basis of principles and logic; e.g. the rule requiring a formal release of a sealed instrument is based on the principle of logic that "things are dissolved as they be contracted"; some of his maxims are either from or mirror those in the Sext,[99] as do four of the 214 maxims in Wingate's *Maxims of Reason or the Reason of the Common Law of England* (1658).[100]

MAXIMS IN ENGLISH ECCLESIASTICAL LAW: THE ENLIGHTENMENT

In England, the eighteenth century is important for the publication of

96. Co. Litt., 1628: 10b–11a (maxim); 343a (maxim/principle); 10b, 343a (detailed rules); 49b, 2 Inst. 65 (proverb); 70b, 355b, 356a (logic and principle); 97b ("common law itself is nothing else but reason").

97. 2 Co. Rep. 3b; VI 5.13.13: Stein, op. cit., 160.

98. Stein, op. cit., 171–174; as Attorney-General, in 1616 Bacon also proposed as part of law reform the creation of a book of maxims *De regulis iuris* which are "the general dictates of reason."

99. Stein, op. cit., 175: Book I has about 100 maxims, all in English: no. 92 is VI 5.13.72; no. 16 compares with VI 5.13.35; no. 22 with VI 5.13.35; no. 25 with VI 5.13.42, and no. 36 with VI 5.13.45. Noy, *Treatise of the Principall Grounds and Maxims of the Lawes of this Kingdome* (1641) follows Finch; there are 36 maxims: No. 9 is VI 5.13.18; the variants are: Nos. 14, 35, and 47; two are from the Digest: Nos. 24 and 27.

100. Wingate, no. 24 is a variant of VI 5.13.79; no. 49 is VI 5.13.54, no. 122 is VI 5.13.27; and no. 124 is VI 5.13.10.

numerous practitioner works on the law applicable to the Church of England.[101] Three of these are notable for their use of "maxims." However, there is little in many of these maxims that is proverbial, or that has an obvious link with natural law or reason; most have a particularity more reminiscent of rules rather than general principles, and many articulate well the entanglement of common law and ecclesiastical law. The first work is that of Edmund Gibson, his *Codex Juris Ecclesiastici Anglicani, or, The Statutes, Constitutions, Canons, Rubrics and Articles of the Church of England* (1713), "Methodically digested under their proper heads with a commentary historical and juridical"; it was intended "for the service of the clergy, and in support of the rights and privileges of the Church," and treats "the Rules of Common and Canon Law."[102] The work uses "maxims" throughout, often in Latin,[103] sometimes to support a particular "rule,"[104] and sometimes citing Coke for a "maxim of law."[105] Gibson uses maxims across the various fields of ecclesiastical law, such as in that of church governance,[106] including the royal supremacy in ecclesiastical af-

101. For example: W. Nelson, *The Rights of the Clergy of Great Britain: As Established by the Canons, the Common Law, and the Statutes of the Realm* (London, 1709) 8: abjuration: "for if goods were stolen, *Et reus ad ecclesiam confugisset, vitam habeat* [and the accused had fled to the church, he should have his life]; that was the doctrine at the time."

102. *Codex* I, Title page, 1713 edition and Preface, viii; see Baker, *Monuments of Endlesse Labours*, 95.

103. *Codex* I, xxviii: "*maxime, cum de jure communi quilibet hujusmodi ordinarius, in causarum cognitionibus committere valeat vices suas* [this is especially the case with the common law when any ordinary of this kind has power to depute his powers]; i.e. to commit them to what hands they please."

104. *Codex* I, xx: "And as to the second rule, viz., the trial of the incident matter, by that Court which hath the proper cognisance of the principal; this hath not only a plain maxim on its side (*cognitio accessarii in causa christianitatis non impediatur, ubi cognitio causae principalis ad forum ecclesiasticum noscitur pertinere;*) [the cognizance of an accessory matter is not to be impeded in an ecclesiastical court where the cognizance of the principal matter is seen to pertain to the ecclesiastical jurisdiction] but the very denial of a right in the spiritual court to write to the temporal on such occasions," which "infers a right to try all incidental matters by their own rules."

105. *Codex* I, xxi: "For though the rule laid down by my Lord Coke as a maxim of law (that when in any case remedy is given *in foro seculari* by a statute law, the jurisdiction of the spiritual court ceases, unless it is generally saved)"; see also II, 710: a "maxim of Coke."

106. *Codex* I, xxv: "And as to the notion, founded on the Maxim of the Chancellor's having the same consistory with the Bishop, as if the Bishop had divested himself of all

fairs,[107] and the subjection of clergy to statute.[108] Occasionally, he presents a proposition as "a known maxim of the canon law,"[109] or else as "a rule of the canon law."[110] Elsewhere, he presents a proposition as, variously: a "maxim of the common law";[111] a maxim in the "temporal law";[112] a maxim "declared" by the courts;[113] a maxim which is "laid down in the books of the common law";[114] and an "equitable maxim."[115]

---

judicial authority and coercion, and, by construction of law, had invested the Chancellor with the whole; ...as none of these things are conveyed to the Chancellor by operation of law, so the maxim cannot be applied to the execution of episcopal authority in things which directly and immediately belong to the episcopal office, as such."

107. *Codex* I, 5: "And it is pursuant to a maxim of our laws, *Ecclesia est infra aetatem, et in custodia Domini regis, qui tenetur Jura et haereditates suas manu tenere et defendere*" [The Church is under age and in the custody of the Lord king, who is bound to uphold and defend its rights and inheritances].

108. *Codex* I, 22: a "declared maxim, That the Clergy are liable to all public charges imposed by Parliament, where they are not specially excepted."

109. *Codex* II, 689: "the known maxim of the canon law, *Ecclesia decimas solvere ecclesiae non debet*" [A church is not obliged to pay tithes to (sc. another) church], and *Cleri a clericis decimas non exigent* [Clergy shall not exact tithes from (sc. other) clergy]; II, 797: "maxim of canon law."

110. *Codex* II, 1116: "The Rule of canon Law": degradation may be imposed by a bishop or *cum certo episcoporum numero definito canonibus* [with a set number of bishops fixed by the canons]; this "was the foundation of the maxim, *spiritualia facilius construuntur, quam destruuntur; quia solus episcopus dat ordinem, quem solus tollere non potest*" [spiritual things are more easily granted than revoked: because (sc. though) the bishop may by himself confer an order, he may not by himself take it away]".

111. *Codex* I, 553: "the contrary maxim of the common law"; II, 690: "The general maxim in the books of the common law" is "That before the Council of Lateran [1215]... no parochial right of tithes was fixed here in England"; II, 696: "general maxim: that once discharged, always discharged."

112. *Codex* II, 869: that a bishop cannot resign to dean and chapter is a maxim in the "temporal law."

113. *Codex* II, 1023: "More especially, it hath been declared as a Maxim [in the courts of the common law] that grants of offices being made for their lives, than they had before the statutes."

114. *Codex* II, 1116: "The maxim laid down in the books of the common law is, That what is sufficient cause to deprive a clerk, is a sufficient cause to refuse him at first" (Coke 5 Rep 58 a); see also: II, 810 and 853: the maxim *nullum tempus occurrit regi* [time never runs against the king] and II, 1077: where common law or statute give remedy, the jurisdiction of the church courts ends.

115. *Codex* II, 1073: "the equitable maxim of principal and accessory may be extended to such latitude, as the quick and easy administration of justice evidently calls for."

Similar use is made of maxims by Richard Grey in *A System of English Ecclesiastical Law* (1730),[116] presented primarily in terms of the "rules" of canon law,[117] and "the rules of the common law" (operative under "the law of God"),[118] and expounded by reference to both the "tenor" and the "strictness" of the law.[119] Grey writes of the "known maxims of the canon law,"[120] or those of the common law,[121] considers that some "maxims" are contrary to "the ancient law" of the church,[122] or else invokes propositions without naming them explicitly as canonical maxims;[123] other legal propositions he presents as grounded in reason or conscience, or else as "canonical reasons."[124] Indeed, Grey employs a wide range of juridical categories, such as: custom; "general rules" and "exceptions"; "common opinion"; "equitable

116. Richard Grey DD (a rector), *A System of English Ecclesiastical Law*, 3rd ed. (1735): he uses a catechetical method (of question and answer). He distinguishes: 314: "the Law, as well of the State, as of the Church"; 214: "The Laws of the Church."

117. *System*, 42: as to "rules" on the appointment of coadjutors: "There are many in the Canon Law, but the Use of them has long been set aside"; for the law of God see e.g. 26, 139.

118. *System*, 111: "the Rules of Common Law concerning church ways."

119. *System*, 90: "the plain Tenor and Letter of the Law"; 338: the "tenor" of a statute; 219: "the Tenor of the Act"; 230: "in strictness of Law" the cure of souls vests in the rector and vicar.

120. *System*, 189: "the known Maxim of the Canon Law, *Ecclesia decimas ecclesiae solvere non debet* [A church is not obliged to pay tithes to (sc. another) church] and *Clerici a clericis decimas non exigant* [Clergy are not to exact tithes from (sc. other) clergy]."

121. *System*, 188: "that Maxim in the Common Law, That the Fee-Simple of the Glebe is in abeyance"

122. *System*, 193: "Tithes shall not be paid of such things as are *ferae naturae* [wild in nature—e.g. deer]: "This Maxim is contrary to the ancient Law of the Church of England."

123. *System*, 287: "whoever elects an unfit person is *ipso jure* deprived of the power of electing, and therefore *Potior qui Prior* is the Rule of the Canon Law in this Case"; 381: a spiritual judge "can only punish *pro salute animae*" [for the saving of a soul]; see 394 for the same maxim. See also 258: *nullum tempus occurrit regi* [time never runs against the king].

124. *System*, 255: commerce in advowsons "is not easily reconciled either to the Laws of the Church, which expressly forbid it, or to the ancient Laws of the land"; rather, they ought "of Reason and good Conscience to be considered" as trusts "for the benefit of men's souls"; 290: the bishop has "the cure of souls in his diocese, and is bound in Conscience to see them well cared for"; 353: churchwardens are to "discharge their consciences" in making presentments; 334: "canonical reasons" for the union of churches (e.g. hospitality); see also 355: "on the foot of long usage and custom."

rules"; "equity and prudence"; and "spiritual law."[125] Moreover, Grey classi-fies some propositions as a "principle" attributable to reason; for example: "The Doctrine of the Canon Law" is that the innocent party in adultery may re-marry; "it seems unreasonable that the Innocent should suffer for the Crime of another; and upon this Principle several Acts of Parliament, for the Divorce of particular persons in the Case of Adultery, have express-ly allowed a Liberty to the innocent Person of marrying again."[126] There are also general propositions which Grey classifies as neither maxims nor principles.[127]

Richard Burn makes much more extensive use of "maxims" in his *Ecclesiastical Law* (1763), a treatment of the civil law, canon law, common law, and statute applicable to the Church of England.[128] Time and again Burn uses the idea of a "rule of law," a "general rule," or a "rule of the canon law";[129] for instance: "the rules which the ancient canon law hath laid down" provide that the election of a cathedral chapter must be in accordance with the cathedral statutes; and: that "A church once consecrated cannot be con-secrated again," is a "general rule of the canon law."[130] These "rules of law" Burn distinguishes from legal "maxims" which may be found in Roman

125. *System*, 199: "The manner of payment of tithes is for the most part governed by the Custom of every Parish"; 201: "general rules" and "exceptions...to this Rule"; 229: "Rectors...long excluded from Residence, are, in common Opinion, discharged from the Cure of Souls"; 250: "great hardship" incurred by the law on dilapidations is tempered by "equitable rules"; 268: "equity and prudence"; 409: "equity"; 274: "spiritual law"; 281: "Court Christian"; 418: "usage of the Church of England."

126. *System*, 147.

127. *System*, 112: "No man shall sit covered in the time of divine service"; "No one shall walk, or talk, or depart out of the church, without urgent and reasonable cause"; 116: "No stranger shall be suffered to preach, without showing his licence"; 129: "None shall be admitted to the Holy Communion, until such time as he be confirmed, or be ready and desirous to be confirmed."

128. In 4 volumes, this was in a "dictionary form" arranged alphabetically. See J. H. Baker, *Endlesse Labours*, 115: the respective authorities of these bodies of law were under-stood by Burn in that order.

129. Burn, *Ecclesiastical Law*, 2nd ed. (1767), I, 480: "rules of law"; I.129: "No person may present himself: and it is according to the rule of the canon law."

130. Burn, I, 255: cathedrals; I, 381: "the rule of the ancient canon law"; I, 307: consecration.

law, canon law and common law; thus, he refers to: "a maxim in law";[131] "a maxim in the temporal law and...applied to the ecclesiastical law";[132] a "known maxim of the canon law, that the church shall not pay tithes to the church";[133] the "general maxim...once discharged, always discharged";[134] and "an inviolable maxim that an inheritance cannot ascend."[135] Also, a legal rule may be "grounded on a maxim" (of Roman law),[136] and the "equity" of certain arrangements may be the basis of a "maxim of the canon law" upon which other "rules" of law rest.[137] For Burn, maxims are "declared," "established" or "unanimous."[138] Other associated juridical categories used

131. Burn I, 124: the king is patron paramount of all the benefices: "And because it is a maxim in law, that the church is not full against the king, till induction; therefore though the bishop hath collated, or hath presented, and the clerk is instituted upon that presentation, yet will not such collation or institution avail the clerk, but the right of presenting devolves to the king"; II, 427: "yet no maxim in the law is more established, than that a subsequent contrary act virtually repeals a preceding act, so far forth as it is contrary"; II, 312: "But it being a maxim in law, that *nullum tempus occurrit regi*" [time never runs against the king].

132. Burn III, 298: "And resignation can only be made to a superior. This is a maxim in the temporal law, and applied by Lord Coke to the ecclesiastical law, when he says, that therefore a bishop cannot resign to the dean and chapter but it must done to the metropolitan from whom he received confirmation and consecration. Gibs[on] 822"; IV, 133: maxim and estates of land.

133. Burn, II, 256 and III, 380.

134. Burn, III, 424: no tithe is payable on oak under 20 years of age; it is privileged (even if rotten).

135. Burn, IV, 304: "an inviolable maxim that an inheritance cannot ascend."

136. Burn, IV, 84: "the credit of a witness could not be purged or varied by an act subsequent to the attestation; which [Lee CJ] grounded on a maxim of the Roman law, *conditionem testium inspicere debemus eo tempore cum signarent*" [we ought to examine the state of the witnesses at the time when they were affixing their seal].

137. Burn, I, 9: "The equity of which union of the advowson to the manor, seems to be the foundation of that maxim of the canon law, *jus patronatus transit cum universitate nisi specialiter excipiatur* [the right of patronage is transferred with the rest unless it is specifically excepted], upon which, the rule of the law is, that he who purchases an advowson ought not to be deprived thereof."

138. Burn, II, 45: "it hath been declared, as a maxim" (on reversions); II, 48: "there is a maxim in the law [no] better established, than that the ecclesiastical court hath no cognizance or jurisdiction in cases of treason or felony"; III, 61: "The bounds of parishes, though coming in question in a spiritual matter, shall be tried in the temporal courts. This is a maxim, in which all the books of the common law are unanimous; although our

by Burn are "rules of equity" and "doctrine,"[139] and he uses the idea of "a principle," but there is little to distinguish a principle in terms of juridical form from the maxims he cites.[140]

At the same time, commentators use "maxims" in their treatment of the common law and equity, such as Wood in his *Institutes of the Laws of England* (1722),[141] and Francis, in his *Maxims of Equity* (1727).[142] Indeed, in Jacob's *Law Dictionary* (1744) we read (after the manner of the seventeenth century): "Maxims in law are positions and theses, being conclusions of reason, and universal propositions, so perfect, that they may not be impugned or disputed"; "The alterations of any of the maxims of the common law are dangerous"; "Maxims are principles and authorities, and part of the general customs or common law of the land; and are of the same strength as acts of parliament, when judges have determined what is a maxim; which belongs to the judges"; and maxims are held "for law."[143] Moreover, whilst the "maxims of equity" find no equivalent in books of common law,[144] several more or less equate with those in the Sext; for example: he who seeks

---

provincial constitutions do mention the bounds of parishes, amongst the matters which merely belong to the ecclesiastical court, and cannot belong to any other. Gibs[on]. 212."

139. Burn I, Preface ii: "the rules of equity"; I, 10: "the doctrine and language of all the books."

140. Burn I, 342: "By a principle of law, in every land there is a fee simple in some body"; II, 65: "a principle which perhaps will not be admitted...at common law"; III, 131: "a principle at least doubtful."

141. Wood sets out "rules" of law, custom and statute, including legal proverbs, maxims (with some from the Sext), and principles; e.g. "Common law is common right"; "The law respects the order of nature."

142. See also Branche: *Principia Legis et Aequitatis* (1753), citing some Sext maxims; Blackstone in his *Commentaries* elucidates "rules and maxims of the common law" (I.68), "general rules and maxims" for the construction of instruments (II.378), and "rules" for the interpretation of statutes (I.87ff).

143. G. Jacob, *New Law Dictionary*, 5th ed. (London, 1744): this cites e.g. Co. Litt. 10.b 11.1, 343; Pl. C. 27b; Coke 2 Inst. 210; 12 Mod. 482: "the principles are borrowed from the Civil law."

144. J. E. Martin, ed., *Hanbury & Martin: Modern Equity*, 19th ed. (London, 2012), 29–34.

equity must do equity;[145] delay defeats equity;[146] where the equities are equal, the first in time shall prevail;[147] he who comes to equity must come with clean hands;[148] and: equity looks upon as done that which ought to be done.[149] Equity lawyers, then, had an intellectual fondness to hang their ideas upon the convenient pegs that were (and are) the maxims. This closeness between civilian, canon and equity lawyers, and the fact that certain equitable maxims are identical to those found in canon law, does not prove that the maxims of equity sprang only from that source, but it does at least suggest a likely point of borrowing.

Maxims in the specifically equitable context have been sniffed at in some circles. No less a work of high authority than Snell's *Equity* refers to equitable maxims as the Emperor's new clothes and says that the common law wisely saw through them for what they were.[150] Two reasons are given for this criticism. First, there might be a tendency to treat maxims as a substitute for transparent reasoning, allowing the judge to gloss over areas requiring careful analysis. Secondly, maxims—like proverbs—can conflict and so are at best unreliable guides.[151] Taken to extremes, the same has been said of the whole of Snell's *Equity*. If equity is a gloss on the common law, what sense does it make to look at the law and practice of the now abolished Courts of Chancery or its successor the Chancery Division by itself? If one had a book solely about the common law and its maxims, one would learn little of the many contributions made to contract law by the equitable ju-

145. R. Pound, "On Certain Maxims of Equity," in G. G. Alexander, ed., *Cambridge Legal Essays* (Cambridge, 1926), 259–277 at 260–263; VI 5.13.5: "A wrong is not pardoned save when [sc. the doer of it has been] corrected." Pound appears not to take this point, since he states (275) that for the greater part these maxims go back no further than Francis' *Maxims of Equity* (1728). He allows one possible reference in *Doctor and Student*, but nothing else. On comparison with the Sext, we can see that this is plainly not the case.

146. 2 Co. Inst. 690; VI 5.13.25: "Anybody's own delay is harmful to him";

147. *Brace v. Duchess of Marlborough* (1728) 2 P. Wms 490 at 495; VI 5.13.54: "The earlier in time is stronger in law."

148. *Dering v. Earl of Winchilsea* (1787) 1 Cox Eq Cas 318 at 319; VI 5.13.59: "He acts dishonestly who seeks that which he ought to restore."

149. R. Pound, "On Certain Maxims of Equity," 273–5; VI 5.13.66: "When there is no reason why a condition may not be fulfilled by him who ought to do it, it ought to be regarded just as if it had been fulfilled."

150. J. McGhee, ed., *Snell's Equity*, 32nd ed. (London, 2010), 105.

151. Ibid., 106.

risdiction (e.g. specific performance, promissory estoppel and the rest). The simple answer must be that English law did not spring into being from one source at one moment. It is perfectly rational, whilst recognizing the unity of, say, contract law as a subject, to see that it is made up of rules that originated in different times and places. Where the law of trusts in concerned, of course, there is even less force in the criticism. The Chancery Division is not deaf to what is said in Snell. In *HR Trustees Ltd v. Wembley plc (in liquidation) & Anor*, Vos J cited the criticisms of Snell *in extenso* in a case that required him to consider the force of the maxim "equity views as done that which ought to be done."[152] There is every reason to believe that this maxim is at least as old as the Sext.[153] The judge did not use it as a fig-leaf to conceal woolly thinking; rather, he used it as a point of departure for a detailed study of relevant cases that seemed to embody this principle. He concluded, "...this is not the exercise of an exorbitant or unpredictable or even unorthodox jurisdiction. It is the stuff of equity, refined and clarified over many years."[154] We can thus see that, in the end, maxims are convenient pegs upon which lawyers may hang their learning for ease of rapid retrieval. They are not a substitute for knowledge of cases and statutes, but are a practical way of organizing such knowledge.

PRINCIPLES IN MODERN CHURCH LAW: 1800 TO THE PRESENT

Whilst in the nineteenth century Herbert Broom published his *Legal Maxims*, some of which deal with ecclesiastical matters,[155] the canonical

---

152. [2011] EWHC 2974 (Ch), esp. [53]–[67].

153. VI 5.13.66: *Quum non stat per eum, ad quem pertinet, quo minus conditio impleatur: haberi debet perinde, ac si impleta fuisset* (Lit. "When there is no reason why a condition may not be fulfilled by him who ought to do it, it ought to be regarded just as if it had been fulfilled").

154. [2011] EWHC 2974 (Ch) at [67].

155. H. Broom, *Legal Maxims*, 3rd ed. (London, 1852): e.g. 323: *consensus, non concubitus, facit matrimonium* [it is consent, not sleeping together, that makes a marriage]; adopted from D 50.17.80; 330: "rule of civil and canon law, *pater est quem nuptiae demonstrant*" [the father is he whom the marriage vows indicate]; subsequent marriage between parents legitimizes a son born out of wedlock.

literature abandons explicit reference to "maxims" in favor of "principles."[156] The literature is dominated by the work of Blunt and Phillimore. In *The Book of Church Law* (1873), Blunt refers to a "recognised principle," a "general principle," a "principle,"[157] "a principle of the common law,"[158] or a "general principle of the canon law," to which he may attribute great antiquity.[159] Blunt finds principles laid down in, for example, the Thirty-Nine Articles of Religion of the Church of England, in the case-law (typically in the formula "the principle in [a named] case"),[160] and in canon law, such as: "It is a principle of the canon law that no church can be erected without the permission of the bishop of the diocese in which it is situated";[161] again: "this plain principle of law should be strictly recognised, and access to the church obtained" through the incumbent who has a right to the church keys in the custody of the churchwardens.[162]

More extensive use was made of principles by Robert Phillimore in his two-volume *Ecclesiastical Law* (1873, second edition 1895). In the preface

156. The Divorce and Matrimonial Causes Act 1857, s. 22 required the new court for divorce and matrimonial causes to act and "give Relief on Principles and Rules which, in the Opinion of the said Court, shall be as nearly as may be conformable to the Principles and Rules on which the Ecclesiastical Courts have heretofore acted and given Relief." For background to the statute, see R. B. Outhwaite, *The Rise and Fall of the English Ecclesiastical Courts 1500–1860* (Cambridge, 2006) 159.

157. Blunt, 6: "It is now a nearly recognised principle of the English constitution that Parliament is supreme"; 7: "The general principle...is, that the Crown possesses a visitatorial and corrective jurisdiction in the Church of England"; 311: "That which is so transferred to God cannot be alienated from Him without sacrilege," is a "principle."

158. Blunt, 358: that ecclesiastical incomes are dealt with by ecclesiastical persons.

159. Blunt, 15: the canons of the Oxford Synod 1222 are "arranged by Lyndwood on the principle adopted by Gratian in...the *Decretum*"; 22: the Submission of the Clergy Act 1533 contains "the principle that convocation has no authority to pass laws except by licence from the Crown"; 38: "As regards lunatics the custom is to baptize them, if...in danger of death, on the principle laid down in the Elviran canon"; 41: "The principle" set down by St. Cyprian on baptism; 179: "the general principle of the canon law" (on suicides and burial); 331: "But after the early ages of the Church, the simple principle of tithes...passed away."

160. Blunt, 116: Article 23 states "a principle of the Church of England" that it is not lawful to preach unless authorised; 94: "the principle of the decision in *Liddell v. Westerton*, held that ornaments or vestments...were...not unlawful"; 140: the "principle of interpretation" in *Harrison v. Burwell*; 294: the principle in *R v. Barrow* LR 4 QB 577.

161. Blunt, 298; Canon of Westminster 1138; J. Johnson, *Collection of All Ecclesiastical Laws* (1720).

162. Blunt, 267; he cites *Lee v. Matthews* (1830) 3 Hag Ecc 169.

to the first edition, Phillimore states that his aim is "to produce the law in the form of a system arranged according to the principles of science" and, to this end, he uses the category "General principles of the law of the Church of England"; moreover, the Church of England "has adhered in all matters of importance to the general principles of the law of the Eastern and Western Church."[163] As well as "propositions,"[164] without reference to law he uses the categories "principles," "principles of public policy," "principles of religion," "principles of Christian faith," "principles and authorities," principles which are "the foundations of the church," and "principles of the Church of England."[165] On the basis of his category of "legal principles" (and the "reasons" which may underlie them),[166] on other occasions he attributes a proposition to, variously: "a principle of law," "a general principle of law" (as contained typically in a particular judicial decision), or the principles of a particular legal field (such as marriage law).[167] Again, he often asserts that a particular court decision "contains" a principle or is "governed" by a

---

163. *Ecclesiastical Law*, 2nd ed. (1895), I, 11; criticizing Burn: "No philosophical connection of parts—no historical and legal development of principles is consistent with the alphabetical form."

164. Phillimore, I, 20–21: "that the bishops exercised the chief influence in the election of another bishop (*electores primarios fuisse episcopos*)" and "that though the people were always among the electors, their voice carried with it less weight than that of the clergy (*clero plus tributum quam populo*)."

165. Phillimore, I, 131: "Upon the same principles the dean and chapter have power to remove a chorister, subject to an appeal to the visitor"; I, 141: "It was said not to fall under the principles of public policy, on which the income of a benefice, pay, pensions, etc, are holden inalienable" (*Grenfell v. Dean of Windsor*); I, 171, 468 and 469: instructing pupils in the "principles of religion"; I, 511: principles of Christian faith; I, 246: *Rex v. Blooer*: The court said "That they reconsidered the point, and weighed all the principles and authorities applicable to it"—*mandamus* lies to determine a right to officiate; I, 711: "the principles upon which the foundations of the church are founded"; I, 5: 26 Geo III c. 84: "the principles of the Church of England"; I, 765: "the distinguishing principles of the Church of England"; II, 1455: "same principle"; II, 1529: "Catholic teaching and principle."

166. Phillimore, I, 331: *Graham*: "the reasons must be considered upon legal principles."

167. Phillimore, I, 582: *Wakefield v. Wakefield* explains the general principles of law applicable to banns"; I, 544: principles of evidence law; 551: principles of marriage law; II, 864: "the well-known principle of law, that the provisions of an act of parliament shall not be evaded by shift or contrivance"; II, 1817: "a principle of constitutional law"; II, 1559: the *cy près* principle in charity law.

principle,[168] by a principle of construction,[169] or by a principle underlying a statutory provision.[170] Phillimore also suggests that particular rules of the unwritten ecclesiastical law may be derived from principles; for example: "It is true that generally the existence of the *jus non scriptum* ("unwritten law") is ascertained by reports of adjudged cases; but it may be proved by other means: it may be proved by public notoriety, or be deducible from principles and analogy, or be shown by legislative recognition."[171]

Phillimore's principles cover a wide range of subjects. The following are offered by way of illustration. First, in church governance: "In England the authority and power of the ecclesiastical courts as to the laity is founded on a principle recognized by the unwritten common law, and in part by statute law, that the ordinary ought in certain matters to administer justice over all persons *pro salute animae*" [for the salvation of the soul]; the courts have acquired a wide jurisdiction "under colour of this principle"; also: "The canon law founds the authority of the pope upon this principle."[172] Secondly, in ministry: "There is, indeed, no general principle of ecclesiastical law more firmly established than this: that it is not competent to any clergyman to officiate in any church or chapel within the limits of a parish without the consent of the incumbent."[173] Thirdly, in marriage: a wife might sue for restitution of conjugal rights and the husband's defense is that the wife is guilty of adultery; if he succeeded, sentence of divorce *a mensa et thoro* (lit. "from table and bed") is issued against the wife: "On the same principle a husband, against whom a wife had instituted a suit for

---

168. Phillimore, II, 871: "the principles which governed" the decision in *Bishop of London v. Ffytche*; II, 1365: n. r: *Whidborne v. Ecclesiastical Commissioners*: "no general principle can be deduced from the decision"; II, 1263: *Wise v. Metcalfe*: the incumbent must keep the parsonage and chancel in good repair; in an action for dilapidations against the executors of a deceased rector by the successor, the damages would be calculated "on this principle"; see also II, 1377 and II, 1489.

169. Phillimore, I, 534: "principles of construction"; I, 772: "legal principles of construction."

170. Phillimore, II, 1181: Tithe Commutation Acts "must be considered as constituting one enactment, their principle being to substitute a corn-rent payable in money... for all tithes." See also II, 1558: the principle "illustrated" in Convocation proceedings (of 1709).

171. Phillimore, I, 708: construing rubrics on the same principles as statutes.

172. Phillimore, II, 827.

173. Phillimore, II, 907.

divorce on the ground of adultery, might plead her adultery in a responsive allegation, and was not compelled to take out any separate or cross citation for this purpose."[174] Fourthly, in property: it is a "principle that a legal origin ought to be presumed if a legal origin be possible"; thus, "a pew may be annexed to a dwelling house by faculty and a faculty may be presumed upon evidence of exclusive possession and repair for a long period."[175] Some of Phillimore's principles are axiomatic: "on the principle that a man cannot visit himself, a beneficial interest in the charity disqualifies a person for the office of visitor."[176] The church courts also use the idea of a "general rule,"[177] as did equity,[178] and common law (often invoking principles reminiscent of the *regulae iuris*).[179] In the early twentieth century, a court of the common law pronounced: "'A principle' means a general guiding rule, and does not include specific directions, which vary according to the subject matter."[180]

174. Phillimore, II, 956.

175. Phillimore, II, 1429; he cites *Philipps v. Halliday*.

176. Phillimore, II, 1605: he cites *R v. Bishop of Chester*; II, 997: "As a general principle, where an offence has been committed, the expense of correcting it is to be borne by the offender"; II, 1610, on colleges: "The same or a closely analogous principle as to the preference of founders' kin is to be found in foreign charitable foundations. This principle may be clearly traced to the canon law as its fountain"—Gibson 188; II, 1800: the extension of the episcopate to India occurred on "the voluntary principle."

177. *St Ethelburga* (1878) Trist 69: "It is impossible to lay down any general rule for the guidance of the Court in the exercise of its discretion in all cases."

178. D. R. Klinck, "Lord Eldon on 'Equity'," *Journal of Legal History* 20 (1999), 50; *Gee v. Pritchard* (1818) 36 ER 670 at 925: "The doctrines of this Court ought to be as well settled and made as uniform almost as those of the common law"; *Sitwell v. Bernard* (1801) 31 ER 1174 at 1182: the Court uses "principles of convenience" and "general rules of justice and convenience; though in particular cases both convenience and justice may be disappointed"; *Moggridge v. Thackwell* (1802) 32 ER 15 at 125: "the cases have gone a length, upon which principles wise or otherwise is not for me to determine, which has formed a precedent, that binds me in this Court." For the earlier axiomatization of equity by e.g. Lord Hardwicke (Chancellor, 1737–1756), see: *Ives v. Medcalfe* (1737) 26 ER 42 at 42: "I must determine [the case]...by the rules of law, and of this court"; however, for his use of conscience, see *Jenkins v. Hiles* (1802) 31 ER 1238 at 1241–1242; *Evans v. Bicknell* (1801) 31 ER 998 at 1006.

179. *Bartlett v. Rendle* (1814) 3 M & S 99: if a man has a power to lease for 10 years, and he leases for 20, the lease for the 20 years is good for 10 years of the 20; VI 5.13.35: "The more includes the less."

180. *McCreagh v. Frearson* [1922] W.N. 37 *per* Shearman J at 37, 38: R. Burrows, general editor, *Words and Phrases Judicially Defined* (London, 1944), 342.

The appeal of principles is no less great today. As well as the commentators,[181] the Chancellors of the diocesan Consistory Courts of the Church of England, in the exercise of the faculty jurisdiction, commonly invoke "principles," some of which echo the maxims of the canonical tradition. A study of their decisions from 2012–2013 reveals that the Chancellors may find a principle latent in the Canons of the Church of England (e.g. on the location of a font, that it should be as near as possible to the principal door of a church building),[182] "extract" a principle from earlier decisions (e.g. the "presumption" that things should remain unchanged, applied to proposed alterations to historic church buildings),[183] or use a "proposition" (e.g. as "ownership of the churchyard vests in the incumbent," "a monument…cannot be removed without the sanction of the Ordinary").[184] Often, the task which the court sets itself is to "consider the legal principles" which apply to the matter;[185] sometimes it considers itself bound by a principle (because it has been enunciated by a superior court, not because of its inherent value),[186] as bound to have regard to a principle (e.g. that exhumation will be

181. For recourse to principle, see e.g. H. W. Cripps, *A Practical Treatise on the Law relating to the Church and Clergy*, ed. K. M. Macmorran, 8th ed. (London, 1937), 7: that canons "could not bind the laity" is a "proposition"; 147: "principle"; M. Hill, *Ecclesiastical Law* (Oxford, 2007) par. 126: "principle"; par. 1.43: "The principle of religious liberty"; Halsbury, *Laws Of England*, vol. 34, *Ecclesiastical Law*, 5th ed. (London, 2011), par. 1039, n. 2: "the constitutional principle of the separation of powers"; par. 1072: "Principles and practice of the faculty jurisdiction."

182. *St Paul's Church, Herne Hill* [2012] Southwark CC, Petchey Ch., par. 57: "relevant principles" and Canon F1(2)). See also *Alrewas: All Saints* [2012] Lichfield CC, Eyre Ch., par. 3: "the principles governing the movement of fonts"; par. 15: "The relevant legal principles."

183. *St Stephen, Selly Park* [2013] Birmingham CC, Interim Judgment, par. 21 (analogous to VI 5.13.11), par. 17: "I extract the following principles" from *St Alkmund, Duffield* (Court of Arches): if a (secular) local authority has granted planning permission for work on an historical church, the Court may take that as a "starting point"; Judgment, 12-7-2013: "It seems to me logical…."

184. *St Thomas Kilnhurst Churchyard* (11-7-2013) Sheffield CC, McClean Ch., par. 10: proposition; par. 13, Coke. This decision echoes VI 5.13.79: no one can transfer more rights than he possesses.

185. *Holy Trinity Church, Sutton Coldfield* [2012] Birmingham CC, Powell Ch., par. 21: "I propose…to consider the legal principles under which I must act and then see how the individual proposals fit into that legal framework."

186. *Wootton St Lawrence Armet* [2013] Winchester CC, Clark Ch., par. 33: "I accept…that principles of law laid down by the Court of Arches are binding" unless the

allowed only in exceptional circumstances),[187] or as not "strictly bound" by a principle which is nevertheless "highly persuasive."[188] Principles are conceived variously as: underlying legal rules (and as such may be theological in character);[189] "well-known," or of "long-standing" (e.g. "the principle of the permanence" of burial);[190] or designed to "guide" the court.[191] Principles include the propositions that: the more valuable an item the weightier the reason needed to justify its sale ("the principle of gradation of proof");[192]

---

facts suggest otherwise; *Standon: All Saints* [2013] Lichfield CC, Eyre Ch., par. 13: "I have to apply those principles to the current petition"; *Chell: St Michael and All Angels* [2012] Lichfield CC, Eyre Ch., par. 13: "The applicable principles."

187. *Dunkworth: St Peter: Re Geoffrey Lloyd Porter Williams* [2103] Lichfield CC, Eyre Ch.: the court must have regard to "the straightforward principle that a faculty for exhumation will only be exceptionally granted"; *Re John Ashton McGarry Deceased* [2013] Manchester CC, Tattersall Ch., par. 10: "The legal principles to be applied" (presumption against exhumation); par. 17: the "principle" that faculties for exhumation must be granted sparingly; *Petition by Mrs K. Wilkes* [2013] Bradford CC: par. 2: "principles governing the circumstances in which [the presumption] can be displaced."

188. *Meir Heath: St Francis of Assisi* [2013] Lichfield CC, Eyre Ch.: "Even if [the] decision [Birmingham CC [2011]] were such as to lay down a legal principle it would not be one by which I would be strictly bound, although it would be highly persuasive"; it did not lay down "principles of wide application."

189. *Eccleshall: Holy Trinity* [2013] Lichfield CC, Eyre Ch., par. 8: "the underlying principle that all that is done for the glory of God, including objects placed in churchyards consecrated to him, must be of the highest possible quality."

190. *Hungarton, St John the Baptist* [2012] Leicester CC, Blackett-Ord Ch., par. 30: "The principles to be applied are well known": to allow exhumation because the family move house "would make unacceptable inroads into the principle of permanence of Christian burial"; *Plumstead Cemetery* [2012] Southwark CC, Petchey Ch., par. 8: the "long standing principle" of permanence; par. 51: he allowed exhumation to consolidate a family grave: "Absent authority and as a matter of principle...the weight attaching to this factor should be much the same in all cases"; he was prepared to depart from "the norm of permanence" as "economical in the use of grave space and...expressive of family unity."

191. *Holy Trinity, Hurstpierpoint* [2012] Chichester CC, Hill Ch., par. 13: "A guiding principle is that the proposals be minimally invasive and maximally reversible"; removing pews for "fellowship space."

192. *Wootton St Lawrence Armet*, par. 14: "The general principles to be applied were first set out by the Court of Arches" in *Re St Gregory, Tredington* [1971] 3 All ER 269; par. 28: "the principle of gradation of proof"; par. 34: "the principle...that the more valuable the article, the weightier will need to be the reasons such as to justify a sale." See also *Lacock, St Syriac* [2012] Bristol CC, Gau Ch., par 20: "the principles [on] disposal of movable property"; par. 46: "whilst applying the principles, I can distinguish the facts in this case" from *St Peter Draycott* [2000] Fam. 93.

a petitioner is entitled to have a case taken as a whole;[193] analogies may be drawn in the exercise of the faculty jurisdiction with secular planning policy ("the principle of equivalence");[194] the introduction of a lavatory in a church is "in principle wholly desirable";[195] a parishioner has a right to burial in the parish churchyard;[196] and the grant of a faculty required to authorize work in a churchyard is subject to "the general principle" *de minimis non curat lex*, though this will not override any contrary and explicit statutory rule.[197]

The articulation of principles of law has also made its mark in contemporary global Anglicanism. The worldwide Anglican Communion has no formal body of law applicable to its forty-four member churches; each

193. *St Alkmund, Duffield* [2011] Derby CC, Bullimore Ch.: par. 20: "In principle, the petitioners are entitled to have their case taken as a whole"; par. 52: "there are...interlocking concepts or principles here" (e.g. on Holy Communion); par. 80: "In principle, arguments based on theological or doctrinal grounds are deployable in faculty matters." The decision was overturned by the Court of Arches (1-10-2012) "following the principles" set out in *In re St Mary, Sherborne* [1996] 3 All ER 769 at 746–756.

194. *St Mary the Blessed Virgin, Eastry* [2012] Canterbury CC, Ellis Ch., par. 35: "The principle of equivalence"—"national planning policy can be an aid to deliberations... because of the desirability of achieving general equivalence in the treatment of listed buildings across the two systems"; par. 39: "The legal principles relevant to this determination are quite clear"; par. 60: *St Mary, Sherborne* [1996] 3 All ER 769 at 746–756: the Court of Arches laid down "general principles" about costs.

195. *Mobberley: St Wilfrid* [2012] Chester CC, Turner Ch., par. 28.

196. *St Nicolas, Pevensey* [2012] Chichester CC, Hill Ch., par. 8: "principles" include the right of a parishioner to burial; par. 18: "Some dioceses have formulated rigid guidelines, but all apply this general principle as it is a matter of ecclesiastical law" (i.e. where space in a churchyard is limited, "it would be wrong...to grant the reservation of a grave space such as to prejudice future burials").

197. *St Peter in the East, Oxford* [2013] Oxford CC, McGregor Dep. Ch.: the Disused Burial Grounds Act 1884 s. 3 forbids erecting "buildings" on a disused burial ground except to enlarge a church—a faculty was sought to erect a gardener's office, greenhouse and tool shed; par. 44: "a structure that is *de minimis* might not amount to a building, on the basis of the general principle *de minimis non curat lex*"; however, par. 47: "I cannot see how such principle could be established contrary to the express provisions of the 1884 Act. I cannot identify any principle of statutory construction [to construe the Act] as excepting from the prohibition...a building...necessary for maintaining the churchyard"; in short, par. 56: "I do not accept that there is a principle of law that permits buildings...ancillary to the function of a churchyard as an open space as an exception to the prohibition in the 1884 Act."

church is autonomous with its own legal system. The Communion is held together by "bonds of affection": shared loyalty to scripture, creeds, baptism, Eucharist, historic episcopate, and its institutional instruments of communion (Archbishop of Canterbury, Primates' Meeting, Lambeth Conference, and Anglican Consultative Council); but these institutions cannot make decisions binding on churches.[198] However, the *Principles of Canon Law Common to the Churches of the Anglican Communion* was launched at the Lambeth Conference in 2008. This document is not a system of international canon law but a statement of principles of canon law which articulate the common ground between the legal systems of each of the churches of the global Communion; the document defines a "principle of canon law" as "a foundational proposition or maxim of general applicability which has a strong dimension of weight, is induced from the similarities of churches, derives from the canonical tradition or other practices of the church, expresses a basic theological truth or ethical value, and is about, is implicit in, or underlies canon law."[199] Many of the principles echo or equate with the traditional canonical maxims: "Laws cannot oblige a person to do the impossible";[200] "Persons cannot give what they do not have";[201] a declaration to comply with ecclesiastical jurisdiction binds the person who makes that declaration;[202] "bodies or persons who exercise ecclesiastical functions may delegate to others only such functions as they are not required to perform themselves";[203] the judges of church courts are "to exercise their office impartially, without fear or favor";[204] consecrated property "may not be used

198. N. Doe, *Canon Law in the Anglican Communion* (Oxford, 1998), 338.

199. *The Principles of Canon Law Common to the Churches of the Anglican Communion* (Anglican Communion Office: London, 2008); for background, see ibid., 97, N. Doe, "The contribution of common principles of canon law to ecclesial communion in Anglicanism."

200. Principle 7.3; VI 5.13.6: "No-one can be obliged to the impossible."

201. Principle 7.4; VI 5.13.79: "No-one gives more right to another than what he has."

202. Principle 5.6; VI 5.13.27: "To the one who knows and approves, there is neither injury nor malice."

203. Principle 17.4; VI 5.13.68: "Whatever someone can do by himself, he can do it by another (unless the power to act cannot be delegated)."

204. Principle 24.7; VI 5.13.12: "Justice should be rendered without respect to persons."

for purposes inconsistent with the uses of God for which it was set aside";[205] and church trustees are not liable for any financial loss resulting from an investment "unless such loss is due to their own wilful default or culpable negligence."[206] Some principles admit to their own exceptions—they apply to the extent allowed by law.[207]

Finally, the category of "principles of Christian law" is beginning to make its mark in the wider ecumenical enterprise. This is on the basis that whilst dogmas may divide Christians amongst the twenty-two global church families, the profound similarities between the laws of churches link Christians in common norms of conduct which in turn stimulate shared forms of action regardless of the denominational affiliation of the faithful.[208] Indeed, in Rome in November 2013 a symposium took place of jurists from eight global ecclesiastical traditions; it concluded that: (1) there are principles of church law and church order common to the Catholic, Orthodox, Anglican, Lutheran, Methodist, Reformed, Presbyterian and Baptist traditions and that their existence can be factually established by empirical observation and comparison; (2) the churches of each Christian tradition contribute through their own regulatory instruments to this store of principles; (3) these principles have a strong theological content and dimension of weight and are fundamental to the self-understanding of Christianity; (4) these principles have a living force and contain within themselves the possibility of further development and articulation; and (5) these principles demonstrate a degree of unity between the churches, stimulate common Christian actions, and should be fed into the global ecumenical enterprise to enhance fuller visible unity. Moreover, the participants considered that the following principles were implicit in or underlie their respective regulatory instruments: church law and church order exist to serve a church in its mission and in its witness to Christ; laws are necessary to constitute the institutional organization of a church and facilitate and

---

205. Principle 81.5; VI 5.13.51: "Once given to God it should not be transferred to the use of man."

206. Principle 89.4; VI 5.13.62: "No liability arises from advice given provided it was not fraudulent."

207. E.g. Principle 41.6: "Clergy of the diocese are subject to the jurisdiction of the diocesan bishop to the extent provided under the law."

208. N. Doe, *Christian Law: Contemporary Principles* (Cambridge, 2013).

order its public activities but cannot encompass all facets and experiences of the Christian faith and life; laws are the servant of the church and must promote the mission of the church universal; theology shapes law, and law implements theological propositions in the form of norms of conduct; and church laws should conform and are subject ultimately to the law of God, as revealed in Holy Scripture and by the Holy Spirit.[209] This is not surprising: maxims and principles are used in other systems of religious law,[210] and *regulae iuris* are debated in modern human rights law.[211]

CONCLUSION

Whilst the use of axioms is constant across the history of church law, the terminology for their designation changes from period to period, as do understandings about their nature and their relationship to the details of the positive law of the church. The *regulae iuris* of medieval canon law, borrowed from classical Roman law, were the subject of extensive debate by the canonists of the Latin Church (particularly whether they were themselves laws or derived from laws), and many surfaced in the medieval English common law. At the time of the Reformation and beyond, into the eighteenth century, "maxims" were used as a vehicle to characterize axioms in the context of the law of the established Church of England, which, with the common law, embarked on the development and articulation of new axioms to meet the needs of ecclesial life. This also echoed the tendency of the common lawyers to reduce the fundamentals of the temporal common law to maxims as well as the chancery lawyers to reduce their jurisdiction to the maxims of equity. However, the concept of "maxims" was displaced by the lawyers of the English church in the nineteenth century with that of "principles" of church law, but many are indistinguishable from more detailed

209. See https://sites.google.com/site/christianlawgroup/home.

210. See e.g. H. A. Ghani, "A Study of the History of Legal Maxims in Islamic Law," *International Journal of Arts and Commerce* 1 (2012), 90.

211. G. Fortman, "Human Rights as *regulae iuris*: An Inquiry into the Dialectics of Legality Versus Legitimacy," *European Review of Private Law* 20 (2012), 409–424. *Regulae iuris* also continue to be important in modern Roman Catholic canon law: G. Sheehey, et al., *The Canon Law: Letter and Spirit: A Practical Guide to the Code of Canon Law* (Dublin, 1995), 18–19: "the general principles of law" (Code, canon 19) are equated with the *regulae juris* of the canonical tradition.

legal rules and few lawyers explicitly equated such principles with natural law or reason. Nevertheless, this deployment of principles continues not only in modern English ecclesiastical law (particularly in the decisions of Consistory Courts), for the practical resolution of cases in the exercise of the faculty jurisdiction, but also for the promotion of greater visible ecclesial unity, in the juridical life of the worldwide Anglican Communion, and, more recently, in the wider ecumenical context—and in both contexts the principles are not themselves laws but are derived from laws in the sense of prescriptive summaries of similarities induced from the comparison of laws. This durability of maxims in the history of church law neatly illustrates what Richard Helmholz has taught us about the essential continuity of the Christian *ius commune*.

Canon Law: The Discipline of Teaching and the Teaching of the Discipline

Mark Hill

Professor Richard Helmholz is unrivaled both for his teaching of legal history and for his systematic research into the manner in which canon law was taught in the past. As my modest contribution to this timely *Festschrift* to mark Dick's work and achievement, I should like to touch on each of these aspects and venture some observations concerning the teaching of canon law, refracted through the prism of the history. In doing so I am pleased that I can draw upon the work of the Colloquium of Anglican and Roman Catholic Canon Lawyers who for more than a decade have engaged in systematic comparative analysis of the legal systems of their two traditions and, particularly the largely unpublished work in this area by the Reverend Robert Ombres OP of Blackfriars, Oxford and Professor Norman Doe, Director of Cardiff University's Centre for Law and Religion. Both have been fellow members of the Colloquium since its inception and, with Dick Helmholz, sit on the Editorial Board of the *Ecclesiastical Law Journal* which for upwards of a quarter of century have been key players in the renaissance in the study and teaching of canon law in the United Kingdom.

Let us start this exploration with a journey into history.[1] By the 1190s a law school had been established at Oxford, probably connected with the

---

1.   For authoritative coverage, see J. Brundage, *The Medieval Origins of the Legal Profession: Canonists, Civilians and Courts* (Chicago, 2008).

ecclesiastical courts there and, whether or not Vacarius ever taught in Oxford, his *Liber pauperum* or digest of classical Roman law composed by the
1180s at the latest had become the staple of canon law students at Oxford.[2]
The first known doctor of canon law there, in c. 1235, was St. Richard of
Chichester, while William of Drogheda is the first known doctor of civil
law in the same decade.[3] At that time the Cambridge canon law faculty was
also established. Universities became very influential institutional concen-
trations of academic achievement, but canon law was studied, and had to
be studied, elsewhere.[4]

Each law faculty in principle set its own curriculum, but the basic
features were common. Lectures in Latin were the primary mode of instruction, and they were text-centered. Candidates for degrees had to hear
a minimum number of lectures on each book in the civil or canon law
corpus. Lectures followed in sequence the order of the texts. Later it was
obligatory to comment on the ordinary gloss as well as the text. The core
of the curriculum was Gratian's *Decretum* joined from 1234 onwards by the
Liber Extra and, in time and with more papal legislation, Gratian's text
became less central. Lectures sometimes included additional material from
private decretal collections in circulation. England had been prominent in
collecting and ordering decretals from the twelfth century. The academic
year went from October to July, with lectures on week days. Hostiensis
(d. 1271) described in his *Summa* the practice current at Bologna: a teacher
ought to begin by explaining the *casus*, that is, the factual situation that
gave rise to a particular law or canon. He should then read out the text,
explaining its meaning as he went along, then point out analogous cases
where the same rules might apply and contrary cases where they would
not. He should then address particular questions that a particular passage
might raise and how to solve them. Finally he should summarize the major themes (*notabilia*) of the text he was discussing and their application in

---

2.   Vacarius (c. 1120–1198) was an Italian who came from Bologna in the 1140s to
assist the Archbishop of Canterbury with administration and remained in England till his
death. He practiced and wrote on law, and was a papal judge delegate.

3.   For a perceptive portrait and appreciation see R. Helmholz, "Notable Ecclesiastical Lawyers: IV, William of Drogheda (c. 1200–1245)," *Ecclesiastical Law Journal* 16
(2014), 66–71.

4.   J. Brundage, *Medieval Canon Law*, 54.

practice.⁵ What Hostiensis described came to be known as the *mos Italicus*, the Italian method. The Paris faculty even prescribed the speed at which lecturers should speak.

In addition to formal lectures, law faculties also expected students to attend review sessions called *repetitiones*. These generally took place in the late afternoon or evening. The *repetitor* in charge of these sessions was often a senior student who went through the material covered in the morning ordinary lectures, commented on the main points, and tried to explain the more intricate technical issues. The students started to learn how to memorize large chunks of material required for both teaching and practice. There survives a fine set of *reportata* from Oxford which includes not only very complete *repetitiones*, but also some of the ordinary lectures of nineteen doctors.

After lectures, the most important learning exercise were disputations. They provided degree candidates in both laws experience in framing oral arguments on legal issues and responding to the arguments of others. One of the masters chaired disputations, and they were obligatory for both teachers and students in varying numbers. The presiding master determined the outcome with a reasoned solution supported by ample citations of legal texts. The masters also provided the official booksellers with a written record of their disputation for the archives and for sale.⁶

Rivers reflects that even though medieval universities also engaged in practices which might bring the student closer to real-life problems (*disputationes* and *quaestiones*), what was inculcated was more a mass of concepts and a mode of thought and argument. Education was through immersion in the authoritative texts as well as their subsequent glosses and comments.⁷

Bologna furnished the model for the Curriculum, which was replicated elsewhere. Oxford and Cambridge (unlike Bologna or Paris) demanded two years of attendance at lectures on the Bible for the J.C.B. The earliest

5. Odofredus, a thirteenth-century teacher of civil law, describes a similar teaching method: J. Brundage, *Medieval Canon Law* (London, 1995), 52.

6. See for example, the transcript of a Cambridge disputation about rights of presentation, identified in D. Owen, *The Medieval Canon Law: Teaching, Literature and Transmission* (Cambridge, 1990), 4.

7. J. Rivers, "Theology and Legal Education," in O. D. Crisp, G. D'Costa, M. Davies and P. Hampson, eds., *Christianity and the Disciplines: The Transformation of the University* (London 2012), 150–1.

Bologna statutes contain detailed directions for the schedule of lectures
in civil and canon law and the time allotted for individual sections of each
text. In the canon law curriculum, lectures on the *Decretum* and the *Liber
Extra* were scheduled in two cycles, so that the students could hear two ordinary lectures each morning. In the afternoon the students also heard extraordinary lectures and attended review sessions. The statutes laid down
provisions for the various books of Justinian's Code and Digest. On the
days no ordinary lectures were scheduled, students could hear extraordinary lectures. By the fourteenth century, especially in England, universities
were even pressing students with just a J.C.B. into service to give ordinary
lectures.[8]

Helmholz, in his 2010 Lyndwood Lecture,[9] looked at lecture notes
from the English universities; the records of disputations in the law faculties; notebooks compiled by students in the course of their studies; and
commentaries on practice in the ecclesiastical courts which show something of the result of university legal education. From the evidence adduced, Helmholz concludes that the needs of medieval legal practice were
not those of today and were met by university education, and that legal
change did occur precisely through the "backward-looking" syllabus and
how it was taught. The authoritative text was central. Canon law studies
were related to those of (Roman-)civil law, and indeed the two laws in some
ways amalgamated to form a *ius commune*.[10] The basic civilian texts, e.g. of
Justinian, were retained in university studies even though much in them
lost its direct relevance and application. It is less strange then, that after
the Reformation although the English canon law faculties were suppressed,
the teaching of canon law continued to some extent in the civil law faculty.

On this, Leonard Boyle was emphatic; competence in canon law was
the goal, expertise in civil law the means. At Oxford, although there were
distinct faculties of canon law and civil law, all were in fact ecclesiastical

8.   L. Boyle, "The Curriculum of the Faculty of Canon Law," in *Oxford Studies
Presented to Daniel Callus* (Oxford, 1962), 135–162.
9.   R. Helmholz, "University Education and English Ecclesiastical Lawyers
1400–1650," *Ecclesiastical Law Journal* 13 (2011), 132–145.
10.   Before admission to the status of lecturer in the canon law faculty at Oxford
a candidate was to have heard lectures in civil law for at least 3 years. In order to become
a bachelor in canon law at Cambridge it was the same: R. Helmholz, *The Canon Law and
Ecclesiastical Jurisdiction from 597 to the 1640s* (Oxford, 2004), 188–9.

lawyers. Irrespective of their affiliation, what they were about was canon law. It mattered little in the long run which of the two faculties one entered. The student of law at Oxford and Cambridge was a student of canon law.

There were provisions for different kinds of examinations and the awarding of different qualifications. The emergence of canonists as a profession is in part signaled by the formalizing of studies and the granting of distinct degrees in contrast to a much more fluid earlier situation. This professionalization also established an identity for canon law differentiated from theology and civil law.

As for degrees, in this too, Bologna was the basic model.[11] Students received the bachelor's degree without examination. Instead, advanced students upon nomination were appointed to incept, that is to start teaching. Inception automatically carried with it the style and title of bachelor. After teaching for a year or two, bachelors were eligible to proceed to the first of the examinations leading to a license, and then continue to the doctorate. The custom of using post-nominal initials started after the Reformation.

Honorius complained in *Super specula* (1219) that while trained theologians were in short supply, students were flocking to the schools of law in the hope that legal qualifications would make them wealthy. For all but twenty years of the long period 1333–1454, the See of Canterbury was occupied by a glittering succession of lawyers. The medieval popes included many lawyers. The clerical students at the Roman curia's own university, founded by Innocent IV in 1245, routinely studied civil law as well as canon law and theology, provided they had not yet been ordained priests. In time, monks could study civil law in their monasteries.

Despite significant contributions concerning the making, collection and ordering of decretals before 1234,[12] taken by some to be the time of the most original and distinctive contributions by English canonists to the history of canon law, medieval English canonists of note were few, and attracted little attention elsewhere.[13] An academic tradition of canon law never

---

11. J.C.B.: *iuris canonici baccalaureus*; J.C.L.: *iuri canonici licentiatus*; J.C.D.: *iuris canonici doctor*; J.U.D.: *iuris utriusque doctor*.

12. R. Helmholz, "Roger, Bishop of Worcester (c. 1134–1179)," *Ecclesiastical Law Journal* 15 (2013), 75–80.

13. J. H. Baker, *Monuments of Endlesse Labours: English Canonists and Their Work 1300–1900* (London, 1998) tells the story, beginning with the initial twelfth-century flow-

took hold in Oxford or Cambridge. William Paull, John Ayton and William Lyndwood were the most distinguished English canonists.[14] Helmholz has speculated as to the relative unimportance of English canonists: the dominance of common law; the geographical distance from Bologna, the absence of secular tribunals where Roman law was used, a distinctively Anglo-Saxon approach, coupled with the brevity of academic careers in underfunded faculties.[15]

The medieval universities of Oxford and Cambridge were essentially religious foundations, each with its own faculty of theology. Following the Reformation in the sixteenth century (and after it as a result of the Act of Uniformity of 1662) until the nineteenth century, in England there were religious tests for admission to Oxford and Cambridge universities which meant that only members of the Church of England were eligible to study in them. Oxford maintained this religious test until the University Reform Act of 1854. Those who did not belong or conform to the Church of England either studied in Scotland, or abroad (such as Protestant students at Utrecht or Catholic seminarians at the English College in Rome, founded 1579), or they attended the so-called "Dissenting Academies" run by Non-Conformists. For instance, from 1690 the "Presbyterian Fund Board" provided scholarships for ministry training at these, and from 1743 the Coward Trust funded the Daventry Academy within the Congregational tradition. The Schism Act (1714 to 1718) resulted in closure of several.[16]

However, the nineteenth century witnessed the establishment of secular higher education institutions, such as University College, London— its foundation in 1826 was opposed by the Church of England and it was not until 1836 that it acquired the right to award degrees. Today it has an Institute of Jewish Studies (established in 1959). In response, King's College, London was set up as a Church of England establishment, and the

---

ering especially in cathedral towns. He has separate chapters on Paull, Ayton and Lyndwood, and also considers William Bateman and Thomas Fastolf. R. Helmholz, *Canon Law*, 186–206 is an excellent survey of medieval English canonical scholarship.

14. Boyle, "Canon Law Before 1380," 556–7. The men that the Oxford faculty produced were able administrators, officials and practical legists and often possessed personal libraries rich in legal texts.

15. R. Helmholz, *The Canon Law*, 194–5.

16. See e.g. J. W. Ashley Smith, *The Birth of Modern Education: The Contribution of the Dissenting Academies 1660–1800* (London, 1954).

University of Durham was founded in 1832 under the control of the Dean and Chapter of Durham Cathedral. Religious tests were removed with the enactment of the Universities Tests Act 1871.

At the start of the nineteenth century, one ambition of the bishops of the established Church of England was that all clergy should be university graduates. The ambition did not come to fruition. Instead it was proposed that any non-graduates prior to ordination should have sufficient education for effective ministry in new theological colleges to be sponsored by the Church of England. Theological colleges were set up, for example, at Lampeter in Wales, to obviate the need for travel to Oxford and Cambridge. A centralized system of church examinations was introduced in the 1870s but the institutions were very much free in terms of their internal governance.[17]

Thus we move rapidly to the present day, where the teaching of theology in universities is academic rather than confessional. A small number of professorial chairs, somewhat anachronistically, are annexed to cathedral canonries and thus open technically only to members of the Church of England. Universities are public institutions usually set up by royal charter and funded by various public higher education funding bodies and councils.

Clerical Formation

The training of ministers of religion is regulated primarily by the norms of religious organizations and those created by their own educational institutions. These address the establishment of such institutions, their governance, discipline within them (including academic discipline on the admission of students, the course of study, and exclusion of students), and their dissolution.[18] Institutions to train ministers of religion are also subject to civil law applicable to them directly or indirectly: for example, the law of trusts (applicable to their trust property); employment law (applicable to

---

17. D. A. Dowland, *Nineteenth-Century Anglican Theological Training: The Redbrick Challenge* (Oxford, 1997).

18. For Christian theological colleges and seminaries, see e.g. N. Doe, *Christian Law: Contemporary Principles* (Cambridge, 2013), 203–209.

staff who function under contracts of employment); and immigration law (applicable to students and ministers of religion from overseas).[19]

Denominational institutions—theological colleges and seminaries— provide in-house training, enable ministry students to attend courses on the basis of agreements with local or other public universities in their departments of theology and/or religious studies. These prepare students for qualifications either awarded or validated by a university. Whilst public universities subscribe to the Quality Assurance Agency, theological colleges of the Church of England, Methodist Church, Baptist Union of Great Britain, and United Reformed Church have all subscribed to a separate regime of quality assurance (which includes inspection, curriculum approval, and moderation).[20]

Church of England: According to the canon law of the established Church of England, candidates must be "called, tried, [and] examined" prior to ordination, and the Ministry Division of the Archbishops' Council, and its Vocation, Recruitment and Selection Committee advises the Council and House of Bishops on ministry strategy.[21] The candidate must: have been involved with the Anglican Church for some time; consult his incumbent priest; contact his Diocesan Director of Ordinands, and obtain approval; attend the Bishops' Advisory Panel and once approved may commence training. Provision is made for Initial Ministerial Education, Continuing Ministerial Education, funding for ministerial training, the validation of courses at Church of England theological colleges, their enjoyment of higher education funding, and the evaluation of new training proposals.[22]

19.   For ministers of religion under UK immigration law, see D. McClean, "Immigration and religion in the United Kingdom," in A. Motilla, ed., *Immigration, National and Regional Laws and Freedom of Religion* (Leuven, 2012), 247 at 251.

20.   Quality Assurance and Enhancement in Ministerial Education: Inspection, Curriculum Approval, and Moderation—Handbook 2010 (e.g. in the Church of England the House of Bishop oversees inspection).

21.   Canon C1; see M. Hill, *Ecclesiastical Law*, 3rd ed. (Oxford, 2007), par. 4.04.

22.   House of Bishops' Regulations for Training; Higher Education Funding (GS Misc. 990 (2011)); Funding Ministerial Training (GS Misc. 990A); Principles for the evaluation of new training proposals agreed by the House of Bishops in May 2010; Formation and Assessment in Curacy (approved by the House of Bishops in May 2010); The Learning Outcomes for IME (as approved by the House of Bishops in May 2005); see also The Hind Report: Formation for Ministry within a Learning Church, 2003.

The training delivered at Ridley Hall, Cambridge (founded 1881) is typical; the college is not part of the University of Cambridge but students there training for ministry may be awarded degrees of (and designed by) Cambridge University as well as qualifications validated by other public universities (such as Anglia Ruskin University).[23] Students under 32 who do not already have a theology degree must complete one of the following three year courses offered by the University of Cambridge: Bachelor of Arts (B.A.) in Christian Theology, "a full vocational degree in Christian Theology which leads to ordination"; Bachelor of Theology, "a vocational degree for Christian ministry leading to ordination" combining "theological and practical study"; and Bachelor of Arts in Theological and Religious Studies combined with a Certificate in Theology for Ministry: this two-year B.A. is "appropriate for [those] who want a more academic focus" and the one-year course "covers the ordination requirements for a theology graduate." Those aged over 32, or those with a significant amount of theological study already, must complete one of the following two year courses (unless permission is granted for them to train for an alternative amount of time): Foundation Degree Award, "a vocational degree for Christian ministry leading to ordination" (made up of the first two years of the B.A. course); Bachelor of Arts in Christian Theology; the two year Bachelor of Theology; and the Certificate in Theology for Ministry. The three-year B.A. covers Biblical Hebrew; New Testament Greek; Psychology and Religion; Christian Culture in the Western World; Christian Ethics; Church History; Judaism, Christianity and Islam in Encounter; and Feminist Theology. There is also provision for optional modules in Judaism, Islam, Hinduism and Buddhism.[24]

Church in Wales (Anglican): The training of those preparing for ordination in the Church in Wales is regulated by the norms of the church and the Bench of Bishops plays a key role in its oversight and the church administers a fund (derived primarily from the donations of the faithful) to train

23. http://www.ridley.cam.ac.uk; most residential students are training to be ordained ministers in the Church of England, but some are training for Ordained Pioneer Ministry (to work in "fresh expressions" churches).

24. www.theofed.cam.ac.uk; http://www.ridley.cam.ac.uk/images/documents/courses/ba-tripos.pdf.

candidates.[25] The church has one institution to train its candidates for ordination: St. Michael's Theological College in Cardiff. This is also recognized
as a training college for lay, reader and ordained ministry by the Church of
England and the Methodist Church and it works closely with the South
Wales Baptist College.[26] Initial ministerial training can be either residential (the norm) or non-residential. For those who undertake residential
training, the course taken depends on the individual's previous education,
for example: a Diploma in Higher Education, a Bachelor of Theology degree, a Bachelor of Arts degree in Theological Studies or a Graduate Diploma in Theology. Non-residential students normally take a Diploma in
Practical Theology.

Catholic: Clerical formation in the Roman Catholic Church is governed
inter alia by the Code of Canon Law 1983 and particular norms (including
those issued by national episcopal conferences, such as those published by
the Bishops' Conference of Scotland in 2005).[27] Under the auspices of the
Bishops' Conference of England and Wales, the National Office for Vocation exists to build a culture of vocation and to promote the calls to specific
vocations, including the priesthood and the diaconate.[28] Clerical formation
is delivered at several seminaries, such as Allen Hall in London.

Methodist: In the Methodist Church of Great Britain, training is compulsory prior to ordination.[29] Wesley House, Methodist Theological College, Cambridge, works in partnership with Cambridge University, Anglia Ruskin University, and Cambridge Theological Federation "to train
presbyters, deacons and lay people for ministry in the British Methodist

---

25. N. Doe, *The Law of the Church in Wales* (Cardiff, 2002), 147 (the bishops) and
343 (the fund).

26. http://www.stmichaels.ac.uk/index.php. Ordination candidates often train
outside Wales (at e.g. English theological colleges of which Wycliffe Hall and St Stephen's
House in Oxford are popular).

27. See J. Conn, S.J., "Norms for Priestly Formation in the Latin Church: Universal and Particular," in N. Doe, ed., *The Formation and Ordination of Clergy in Anglican and
Roman Catholic Canon Law* (Cardiff, 2009).

28. The inspiration for its creation is *New Vocations for a New Europe* 1997 (*In
Verbo Tuo*).

29. See Doe, *Christian Law*, 82.

Church." It is prescribed that "benchmarks are set by the Methodist Conference and the progress of each student is monitored by the local Oversight Committee of the Methodist Church."[30]

As to curriculum, the Foundation Degree in Mission and Ministry comprises both content-based and practice-based modules. Optional modules include: Foundations in Christian Worship; Black and Asian Christian Theology; Pastoral Theology; and Introduction to Christian Mission.

Baptist: In the Baptist Union of Great Britain, candidates to train for ministry must satisfy various religious tests.[31] Bristol Baptist College offers a wide range of courses to prepare people for ordained ministry, youth or children's ministry, ministry as a lay pastor, or those seeking to study theology their own development and growth.[32] There are three possible routes to ministry: a college-based course, congregation-based learning, and mission-context based training. Each of these routes "can be accompanied by different degree or diploma courses up to Ph.D. level."

Presbyterian: Presbyterian churches have complex norms on the process leading to ordination, a process which is characterized typically by the participation of the local (Kirk) Session, the regional Presbytery, and the national General Assembly.[33] The normal route for initial ministerial training is the Bachelor of Arts in Theological Studies. In the Church of Scotland, potential Ministers of Word and Sacrament and potential candidates for Ordained Local Ministry go through the following process: the call to ministry (run by the Ministries Council); Vocations Conference (which involves Enquiry and Assessment); Extended Enquiry (which usually involves a placement); Local Review followed by a national Assessment Conference (including interviews by Church Assessors and a Psychologist Assessor).

Islamic: In the Islamic College, London, although there is no specific Imamship Program, the Hawaza Program "provides students with an excellent

---

30. http://www.theofed.cam.ac.uk.

31. See, by way of example, the information contained in "Called to be a Nationally Recognised Pastor" (Baptists Together, September 2013), available at http://www.baptist.org.uk/Articles/368853/Called_to_be.aspx.

32. http://www.bristol-baptist.ac.uk.

33. Doe, *Christian Law*, 83.

platform for a career as an Islamic lecturer and researcher or as a minister of religion."[34] The Hawaza Program consists of a Bachelor of Arts in Hawaza Studies plus Complementary Hawaza Studies. The Muslim College, London, is "a post-graduate Islamic seminary based in West London that is geared towards engagement with wider society by providing comprehensive studies of Islam to its students and visitors."

Jewish: The Leo Baeck College, London, for example, offers rabbinical training for "Progressive Judaism."[35] The normal route is the five-year Rabbinic Program consisting of academic studies, placements and apprenticeships, and vocational modules. For the Rabbinic Program, the "General Criteria for Admissions" include: appropriate motivation; academic ability to complete the program; willingness and potential to grow and develop through the program; religious commitment and personal integrity; dedication to "the Principles of Progressive Judaism;" and intellectual maturity. All rabbinic candidates are interviewed over a period of three days and this includes an academic interview, and structured and unstructured group interviews. Psychological assessment of the candidate is also required.

TRAINING IN CANON LAW

The theological colleges and seminaries of the Christian denominations studied here usually provide that students training for ministry are required to be introduced to at least elements of their own systems of church law and church polity. Since its establishment in 1987, the Ecclesiastical Law Society has undertaken several initiatives to encourage the study of ecclesiastical law as part of initial and continuing ministerial education in the Church of England,[36] including a guide and teaching aid on canon law for the newly ordained—to meet the expectation of the Ministry Division of the Church of England that, at the point of ordination, candidates

34. http://www.islamic-college.ac.uk. Also, the Hijaz College Islamic University (Nuneaton near Birmingham) offers a Diploma in Islamic Law and the London University external LL.B.: http://www.hijazcollege.com/.

35. http://www.lbc.ac.uk.

36. *An Ordered Church: A Syllabus Introducing the Canon and Ecclesiastical Law of the Church of England,* Ecclesiastical Law Society in Conjunction with the Ministry Division of the Archbishops' Council (1999).

should "demonstrate familiarity with the legal, canonical and administrative responsibilities appropriate to the newly ordained and those working under supervision."[37]

The guide asserts: "All clergy are, to a certain extent, practitioners of ecclesiastical law and should be aware of their legal responsibilities" on the basis that: "The general public are entitled to expect the same level of service and expertise from the clergy as they would expect from any professional person."[38] Nevertheless, there is still no national formal freestanding provision in the Church of England itself, or its theological colleges, to train its clergy (as part of initial or continuing ministerial education) or its legal officers in the canon and ecclesiastical law they administer;[39] rather, the teaching is on an *ad hoc* basis. There are in UK law schools courses in canon law,[40] or aspects of it are treated in courses on law and religion.[41]

In the Catholic Church, the study of canon law as part of priestly formation is designed to enable seminary students to understand how canon law applies to every-day ministry as parish priests, for them to know, explain and apply the law with confidence in the decisions they make which affect people; teaching is also provided at a more advanced level in the faculties of canon law at pontifical universities to prepare those to be engaged in the exercise of administrative and judicial offices, and the licentiate (J.C.L.) takes three years.[42] The Sacred Congregation for Catholic Education provides that teaching should cover: the theological foundations of canon law;

---

37.   The Ecclesiastical Law Society, in association with the Ministry Division of the Church of England, *Canon Law for the Newly Ordained: A Brief Guide and Teaching Aid*, L. Yates and W. Adam, 3rd ed. (2011).

38.   Ibid., 9, 18.

39.   Canons of the Church of England, Canon G4: to qualify for appointment as provincial and diocesan registrars, candidates must be "learned in the ecclesiastical laws," but no formal training is provided by the church; no such requirement attaches to candidates for the office of diocesan chancellor: Canon G2.

40.   The Cardiff LL.M. in Canon Law deals critically with the laws of the Church of England and other churches in the global Anglican Communion, as well as comparative church law.

41.   Ecclesiastical law appears in LL.B. law and religion modules at Bangor, Cardiff and Oxford Brookes.

42.   J. Conn, S.J., "The teaching of Canon law in the Roman Catholic Church," unpublished paper delivered at the 14th Colloquium of Anglican and Roman Catholic Canon Lawyers, Rome, 26–27 April 2013.

the application of canon law to concrete circumstances of pastoral life; administrative and judicial practice; and ecumenical aspects of canon law; also, canon law should be treated in the continuing education of clergy.[43] In terms of the purpose of training: "Competent canonists are needed in teaching theology, in the structures of diocesan curial offices, in regional Church tribunals, [and] in the governmental structure of Religious Families"; moreover: "even a priest who is directly occupied with the care of souls needs an adequate training in law to carry out suitably his pastoral ministry in the way a shepherd should."[44] As to the methods of study: "Canon law should be taught in relation to the mystery of the Church as more profoundly understood by the Second Vatican Council. While explaining principles and laws, the point should be made plain, apart from anything else, how the whole system of ecclesiastical government and discipline is in accord with the salvific will of God, and, in all things, has as its scope the salvation of souls."[45]

The Queen's Foundation, Birmingham, teaches "Methodist law and polity" as a compulsory subject for all Methodist pre-ordination students as part of their leadership work; it is designed to introduce students to the concept of living within authority.[46] Teaching begins with the foundational documents, the Deed of Union (1932) and the Constitutional Practice and Discipline of the Methodist Church.

In the Church of Scotland, students in their years of ministerial training attend conferences at which "the Church's practice on matters such as Baptism, Communion, Ordination etc. are taught" and in their fi-

---

43. Ibid; Conn cites the Circular Letter 2 April 1975, On the Teaching of Canon Law to those Preparing to be Priests, and other key instruments on the teaching of canon law such as *Sapientia Christiana* 29 April 1979, Art. 75 of which states: "A Faculty of Canon Law, whether Latin or oriental, has the aim of cultivating and promoting the juridical disciplines in the light of the law of the Gospel and of deeply instructing the students in these, so as to form researchers, teachers, and others who will be trained to hold special ecclesiastical posts."

44. Circular Letter 2 April 1975 (supra).

45. *Ratio fundamentalis institutionis sacerdotalis* (Congregation for Catholic Education, 1970) 174: see Conn.

46. Rev. Helen Cameron, Oversight Tutor, Co-Director of the Centre for Ministerial Formation, The Queen's Foundation, Birmingham (UK) (email 15 April 2013).

nal year all probationers are taught the "Church of Scotland Law."[47] This study is "compulsory for all new entrants and for ministers coming from other churches and from other Presbyterian churches overseas" and is taught over four years.

In the Baptist colleges, the study of Baptist "polity," "principles," or "ecclesiology" is often a compulsory part of the course for ministerial students. One purpose of the course at the Bristol Baptist College, on Baptist History and Principles, is to ensure that "a genuinely Baptist Christian culture is ingrained into the way we do things and relate to one another."[48]

SUMMARY

There is no distinct body of State law in the United Kingdom which explicitly addresses the training of ministers of religion. This is in marked contradistinction to the position in continental Europe.[49] Historically, in the medieval period clergy obtained their theological education at the ancient universities in England and Scotland. Today most universities have faculties or departments of theology and/or religious studies. These are funded wholly or partly from public funds. However, following the Reformation in the sixteenth century, in England the bar to admission to the ancient universities meant that religious groups other than the Church of England set up their own "dissenting academies" or else their members trained for ministry abroad. The nineteenth century witnessed the rise of Church of England, Roman Catholic, and other theological colleges to train candidates for ordained ministry.

The twentieth century, and the religious pluralism which has emerged during it, has seen the rise of Islamic and Jewish colleges for the training of imams and rabbis. Broadly, these religious colleges offer courses for ministry candidates which are either validated by or delivered at the theology and/or religious studies departments of public universities (themselves subject to State higher education law and independent quality assur-

47. The Acts of General Assembly: http://www.churchofscotland.org.uk/about_us/church_law/acts
48. Stephen Finamore (email 16 April 2013).
49. See F. Mesner, ed., *Public Authorities and the Training of Religious Personnel in Europe* (2014).

ance standards). Some religious colleges provide training in other faiths, civil culture and civil law. The colleges are subject to the general law (such as employment and charity) but may enjoy exemptions from equality law (to restrict admission to students within the faith in question). There are also specific rules in immigration law about ministers of religion and those training for this. The colleges may be regulated by means of trust deeds and other associated instruments which provide for their governance, inspection, admission, staff, property and academic discipline.

What is regrettably clear, however, is that education in canon law has become marginalized. The shift from the medieval position to the present day could not be more marked. Then canon law was a component part of the general law which was to be studied by all those wishing to practice law, as well as those called for ordained ministry. Today, in the Church of England in particular, clergy are routinely ordained as deacon and priest and then inducted into a cure of souls with only the most cursory knowledge of canon law. A few straws in the wind might tend to suggest that change is afoot. The achievement of the Ecclesiastical Law Society has been to rekindle an understanding of the importance of canon law to the mission of the church, and a form of "applied ecclesiology."[50] The work of the Centre for Law and Religion at Cardiff University has revived canon law as an academic discipline. The unfortunate, but all too predictable, failure of the draft measure for the consecration of women bishops to achieve the necessary majorities,[51] demonstrated how the Westminster parliamentary model of synodical government had failed the church. There is hope for the future in the structured dialogue facilitated by trained mediators and the recovery of institutional consensus as a means of decision making, rather than adversarial engagement on "party" lines.

But this is not the only beacon of hope. The work of Richard Helmholz and others in tracing the historical basis by which the church legislated for itself and operated that law in practice shows that in terms of its sources and purpose, little is changed. As the current renaissance in the study of canon law takes hold, the recovery of a fuller understanding of the historic position of the law of the church in facilitating its mission

50. A term first coined by R. Ombres in, "Why then the Law?," *New Blackfriars* 55 296–304.

51. M. Hill, "A Measure of Credibility," *Ecclesiastical Law Journal* 15 (2013), 1.

and as a dynamic force in the ecumenical movement can be discerned. The contribution of Professor Richard Helmholz to this is significant, and I am pleased and proud to be able to record it within this volume.

Agreed Payment for Non-Performance in European Contract Law

Reinhard Zimmermann

Introduction

Europe may be on its way towards a Code of Contract Law.[1] On 11 October 2011 a Proposal for a Regulation of the European Parliament and of the Council on a European Sales Law was published[2] which, should it one day be enacted, will constitute a significant milestone along that path. The proposal was preceded by a sequence of official Communications[3] and a string

---

1.   Or even towards a European Civil Code? See Arthur Hartkamp, Martijn Hesselink, Ewoud Hondius, Chantal Mak, and Edgar du Perron, *Towards a European Civil Code*, 4th ed. (Nijmegen, 2011) and the many volumes edited by the "Study Group on a European Civil Code" founded by Christian von Bar; but see also Reinhard Zimmermann, "The Present State of European Private Law," *American Journal of Comparative Law* 57 (2009), 479 ff. On the Study Group, see Martin Schmidt-Kessel, in Jürgen Basedow, Klaus J. Hopt, and Reinhard Zimmermann, ed., *The Max Planck Encyclopedia of European Private Law* (Oxford, 2012) [*MaxEuP*], 1611 ff.; on a European civil code, cf. also Martin Schmidt-Kessel, in the same volume, 553 ff. and Nils Jansen and Lukas Rademacher, in Jan Smits, ed., *Elgar Encyclopedia of Comparative Law* (Cheltenham, 2012) 299 ff.
2.   COM (2011) 635 final. The proposed Common European Sales Law (CESL) constitutes Annex I to the Proposal for a Regulation (PR CESL).
3.   Starting with the Communication on European Contract Law of 11 July 2001, COM (2001) 398 final.

of unofficial model laws, drafted by international groups of academics.[4] The preparatory documents culminated in a Green Paper on policy options for progress towards a European Contract Law for consumers and businesses of 1 July 2010[5] and a Feasibility Study for a future instrument in European Contract Law of 3 May 2011, drafted by a Commission Expert Group on European Contract Law.[6] In academic circles, the proposed CESL has had a somewhat mixed reception.[7] Its fate is unclear, at the moment because, even though it is presently debated in the two Committees of the European Parliament responsible for various aspects of it, i.e. the Legal Affairs Committee and the Internal Market and Consumer Protection Committee, it will not be possible to secure its enactment before the European elections in 2014. Moreover, it now appears likely that its scope of application will be limited to international distance transactions.[8] Also, even if the CESL should be enacted in the course of 2015 or 2016, its practical impact may be limited as a result of the fact that it will only be available to contracting par-

---

4.   For details, see Reinhard Zimmermann, "'Wissenschaftliches Recht' am Beispiel (vor allem) des europäischen Vertragsrechts," in Christian Bumke and Anne Röthel, ed., *Privates Recht* (Tübingen, 2012), 21 ff.

5.   COM (2010) 348 final. On that Green Paper, see Max Planck Institute for Comparative and International Private Law, "Policy Options for Progress Towards a European Contract Law," *RabelsZ* 75 (2011), 371 ff.

6.   The Feasibility Study (FS) is easily accessible in Reiner Schulze and Reinhard Zimmermann, *Europäisches Privatrecht: Basistexte*, 4th ed. (Baden-Baden, 2012), sub III.30.

7.   See Horst Eidenmüller, Nils Jansen, Eva-Maria Kieninger, Gerhard Wagner, and Reinhard Zimmermann, "The Proposal for a Regulation on a Common European Sales Law: Deficits of the Most Recent Textual Layer of European Contract Law," *Edinburgh Law Review* 16 (2012), 301 ff.; and the contributions to Gerhard Wagner and Reinhard Zimmermann, "Sondertagung der Zivilrechtslehrervereinigung zum Vorschlag für ein Common European Sales Law," *Archiv für die civilistische Praxis* 212 (2012), 467 ff. The European Law Institute has proposed a number of amendments, see Statement of the European Law Institute on the Proposal for a Regulation on a Common European Sales Law COM (2011) 635 final, available at http://www.europeanlawinstitute.eu.

8.   See Commission Memo 13/792 of 17 September 2013, available at http://www.europa.eu/: "The European Parliament's Legal Affairs Committee is backing the adoption of an optional instrument limited to distance contracts, notably online contracts. It strikes a balance between allowing SMEs to market the goods on the basis of one single law and one single IT platform in cross-border trade and the need to ensure consumer confidence through the high level of protection standards."

ties as an "optional instrument."⁹ But be that as it may, the CESL is likely to become the central reference text for the discussion and further development of European contract law. Thus, it deserves careful examination. Each rule should be scrutinized in historical and comparative perspective in order to assess its specific profile and in order to draw attention to national experiences and to comparative legal literature that may facilitate its understanding and interpretation. This is all the more important in view of the fact that any motivation for the rules is lacking. Nor have comparative notes been appended to the text of the CESL.

The CESL has rules on contracts of sale and on "related service contracts." In addition it contains rules of general contract law: formation of contract, pre-contractual information duties, interpretation, contents and effects, etc. At the same time, and surprisingly in view of the relatively comprehensive coverage in the predecessor model rules,¹⁰ the CESL contains large gaps.¹¹ The failure to include rules on illegality and immorality, representation, plurality of debtors and creditors, assignment, and set-off is admitted in recital (27) to the proposed regulation itself. But there are a number of other gaps not, evidently, contemplated by the draftsmen of the CESL. As far as these are internal gaps, courts will have to resort to the general principles underlying the instrument and, ultimately, to the general

---

9.   For an exploration of what that means, see Max Planck Institute, "Policy Options," 398 ff.; and see Eidenmüller et al., "The Proposal for a Regulation on a Common European Sales Law," 312 ff.

10.   The most important ones, for present purposes, are: the Principles of European Contract Law (PECL: *Principles of European Contract Law, Parts I and II*, ed. Ole Lando and Hugh Beale [The Hague, 2000]; *Principles of European Contract Law, Part III*, ed. Ole Lando, Eric Clive, André Prüm, and Reinhard Zimmermann [The Hague, 2003]); the UNIDROIT Principles of International Commercial Contracts (PICC: *UNIDROIT Principles of International Commercial Contracts* [Rome, 1994, 2004, 2010]), the Draft Common Frame of Reference (DCFR: *Principles, Definitions and Model Rules of European Private Law: Draft Common Frame of Reference (DCFR), Outline Edition*, ed. Christian von Bar, Eric Clive, and Hans Schulte-Nölke [Munich, 2009]; *Principles, Definitions and Model Rules of European Private Law: Draft Common Frame of Reference (DCFR), Full Edition*, ed. Christian von Bar and Eric Clive [Munich, 2009]) and the Feasibility Study, mentioned above, n. 6.

11.   For comment, see Eidenmüller et al., "The Proposal for a Regulation on a Common European Sales Law," 308 f.

principles of contract law common to the EU member states.[12] In order to establish such general principles, resort may be had to instruments such as the PECL which are based on comparative research and international collaboration.[13] While, therefore, the CESL is far from revealing a complete picture of European contract law, it may be supplemented by rules drawn from these other instruments and set against their comparative background. The present paper will attempt to do this with regard to one specific issue which is not dealt with in the CESL. Since it is to appear in a collection of essays dedicated to Richard Helmholz, I have chosen an issue where the influence of classical canon law is still easily perceptible today. Since my time in the Chicago Law School in 1993 I have had the great pleasure to meet Richard in many different places and on many different occasions; one particularly memorable experience we shared was a year as Goodhart Professor in Cambridge in 1998–99 and 2000–01, respectively. Richard's work has been, and continues to be, a constant source of inspiration for me.

GENERAL BACKGROUND IN THE NATIONAL LEGAL SYSTEMS

A frequent feature of both domestic and international sales contracts are provisions according to which a party who fails to perform has to pay a specific sum to the party to whom the performance was due.[14] Such provisions are known, in the international model rules, as "contract clauses for an agreed sum due upon failure of performance"[15] or, more succinctly, "agreed

---

12.   See Max Planck Institute, "Policy Options," 409 ff.

13.   Reinhard Zimmermann, "Principles of European Contract Law," in *MaxEuP*, 1325.

14.   Lando and Beale I and II (n. 10), 454; *UNIDROIT Principles of International Commercial Contracts* (n. 10), 284 ("... frequency in international contract practice"); Pascal Hachem, *Agreed Sums Payable upon Breach of an Obligation* (The Hague, 2011), 21; Ingeborg Schwenzer, Pascal Hachem, and Christopher Kee, *Global Sales and Contract Law* (Oxford, 2012), no. 44.266.

15.   "UNCITRAL Uniform Rules on Contract Clauses for an Agreed Sum Due upon Failure of Performance," *UNCITRAL Yearbook* XIV (1983), 272.

payments for non-performance."[16] These terms are neologisms, in English as well as in other languages,[17] intended to avoid the two expressions commonly used in the national legal systems, i.e. liquidated damages clauses (*Schadenspauschalen, réparation forfaitaire, rimborso a forfait*) and conventional penalties (penalty clauses, *Vertragsstrafen, clauses pénales, clausole penali, boetebedinge*). Liquidated damages clauses are intended to provide a genuine pre-estimate of the loss likely to be occasioned by a breach of contract, and they thus serve as a convenient means for the creditor who wants to bring a claim for damages to be relieved of the necessity of assessing and proving whatever loss he has actually suffered.[18] It is hardly surprising, in view of the generally acknowledged principle of *pacta sunt servanda*,[19] that such clauses are held to be valid in all legal systems in Europe. Conventional penalties (or penalty clauses) are commonly held to be more problematic. For while, like liquidated damages clauses, they make it easier, or even unnecessary, for the creditor to prove that he has suffered loss as a result of the debtor's non-performance, or to prove the extent of such loss, they also serve as a means of exercising pressure upon the debtor to comply with his obligations.[20]

16. Art. 9:509 PECL; Art. 7.4.13 PICC; Art. III.-3:712 DCFR; Art. 170 FS. (The latter two instruments use the term "stipulated" payment for non-performance. But modern contracts have nothing in common, either genetically, or formally, with "stipulation" in the original meaning of the word.)

17. See the official French and German translations of the title of Art. 9:509 PECL: "Clauses relatives aux conséquences pécuniaires de l'inexécution," "Vereinbarte Zahlung wegen Nichterfüllung."

18. See, e.g., Jack Beatson, Andrew Burrows, John Cartwright, *Anson's Law of Contract*, 29th ed (Oxford, 2010), 565 ff.; Peter Gottwald, in *Münchener Kommentar zum BGB*, vol. II, 6th ed. (Munich, 2012), Vor § 339, no. 34. For France see Philippe Malaurie, Laurent Aynès, and Philippe Stoffel-Munck, *Les obligations*, 5th ed. (Paris, 2011), no. 989; François Terré, Philippe Simler and Yves Lequette, *Les obligations*, 10th ed. (Paris, 2009), no. 625. For Italy see Grazia Baratella, *Le pene private* (Milan, 2006), 32.

19. See, e.g., Art. 1:102 PECL; Art. 1.1 PICC; Art. 1 CESL.

20. On these two purposes of conventional penalties, see G. H. Treitel, *Remedies for Breach of Contract: A Comparative Account* (Oxford, 1988), 212 f.; Isabel Steltmann, *Die Vertragsstrafe im Europäischen Privatrecht* (Berlin, 2000), 24 ff., 32 ff., 56 ff.; Harriët Natalie Schelhaas, *Het Boetebeding in het Europese Contractenrecht* (Deventer, 2004), 3 ff.; Hachem (n. 14), 43 ff.; Marcus Baum, "Penalty Clauses," in *MaxEuP*, 1259; Hans-Georg Hermann, *Historisch-kritischer Kommentar zum BGB (HKK)*, ed. Mathias Schmoeckel, Joachim

The Roman lawyers, from whom the civilian systems derive their rules on conventional penalties, were familiar with both these functions.[21] Their conventional penalty was usually cast in the form of a stipulation (hence: *stipulatio poenae*). The use of such *stipulationes poenae* was highly recommended in Justinian's Institutes,[22] though a number of issues remained controversial among the Roman lawyers. What, for example, was the relationship between the debtor's primary obligation and the penalty, once the former had become due?[23] Could the penalty be claimed when the primary obligation had not been complied with, or only when the debtor was in some way responsible for such non-compliance?[24] The Roman lawyers also realized that dangers were inherent in conventional penalties for the debtor of an obligation, and they thus recognized certain ways and means of assisting him against his creditor claiming the penalty.[25] They did not, however, permit the judge to reduce excessive penalties to a reasonable amount. Such interference with what the parties had agreed upon could not be justified in a legal system where contracting parties could typically be relied upon to look after their own interests.

The problem of excessive penalties, however, became the subject of debate in later times.[26] This was due largely to the question whether the poorly drafted enactment limiting the amount of damages to twice the value of what had been promised (C. 7.47.1)[27] was applicable to conventional penalties. It was argued that if the penalty, with regard to its nature and its function, is a substitute for the recovery of whatever damages had aris-

---

Rückert, and Reinhard Zimmermann, vol. II/2 (Tübingen, 2007), §§ 336—345, nos. 11, 31 ff.

21.　For details, see Rolf Knütel, *Stipulatio poenae* (Cologne, 1976), 45 ff.; Reinhard Zimmermann, *The Law of Obligations: Roman Foundations of the Civilian Tradition* (Oxford, 1996), 95 ff.

22.　Inst. 3.15.7; cf. also Ven. D. 46.5.11. In Roman law, *stipulationes poenae* served another important function; see below, p. 369.

23.　See Zimmermann, *Law of Obligations*, 100 ff.

24.　Ibid., 104 ff.

25.　Ibid., 110 ff.

26.　Ralf-Peter Sossna, *Die Geschichte der Begrenzung von Vertragsstrafen* (Berlin, 1993), 101 ff.; *HKK*/Hermann (n. 20), §§ 336—345, nos. 27 f.; Zimmermann, *Law of Obligations*, 106 ff.

27.　See Zimmermann, *Law of Obligations*, 828 ff.

en, its amount should be limited in the same way as damages.[28] Others did not apply C. 7.47.1 to conventional penalties. That, however, only led some of these authors to conclude that the parties were completely free to determine the extent of the penalty.[29] It had come to be widely recognized that if the penalty was much larger than the loss suffered, it was within the competence of the court to reduce it to a reasonable amount. "By the customs of today," in the words of Johannes Voet, "when a huge penalty has been attached to a covenant, the whole penalty should not be awarded, but it ought rather to be so softened in the discretion of the judge that it is brought down and limited nearly to the amount which can reasonably be that of the [claimant's] damages."[30] The source of inspiration for this judicial power of reduction was, ultimately, the *aequitas canonica*: a creditor should receive his interest but he should not be allowed to enrich himself on account of the defaulting party's breach. This *leitmotif* was sounded in the Decretals of Pope Gregory IX where the bishop of Spoleto was advised that it was hardly fitting "in tantum pontificalis modestiae oblivisci, ut inhonestis quaestibus anhelando desideres cum aliena iactura ditari"; the subsequent canon lawyers tended to use this text as a starting point for their discussions on excessive penalty clauses.[31]

28. See, e.g., Cornelis van Bynkershoek, *Quaestiones Juris Privati* (Lugduni Batavorum, 1744), Lib. II, Cap. XIV.

29. See, e.g., Arnold Vinnius, *In Quatuor Libros Institutionum Imperialium Commentarius Academicus et Forensis* (Lugduni Batavorum, 1726), Lib. III, Tit. XVI (Inst. 3.15), 7 Commentarius no. 5 ("[N]eque vero hic poenam promissor effugiet paratus praestare quod interest: nec amplius quaeritur, an et quanti intersit, sed an tantum poenae nomine promissum sit"); see also Arnold Vinnius, *Institutionenkommentar, Schuldrecht: Text und Übersetzung* (Heidelberg, 2005), 142 f.; cf. also Gerard Noodt, *De Foenore et Usuris Libri Tres*, in *Opera Omnia*, vol. I (Lugduni Batavorum, 1760), Lib. II, Cap. XIII ("[D]istinguitur igitur poena ab usuris: et quamquam usura non possit centesimam egredi; tamen nil vetat, poenam in duplum, triplum aut quadruplum, promitti").

30. "Denique moribus hodiernis volunt, ingente poena conventioni apposita, non totam poenam adjudicandum esse, sed magis arbitrio judicis eam ita oportere mitigari, ut ad id prope reducatur ac restringatur, quanti probabiliter actoris interesse potest": *Commentarius ad Pandectas* (Parisiis, 1829), Lib. XLV, Tit. I, XIII (translated by Percival Gane, *The Selective Voet*, vol. VI (Durban, 1957), 637; cf. also Simon Groenewegen van der Made, *Tractatus de legibus abrogatis et inusitatis in Hollandia vicinisque regionibus* (Lugduni Batavorum, 1649), ad C. 7.47, no. 10.

31. See André Fliniaux, "L'évolution du concept de clause pénale chez les canonistes du Moyen Âge," in *Mélanges Paul Fournier* (Paris, 1929), 233 ff.; Sossna (n. 26), 54 ff.,

A more drastic way of protecting debtors against excessive penalties is to reject penalty clauses altogether. That is the approach adopted in English law which thus, in this respect, curtails the parties' freedom of contract:[32] clauses "stipulated *in terrorem* of the offending party" are held to be unenforceable.[33] Historically, this restriction originated in the jurisdiction of the Chancellor (i.e. in the body of law known as Equity) who felt compelled, under certain circumstances, to grant relief against "penal bonds"; in doing so, the Chancellors were almost certainly influenced by canon law doctrine.[34] At the same time, it may be a reflection of the general reluctance in English law to award specific performance.[35] Whether a provision in a contract constitutes a genuine pre-estimate of the likely loss or a penalty

---

74 ff.; cf. also Schelhaas, *Boetebeding* (n. 20), 4; *HKK*/Hermann (n. 20), §§ 336—345, no. 28. The canon lawyers became interested in penalty provisions, in the first place because, and insofar as, they could be used to circumvent the prohibition on usury. It appears to have been Hostiensis (Henricus de Segusio) who related the extent of the penalty to the creditor's interest. Andreas Alciatus discussed and ultimately accepted the canon law doctrine, and so did subsequent humanists such as Hugo Donellus, Charles Dumoulin and Fraçois Hotman. In France, the judicial power of reduction thus became widely accepted; see, e.g., Robert Joseph Pothier, "Traité des obligations," in *Traités sur différentes matières de droit civil*, 2nd ed., vol. I (Paris, 1781), no. 346. In Germany, on the other hand, the view prevailed that the parties are free to determine the sum of the penalty; for details, see the references in Sossna (n. 26), 114 ff.

32. It is for this reason that a court will be cautious to conclude that a particular provision is a penalty clause and, therefore, unenforceable. See *Philips Hong Kong Ltd v. Attorney-General of Hong Kong* [1993] HKLR 269; Hachem (n. 14), 84 ff.

33. See Treitel, *Remedies* (n. 20), 229 f.; Zimmermann, *Law of Obligations* (n. 21), 107 f.; Schelhaas, *Boetebeding* (n. 20), 155 ff.; Steltmann (n. 20), 37 ff.; Hachem (n. 14), 34 ff.; Baum (n. 20), 1261; Oliver Remien, *Zwingendes Vertragsrecht und Grundfreiheiten des EG-Vertrages* (Tübingen, 2003), 521 ff. The quotation is from the leading case of *Dunlop Pneumatic Tyre Co Ltd v. New Garage and Motor Co Ltd*, [1915] AC 79 (HL) 86; for the crucial passages of Lord Dunedin's speech, see also Hugh Beale, Bénédicte Fauvarque-Cosson, Jacobien Rutgers, Denis Tallon, and Stefan Vogenauer, *Cases, Materials and Text on Contract Law*, 2nd ed. (Oxford, 2010), 1052 ff.

34. For the historical development, see A. W. B. Simpson, "The Penal Bond with Conditional Defeasance," *Law Quarterly Review* 82 (1966), 392, 411 ff.; *idem, A History of the Common Law of Contract* (Oxford, 1975), 113 ff., 123 f.; Schelhaas, *Boetebeding* (n. 20), 145 ff.; cf. also Treitel, *Remedies* (n. 20), no. 167; Hachem (n. 14), 34 f.; Baum (n. 20), 1261. Once again, originally, circumvention of the ban against usury appears to have been a central concern.

35. Beale et al., *Cases, Materials and Text on Contract Law* (n. 33), 1060.

clause is dependent upon the parties' intention at the time when they concluded the contract,[36] and the English courts have identified a number of factors to assist them in determining that intention.[37] From a comparative perspective it must be noted that English law, focusing on the *in terrorem* aspect, traditionally defines conventional penalties more narrowly than the civilian systems.[38]

Modern German law perpetuates the traditional civilian concept of a penalty clause, and thus emphasizes its bi-functional nature.[39] At the same time, like English law, it draws a distinction between conventional penalties and liquidated damages clauses.[40] Unlike English law, however, it recognizes both types of contractual provisions as valid, though it applies different rules to them: in particular, the judicial power to reduce an amount that is found to be excessive does not pertain to liquidated damages clauses. French and Dutch law, on the other hand, while also recognizing both types of clauses as valid, subject them to the same rules, including the judicial power of reduction of the agreed sum.[41] Finally, there is also at least

36. See *Dunlop Pneumatic Tyre Co Ltd v. New Garage and Motor Co Ltd*, [1915] AC 79 (HL) 86 f.; Hachem (n. 14), 60 f.

37. *Dunlop Pneumatic Tyre Co Ltd v. New Garage and Motors Co Ltd*, [1915] AC 79 (HL) 86 ff.; Treitel, *Remedies* (n. 20), nn 1.79 f.; *Anson's Law of Contract* (n. 18), 566 ff.; Schelhaas, *Boetebeding* (n. 20), 158 ff.; Hachem (n. 14), 61 ff.

38. See also Treitel, *Remedies* (n. 20), no. 164, stating that the difference in terminology gives rise to some awkwardness in a comparative discussion of the institution; Hachem (n. 14), 27 (fallacy of terminology). In addition, many civilian legal systems do not draw a distinction between conventional penalties and liquidated damages clauses, while others do (see the next paragraph in the text). Thus, the terms *clause pénal* and *Vertragsstrafe*, used in France and Germany for "conventional penalties" are not synonymous.

39. Gottwald (n. 18), Vor § 339, no. 6. For Austria, see Karl-Heinz Danzl, in *Kurzkommentar zum ABGB*, ed. Helmut Koziol, Peter Bydlinski, and Raimund Bollenberger, 3rd ed. (Vienna, 2010), § 1336, no. 2.

40. Treitel, *Remedies* (n. 20), no. 178; Schelhaas, *Boetebeding* (n. 20), 211 ff.; Steltmann (n. 20), 65 ff.; Gottwald (n. 18), Vor § 339, no. 34. For Austria, see Danzl (n. 39), § 1336, no. 2.

41. Art. 1152 *Code civil*; Art. 6:91 BW; for details, see Schelhaas, *Boetebeding* (n. 20), 63 ff. For Italy, see Art. 1382 ff. *Codice Civile*; Alessandra Mari, in Luisa Antoniolli and Anna Veneziano, *Principles of European Contract Law and Italian Law: A Commentary* (The Hague, 2005) 472; Alessio Zaccaria, in *Commentario breve al codice civile*, ed. Giorgio Cian and Alberto Trabucchi, 6th ed. (Padova, 2010), Art. 1384 II. For France, see Malaurie et al. (n. 18), no. 991; Terré et al. (n. 18). no. 627.

one civilian legal system, Belgium, which has adopted an approach that is similar to the English one.[42]

THE INTERNATIONAL MODEL RULES

The international model rules have essentially endorsed the civilian approach in the shape that it has taken in France and in the Netherlands. This is to be welcomed, for the distinction between liquidated damages clauses and conventional penalties, however the latter may be conceptualized, is notoriously difficult as both the English and German experiences demonstrate.[43] Also, a pre-estimate of the loss that is likely to arise as a result of the non-performance of an obligation can turn out to be as oppressive for the debtor as a penalty clause, considering that the pre-estimate is made at the time of conclusion of the contract and not at the time of non-performance.[44] The rules laid down in Art 9:509 PECL, Art 7.4.13 PICC, Art III.-3:712 DCFR, and Art 170 FS are virtually identical; their differences are of a merely terminological nature. It is surprising in view of the consistency of approach (endorsing a growing international consensus),[45] and of the practical importance of the matter, that the CESL does not contain any rule on agreed payment for non-performance at all.[46] It does not, in that respect, constitute an advance over the CISG which has

42.   See Schelhaas, *Boetebeding* (n. 20), 178 ff.

43.   For England, see Treitel, *Remedies* (n. 20), no. 180: "The common law rules for distinguishing between penalties and liquidated damages manage to get the worst of both worlds." For a detailed and critical discussion of the English approach in comparative and economic perspective, see Hachem (n. 14), 83 ff.; for criticism in England concerning the rule on penalty clauses see, e.g., T. A. Downes, "Rethinking Penalty Clauses," in Peter Birks, ed., *Wrongs and Remedies in the Twenty-First Century* (Oxford, 1996), 249 ff.; Mindy Chen-Wishart, "Controlling the Powers to Agree Damages," in Birks, *Wrongs and Remedies*, 271 ff. For Germany, see Gottwald (n. 18), Vor § 339, no. 34 f.; Schelhaas, *Boetebeding* (n. 20) 219 ff.

44.   See Art. 85 (e) CESL and Annex 1. e) of the Unfair Terms Directive.

45.   Cf. also the last paragraph of Comment A to Art. III.-3.712 DCFR that has been added to what otherwise is a copy of Comment A to Art. 9:509 PECL.

46.   But see the reference to such provisions in Art. 85 (e) CESL; for comment, see Eidenmüller, et al., "The Proposal for a Regulation" (n. 7), 328 ff.

also failed to provide a regulation.[47] UNCITRAL subsequently presented a set of "Uniform Rules on Contract Clauses for an Agreed Sum Due upon Failure of Performance";[48] this initiative has not, however, led to an international Convention but merely to a recommendation in 1983 on the part of the General Assembly of the United Nations to its member states to give serious consideration to these rules and, where appropriate, their introduction.[49] Even earlier, in 1973, the Benelux countries had prepared a *Convention relative à la clause pénale* (*Overeenkomst betreffende het boetebeding*) which was, however, never ratified.[50] Both documents pursue the same approach as, but contain a more detailed regime than, PECL, PICC, DCFR and FS.[51] This is the text on which the following discussion is based:[52]

47. On agreed payment clauses under the CISG, see Ingeborg Schwenzer, in Peter Schlechtriem and Ingeborg Schwenzer, *Commentary on the UN Convention on the International Sale of Goods (CISG)*, 3rd ed. (Oxford, 2010), Art. 74, nos. 58 f.

48. See above, n. 15.

49. See Remien, *Zwingendes Vertragsrecht* (n. 33), 524 f. with references; Hachem (n. 14), 41; on the UNCITRAL rules cf. also Baum (n. 20), 1262.

50. *Bulletin/Publikatieblad* Benelux 1973—7; see Baum (n. 20), 1261 who also states that this Convention influenced a Resolution passed by the Council of Europe in 1978, on which cf. also Remien, *Zwingendes Vertragsrecht* (n. 33), 524. The Gandolfi *Avant-projet* (*Code Européen des Contrats: Avant-projet*, vol. I [Milan, 2004]) has a rule on *clause pénale* in Art. 170. At least equally interesting is the South African Conventional Penalties Act 15 of 1962 which was enacted in view of the very unsatisfactory common law position previously prevailing: South African courts had followed the English approach (see, in particular, *Commissioner of Public Works v. Hills*, 1906 AC 368 (PC)), until the Appellate Division attempted to re-introduce certain principles of Roman-Dutch law (*Pearl Assurance Co Ltd v. Union Government*, 1933 AD 277). The mastermind behind the Conventional Penalties Act was South Africa's most influential academic of the twentieth century, Professor J. C. de Wet of the University of Stellenbosch. He managed to bring South African law in line with the modern continental codifications; see "Straf- en verbeuringsbedinge: memorandum vir die regshersieningskommissie" (1955) and "Penalties and Liquidated Damages," both in J. C. de Wet, *Opuscula Miscellanea*, ed. J. J. Gauntlett (Durban, 1979). For a general assessment, see Franziska Myburgh and Reinhard Zimmermann, "J. C. de Wet and the Conventional Penalties Act 15 of 1962," in J. E. du Plessis, ed., *A Man of Principle—The Life and Legacy of J. C. de Wet* (Claremont, 2013), 270 ff.

51. This also applies to Art. 170 *Avant-projet* and, in particular, to the South African Conventional Penalties Act 15 of 1962.

52. Paragraph (1) follows Art. 170 (1) FS with one deviation: Art. 170 (1) FS refers to a debtor "who fails to perform the obligation"; cf. also Art. III.-3:712 (1) DCFR. The term "the obligation," however, lacks a point of reference and hence, in line with Art. 9:509 (1) PECL and Art. 7.4.13 (1) PICC it has been left out. Paragraph (2) is identical with Art.

(1) Where the contract provides that a debtor who fails to perform is to pay a specified sum to the creditor for such non-performance, the creditor is entitled to that sum irrespective of the actual loss.

(2) However, despite any agreement to the contrary, the sum specified may be reduced to a reasonable amount where it is grossly excessive in relation to the loss resulting from the non-performance and the other circumstances.

Systematically, PECL, PICC, DCFR and FS all deal with the matter in the context of their rules on damages (as does French law). For a German or Italian lawyer this may be surprising.[53] But it should not be taken as an indication that "agreed payment for non-performance" is tantamount to liquidated damages clauses. It is clear beyond doubt that both liquidated damages clauses and conventional penalties are covered (and thus subjected to one and the same regime).[54] This also appears to be the reason for the neologism "agreed payment for non-performance."

9:509 (2) PECL, except that a comma has been added after "contrary." The differences to Art. 7.4.13 (2) PICC, Art. III.-3.712 (2) DCFR and Art. 170 (2) FS are merely terminological in nature.

53. In Germany the regulation of *Vertragsstrafen* (§§ 339–345 BGB) occupies its own title (together with the "earnest") in the general part of the law of obligations, quite apart from the rules on damages. In Italy, the *clausola penale* (Art. 1382–1384) is dealt with in a chapter on the effects of the contract, while the regulation of damages is part of another chapter on non-performance. The BW (Art. 91–94) rules on *boetebeding* are part of the regulation on the consequences of non-performance; they are immediately followed by a section on damages which is, however, systematically separate. For France, see Art. 1152 (part of a section of the code devoted to "Des dommages et intérêts résultant de l'inexécution de l'obligation") and Art. 1226–1233 (forming part of a chapter on "Des diverses espèces d'obligations").

54. Comment 1 to Art. 7.4.13 PICC specifically states that the definition given for an agreed payment for non-performance is intentionally broad, so as to cover both liquidated damages clauses and conventional penalties. The Comments to PECL and DCFR are less specific on this point but have to be understood in the same way.—Strangely, on the other hand, Art. 85 (e) CESL does appear to draw a distinction between liquidated damages clauses and conventional penalties: a contract term is presumed to be unfair if it requires a consumer who fails to perform an obligation under the contract not only to make an agreed payment for non-performance but also "to pay a disproportionately high amount by way of damages."

AGREED PAYMENT SPECIFIED

As is apparent from the latter term (as well as from the definition of an "agreed payment" in PECL, PICC, DCFR and FS), the payment must have been agreed upon for cases in which a party to the contract fails to perform (one of his contractual obligations). In traditional civilian terminology this is a "genuine" conventional penalty: it is of an accessory nature in that the obligation to pay presupposes (breach of) another, principal obligation. Roman law, however, also recognized "non-genuine" (or "non-accessory," or "independent") conventional penalties.[55] They served as an incentive to make someone else perform something that he was not (usually: could not be) contractually bound to perform. A prominent example was what we refer to as a contract in favor of a third party. A *stipulatio alteri*, designed to enable a third party to claim performance from the promisor, was not enforceable.[56] Yet, by means of a *stipulatio poenae* the promisor could be put under pressure to perform towards the third party rather than having to pay the penalty to the promisee: "[E]rgo si quis stipuletur Titio dari, nihil agit, sed si addiderit de poena 'nisi dederis, tot aureos dare spondes?' tunc committitur stipulatio."[57] Most modern codifications no longer deal with independent conventional penalties.[58] This is due to the broadening of the contractual freedom of the parties: they are now able to agree upon— and thus make enforceable directly—what they could not agree upon in Roman law (e.g. to invest a third party with a right to claim performance from the promisor).[59] The German Civil Code mentions the independent

55. See Zimmermann, *Law of Obligations* (n. 21), 98 f.

56. Ibid., 34 ff.

57. Inst. 3.19.19; cf. also Ulp. D. 45.1.38.17.

58. See, e.g., Schelhaas, *Boetebeding* (n. 20), 28 ff., 38, emphasizing the accessory character of the *boetebeding* in the Netherlands and of the *clause pénale* in France. For Italy, see Mari, in Antoniolli and Veneziano (n. 41), 472 (requirement always: non-performance); for liquidated damages clauses in England, see *Anson's Law of Contract* (n. 18), 569 f.; for South Africa, see the discussion in Myburgh and Zimmermann (n. 50), 282 ff.; generally, Treitel, *Remedies* (n. 20), nos. 166, 168 (who does not regard agreements for the payment of money in events other than non-performance as penalty clauses).

59. That the parties were unable to do so in Roman law is a consequence of the principle of *omnis condemnatio pecuniaria* and of the closely related fact that for a *stipulatio alteri* there was no "interest" that could be assessed in monetary terms; see Zimmermann, *Law of Obligations* (n. 21), 35 f. These impediments towards recognizing contracts in favor of

conventional penalty but it does so in passing and without devoting to it a fully-fledged regulation.[60] The only thing that is clear is that the right of reduction provided in § 343 (1) BGB has to be applied. Doctrinally, an independent conventional penalty is widely held today to be a (non-accessory) guarantee.[61]

Under which circumstances exactly the agreed sum is triggered is to be determined, in the first place, by the parties themselves.[62] They can link the agreed sum to non-performance in general, or to specific types of non-performance such as delay, or non-conformity. And they can also specify the requirements for non-performance, or the pertinent type of non-performance, particularly whether the non-performance must be in some way or other imputable to the debtor. Generally speaking, however, the parties can be taken to have intended to make payment of the agreed sum dependent on whatever criterion the applicable law generally uses for imputing a failure to perform to the debtor; for the CESL (and for the international model rules preceding it) this would mean strict liability, limited by *force majeure*.[63] In the same way, the approach adopted in the national legal systems reflects, absent an agreement to the contrary, what is recognized for non-performance in general.[64] The matter is addressed in Comment 2 to Art 7.4.13 PICC where it is noted that the non-performance

---

a third party, of course, no longer exist (which is why the contractual freedom of the parties could be extended in that respect).

60. § 343 (2) BGB; for details, see *HKK*/Hermann (n. 20), §§ 336–345, no. 15; Gottwald (n. 18), Vor § 339, no. 2; § 343, nos. 28 ff.; Schelhaas, *Boetebeding* (n. 20), 415 f.

61. Gottwald (n. 18), § 343, no. 24.

62. In other words: freedom of contract prevails. Cf. Hachem (n. 14), 136; Gottwald (n. 18), § 339, no. 35; Mari (n. 41), 473; Schelhaas, *Boetebeding* (n. 20) 25, 37; Art. 9 UNCITRAL Rules. In some legal systems (Italy, France), if the parties are ad idem that the agreed sum is due also in the event that the debtor has not been at fault in failing to perform, this is no longer regarded as a conventional penalty. For France, see Malaurie et al. (n. 18), no. 992; Terré et al. (n. 18), no. 624. For Italy, see Zaccaria (n. 41), Art. 1382 no. I.10: such a provision is valid but is not subject to the rules governing penalty clauses (Art. 1382-1386 *Codice Civile*).

63. Art. 159 CESL.

64. For Germany, see Gottwald (n. 18), § 339, no. 34; for Italy, see Mari (n. 41), 473; for the Netherlands, see Art. 92 (3) BW; for France, see Schelhaas, *Boetebeding* (n. 20), 25, 36; generally, see Treitel, *Remedies* (n. 20) no. 168; Hachem (n. 14) 135 ff.

must normally be "one for which the non-performing party is liable";[65] exceptionally, however, the agreed-payment clause may be intended by the parties "also to cover non-performance for which the non-performing party is not liable," i.e. in a *force majeure* situation.[66]

"Irrespective of the actual loss" (above, p. 366, under (1)) includes situations where the creditor has not suffered any loss at all.[67] This might have been clarified by adding the words "if any." The agreed payment clause is designed, *inter alia*, to save the creditor *any* trouble relating to proof of loss.

AGREED PAYMENT, DAMAGES CLAIM, SPECIFIC PERFORMANCE

The specific structure of a (genuine) conventional penalty, and thus also of what the international instruments term "agreed payment for non-performance," raises the question whether, once the non-performance has occurred, the creditor can only claim the penalty, or whether he can still resort to a claim for damages. Where the loss that has arisen actually exceeds the penalty, he will normally want to pursue the latter course. In the first place, the matter is one of contract interpretation, for the parties are free to make provision for this issue.[68] As far as the default rule is concerned, modern continental codifications are divided;[69] both approaches adopted by them, at least in principle, trace their lineage to Roman law, the one to *stipulationes poenae* attached to a stipulation, the other to those attached to a contract governed by *iudicia bonae fidei*, such as a contract of sale.[70]

---

65. Cf. also Art. 5 UNCITRAL Rules ("The obligee is not entitled to the agreed sum if the obligor is not liable for the failure of performance") and Art. 2 (3) Benelux Convention ("Le créancier ne peut prétendre à l'exécution de la clause pénale lorsque l'inexécution de l'obligation à laquelle elle se rattache ne peut être imputée au débiteur").

66. *UNIDROIT Principles of International Commercial Contracts* (n. 10), 285.

67. Comment 2 to Art. 7.4.13 PICC; Comment A to Art. 9:509 PECL; Hachem (n. 14), 138 ff.; for liquidated damages clauses in England, see *Anson's Law of Contract* (n. 18), 570.

68. See, e.g., Gottwald (n. 18), § 340, no. 3; Art. 1382 (1) *Codice civile*; Steltmann (n. 20), 174; Schelhaas, *Boetebeding* (n. 20), 274 f.; Hachem (n. 14), 163.

69. For a general comparative overview, see Hachem (n. 14) 161 ff.; Baum (n. 20), 1260.

70. See Zimmermann, *Law of Obligations* (n. 21), 100 ff.

According to French, Dutch, and Italian law, the penalty is seen to replace the claim for damages with the result that the creditor is limited to claiming the penalty.[71] French law makes an exception for cases of *dol* and *faute lourde*, where the creditor is not limited to the agreed sum but may claim full damages.[72] Dutch law, on the other hand, grants the courts the power to award damages, in addition to the agreed sum, "if it is evident that equity so requires."[73] Also, the parties can determine that the creditor may claim damages exceeding the penalty. The *Codice civile* contains a specific provision to this effect (Art. 1382).[74]

By contrast, under the German Civil Code, the creditor retains his claim for damages and is allowed to choose between claiming damages and the penalty. He may even claim the penalty plus whatever damages are not covered by it.[75] The penalty thus, effectively, constitutes a minimum amount of damages. Obviously, the German approach favors the creditor. The agreed-payment clause has, after all, been introduced into the contract in his interest. On the other hand, it may be argued that he could have fixed a higher sum in the first place. If the agreed-payment clause is supposed to relieve him of the cumbersome necessity of having to prove his loss, he should also have to suffer the potentially disadvantageous consequences following from this course of action.

Strangely, the PECL, PICC, DCFR and FS do not deal with the issue. The Benelux Convention followed the first of the above-mentioned approaches when it stated in Art 2 (2): "Ce qui est dû en vertu de la clause pénale est substitué aux dommages et intérêts en vertu de la loi."[76] The UNCITRAL Rules, in turn, obviously attempted to devise a compromise

---

71.   See Art. 1229 *Code civil*; Art. 6:92 (2) BW; Art. 1382 (1) *Codice civile*; Schelhaas, *Boetebeding* (n. 20), 267 ff.; Steltmann (n. 20), 173 ff.; Mari (n. 41), 473 f.; for liquidated damages clauses in England, see Schelhaas, *Boetebeding* (n. 20), 281 f.; cf. also s. 2 (1) (South African) Conventional Penalties Act 15 of 1962 (on which, see Myburgh and Zimmermann (n. 50), 288 ff.); Hachem (n. 14), 161 ff.

72.   Terré et al. (n. 18), no. 625; Beale et al. (n. 33), 1052; Steltmann (n. 20), 174 f.

73.   Art. 6:94 (2) BW.

74.   For France, see Steltmann (n. 20), 174; Terré et al. (n. 18). no. 625; for the Netherlands, see Schelhaas, *Boetebeding* (n. 20), 269; generally, see Hachem (n. 14), 163.

75.   Art. 340 (2) BGB; cf. also § 1336 (3) ABGB; Hachem (n. 14), 165.

76.   See also Art. 170 (1) Gandolfi *Avant-projet* (with misleading German translation of this rule).

solution: Art 7 first states that the creditor "may not claim damages to the extent of the loss covered by the agreed sum." But it then carries on to provide that "[n]evertheless, he may claim damages to the extent of the loss not covered by the agreed sum, if the loss substantially exceeds the agreed sum." This does not appear to be a very happy solution because the meaning of the phrase "loss covered by the agreed sum" is unclear: it can hardly mean that the agreed sum serves as a Cap. in view of the fact that the second sentence only allows the creditor to claim damages if the loss "substantially" exceeds the agreed sum. The Comments to Art 9:509 PECL and III.-3:712 DCFR[77] (they are identical) appear to indicate that the draftsmen of these documents assumed that the claim for the agreed sum normally replaces the damages claim: for they allow the creditor to recover a higher figure only if "the contract specifies merely the minimum sum payable by the non-performing party" (and, provided he can prove a loss exceeding [not: substantially exceeding!] the minimum sum). The implication thus appears to be that the parties must specifically designate the agreed sum as a minimum sum and thus contract out of the normal regime, if they intend the creditor to be able to sue for damages rather than to invoke the agreed-payment provision.

The continental codifications also normally deal with the relationship between the claims for the agreed sum and for specific performance. In German law, for example, the creditor may not cumulate these claims, unless the penalty has been agreed upon for cases in which the debtor fails to fulfill his obligation properly (i.e. delay or non-conformity).[78] This approach is based on the notion of *Interessenidentität* (identity of interests): The creditor is not to be allowed to recover the same interest twice, but where the two claims are not designed to cover the same interest, they may be brought together.[79] Many other codifications essentially pursue the same approach, even though they primarily think of cases of delay rath-

---

77. Lando and Beale I and II (n. 10), 454; von Bar and Clive, full edition, vol. I (n. 10), 962.

78. §§ 340 (1), 341 (1) and (3) BGB.

79. Steltmann (n. 20), 163; Schelhaas, *Boetebeding* (n. 20), 289; Hachem (n. 14), 156; Baum (n. 20), 1261.

er than improper performance in general.[80] Article 6 of the UNCITRAL
Rules also, at first, singles out "delay in performance" but then carries on to
state, more generally, that if the agreed sum "cannot reasonably be regarded as compensation for [a specific] failure of performance," the creditor is
entitled to both performance of that obligation and the agreed sum.[81] Once
again, the issue is not dealt with by PECL, PICC, DCFR or FS but it appears to be reasonable to assume that those who will have to resolve it will
be guided by the solution favored in the majority of national legal systems
and also adopted in the UNCITRAL Rules.[82]

In view of the fact that the two issues just discussed are traditionally
covered by rules in the national codifications, and also by two of the international instruments, it is suggested that the following two additional rules
be inserted into the provision on agreed payments:

(1a) The specified sum replaces the creditor's right to damages for loss
caused by the non-performance.

(1b) The creditor is not allowed to claim the specified sum and performance of the obligation for the non-performance of which the sum has
been agreed upon, unless the specified sum cannot reasonably be regarded
as compensation for the non-performance.

The first of these rules is modeled on Art. 2 (2) of the Benelux Convention, the second on Art. 6 (2) of the UNCITRAL Convention.

POWER OF REDUCTION OF THE AGREED SUM

Conventional penalties, as well as "agreed payments" serving the same two
functions as conventional penalties do, are dangerous for a number of rea-

---

80.   Art. 1229 (2) *Code civil*; § 1336 (1) third sentence ABGB; Art. 1383 *Codice civile*;
Art. 170 (3) Gandolfi *Avant-projet*; Hachem (n. 14), 156. But see Art. 92 (1) BW and Art. 2
(1) Benelux Convention, which contains a general prohibition upon the cumulation of both
claims.

81.   This is preceded by the following general rule: "[i]f the contract provides that
the [creditor] is entitled to the agreed sum upon a failure of performance other than delay,
he is entitled either to performance or to the agreed sum." The way in which this rule is
structured appears to be less than ideal.

82.   Hachem (n. 14), 158.

sons.[83] The agreement is made at a time when the loss resulting from breach can only be estimated. The amount fixed as a true penalty, i.e. in order to exert pressure on the debtor, can be quite arbitrary, and it is usually effectively determined by the creditor. Furthermore, as under a suretyship obligation, the debtor is not exposed to an immediate obligation to pay, but only to a conditional one; and thus, the natural confidence in his own ability to perform his principal obligation will often lead the debtor to underrate the gravely detrimental nature of the clause. Unlike in the case of suretyship contracts, the national legal systems, followed by the international instruments, have not usually relied on statutory form requirements to protect the debtor.[84] They have taken the more drastic step of curtailing the parties' private autonomy: either by disallowing conventional penalties altogether, or by granting the courts the power to reduce excessive penalties.[85]

The latter mechanism, while more liberal than the approach of the common law, is still an interference with contractual freedom—which is why it was only adopted into the BGB after much controversy and as something highly exceptional.[86] The legal systems closely associated with German law have always had similar provisions in their codes,[87] while the power of reduction was introduced into the *Code civil* only in 1975[88] and into Dutch law in 1992.[89] Today, it is commonly recognized in civilian legal

83. Cf. also Hachem (n. 14), 51 f. ("...it is the protection of the debtor that lies at the heart of the issue of agreed sums").

84. For a discussion, see Hachem (n. 14) 52 ff.

85. See above, pp. 360–63.

86. § 343 BGB; see "Protokolle," in Benno Mugdan, *Die gesammten Materialien zum Bürgerlichen Gesetzbuch für das Deutsche Reich*, vol. II (Berlin, 1899), 722 ff.; *Verhandlungen des 20. Deutschen Juristentages*, vol. II (1889), 23 ff., 43 ff.; Heinrich Siber, in Gottlieb Planck, ed., *Kommentar zum Bürgerlichen Gesetzbuch*, vol. II/1, 4th ed. (Berlin, 1914), § 343, 1. This was in conflict with contemporary Roman law prevailing in nineteenth-century Germany; see Bernhard Windscheid and Theodor Kipp, *Lehrbuch des Pandektenrechts*, 9th ed. (Frankfurt, 1906), § 285; Heinrich Dernburg, *Pandekten*, vol. II, 6th ed. (Berlin, 1900). § 46, 4.

87. § 1336 (2) ABGB; Art. 409 *Astikos Kodikas*; Art. 163 (3) OR; Art. 1384 *Codice civile*.

88. Act 75-597 of 1975 which introduced the second paragraph of Art. 1152 *Code civil*.

89. Art. 94 (1) BW; the reform was brought about by the new BW in 1992.

systems,[90] and this very widespread recognition is reflected in the international instruments.[91]

The power of reduction, as in the national legal systems,[92] is of a mandatory character. Contrary to German law[93] it also applies to contracts concluded between merchants. That a restrictive approach has to be followed is made clear by the words "grossly excessive" (PECL, PICC, DCFR, FS), "substantially disproportionate" (UNCITRAL Rules), "si l'équité l'exige manifestement" (Benelux Convention), "manifestamente excessivo" (Italy), "manifestement excessive" (France), "indien de billijkheid dit klaarblijkelijk eist" (the Netherlands) or, less emphatically, "unverhältnismäßig hoch" (Germany). The national codifications are not usually very specific when it comes to rendering this yardstick operational: obviously, they all envisage a comparison between the agreed payment and something else[94] without, however, specifying this something else. PECL, PICC, DCFR and FS are somewhat more explicit[95] when they determine that the agreed payment must be assessed in relation to the loss resulting from the non-performance (meaning the loss actually suffered by the creditor rather than the loss legally recoverable in terms of the foreseeability principle)[96] and considering all circumstances of the case such as whether there has been part perfor-

---

90. For a detailed list (to which s. 3 Conventional Penalties Act 15 of 1962 for South Africa may be added), see Hachem (n. 14), 33.

91. Art. 9:509 (2) PECL; Art. 7.4.13 (2); Art. III.-3:712 (2) DCFR; Art. 170 (2) FS. Cf. also Art. 4 Benelux Convention; Art. 8 UNCITRAL Rules; Art. 170 (4) Gandolfi *Avant-projet*.

92. See, e.g., Art. 1152 (2) second sentence *Code civil*; Art. 84 (3) BW; Gottwald (n. 18), § 343, no. 2; Mari (n. 41), 474; Hachem (n. 14), 118 f.

93. § 348 Commercial Code (*Handelsgesetzbuch* = HGB). This used to be the position also in Austria until 2007; see Danzl (n. 39), § 1336, no. 1. That the right of reduction does not apply in cases where a merchant has promised to pay a conventional penalty does not mean that merchants who have promised to pay an excessive penalty are entirely without protection; for details, Gottwald (n. 18), § 343, nos. 3 f.; Schelhaas, *Boetebeding* (n. 20), 230 ff., 233 ff.; Hachem (n. 14), 123 f.

94. Treitel, *Remedies* (n. 20), no. 177.

95. Cf. also Art. 8 UNCITRAL Rules ("...the loss that has been suffered by the obligee"); Art. 170 (4) Gandolfi *Avant-projet* ("...l'intérêt que le créancier avait à l'exécution"); s. 3 (South African) Conventional Penalties Act 15 of 1962 ("...the prejudice suffered by the creditor").

96. Lando and Beale I and II (n. 10), 455; von Bar and Clive, full edition, vol. I (n. 10), 963; cf. also *UNIDROIT Principles of International Commercial Contracts* (n. 10), 285;

mance,[97] the seriousness of the non-performance and also certain aspects relating to the position of the debtor.[98]

On other questions, too, the national codifications offer little guidance. One of these questions relates to the moment relevant for the assessment of whether the specified sum is grossly excessive. Since the actual loss suffered by the creditor is a key factor in that respect, it cannot be the time of conclusion of the contract. Thus, it will either have to be the time when the agreed sum becomes due to be paid, or when the case is heard before a court or arbitral tribunal.[99] Another question is by how much, or to what level, the agreed sum has to be reduced. Many codifications do not address this question at all, while the BGB states that the penalty may be reduced to a reasonable amount.[100] This is less unhelpful than it may sound, for it may be taken to indicate that the sum should not merely be reduced to a level which, while still harsh, is no longer manifestly unfair.

In Germany and in the Netherlands, a penalty can be reduced only upon request of the debtor.[101] There is no need for the law to foist its protection upon a debtor who is not willing to be protected. Also, the argument has been advanced that it is not conducive to legal certainty if a judge could *mero motu* consider reduction of a penalty.[102] Moreover, in order to determine whether and to what extent a penalty should be reduced, a court needs to be in possession of a certain amount of information that can only

---

Hachem (n. 14) 129 f. This corresponds to the way in which s. 3 of the (South African) Conventional Penalties Act is understood; see Myburgh and Zimmermann (n. 50), 298.

97. Part performance is specifically dealt with in Art. 1231 *Code civil*; Art. 1384 *Codice civile*; for further references, see Hachem (n. 14), 128.

98. Hachem (n. 14), 128 ff.

99. The issue is canvassed by Hachem (n. 14), 132 f.

100. § 343 (1) first sentence BGB; the same formula can be found in the relevant provisions of PECL, PICC, DCFR, and FS. Art. 94 (1) BW specifies that the court must not award the creditor less than "de schadevergoeding op grond van de wet"; for Germany, see Gottwald (n. 18), § 343, no. 21. The Comments to PECL (and DCFR), on the other hand, state that the court should not reduce the award to the actual loss; "the court has to fix an intermediate figure": Lando and Beale I and II (n. 10), 454; von Bar and Clive, full edition, vol. I (n. 10), 963; along the same lines *UNIDROIT Principles of International Commercial Contracts* (n. 10), 285; cf. also Myburgh and Zimmermann (n. 50), 299 f.

101. § 343 (1) BGB; Art. 6:94 (1) BW; but see Hachem (n. 14), 126 pointing out that this requirement is interpreted liberally.

102. See, e.g., Schelhaas, *Boetebeding* (n. 20), 72.

be supplied by the debtor. The position is different in France where Art 1152 *Code civil*—as amended in 1975—grants judges the power to reduce excessive penalties even *mero motu*, in order to maximize the protection of the debtor.[103] Italy presents the example of a legal system where, though its code merely states that the penalty "may be reduced by the court," at least in the past "a strong majority of decisions used to hold that the exercise of the power [to reduce] presupposes an express request by the non-performing party."[104] On the international level, while the Benelux Convention requires "[une] demande du debiteur," the UNCITRAL Rules, PECL, PICC, DCFR and FS do not mention such a requirement and thus appear to be in line with the French approach.[105] Whether reduction only takes place upon a request by the debtor or not, the onus of proving that the requirements for reduction are met is on the debtor.[106] Unlike under the *Code civil*, and contrary to the *Principes Contractuels Communs* (PCC),[107] the courts do not have the power to increase the agreed sum if, in relation to the loss, it appears to be "dérisoire."

Whether, and if so, under which circumstances, the rules on agreed payment for non-performance, particularly the protective mechanisms set out above, apply to forfeiture clauses is unclear. This is due not only to the fact that the notion of a forfeiture clause in general is notoriously difficult

103. Schelhaas, *Boetebeding* (n. 20), 131; Terré et al. (n. 18), no. 627; Malaurie et al. (n. 18), no. 991.

104. Mari (n. 41), 475. Cf. also Zaccaria (n. 41), Art. 1384 V, who emphasizes the judges' power to reduce penalties *ex officio* but also notes that the party claiming the penalty bears the onus of proof for the requirements of Art 1384 *Codice civile*, including the disproportionality. For Austria, see Danzl (n. 39), § 1336, no. 10.

105. Hachem (n. 14), 126 concludes that the wording of the uniform projects "is not conclusive in the one or the other direction." On the case law revolving around this question in South Africa, see Myburgh and Zimmermann (n. 50), 296 ff.

106. For discussion and references, see Hachem (n. 14) 133; on the South African discussion relating to this point, see Myburgh and Zimmermann (n. 50) 293 ff.

107. Art. 1152 (2) *Code civil*; Art. 10:509 (2) PCC (the PCC constitute a proposed revision of the PECL by a French working group: Association Henri Capitant des Amis de la Culture Juridique Française and Société de Législation Comparée, *Principes Contractuels Communs* [Paris, 2008]). Cf. also Art. 6:94 (2) BW, granting courts the power to award additional damages, over and above the agreed sum, if it is evident that equity so requires; see above, at n. 73.

to define.[108] It also arises from the distinction drawn, in that respect, in Comment 4 to Art 7.4.13 PICC between a deposit and a clause according to which the creditor may retain whatever sum the debtor has already paid as part of the price.[109] Only the latter clause is said to fall within the scope of Art 7.4.13. Illustration 2 to Art 9:509 PECL, on the other hand, appears to assume that forfeiture of a deposit is covered by Art 9:509 PECL.[110] Another type of clause often subsumed under the heading of "forfeiture" are acceleration clauses.[111] Here a general guideline may be that the rules on agreed payments do not apply unless, under the clause in question, the creditor becomes entitled to something which would not otherwise have been due to him—if, for example, the debtor not only has to accelerate the repayment of a loan but, in addition, has to pay interest for a period of time during which he did not have the benefit of the money lent to him.[112]

---

108. Treitel, *Remedies* (n. 20), no. 166; cf. also Beale et al., (n. 33), 1060 ("a complex topic"). The South African Conventional Penalties Act also covers forfeiture clauses and defines them in s. 4 as follows: "A stipulation whereby it is provided that upon withdrawal from an agreement by a party thereto under circumstances specified therein, any other party thereto shall forfeit the right to claim restitution of anything performed by him in terms of the agreement, or shall, notwithstanding the withdrawal, remain liable for the performance of anything thereunder." For comparative discussion relating to France, England, and Germany, see Schelhaas, *Boetebeding* (n. 20), 374, 383 ff., 397 ff., 413 f. As far as English law is concerned, see Beale et al. (n. 33), 1062 ff. where the authors wonder why forfeiture clauses should not be subject to the penalty clauses rules: "After all, they seem to have the same function."

109. *UNIDROIT Principles of International Commercial Contracts* (n. 10), 286; see the discussion by Ewan McKendrick, in *Commentary on the UNIDROIT Principles of International Commercial Contracts (PICC)*, ed. Stefan Vogenauer and Jan Kleinheisterkamp (Oxford, 2009) Art. 7.4.13, nos. 8 ff.

110. Lando and Beale I and II (n. 10), 454; cf. also von Bar and Clive, full edition, vol. I (n. 10), 962 (correcting the obvious mistake in illustration 2 to Art. 9:509 PECL: the deposit may be kept by A, A does not forfeit it). According to Beale et al. (n. 33), 1066 "there is no doubt that [the rules on agreed payments] could be applied by analogy."

111. For discussion and references, see Hachem (n. 14), 149.

112. See the South African case law discussed in Myburgh and Zimmermann (n. 50), 284 ff.

POSTSCRIPT

This essay was submitted early in 2014 and reflects the state of affairs as at the end of 2013. At the time of correction of the proofs (January 2015) the fate of the proposed CESL is even less clear than it was at the end of 2013 (see above, p. 338). After a first reading in the European Parliament (February 2014) the European elections have taken place (May 2014). In December 2014 the new Commission under President Juncker announced its intention to withdraw the present proposal and to submit a modified proposal "in order to fully unleash the potential of e-commerce for the Digital Single Market." One will have to wait and see what that means; and whether the new proposal will perhaps contain a provision on agreed payments for non-performance.

Lightning Source UK Ltd.
Milton Keynes UK
UKOW04n1351220515

252133UK00001B/34/P